**Resolutions and Decisions of the
Communist Party of the Soviet Union**

General Editor: Robert H. McNeal

This set of five volumes is an indispensable reference work for the study of modern Russia in general and Soviet Communism in particular. Ever since its foundation on the eve of the twentieth century, the organization now called the Communist Party of the Soviet Union has been embodying its major policies in documents called 'resolutions and decisions.' These form a much more continuous and extensive record of the evolution of Soviet Communism than the writings of any single leader, yet most of this essential material has been available only in Russian, and has been marred by selectivity and editorial comment that is often politically motivated.

At last students of modern Russian studies have access to a multi-volume work that not only presents the most important Communist Party resolutions and decisions in English, but provides editorial explanation that is independent of Kremlin politics. The rich store of materials in these five volumes ranges from the formation of the party through the Brezhnev years. The clearly organized volumes each contain a major introductory essay as well as shorter background essays on each party congress, conference, or Central Committee plenum. The centralist operation of the party in power has been such that many of the most vital decisions have been issued in the name of the Central Committee when there was no meeting of that body at all. It is one of the signal achievements of these volumes that the selection of materials included was based on a list of *all* known party decisions, whether or not they have been included in the main Soviet reference work.

The five volumes in this series are edited as an integral set. Each contains a subject index in which Russian abbreviations and acronymic names are trans-lated. Tables summarizing the personnel of the main party executive bodies since 1917 are also provided. At the same time each of the volumes is built around a coherent period in the development of Russian Communism, and each reflects the special features of its time.

Volume 5 covers Brezhnev's consolidation of power; the limits set on his rule are traced through leadership changes, institutional reforms, and policy development. The major industrial and agricultural reforms introduced under Brezhnev are documented, as are the struggle to implement the reforms, the resistance of managerial elites and workers, and Brezhnev's attempt to modernize the Soviet economy and improve levels of efficiency and productivity.

Internal party changes reflecting the stable oligarchy that emerged after Khrushchev's removal are included, as well as Brezhnev's commitment to security of tenure for cadres and the changing nature and role of the purge. Party efforts to upgrade recruitment procedures, to change the qualitative composition of the party, to improve the procedures for ensuring routinization and responsiveness in the conduct of party business, and to upgrade the party education system are also documented. Evidence is provided of the party's struggle with corruption in the Georgian Republic and the regime's inability to cope effectively with the widespread growth of social problems. The volume conveys the flavour of oligarchic and bureaucratic politics that emerged with Brezhnev's style of leadership.

DONALD V. SCHWARTZ is a member of the Department of Political Economy at the University of Toronto.

**Resolutions and Decisions of the
Communist Party of the Soviet Union**

Volume 5
The Brezhnev Years
1964–1981

Editor: Donald V. Schwartz

University of Toronto Press
Toronto Buffalo London

© University of Toronto Press 1982
Toronto Buffalo London
Printed in Canada

ISBN 0-8020-5552-4

Canadian Cataloguing in Publication Data

Kommunisticheskaia partiia Sovetskogo Soiuza.
Resolutions and decisions of the Communist Party
of the Soviet Union

Contents: v. 5. The Brezhnev years, 1964-1981 /
editor: Donald V. Schwartz.
ISBN 0-8020-5552-4 (v. 5)
1. Kommunisticheskaia partiia Sovetskogo Soiuza.
2. Soviet Union – Politics and government – 20th
century. I. Schwartz, Donald V. (Donald Victor), 1941-
II. Title.
JN6598.K7K75   324.247′075   C75-0467-3

General Editor's Preface

It has proven difficult to synchronize this documentary series with Soviet political history. When the work was planned, Khrushchev had only lately retired, and the editors believed that it would be possible to prepare a four-volume series, the last volume of which would cover the entire period since the death of Stalin. Grey Hodnett, the editor of volume 4, in fact collected materials and drafted a volume that included Soviet Communist Party decisions through the 1960s. But we were excessively optimistic about the tempo of our work and increasingly aware that the Brezhnev administration was assuming an historic identity of its own. Thus we decided to terminate volume 4 with the fall of Khrushchev and to add a fifth volume to cover the Brezhnev years. Donald V. Schwartz of the University of Toronto assumed responsibility for this project, taking over the material that Grey Hodnett had prepared, to be reworked for inclusion in a new context.

At this point, in the early 1970s, it did not seem plausible that Leonid Brezhnev would carry on as party leader into the next decade. As Donald Schwartz approached the completion of his work in the latter half of the 1970s, the health of the General Secretary was reported to be in decline, and it seemed that we could bring out a volume on the Brezhnev era shortly after its close. But the political and physical resiliency of the Soviet leader has confounded this plan. The XXVI Party Congress came and went in February/March 1981 with no hint that Brezhnev was contemplating retirement for reasons of age or ill health. We now faced a dilemma. Donald Schwartz had a finished volume in manuscript that would serve well the interest of many students of Soviet affairs. Was it better to withhold publication until the end of the Brezhnev administration, which surely could not be postponed indefinitely, or to publish it knowing that it would lack an unknown number of months or years of coverage of this administration? We concluded, with some reluctance, that it would be better to sacrifice this element of completeness in favour of the interests of the potential users of the work. Given Brezhnev's remarkable durability, it *could* be years before the era ends, just as it *could* happen with perverse suddenness a few weeks after the work was handed to the printer.

The Soviet editors of the roughly corresponding series, *Kommunisti-cheskaia Partiia Sovetskogo Soiuza v rezoliutsiiakh i resheniiakh s"ezdov, konfer-*

entsii i plenumov TsK (Communist Party of the Soviet Union in Resolutions and Decisions of Congresses, Conferences, and Plenums of the Central Committee) have not had to deal with our problem in the same form. The eighth edition of this work, which began publication in 1970, has been gradually extended as the years and documents accumulate. Volumes xi-xii, published in 1978, have covered the Brezhnev era through 1977, and one may assume that additional volumes will appear every few years. This series remains one of the basic reference works in the Soviet Union, one of the fundamental records of the system, and a foundation of political orthodoxy. Along with the collected writings of Lenin (which obviously do not deal with events after 1923), the Soviet series appears to be the most frequently cited authority in Soviet writing on twentieth-century history and politics. The Institute of Marxism–Leninism no doubt had this in mind when they published in 1973 a volume of 271 pages, entitled *Spravochnyi tom k vos'momu izdaniiu KPSS v rezoliutsiiakh i resheniiakh s"ezdov, konferentsii i plenumov TsK* (Index Volume to the Eighth Edition of cpsu in Resolutions and Decisions of Congresses, Conferences, and Plenums of the Central Committee).

Robert H. McNeal

Editor's Preface

The fifth volume in the series *Resolutions and Decisions of the Communist Party of the Soviet Union* was compiled and written after the publication of the first four volumes. The early volumes were edited by a collective of scholars who worked out the principles of selection and analysis together. These principles are identified in the General Editor's introduction to volume 1. I have tried to follow the established editorial and selection principles as closely as possible. I have operated under the assumption identified in volume 1 that the decisions of the CPSU are considered to be formal and binding expressions of the whole party, that they are operating commands, and that they draw their authority from the party bodies that issued them. Decisions that refer to the activities of specific party organizations are assumed to imply universalistic messages for all party organizations charged with similar responsibilities. I have excluded decisions issued by any authority other than the party, as well as decisions issued jointly by the party and another organization. Despite the importance of foreign policy as a sphere of party decision making, I have continued the principle established in the earlier volumes and excluded material relating to foreign affairs. An additional constraint, imposed by the party, has been a lack of published decisions in areas considered crucial to understanding the Brezhnev regime by many Western observers (e.g. the Soviet military build-up and the treatment of dissidents).

Despite attempts to provide continuity with the principles of the previous four volumes in the series, circumstances have dictated that some discontinuities also emerge, although these appear to be minor. The translator of the fifth volume, Ms Barbara Richmond, worked independently of the previous translators. However, Barbara and I have tried to provide translations that adhere closely to the style of the party resolutions so as to convey the flavour of the documents in a manner similar to the earlier volumes. Included in this volume are the brief resolutions approving Brezhnev's Central Committee Report to the XXV and XXVI Party congresses. Although these resolutions contain nothing of substance, they are important indicators of Brezhnev's increased authority and they have proved to be useful for providing some analysis of the content of Brezhnev's reports, which served as surrogates for party decisions. Finally, the previous volumes in the series had the advantage of focusing on completed periods of history. The editors could view the party decisions from the perspective of observers of integrated and unified stages in the development of the party. The editor of the fifth volume has not been blessed with such a luxury. The present volume has been in process since the mid-1970s and therefore judgment in selecting documents and providing commentary has had to be tempered by the realization that each decision chosen for inclusion may not be the last word of the party under Brezhnev's leadership. Nevertheless, at the time when the manuscript went to press (mid-1981), certain trends seemed evident. The major decisions giving direction to party organization and policy were made in the first decade of Brezhnev's tenure. Since the mid-1970s, there has been nothing of substance in the party's treatment of its internal organization, its relations with other institutions, and its domestic policy initiatives that would appear to alter dramatically the course of events giving the Brezhnev years their distinct character. Continuity and incremental changes have dominated party policy since the establishment of the basic directions at the XXIII and XXIV Party congresses. At present, it appears that any significant shifts in party policy will have to await a new leadership and, perhaps, a new generation of leaders.

Russian terms are translated if a generally accepted English form exists, but are transliterated otherwise. In the latter case the term (e.g. oblast) is treated as an anglicized expression, without hard and soft signs (except in titles), to simplify the appearance of the text. The index of the volume provides parenthetical translations of transliterated terms.

Document numbers (e.g. 5.44) are supplied by the editor of the volume; the prefix '5.' indicates the volume number in the present series. Throughout the book such a decimal number implies reference to a document number.

Square brackets [ ] enclose material added by the editor of this volume, while parentheses appearing in documents are in the original Russian text. Ellipses (...) indicate omissions of part of the original document by the editor, unless otherwise specified. To assist the reader in identifying changes in the party Rules, bracketed notes are inserted with each article, indicating whether it is a new or revised article with respect to the existing version of the Rules.

At the end of each document or group of documents adopted at a congress or Central Committee plenum, source attributions are provided. On the left the earliest published source that was accessible to the editor is cited. On the right the location of the material in the standard Soviet reference work is cited: *Kommunisticheskaia Partiia Sovetskogo Soiuza v rezoliutsiiakh i resheniiakh s"ezdov, konferentsii i plenumov TsK* (Communist Party of the Soviet Union in Resolutions and Decisions of Congresses, Conferences, and Plenums of the Central Committee), 8th edition, Moscow, 1970–1972, 1978 (hereafter abbreviated *KPSS v rezoliutsiiakh*). Not all documents published in the present work appear in *KPSS v rezoliutsiiakh*, so citations of this source do not appear in every case. Translations are based upon the version of the decision or resolution published in *KPSS v rezoliutsiiakh*. Where this is not available, the version in the place of first publication is used.

The end of each set of documents emerging from a congress or Central Committee plenum is indicated by the following symbol: ☼

The editor of the present volume wishes to express his thanks to the Canada Council and the Centre for Russian and East European Studies (University of Toronto) for their support during the research and writing stages. This book has been published with the help of a grant from the Social Science Federation of Canada, using funds provided by the Social Sciences and Humanities Research Council of Canada, and a grant from the Publications Fund of the University of Toronto Press.

Contents

The Brezhnev Years
1964–1981

Introduction

After Khrushchev was ousted from his offices in October 1964 a number of Soviet leaders shared power. Brezhnev, as First Secretary, undoubtedly held the key position and there is no evidence that his occupation of the post was contested. However, his manoeuvrability and power were explicitly circumscribed by the arrangements that had been agreed upon by the new leadership. Kosygin was placed in the position of head of the government when he was named Chairman of the USSR Council of Ministers. Apparently, there was an implicit agreement that the two positions of head of the party and head of the government should not be combined in the hands of a single individual as under Khrushchev.[1] In addition, there is good evidence that Brezhnev's power within the party was limited. N.V. Podgorny emerged clearly as second in command in the Secretariat, with a strong influence over internal party organizational matters. A.N. Shelepin had been promoted to full membership in the Presidium as part of the October 1964 accord and appeared to be in a position to enhance his power because of his age (46) and his holding of a post in the party Secretariat as well as the chairmanship of the Party-State Control Committee. M.A. Suslov was the person with the greatest seniority in the leadership and the recognized leading ideologist. While none of these individuals posed a direct challenge to Brezhnev's

---

1   Several Western observers make reference to a Central Committee decision to enforce the separation of the offices of First Secretary and Chairman of the Council of Ministers. See T.H. Rigby, 'The Soviet Leadership: Towards a Self-Stabilizing Oligarchy?' *Soviet Studies* XXII, 2 (October 1970): 175; D.P. Hammer, 'Brezhnev and the Communist Party,' *Soviet Union* II, Part 1 (1975): 6. The original source of the information is P.A. Rodionov, *Kollektivnost'– vysshy printsip partiinogo rukovodstva* (Moscow 1967). In the original edition Rodionov notes that the October 1964 Central Committee Plenum 'recognized as inexpedient in the future the combining in one person of the responsibilities of the Central Committee First Secretary and the Chairman of the USSR Council of Ministers' (p. 219). In the second edition of the book, published in 1974, Rodionov omits this specific passage and talks only in general terms (p. 225). Grey Hodnett reports through another source that the decision to keep the two positions in separate hands took the form of a closed circular letter issued by the Central Committee. See his 'Succession Contingencies in the Soviet Union,' *Problems of Communism* XXIV, 2 (March–April 1975): 5.

position, the diffusion of power among a number of leaders after October 1964 indicates clearly that Brezhnev began his tenure with severe limitations on his own power. There is strong evidence suggesting that the new leadership took a number of deliberate steps to ensure the emergence of a stable oligarchy in which Brezhnev, by common consent, held the leading position.[2]

There were several overt indicators after the beginning of 1965 that Brezhnev was moving to enhance his power.[3] In policy, Brezhnev was the leading figure at the March 1965 and May 1966 Central Committee plenums, which gave approval to his personal initiative for the basic lines of agricultural development. In the area of personnel, changes were made during 1965 in the Secretariat, with several of Brezhnev's former associates gaining positions. The key change in the Secretariat was the replacement of Podgorny with Brezhnev supporter A.P. Kirilenko, who was put in charge of cadres. In December 1965 Podgorny was removed from the Secretariat and given a largely ceremonial position as Chairman of the Presidium of the USSR Supreme Soviet, while Shelepin was deprived of his chairmanship of the potentially powerful Party-State Control Committee when it was dissolved. In 1967 Shelepin was completely removed as a possible rival when he was forced to resign from the Secretariat in conjunction with his appointment as Chairman of the Trade Unions' Council. During the 1970s Brezhnev gradually consolidated his position as potential rivals or opponents on policy issues were removed from the Politburo.[4] At the same time, Brezhnev was able to advance into the Politburo a number of individuals whose presence strength-

2   For a persuasive argument detailing the mechanisms employed to stabilize the oligarchy, see Rigby, 'The Soviet Leadership,' 167–91.

3   For varying interpretations of the distribution of power immediately after October 1964 and Brezhnev's consolidation of his position see Y. Bilinsky, 'The Communist Party of the Soviet Union,' in J.W. Strong, ed., *The Soviet Union Under Brezhnev and Kosygin* (New York 1971), chapter 3; A. Brown and M. Kaser, eds, *The Soviet Union Since Khrushchev*, 2nd edition (London 1978), chapters 10, 12; Hodnett, 'Succession Contingencies ...' 1–21; J.F. Hough, 'The Man and the System,' *Problems of Communism* XXV, 2 (March–April 1976): 1–17; T. Rakowska-Harmstone, 'Toward a Theory of Soviet Leadership Maintenance,' in P. Cocks, R. Daniels, and N. Heer, eds, *The Dynamics of Soviet Politics* (Cambridge 1976): 51–76; Rigby, 'The Soviet Leadership'; M. Rush, 'After Khrushchev: Problems of Succession in the Soviet Union,' *Studies in Comparative Communism* II, 3 and 4 (July/October 1969): 79–94; M. Tatu, *Power in the Kremlin* (New York 1970), part v.

4   G.I. Voronov and P.E. Shelest in April 1973; Shelepin in April 1975; D.S. Poliansky in early 1976; Podgorny in May 1977; K.T. Mazurov in November 1978; and Kosygin in October 1980.

ened his position.[5] When Kosygin resigned as Chairman of the Council of Ministers in October 1980, he was replaced by a long-time Brezhnev associate, N.A. Tikhonov, who had become a full member of the Politburo only one year earlier. Most of the new recruits into the Politburo were men who had had previous career associations with Brezhnev that were sufficiently strong to identify them as his supporters, or who had been publicly associated with policy issues that reinforced Brezhnev's position within the Politburo. Equally important in understanding the security of Brezhnev's tenure was that, at the time of their promotion to the Politburo, none of these men had the combination of personal characteristics, training, career experience and institutional power base, and age that would make them competitors or logical heirs apparent to Brezhnev's leadership.[6]

There were also a number of symbolic indicators of a gradual but not uncontrolled enhancement of Brezhnev's power and status after October 1964. In late 1964 he was appointed Chairman of the Constitutional Commission, which had been established by Khrushchev. He also took over as Chairman of the RSFSR Bureau of the Central Committee until its dissolution in April 1966. In October 1965 Brezhnev gained a seat on the Presidium of the USSR Supreme Soviet. The XXIII Congress, held in April 1966, served as a symbol of the consolidation of Brezhnev's position. His central role in the congress proceedings was reinforced by moderate praise directed his way in some of the speeches and by his designation as General Secretary of the Central Committee. During the next decade, the outward trappings of Brezhnev's power changed only marginally. It was only in the mid-1970s that Brezhnev's personal career again generated a momentum that raised his status significantly. Party decisions suggested this shift with more frequent reference to Brezhnev and his statements as the source of directives. At the XXV Congress Brezhnev was the focus of an outburst of praise for his personal and leadership qualities that was unrivaled in the post-Stalin period. His Central Committee Report took on the status of a party decision through the technique of giving it perfunctory congress approval rather than the pattern that had been established at previous congresses of issuing a separate detailed resolution on the report. This pattern was repeated at the XXVI Congress in 1981. In May 1976 Brezhnev was created a Marshal of the Soviet Union. In 1977 Brezhnev succeeded in bringing to fruition the new Con-

5   V.V. Shcherbitsky, F.D. Kulakov, D.A. Kunayev, and V.V. Grishin in April 1971; A.A. Grechko, A.A. Gromyko and Iu.V. Andropov in April 1973; G.V. Romanov and D.F. Ustinov in February 1976; K.U. Chernenko in November 1977; N.A. Tikhonov in November 1979; M.S. Gorbachev in October 1980.

6   For a detailed analysis of leadership qualifications of Brezhnev's recruits into the Politburo see Hodnett, 'Succession Contingencies ...'

stitution of the USSR and, in conjunction with this, he was named to succeed Podgorny as Head of State. In terms of the longevity of Brezhnev's reign as the leading party figure, his ability to manipulate personnel appointments at the highest level, and the symbols of power surrounding him, there can be little doubt that the past years have been the 'Brezhnev Years.'

Despite the real and symbolic indicators of Brezhnev's accumulation of power, there were always clear indications of limits on him and resistance to his leadership developing beyond certain undefined bounds. The major economic thrust, the New Economic Reform, was essentially Kosygin's programme and was originally approved in September 1965, sometime before Brezhnev achieved his plateau of power at the XXIII Congress. Brezhnev was not associated with any radical domestic policy initiatives outside of agriculture. Even his new Constitution appeared to be a compromise document. Turnover among the top leadership was extremely slow and stable and recruitment conservative, as reflected in the steadily increasing average age of the Politburo and Central Committee membership.[7]

Brezhnev's political career after 1964 was remarkable for its failure to follow a pattern of consolidation or decline, expected on the basis of previous Soviet succession patterns. Brezhnev never achieved the degree of personal power accumulated by his predecessors. Whether by conscious design of a moderate leader who was satisfied with playing the role of power broker and chose a limited but stable leadership role or by the conscious design of his Politburo colleagues whose support came only on condition of prior limitations and restraints, Brezhnev never achieved the concentration of power in his own person that so many in the West predicted was the inevitable outcome of a Soviet succession struggle.[8] Yet, his tenure, the second longest in Soviet history, certainly belied the label of caretaker or interim leader and exhibited a degree of security that Stalin achieved only through excessive coercion and Khrushchev never attained. Brezhnev became the dominant figure of post-Khrushchev politics and gave the party and the country a leadership style that has left its imprint in most areas of domestic policy.

7   For patterns of leadership turnover at the Politburo and Central Committee levels see R.E. Blackwell, 'Cadres Policy in the Brezhnev Era,' *Problems of Communism* XXVIII, 2 (March–April 1979): 29–42; R.V. Daniels, 'Office Holding and Elite Status: The Central Committee of the CPSU,' in Cocks, Daniels, and Heer, eds, *The Dynamics of Soviet Politics*, 77–95; R.H. Donaldson, 'The 1971 Soviet Central Committee: An Assessment of the New Elite,' *World Politics* XXIV, 3 (April 1972): 382–409; Rigby, 'The Soviet Leadership'; R. Taagepera and R.D. Chapman, 'A Note on the Ageing of the Politburo,' *Soviet Studies* XXIX, 2 (April 1977): 296–305.

8   Hough develops the argument that Brezhnev willingly accepted the limits placed on him and consciously chose to delegate much authority to subordinates. See Hough, 'The Man and the System,' 5–6.

PARTY ORGANIZATION AND COMPOSITION

Khrushchev's style of rule had been to introduce a number of organizational changes and experiments that challenged the corporate integrity of the party and the security of its personnel. Under Brezhnev there was an immediate move to restore the party's authority and power.[9] Within one month after the removal of Khrushchev the new leadership had reached agreement on basic reform of the party's structure. The essence of this reform (5.2) was to revoke Khrushchev's bifurcation of the party organization that had split the local party organs into separate bureaus for industry and agriculture (4.37 and 4.39). The party organization was restored to its traditional basis on the territorial-production principle. The reform had the practical consequence of reuniting oblast and krai party organizations that had been divided into agricultural and industrial sections. The major impact occurred in the countryside where the rural raion committees regained their previous position of authority by absorbing the kolkhoz-sovkhoz production administration party committees into rural raion committees and through abolition of the zonal industrial-production party committees. The local party organs were re-established at the raion and oblast level as the unifying and co-ordinating bodies over the entire range of industrial, agricultural, and public organizations at the district level (5.24).

The aim of the reform was to restore the party to its previous level of internal efficiency and external influence by disengaging it from detailed interference in routine economic decision making and re-emphasizing its co-ordinative and supervisory functions. The stage was set for further marginal adaptations to improve performance without numerous and radical reorganizations. The changes in party organization over the next years followed an incremental line aimed at introducing and maintaining stability and routine in the party's structure and procedures and upgrading its status as a corporate entity. This line can be seen in changes and new interpretations in party norms and rules in the areas of membership and recruitment, cadres, party discipline, and the conduct of party business.

Recruitment and membership policy were directed at restoring the authority associated with the party's role as the leading element in Soviet society. The tone for this trend was set by the July 1965 Central Committee resolution on the work of the Kharkov oblast party organization (5.4). Recruitment according to quantitative indicators was judged detrimental to the party's status and functioning. The Kharkov resolution called for an

9 For detailed analysis of the post-Khrushchev party reform and its intended impact, see W.J. Conyngham, *Industrial Management in the Soviet Union* (Stanford 1973), chapter 10; D.P. Hammer, 'Brezhnev and the Communist Party,' 1–21; J.F. Hough, 'Reforms in Administration and Government,' in A. Dallin and T.B. Larson, eds, *Soviet Politics since Khrushchev* (Englewood Cliffs 1968), chapter 2.

upgrading of the quality of candidates recruited into the party, strict adherence to the party Rules in the selection process, adherence to the principle of individual selection, greater attention to the social and occupational composition of new party membership, and increased concern for the ideological consciousness of candidates entering the party and the continued political education of party members. The basic principles stated in the Kharkov resolution were reaffirmed and given concrete expression at the XXIII Congress. Changes were incorporated into the party Rules to tighten up recruitment procedures by limiting recruitment of young people under the age of 23 to admission only through the Komsomol and by requiring those recommending applicants to the party to have party standing of not less than five years (5.8).

Under Brezhnev, the party sought a way out of its traditional dilemma of choosing between being an elite organization and a proletarian party, in part, by recruiting better educated and upwardly mobile workers.[10] There was to be working-class predominance but recruitment also had to take into consideration the choosing of people for their potential leadership qualities regardless of their class background. The party's growth rate slowed down considerably after 1965, thus contributing to the leadership's basic objective of ensuring its elite status. However, the lower growth rate in party membership had a number of effects that were inconsistent with secondary goals associated with the idea of the party as a representative institution. As the number of people entering the party declined, several intermediate goals were retarded such as the desire to shift balances more in favour of younger members, workers, national minorities, the better educated, and women.

Policy on party cadres aimed at providing greater stability and security for personnel. A number of specific measures were taken in this direction. Khrushchev's rigid conditions for turnover of cadres (4.38) were abolished at the XXIII Congress. More flexible provisions were substituted, providing that the general principles of systematic renewal and continuity of leadership both be observed. The party underwent an internal devolution of authority, suggesting a greater confidence in local leaders. For example, amendments to the party Rules gave larger primary party organizations the rights of raion party committees and gave the primary party organizations at large shops in enterprises the right to form party committees while allowing primary party organizations to be set up in the shops of these enterprises. The RSFSR Bureau of the Central Committee was abolished (5.8).

10   See Rigby, 'Soviet Communist Party Membership Under Brezhnev,' *Soviet Studies* XXVIII,
     3 (July 1976): 317–37; *idem*, 'Addendum,' *Soviet Studies* XXVIII, 4 (October 1976): 615;
     and A.L. Unger's response to Rigby 'Soviet Communist Party Membership Under Brezh-
     nev: A Comment,' *Soviet Studies* XXIX, 2 (April 1977): 306–16.

In general it was recognized that competent personnel required ongoing support in the form of formal training and retraining courses, stable patterns of promotion through the ranks, and stability of tenure without unwarranted and frequent transfers if they were expected to work at a higher level of efficiency. There was also recognition of the need for a better balance in cadres policy, combining the promotion of promising young functionaries with regard for experienced veteran cadres and achieving a more satisfactory blend between the qualities of specialist and generalist. Recognition of the need to achieve these balances resulted in a shift in cadres policy, with greater emphasis being placed on qualities such as those exhibited by good organizers and administrators, innovators, and people with a long-range perspective – at the expense of the traditional qualities of political loyalty, knowledge of marxism-leninism, or specialized technical knowledge. While the party did not officially acknowledge a tension among these sets of characteristics, its pronouncements suggested a shift away from political and specialist approaches and towards administrative approaches to party business. Courses for leading party and soviet cadres re-focused their curricula so that they included an increasing component of modern economic management techniques, social psychology, the latest achievements in science, technology, and culture, and the development of leadership qualities. This was achieved at the expense of more traditional ideologically oriented subjects, which had constituted the bulk of the curricula in party schools. The balance was shifted in favour of training oriented towards business and management skills (5.11, 5.36, 5.44, 5.55). In return for ensuring stability and upgrading the status of party officials, the leadership repeatedly indicated expectations for improved performance by the apparat, symbolized by the slogan of 'exactingness' in the behaviour of officials.

The party took a measured, administrative approach to the question of party discipline. Additional pressure was placed on party members to exhibit exemplary behaviour by adding a phase to the introductory section of the Rules at the XXIII Congress that 'the party set itself free of individuals who violate the CPSU Programme, the Rules, and who by their behaviour compromise the lofty title of Communist' (5.8). Penalties for violation of party discipline were made more severe by the abolition of the penalty of transfer of a party member to the status of candidate. Organizational changes were made in the form of the activation of party commissions of local party organs to ensure compliance with party Rules (5.15).

The major decision of the Brezhnev leadership regarding party discipline involved the conducting of an exchange of party documents, announced at the XXIV Congress. The Central Committee Report noted with approval the increased activity of the Party Control Committee and the commissions attached to local party organs in strengthening party discipline. In this connection, an exchange of party documents was placed on the agenda. Such an exchange is normally associated with a purge of the party, a process that has wide-ranging ramifications and symbolism associated with the purges of Stalin (3.19). However, in this case, the leadership took pains to ensure the orderliness and regularity of procedures. Brezhnev noted that the exchange of party documents was to be the first in 17 years and that it was to occur after the expiry of the period of validity of party membership cards.[11] No ominous political developments were associated with the decision. The symbol of Lenin was evoked to give reassurances of an administrative rather than a political meaning to the decision. The official aim of the exchange was to rid the party of inactive and passive members who had failed to engage in the duties of party membership and to intensify discipline among party members so that the party organization could be strengthened.

The image of the exchange of documents as an administrative procedure rather than a political measure was borne out in the two-year delay before the start of the exchange, explained by the lengthy preparatory work required. The Central Committee documents pertaining to the details of the exchange affirmed its limited scope and administrative nature. The initially stated aims were reiterated. Directives were provided to ensure that the exchange of cards was carried out according to a strictly individual procedure directly in the raion and city party committees and in political departments where party members were permanently registered. The exchange was not to be aimed indiscriminately at large groups and each individual's status was to be reviewed by party officials responsible for knowing the record of that person (5.43). The post-exchange documents confirmed the original intent of the procedure. A Central Committee resolution summarized the results of the exchange of documents in terms of its contribution to the organizational efficiency of the party and an improvement in the ability of the party to carry out its mobilization and supervisory work in the economy (5.47). Finally, in his major address to the XXV Congress, Brezhnev closed the book on the exchange of party documents by stressing its contribution to the organizational development of the party (i.e. party discipline) and the increased activeness of party members. He made special note that 'it was not a purge of the party' and that those who did not receive new party cards (about 347,000) were expelled due to the fact that they were inhibiting the party's basic organizational (rather than political) goals by committing deviations from the norms of party life, violating discipline, and losing touch with the party organizations.[12]

11   L. Gruliow, ed., *Current Soviet Policies* VI (1973), 36.

12   *Ibid.*, VII (1976), 23. Rigby makes the point that, if the attrition rate of the late 1960s were projected for the two years of the purge, nearly half of the total party members expelled during the purge would have been dropped from the party ranks in any case. Thus, the

Brezhnev tried to set the tone for internal party business in his reports to the party congresses by citing changes and patterns at the all-union level as examples for local and primary party organizations. At the XXIII Congress he stressed the importance of efficiency, responsiveness, and the principles of collective leadership when proposing amendments to the party Rules.[13] At the XXIV, XXV, and XXVI congresses, Brezhnev cited the procedures of the central party organs as examples to be followed of the frequency and regularity of meetings for executive and policy-making bodies in the party, and he even provided a rough division of responsibility among them.[14] At the XXVI Congress Brezhnev announced the establishment of a new Letters Department of the Central Committee apparatus and the congress approved a resolution noting that the congress Secretariat had examined letters, statements, and appeals from the public and party members and instructing the Central Committee to follow through on this work (5.67). These general indicators of a businesslike approach to party affairs found concrete expression in the emergence of a number of organizational principles stressing and/or redefining the elements of democratic centralism as it applied to internal party business procedures at the local and primary levels and relations among the three party levels. The centre, under Brezhnev, pushed in the direction of increased intra-party responsiveness through improved communications, greater compliance with regime norms by local party organizations, and a campaign to improve various aspects of internal party business.

The issue of responsiveness through improved vertical communications was taken up at the national level where the party leadership incorporated into the party Rules a provision for the convening of general party conferences (moribund since 1941) during the period between congresses for discussion of party issues on a basis broader than a Central Committee plenum but less authoritative than a congress (5.8). This amendment reflected an attempt to balance conflicting demands. On the one hand, the Central Committee apparatus and the members of the Central Committee probably felt strongly about upgrading the status of Central Committee plenums, which had become almost public forums under Khrushehev through expanded attendance and publication of stenographic reports. On the other hand, there were legitimate pressures from regional party secretaries, government officials, and specialists who were not Central Committee members to have a national forum available to voice their opinions on relevant issues.

The Central Committee resolution on the Tbilisi City party organization (5.41) dealt with the issue of responsiveness in terms of the centre's

exchange of party documents resulted in a loss of membership probably not in excess of 1.5 per cent. See Rigby, 'Soviet Communist Party Membership Under Brezhnev,' 322.

13 *Current Soviet Policies* v (1973), 28

14 *Ibid.*, vi (1973), 35; vii (1976), 24; *Current Digest of the Soviet Press* xxxiii, no. 9, 11.

expectations regarding the limits to be imposed on local and primary party organizations in complying with the newly provided rules of the game. While the document was directed to the Georgian party organization, it also had more wide-ranging significance, suggesting to all party organizations that if they did not take action to set limits on irregular procedures and to implement the centre's norms and rules of organizational behaviour, the centre would take strong and forceful action to have the local leadership replaced and to impose its own ideas of what was acceptable on the local party organization.

The issue of responsiveness in the party was elaborated extensively for the local party organs in terms of adherence to certain norms and rules in the conduct of internal business and relations with primary party organizations and state and public agencies. Responsiveness was associated with introducing business procedures that would improve the vertical flow of communication in both directions, increase the accountability of leading party bodies and officials through adherence to the principles of collective leadership, and increase participation of rank-and-file party members in discussing, elaborating, and carrying out party decisions. These principles were detailed in three specific decisions dealing with the practice of conducting party meetings (5.29), report-and-election meetings and conferences (5.45), and the use of criticism and self-criticism in the party (5.48). The ethos of the campaign to improve internal party business procedures was captured in a number of themes applied to desired behaviour of local and primary party organizations and officials in decision making: boesposobnost (fighting efficiency), delovitost (businesslike approach), and nauchnyi podkhod (scientific approach). The essence of the entire campaign was summed up by Brezhnev at the XXV Congress in reference to the Tambov resolution on criticism and self-criticism. He placed stress on the need for objective appraisal of all activity of organizations and officials, comprehensive analysis of short-comings with the aim of eliminating them, intolerance of a liberal attitude to short-comings, a combination of trust in and respect for personnel, high exactingness for assigned tasks, and finally, sincerity and a readiness to take up mistakes and short-comings immediately.[15] The overall aim of the campaign was to institutionalize business procedures and harness them to improving party performance while minimizing their potential disabuse for personal gain or vindictiveness.

There appeared to be limits on what the central leadership could achieve through marginal organizational reform and revision of party principles. The exhortatory nature of the documents and the repetition of their messages in various decisions, at endless party meetings, and through party

15   *Current Soviet Policies* VII (1976), 25

journals suggest that there was strong resistance and apathy towards the changes that the Brezhnev leadership tried to effect. The toughening of the line with the exchange of party documents and the Tbilisi decision, which was accompanied by major personnel changes, confirmed that the central leadership could not expect radical changes in attitudes and behaviour; it was forced to employ more traditional compliance mechanisms such as direct central intervention in local affairs, the imposition of strict party discipline, and, in extreme cases, the application of criminal sanctions.

INDUSTRIAL POLICY AND PARTY GUIDANCE OF THE ECONOMY

The party's economic policies and its role in the economic sector were determined largely by the new priorities the Brezhnev regime set and by certain structural characteristics of the Soviet economy.[16] The major structural characteristics confronting the Brezhnev regime included the institutional inheritance of Khrushchev's reformism and the more serious long-run effects of an economy geared towards quantitative growth confronted with a levelling off of the growth rate, decreasing labour reserves, increasing costs of resource extraction, highly rigid and well-entrenched institutions and approaches for economic planning and administration that had been appropriate to extensive economic development, and ever-increasing demands from long-neglected areas such as the consumer and agricultural sectors. The major priorities of the leadership, which placed additional stress on the economic mechanism, included a desire to maintain industrial growth rates while diverting investments to the consumer and agricultural sectors and transformation of the economy to place more emphasis on efficiency in production and on quality of output by taking advantage of scientific, technological, and organizational innovation. To cope with the pressures exerted by the economy's structural requirements and the regime's increased demands, the new leadership embarked on an economic policy that involved, at first, a return to the pre-khrushchevian institutional structure along with a new set of decision rules and incentives for planners and administrators. When this failed to produce the desired results, the leadership turned to the technique of grafting on additional reforms aimed at improving managerial capabilities, increasing labour productivity, searching out additional production reserves, and reorganizing the intermediate levels of the administrative structure to

16   For an overview of the economic priorities of the Brezhnev regime and the obstacles to achieving economic goals, see Conyngham, *Industrial Management in the Soviet Union*, chapter 10; G. Grossman, 'An Economy at Middle Age,' *Problems of Communism* XXV, 2 (March–April 1976): 18–33; A. Katz, *The Politics of Economic Reform in the Soviet Union* (New York 1972), chapters 7–10; A. Nove, 'Economic Policy and Economic Trends,' in A. Dallin and T.B. Larson, eds, *Soviet Politics since Khrushchev*, chapter 4.

improve the relationship between research and production and to take advantage of certain economies of larger scale economic units without reverting to rigid centralization.

In September 1965 the Central Committee met in plenary session for the third time since Khrushchev's removal. At this session a major set of decisions (5.5) was taken regarding reorganization of the Soviet planning and industrial complex. The economic reform, associated primarily with Kosygin who delivered the major report to the plenum,[17] took aim at Khrushchev's system of regional economic councils (4.16) as a major impediment to the modernization of the Soviet economy. To overcome the difficulties and restraints imposed by the system of territorial administration, the plenum ordered its abolition and a return to the branch principle of industrial administration. However, there was not to be a complete return to the pre-1957 relationships. Several changes were proposed. Excessive central regulation of industrial enterprises was to be eliminated by reducing the number of plan indices imposed on enterprises from above. There was to be increased emphasis on economic levers such as profit, price, bonus, and credit. Planning was to show more adaptiveness and flexibility in response to changing needs. New techniques were to be developed and applied to encourage enterprises to work out higher target plans. The essence of the reform was to combine centralized branch and national planning with a greater degree of deconcentrated administration.

There was an explicit connection between the changes in party structure implemented at the November 1964 Central Committee Plenum and the proposed reforms in economic planning and management. Under the new conditions of increased enterprise autonomy, the local and primary party organs' leading role was redefined to place greater emphasis on making 'political' decisions and exercising supervision over the state economic organization through control of cadres. Party decisions issued after the September 1965 Central Committee Plenum spelled out in detail the nature of party co-ordinating and personnel duties in the production unit, with continuous injunctions that party committees achieve these goals through special party techniques short of direct managerial functions and that they not take over the functions of economic managers nor supplant soviet and economic bodies or assume petty tutelage over them (5.10, 5.12, 5.23). Party organizations were instructed to recruit and then exhibit more confidence in managerial cadres who could cope with the new administrative, technical, and organizational issues raised by the deconcentration of authority granted in the 1965 Statute on the Socialist State Production Enterprise.[18] A clear image was presented of the party organization as a co-ordinative agency,

17   *Current Digest of the Soviet Press* XVII, no. 38, 3–15
18   *Ibid.*, XVII, no. 42, 3–10

consolidating the activities of all the components of the production unit into a synchronized effort aimed at achieving the successful transformation to the new system of economic management.

There was apparently strong resistance to the changes in party activity decreed at the centre. While some work in implementing the reforms was being conducted, it became evident by 1968 that the party had been unable to ensure that the advantages of the new system of management were fully utilized. The key problem seems to have been attaining a degree of stability in progress. There were isolated cases of success, but, on the whole, industry had not been able to achieve stable high rates of development and had not systematically been able to fulfil plans for introducing new technology, for mechanization and automation of production processes, and for raising the quality and technical level of goods produced (5.23, 5.25). The exhortations to improve party supervision of production in the context of the new economic reform continued through most of 1969. At the same time, the entire reform came under sharp scrutiny from the party leadership and there was doubt regarding its continuation. Evidence pointed to strong resistance to the application of the reform's key principles by major participants – party officials, enterprise managers, ministry officials, and planners. Nevertheless, in October 1969 a decision was made to continue attempts to improve selected aspects of the system and extend their application. The case chosen to publicize this decision was the Shchekino Chemical Combine, which had successfully developed and introduced a system of personnel reclassification and dismissal leading to significant increases in labour productivity (5.28).

The Shchekino decision announcing the party's intention to continue at least some key aspects of the new economic reform was only a partial and temporary victory for the proponents of reform. Brezhnev's major report to the December 1969 Central Committee Plenum contained several indicators of substantial change away from the direction of the reform.[19] According to Brezhnev, there were 'insufficiencies, difficulties, and gaps' in the economy that were not petty little things to be ignored and glossed over by emphasizing general statistical indicators and results, especially in the areas of labour productivity and the effectiveness of social production. In addition, 'unpleasant but none the less very important' factors were impeding economic progress, especially personnel problems at the middle-management level. Lack of a feeling of responsibility, violations of discipline, and a lack of conscientiousness had become regular patterns and were being transformed into widespread practice. Brezhnev's position was that the key to developing a successful economic policy lay in understanding that the Soviet Union had achieved a new stage of intensive development requiring new techniques

19 Excerpts from Brezhnev's speech are contained in L.I. Brezhnev, *Ob osnovnykh voprosakh ekonomicheskoi politiki KPSS na sovremennom etape* I (Moscow 1975), 414–29.

and decisions that could deal with qualitative factors in economic growth and increases in the effectiveness of the economy. What was required was a new strategy that accounted for full and rational utilization of existing production capacities, the introduction of the achievements of modern science and technology, and a parsimonious attitude to all resources. Brezhnev's solution lay in the direction of intensification of labour, party and state discipline, and more centralized direction of resources. At this point, the 1965 economic reforms came under direct attack since Brezhnev was identifying the problems they were to overcome while advocating a change in approach, with greater emphasis on centralized administrative control and the use of organization and discipline. However, Brezhnev went out of his way to present himself as a moderate. He explicitly rejected the solution of 'some comrades who wish to return to former times and especially to techniques of administrative fiat.' Brezhnev claimed to be representing an intermediate position in advocating continued trust in cadres but a more intensive application of mechanisms for monitoring behaviour.

The first visible evidence of a change in policy reflecting Brezhnev's position was the announcement in February 1970 of a widening of the scope of those held responsible for economic failures to include higher state and party bodies. Using problems encountered by the meat and dairy industry as an example, economic difficulties were explained by a series of administrative failures of the ministry's party committee to fulfil its supervisory and co-ordinative duties and to report the deteriorating state of affairs to the appropriate Central Committee departments (5.30). To correct this situation, a change was made in the party Rules at the XXIV Congress in April 1971, granting party organizations of ministries, state committees, and other central and local soviet and economic institutions and departments the right to exercise supervision over the work of the apparatus in implementing party and government directives and in the observance of Soviet laws (5.35).

At the XXIV Congress the relative importance of the 1965 economic reforms decreased when an additional factor was officially identified and recognized as critical to the regime's economic goals. The importance of scientific and technological progress was given formal recognition and it was rated as a decisive condition in raising the effectiveness of social production.[20] Two administrative reforms were introduced to cope with the demands of the scientific-technological revolution. First, the congress called for the creation of an intermediate level of administration in the form of science-production associations as the basic unit of production, and provisions were made in the party Rules for the creation of primary party organizations in production associations. Second, the party Rules were amended to give primary party organizations in research, design, educational, and other institutes not performing direct production functions the right of supervision over the administration of the institutes. The main purpose of these changes was to allow the regime to cope more effectively with a problem that had become increasingly severe and damaging to Soviet economic development: the issues of establishing research priorities in the natural and applied sciences and transferring advances in science and technology into direct production improvements. These issues became critical with the appearance of declining growth rates and the commitment of the regime to an increase in the production of consumer goods without a decline in the rate of increase in capital goods. The changes proposed at the XXIV Congress were directed at overcoming the science-technology-production nexus and improving efficiency through structural reform aimed at reducing superfluous administrative subdivisions and increasing the party's co-ordinative and supervisory powers. This was to be reinforced with the wider application of modern organizational techniques, computer technology, automated management systems, and scientific methods of administration and planning. However, a brief examination of the party-state relationship proposed in the two amendments to the party Rules indicates that there were serious structural and behavioural constraints limiting their impact.

The main purpose of establishing associations was to create a new middle level of management between the ministry and the enterprise that could co-ordinate concentration and specialization of production by reallocating production tasks at the enterprise level, improving supplier-customer ties among member enterprises, and improving co-ordination between research and production so that technological advances could be introduced more quickly into production.[21] Central planning was to be improved since there were fewer units to plan for and administration was to be streamlined since the association was to be made directly subordinate to the ministry. A problem arose in redefining the co-ordinating functions of party organizations at the production association level. Obviously, the most desirable situation would have been to establish a unified party organization in the association since the party would then be in an opportune position to co-ordinate all the activities of the expanded production unit. However, this optimal variant was difficult to introduce because of many competing criteria. The party was forced to choose sub-optimal forms of organization through affiliation in which several of the constituent enterprises of an association retained their

---

21 For a detailed description and analysis of the economic functions of production associations, see J. Cooper, 'Research, Development and Innovation in the Soviet Union,' in Z.M. Fallenbuchl, ed., *Economic Development in the Soviet Union and Eastern Europe* I (New York 1975), chapter 5; A.C. Gorlin, 'The Soviet Economic Associations,' *Soviet Studies* XXVI, 1 (January 1974): 3–27; L. Smolinski, 'Towards a Socialist Corporation: Soviet Industrial Reorganization of 1973,' *Survey* 20, 1 (Winter 1974): 24–35.

own primary party organization, often subordinate to a raion or city committee outside the jurisdiction of the chief enterprise of the association. This
resulted in situations where it was not clear to which raion or city committee
many primary party organizations were subordinated and situations where
no party organization could take responsibility for the work of the association
as a whole. Attempts have been made to overcome co-ordination problems
by setting up controversial 'councils of secretaries of party organizations in
production associations' (5.58). The councils of secretaries were mandated
to harmonize and co-ordinate the activities of the constituent party organizations on questions of party guidance over production, work with cadres, and
the organization of socialist competition. They were to have the power to
convene meetings of the party-economic aktiv of the association and to issue
recommendations to the constituent party organizations on issues within
their competence. However, they were limited in the scope of their powers
since they could not make recommendations to the constituent party organizations on issues falling within the competence of the territorial party organs.
Thus, there emerged a sharp discrepancy between what was expected of the
secretaries' councils as co-ordinating mechanisms and their actual powers.[22]

The second proposal of the XXIV Congress aimed at rationalizing the
science-technology-production link involved a change in the party Rules
granting the right to supervise the activity of the administration to primary
party organizations of all design organizations and bureaus, scientific-research
institutes, educational institutions, cultural-enlightenment, medical, and
other institutions and organizations whose administrative functions did not
extend beyond their collectives. This affected approximately 45 per cent of
all primary party organizations. The change was intended, in large part, to
overcome the gap between individual research interests and state interests
and to narrow the gap between research and production. Party committees in
institutes were given an expanded role in directly supervising a number of
areas of management activity (5.32, 5.34, 5.35). However, the expansion of
party rights in institutes also created the basis for a number of conflicts
within the institutes that set limits on the impact of intensified party supervision. The longstanding, informal, and potential conflict between party and
administration was transferred to a level of formal relations where subordinates in the state administrative hierarchy were often expected to pass judgment on their administrative superiors through the parallel hierarchy of the
party. Both party and institute officials had their own ideas as to the way
supervision was to be implemented and its intended effects. Charges were

22   For detailed evidence of the problems encountered by local party organs, primary party
     organizations, and the councils of party secretaries since 1973, see T. Dunmore, 'Local
     Party Organs in Industrial Administration: The Case of the Ob"edinenie Reform,' *Soviet
     Studies* XXIV, 2 (April 1980): 195–217.

laid that the temporary and permanent party commissions set up under primary party organizations to conduct supervision tended to encroach upon, usurp, or undermine the rightful authority of the institute administration. In addition, it was charged that party commissions concentrated their criticism on individuals rather than on policy matters and that they stirred up conflict and internecine struggle in their institutes. Often, even when the result of their work was salutary, it was alleged that the commissions operated improperly in the investigations, failing to consult with management or the party aktiv and bureau, working in secret, and issuing peremptory orders and administrative fiats. There was a great deal of inconsistency in interpreting and applying the new right of supervision. Some primary party organizations took it to mean a licence to examine arbitrarily any and all aspects of management's work. Others were more circumspect, activating their powers only in sectors or situations where difficulties were being encountered or work was lagging. The excesses and inequities in party work and the strong instinctive reaction by management against any criticism, gave rise to resistance from the administration. Some administrators attempted to direct the work of the supervisory commissions, thus provoking the charge that many commissions were simply tools of the administration. Others simply denied party commissions the information needed to carry out their functions, failed to co-operate in their investigations, bypassed them, or ignored their recommendations.

Time and again, the local party organs had to be called in to resolve conflict between the primary party organization and the institute administration arising out of the attempt by the party to exercise its expanded supervisory powers. In part, the long-term resolution of the conflict came through limitation of the party commissions' supervisory functions. The commissions were instructed to adhere to a number of principles circumscribing their work, including clearer definition of the scope of their activity, closer consultation with management and party bureaus, and more scrupulous concern for following appropriate procedures.[23]

Finally, the campaign or mobilization aspects of the post-1969 approach to economic administration were brought out in Central Committee demands for further intensification of ideological work and for improved organization of socialist competition (5.37). The thrust of ideological work was to be towards improving the work attitudes and behaviour of the workers. This production orientation was reinforced by enrolling large numbers of engineering and technical personnel and lower level management personnel in the campaign with the aim of using their authority and expertise to dissemi-

---

23 Accounts of the party-administration conflict and attempts to resolve it are found in *Current Digest of the Soviet Press* XXIII, no. 20, 6–8; no. 34, 1–4; XXIV, no. 2, 15; no. 6, 1–5, 27; no. 8, 18–19; no. 9, 12–14; no. 13, 19–20; no. 21, 13, 22.

nate proper attitudes and relevant knowledge that would lead to increased labour productivity. Socialist competition was to take on new importance, directions and forms determined by the scientific-technological revolution. It was not to be a campaign based simply on traditional Soviet approaches of exhortation and 'Bolshevik will' and measured in terms of gross output indicators. The program was to be based on a belief that more specialized knowledge, including economics, at all levels of the industrial system would produce more rational and committed responses by the participants in the production process. And its success was to be determined by additional criteria such as efficiency and quality (5.38, 5.49).

The limited impact of the Brezhnev–Kosygin reforms on the Soviet economy is evident in the slowdown in economic growth experienced by the Soviet Union in the late 1970s and early 1980s. The frustration and anger of the leadership, and Brezhnev in particular, is evident in Brezhnev's reports to the annual Central Committee plenums on the state plan and budget after 1978. The resistance of planning officials, ministerial executives, and managers to the leadership's attempts to move the economy in the direction of greater efficiency and productivity through administrative reform resulted in a return to more conservative and traditional approaches to economic problems such as increased discipline, more intensive monitoring of economic activity, improved ideological work, and stricter enforcement of legal norms (5.62, 5.63, 5.64).

AGRICULTURAL POLICY
The Brezhnev regime was faced with a situation in agriculture that paralleled industry: certain long-run structural deficiencies had been compounded by the often economically irrational and erratic policies of Khrushchev.[24] Two basic long-run factors affecting Soviet agriculture have been organizational and technical. The system of collective and state farms in the Soviet Union has produced a number of organizational constraints on agricultural productivity, including resistance on the part of the peasants, management problems, and the application of central directives without due concern for local conditions. In addition, the Soviet countryside has traditionally been starved of investments, both in terms of capital and in terms of the skill level of the agricultural labour force. Compounding these long-run factors in the previous decade had been Khrushchev's attempt to solve the Soviet agricultural crisis by employing constant campaigns, shifting the focus of agricultural priorities, and frequently reorganizing the administrative superstructure as substitutes for increased investment, the use of advanced agricultural technology, and a pricing policy that would provide incentives to agricultural

24   For an overview of the short-run and long-run obstacles facing the Brezhnev regime in
      agriculture, see Nove, 'Economic Policy and Economic Trends.'

managers and farm workers. The Brezhnev leadership, with the personal imprimatur of the General Secretary, used two early plenums of the Central Committee (March 1965 and May 1966) to announce the details of a 'new deal' for agriculture, raising its importance in the scheme of Soviet economic development and promising organizational stability, improved terms of trade, scientifically based policies, and capital investments as solutions to agricultural problems.[25]

The March 1965 Plenum dealt primarily with the organizational issue (5.3). Its focus was based on the assumption that failures in the agricultural sector – lagging rates of growth, slowly rising yields, insignificant increases in production of dairy products – had been caused by a number of organizational deviations. The decision of the plenum did not spell out in detail how the organizational obstacles to agricultural efficiency and productivity were to be overcome. However, it did signal the regime's sensitivity to the alienation that had been created in the countryside by Khrushchev's roughshod approach to agriculture. The document appeared almost as an apology to agricultural interests for what Khrushchev had done to them and a promise for an agricultural policy that was more sensitive to objective agricultural needs and was based on a more realistic assessment of agricultural problems and their solutions.

Despite the leadership's general sensitivity to the impact of organization on agricultural productivity, there was little evidence in its actions that showed any real understanding that organizational forms suitable for agriculture may reflect certain distinctive characteristics of rural ways of life. Marginal changes were made in agricultural organization such as easing restrictions on household plots and extending credit to individual peasants for purchase of livestock (5.1), the introduction of a new Model Kolkhoz Charter in 1969[26] and proposals for a nationwide structure of kolkhoz unions.[27] However, the regime was insensitive to the idea that it might be the basic forms of agricultural organization in the Soviet Union that were the source of unre-

25 Brezhnev's personal commitment to the change in agricultural policy is reflected in his speeches at the two Central Committee plenums. See *Current Digest of the Soviet Press* XVII, no. 12, 3–11, 36; XVIII, no. 23, 3–8. For detailed description and analyses of the significance of the reforms, see R.A. Clarke, 'Soviet Agricultural Reforms since Khrushchev,' *Soviet Studies* XX, 2 (October 1968): 159–67; J.F. Karcz, 'The New Soviet Agricultural Programme,' *Soviet Studies* XVII, 2 (October 1965): 129–61; R.D. Laird, 'Prospects for Soviet Agriculture,' *Problems of Communism XX, 5 (September-October 1971): 31–40;* Nove, *'Economic Policy and Economic Trends.'*

26 The text of the Charter is translated in *Current Digest of the Soviet Press* XXI, no. 17, 3–8.

27 For a discussion of the proposed nation-wide structure of kolkhoz unions and the Model Kolkhoz Charter, see R.F. Miller, 'The Future of the Soviet Kolkhoz,' *Problems of Communism* XXV, 2 (March-April 1976): 34–50.

sponsive and noncompliant behaviour in the agricultural sector. A continued commitment was made to the fundamental organizational forms, state and collective farms, and to the idea that only incremental adjustments needed to be made to achieve high levels of efficiency. In addition, a basic assumption underlying the regime's approach was that the direction of incremental changes in agricultural organization could best be determined according to organizational principles and experience in the industrial sector.

The regime's rigid position of imposing industrial forms of organization on agriculture was demonstrated in three organizational reforms of the Brezhnev years. In 1967 there was an attempt to bring the sovkhozes closer to industrial forms of management by transferring them to profit-and-loss accounting (khozraschet) (5.13). The aim was to improve efficiency by tying bonuses and investment funds to profits. In 1967 there was also an attempt to encourage subsidiary enterprises associated with collective and state farms. Small-scale processing of agricultural produce, the production of local building materials and consumer goods, and the development of production links with industrial enterprises were encouraged in order to make fuller use of seasonal surpluses of labour and materials on farms.[28] Finally, after lengthy discussion on the relative merits of delegating meaningful operational autonomy to local agricultural subunits in the form of the zveno (link), Brezhnev was able to impose his own position, which favoured larger scale middle-level units. A series of successful experiments had been carried out, directed at both horizontal and vertical integration in the agricultural sector. At the XXV Congress, Brezhnev announced that the policy would be pursued more systematically and vigorously.[29] Three months later a detailed Central Committee resolution was published outlining the rationale, forms, and procedures for introducing specialization and concentration of agricultural production on the basis of inter-farm co-operation and agro-industrial integration (5.52). What emerged as the major feature in the party's organizational component of its agricultural policy in the mid-1970s was an attempt to transform agricultural organization according to the latest model of industrial organization – the production association – with all of the alleged advantages of centralized planning and direction, middle-level co-ordination, allocation and pooling of regional resources, local responsiveness to specific conditions in carrying out basic directives, and closer ties with industrial suppliers and consumers.

---

28   A discussion of the economic dimensions of vertical integration of agriculture and industry in rural areas is contained in A. Kahan, 'The Problems of the "Agrarian-Industrial Complexes" in the Soviet Union', in Z.M. Fallenbuchl, ed., *Economic Development ... II, chapter 8.*

29   *Current Soviet Policies* VII (1976): 19–20. For the political background to the decision, see Miller, 'The Future of the Soviet Kolkhoz.'

Major changes in agricultural policy that promised to have a significant long-run impact came in the areas of investment, science, and technology (5.9, 5.26, 5.31). In May 1966, the Central Committee plenum announced radical changes in the party's agricultural policies in these areas aimed at filling the gaps left by attacks on the previous regime's approach. Criticisms and solutions were specific and action was required by responsible state officials. To heighten the import of the decisions, Brezhnev's name was directly associated with the proposals. Agricultural policy was obviously an issue of first-rate political importance as well as economic significance. The existing lags in agricultural productivity and efficiency were blamed on a whole series of technical problems. The plenum approved the adoption of several major programmes aimed directly at dealing with these technical constraints: extensive development and improvement of land reclamation and preservation through irrigation, drainage, water resource development, liming, and anti-erosion projects; expanded supply of mechanization, electric power, chemical fertilizers, equipment, building and other materials; more extensive research, decision making based on the results of the research, and rapid implementation of scientific advances; and, improved material incentive systems for employees in the priority-designated areas.

The party's programmatic statements regarding investment priorities within agriculture and between agriculture and other sectors of the Soviet economy that have traditionally been favoured in resource allocation decisions had their impact on the national budget. The Brezhnev years saw a massive redirection of resources into agriculture and related industries. Overall investment in agriculture and direct productive investment in agriculture grew significantly after 1964. Priorities were set to ensure that agricultural development was channelled in a capital-intensive direction, especially with the undertaking of major land-reclamation schemes, the mechanization of agriculture, and the wide use of mineral fertilizers. The terms of trade between the countryside and the city were adjusted in favour of the rural sector through direct subsidies from the state budget and adjustments in purchase prices of agricultural produce and above-plan premium rates. A number of measures were taken to improve the purchasing power of agricultural workers and upgrade their social services and living conditions.[30]

Evidence of the constraints that the regime has imposed on its own agricultural policy and its frustration in dealing with the issue emerged at the

---

30 For a detailed analysis of the changes in investment patterns, pricing, and manpower policies that resulted from the party's shift in agricultural policy and an assessment of their impact, see K. Bush, 'Soviet Agriculture: Ten Years Under New Management,' in Z.M. Fallenbuchl, ed., *Economic Development* ... II, chapter 7; R.A. Clarke, 'Soviet Agricultural Reforms since Khrushchev.'

July 1978 Central Committee Plenum.[31] Over a decade had passed since the introduction and approval of the Brezhnev course in agriculture, sufficient time to assess the impact of higher levels of investment and changes in pricing, planning, incentives, and the organization of agricultural production. Nevertheless, after reviewing the successes of the past, Brezhnev was forced to conclude that 'not everything in this sector is what it should be.' Brezhnev then launched into a blistering attack on the administration of all segments of his agricultural policy. The industrial sector had failed to produce agricultural machinery and herbicides, to develop processing facilities up to capacity, and to expand capacities. There were shortfalls in quality, design, and production of agricultural machinery. Agricultural equipment had been underutilized and abused. Chemical fertilizers had been used improperly. Reclaimed land had been cultivated improperly. There had been many mistakes resulting in shortfalls in animal husbandry. The major reorganization of 1976 aimed at specialization and concentration of agricultural production through the development of inter-farm co-operation and agro-industrial integration had not resulted in any significant breakthroughs because of resistance by planning agencies, ministries, and middle-level management. A host of construction difficulties, short-comings, and bottlenecks had significantly lowered the efficiency of the rural sector. The bottom line was summarized by Brezhnev in the following understatement: 'Each year we allocate more and more capital investments and material resources to the development of agriculture. But it must be said that in some places these investments do not provide the proper return in the form of output ... [T]he return from agriculture is still insufficient when compared with investment.'

On balance, the Brezhnev leadership recognized two major sources of the dismal performance of Soviet agriculture: capital investments and organization. However, for political and ideological reasons, it was able to deal effectively with only part of the problem. The regime pursued a consistent policy of large investments in agriculture and related sectors of the economy aimed at a stable and sustained rate of agricultural growth that would make the Soviet Union self-sufficient at an acceptable level of consumption and it showed itself willing to subsidize the agricultural sector heavily (including large grain imports at times of shortfalls). However, the pay-offs, in terms of high and stable output levels, were not commensurate with the investment. In large part, the failure of returns on investment to reach expected levels can be attributed to the failure of the party to cope more imaginatively with organizational problems endemic to the Soviet economy in general and agriculture in particular.

31   *Current Digest of the Soviet Press*, XXX, no. 27, 1–13

STATE AND PUBLIC ORGANIZATIONS

The party's policy on state and public organizations under Brezhnev was conservative for the most part, lacking in imagination and innovation. A pragmatic approach, largely devoid of utopian dimensions, was taken to the structure and functions of these political organizations, while there was a subtle redefinition of the relationship between their responsibilities and rights. A limited attempt was made to enhance their authority by improving their internal organization, by more clearly defining their jurisdictions, and, in certain cases, by expanding their powers and rights to satisfy certain requirements of their constituencies. However, it must be remembered that all of these changes took place within the context of the principles of democratic centralism and party 'rukovodstvo.'

Under Brezhnev there was a continuation of the policy initiated by Khrushchev (see 4.14) of improving the practical work of the soviets while marginally increasing their power and independence. The soviets' primary function was still defined in terms of mobilization and supervision over the implementation of party and state decisions. In addition, however, increasing emphasis was placed on their duties to solve problems of local significance within their territorial jurisdiction and to co-ordinate and supervise the activities of local branch units of ministries up to the limits of their competence. The soviets were depicted as an important mechanism for ensuring that housing, social, and cultural facilities promised through the plan were delivered and that distribution and maintenance of these facilities were managed efficiently (5.33). The party declared that the soviets must be strengthened institutionally and given more power, authority, and independence from outside interference in carrying out their tasks. Local soviets' rights were to be extended to give them a more active role in co-ordinating and directing the activities of the enterprises and services of direct concern to the locality. Lines of responsibility between different levels of soviets were to be clarified. The soviets were urged to strengthen their administrative apparatus. The careers of selected deputies and staffs of soviets were to be professionalized through the introduction and extension of training and retraining programmes that gave more emphasis to learning managerial skills (5.11, 5.19, 5.38, 5.44). Party guidance of the soviets was to be improved by eliminating petty tutelage and the usurpation of soviet functions by the party. An element of budgetary independence was introduced, with local soviet budgets to come partially from the profits of locally situated enterprises. The responsibility of the soviets was to be ensured by combining responsiveness of deputies to their constituents with hierarchical control over local soviets by the supreme soviets and councils of ministers of the union republics. Despite the calls for upgrading the status and enhancing the impact of soviet work, however, severe limits on their activities remained. There were continuing complaints that the soviets failed to make full use of their rights, that they were limited in their major efforts by branch ministries that were unwilling to co-operate with local officials, that higher standing soviets refused to grant them their new independence, that party organizations were constantly interfering in their work, and that the soviets were unable to attract qualified personnel.

In his Central Committee Report to the XXV Congress, Brezhnev made a number of significant departures from the previous form and substance of his remarks on the state. At the two previous congresses his report on the state was short and dealt mainly with the routine issues of upgrading the status of the soviets, expanding socialist democracy, and improving the administrative apparatus. At the XXV Congress, Brezhnev used his report on the state to convey a political message suggesting a tightening up or conservative law-and-order line in several directions.[32] There was reference to 'the question of improving our legislation and strengthening socialist law and order.' Legal norms and regulations were to play a greater role in regulating new areas of concern such as environmental protection. In addition, they were to be utilized more in regulating economic activity by ensuring compliance with the tasks of improving quality of output, economizing, and counteracting deviant behaviour such as deception of the state, report padding, the theft of socialist property, and manifestations of parochialism. Brezhnev called for the issuance of a code of laws of the Soviet state to increase the stability of the structure of law and order. The administrative bodies responsible for the law – the militia, the procurator's office, the courts and the judicial agencies – were also to improve their activity. Finally, special mention was made of the state security agencies and their work in protecting the Soviet state from foreign subversion. At the same time, however, the state security agencies were reminded that the source of their strength came from the fact that their work was conducted under the party's 'guidance and unremitting control, according to the interests of the people and the state, with the support of the broad masses of working people and on the basis of strict observance of constitutional norms and socialist legality.' Brezhnev's recommendations to the XXV Congress were followed in 1979 by a Central Committee decision detailing the responsibilities of party, state, and public organizations in the struggle against law violations (5.64).

At a later point in his report to the XXV Congress, and possibly in response to Western criticism of the lack of human and civil rights in the Soviet Union, Brezhnev noted that, while there was concern for the rights of citizens in the Soviet Union, 'we at the same time pay due attention to the problems of strengthening social discipline and to the observance by all citizens of their obligations to society ... We might recall Lenin's words to the effect that in our society everything that serves the interests of the construction of communism is moral. Similarly, we can say that for us, that which serves the interests of the people, the interests of communist construction, is democratic.'[33] Brezhnev's position of moral and legal relativism and his definition of civil rights in terms of state interests and compliance with social obligations indicated that the hard line on organized and public dissent would continue. On the issue of dissent, the Brezhnev regime was confronted with a major paradox that was never resolved. The trial of Siniavsky and Daniel in 1965 set the basis for the regime's conservative interpretation of the limits of dissent and this was supported by a broad spectrum of policies: repression through the legal system, harassment, the use of psychiatric hospitals, internal and external exile. Despite these measures, the regime was continuously confronted with a wide range of articulate and semi-organized opposition from a number of sources, including neo-marxists, liberal socialists, national minorities, Russian nationalists, and religious groups. These forces were able to express their views through a wide range of media, which included the publication of illegal underground journals and manuscripts (samizdat), petitions, influence over the editorship of certain journals, and the use of the foreign media and foreign publishers. New individuals and groupings emerged to take the place of the older generation of dissidents and in response to new issues. In at least two cases (Jews and Germans) the regime made major and unprecedented concessions on the right to emigrate.

The consistently conservative thrust of Brezhnev's position was emphasized at the XXVI Congress in his remarks on art and literature, where he served notice that the party's intolerance of the expression of dissent through creative works would continue. He warned that even talented individuals' work could be harmed by lack of principles, philosophical unscrupulousness, and a departure from a clear-cut class assessment of individual historical events and figures. The party could not be indifferent to the ideological orientation of art. Consequently, party organizations in the creative professions were required to take action when works appeared that discredited Soviet reality and to correct those who move away from the mainstream. In discussing the activity of the state security organs, Brezhnev expressed the gratitude of the party and the people for their decisive work in cutting short the activity of persons engaging in anti-state, hostile actions and of those who encroach on the rights of the Soviet people and the interests of Soviet society.[34]

Under Brezhnev the basic function of the trade unions continued to be defined as the mobilization of the work force to fulfil the tasks of economic and cultural construction (5.17). However, a balanced approach was taken to

---

33   *Ibid.*, 30
34   *Current Digest of the Soviet Press*, XXXIII, no. 9, 8

the elaboration of the techniques considered suitable for the trade unions in their work. Heavy emphasis was still placed on the traditional approach to mobilization work through unions as 'schools of administration, schools of management, and schools of communism.' The unions were depicted in a parental relationship with the worker, urging him to maximize his contribution to the general good by ideological work and through the organization of socialist competition and socialist obligations. The work force was seen as a malleable resource that must be shaped by the trade unions to fit the new requirements placed on society by economic reforms and the scientific-technological revolution. However, implicit in the party's approach to trade union work was the idea that a productive worker in modern society requires more than exhortation and identification with the general good to produce efficiently. Consequently, the mobilization functions of the trade unions were balanced by an extension of their functions in the areas of protecting labour rights, ensuring the observance of labour legislation, improving work conditions and enforcing safety provisions, and fulfilling plans for the output of consumer goods such as housing, schools, health facilities and services, trade and public catering enterprises, and social insurance. It was also recognized that the effectiveness of the trade unions depended on the level of education of their members. There was a call for improved educational facilities for workers and trade union cadres.

The party's position on the Komsomol was traditional in its proposals for substance and style of work (5.21). Three primary functions were identified for Komsomol organizations. Labour mobilization was to be intensified and improved through various techniques such as direct organization of young people for specific tasks or projects, the organization of socialist competitions, socialization into proper attitudes towards work and labour discipline, encouragement of education and post-graduation upgrading of skills. Political socialization was to continue on an intensive level through the Komsomol's ideological and political enlightment work and through its influence in educational institutions. Cadre work was to be improved, especially with a view to utilizing the Komsomol as a major base of recruitment for the party. In all this, the party's direct role in Komsomol organization and activity was to be enhanced. Party organizations were held directly responsible for the ideological training of young people, consolidating the party nucleus in Komsomol organizations, and raising the responsibility of all party members for the state of affairs in the Komsomol. Party committees and party organizations were castigated for not going deeply into the substance of the activity of Komsomol organizations and failing to offer concrete daily assistance to them.

At the December 1965 Central Committee Plenum the party abolished one of Khrushchev's populist reforms – the Party-State Control Committee – which had been created at the November 1962 Plenum (4.39). A separate state network of People's Control organs was set up (5.6). The move can be explained in both political and administrative terms. Politically it served as a pretext for removing Shelepin from his position as head of the Party-State Control Committee.[35] However, the reorganization was also consistent with the leadership's general approach to party-state relations, which emphasized a clearer distinction between party and state structures and functions and a downplaying of the populist aspects of Khrushchev's administrative reforms. A decade after its effective withdrawal from meaningful work the regime began to revitalize the People's Control network as an administrative watchdog agency (5.50). The long delay in reactivation and the new principles of its organization and operation served to indicate that there would be significant differences from its predecessor. Its internal organization and activities were to be upgraded and routinized in the fashion of other public agencies and its activities were to reinforce the campaign for economic efficiency and productivity.

IDEOLOGY, PROPAGANDA, AND AGITATION

At first glance, the number of documents issued under Brezhnev's leadership containing ideological pronouncements would seem to contradict the argument that the Brezhnev years were characterized by pragmatism and instrumentalism. The regime availed itself of many occasions to make lengthy statements through party resolutions on questions pertaining to ideology. Official party pronouncements were issued celebrating the fiftieth and sixtieth anniversaries of the Great October Revolution, the one hundred and fiftieth Anniversary of the birth of Marx, the one hundredth and one hundred and tenth anniversaries of the birth of Lenin, the one hundred and fiftieth anniversary of Engels' birth, the seventieth anniversary of the 2nd Congress of the RSDLP and the 1905–1907 Revolution, and more. Almost any of these occasions could have been used to introduce significant new departures relating to the ideology. However, the Brezhnev regime was not noted for its substantive ideological developments.

The major theoretical advance introduced by Brezhnev was the idea that the Soviet Union had now reached a stage of 'developed socialist society.' This is a remarkably ambiguous concept that came into use only gradually and has never been properly canonized through detailed exposition of its characteristics and place in the stages of development towards communism in a formal party document. The concept was first introduced in a policy-making *Pravda* article on 27 December 1966. Brezhnev then made increasing reference to it in speeches, Soviet theoreticians elaborated on its meaning and significance, and it was discussed at length in the party's theoretical journal,

35   For the political background to the reform see Bilinsky, 'The Communist Party of the Soviet Union,' 31–4; Hough, 'Reforms in Government and Administration,' 27–8.

Kommunist. However, it was ignored in the Central Committee Theses celebrating the fiftieth anniversary of the Revolution in 1967 and received some
limited elaboration in the party documents only in early 1972, on the occasion of the fiftieth anniversary of the formation of the USSR (5.40). In the
latter document, the concept was briefly identified in relationship to the state
to include a number of features reflecting the current level of Soviet economic, class, political, ideological and nationality developments. Developed
socialism received full formal recognition as a stage in socialist development
in the new Constitution adopted in 1977.

What emerged from the new self-characterization of socialism in the
Soviet Union was an image of a society that had achieved a relatively high
level of industrial development and now required more intensive and sophisticated approaches to the economic, social, and political problems of a complex society. In the economic sphere this was associated with the need to pay
greater attention to factors such as the scientific-technological revolution and
managerial practices. In the sphere of social relations it meant such things as
more realistic assessment of the timetable for the elimination of differences
associated with the transformation to a communist society, a need to deal
more intensively with the social effects of industrialization and modernization, and continued emphasis on the need for national integration. On the
political level, the concept of developed socialism was associated with a
policy of re-emphasizing the role of the state in planning and administering
the construction of the material-technical base of communism, along with
Khrushchev's stress on the growth of public self-government through social
organizations. In brief, Brezhnev's depiction of the current stage of socialist
development in the Soviet Union provided the ideological legitimization for
a relatively conservative set of policies aimed at maintaining and strengthening the economic, social, and political achievements of the earlier transformationist period in Soviet development.[36] In addition, the incorporation into
the ideology of the stage of developed socialism contributed to Brezhnev's
status. It allowed him to take his place as a leading ideologist who brought
forth the concept of a new stage in the development of socialism, which was
broader than Khrushchev's all-people's state and called for a redirection of
the policies implicit in Khrushchev's formula (without rejecting the formula
itself) in favour of more intensified state activity and increasing popular participation through state organs (the soviets, which were renamed Soviets of
People's Deputies in the new Constitution).

The absence of radical developments in the ideology did not mean that
the party renounced its interest in ideological matters. The party attempted
two parallel and reinforcing approaches to the issue of ideological work. On

---

36   A.B. Evans, Jr, 'Developed Socialism in Soviet Ideology,' *Soviet Studies* XXIX, 3 (July
      1977): 409–28.

one level, the party was involved in the setting of tasks and directions of work for certain groups which make a direct contribution to the substance of the ideology by elaborating on existing principles and relating them to current societal tasks (e.g. the social sciences) or are involved in their dissemination (e.g. literary and art criticism) (5.16, 5.39). The party's general directives identified short-comings, requirements, and immediate tasks in these fields. Party bodies, state agencies and public organizations responsible for the formulation of details and the administration of policy were then charged with implementation. Local and primary party organizations were initially confined to the limited tasks of general guidance and supervision, cadres work, and providing assistance, without too much attention to details of substance. The assumption underlying this approach was that self-discipline by the administrative and creative elites involved would be sufficient to produce the required results, while giving reign to some degree of creativity to improve the quality of the product.

On a second level, the party at times exercised its right to determine that ideological work be intensified and that party organizations become more directly involved and active in performing ideological work. There was no linear pattern to intensified party activity in ideological work. However, a number of such waves can be identified, often in response to specific sets of circumstances. For example, the April 1968 Central Committee Plenum signaled an intensification of the party's concern for ideological work, obviously in response to the emerging situation in Czechoslovakia (5.20). After the December 1969 Central Committee Plenum there was to be a perceptible increase in the party's ideological work associated with the re-emphasis on labour discipline (5.37). The party's ideological machine was also exhorted to energize itself in conjunction with the multitude of anniversaries that were celebrated during Brezhnev's tenure, especially the fiftieth anniversary of the Revolution and the formation of the Soviet state. Finally, a proliferation of resolutions occurred in response to Brezhnev's Central Committee Report to the XXV Congress where he called for a comprehensive approach to ideological work 'that ensures the close unity of ideological-political, labour, and moral upbringing ...'[37] In less than a year, several Central Committee resolutions had been issued detailing tasks and activities and indicating a reformulation of the priorities of party organizations with more emphasis and resources to be placed on ideological work.

Most ideological work under Brezhnev was production oriented, that is, concerned with the mobilization of the labour force to achieve certain economic goals such as increased labour productivity, improved efficiency, lower labour turnover, improved quality of output, etc. To achieve these goals there was an attempt to change the system of ideological work in several directions: greater emphasis on communicating more specialized and economic knowledge; more careful differentiation of audiences according to their skills and needs; intensification of party control over the ideological work of the mass media; improvement in the teaching of the social sciences to specialists while they were still completing their higher education; greater specialization and differentiation among the functions performed by various categories of ideological workers; improved training for ideological workers (5.38, 5.46, 5.53, 5.57, 5.63). However, given the content and nature of ideological work in the Soviet Union, it is doubtful that these marginal changes contributed in any significant way to improving the overall efficacy of either agitation or propaganda.

CONCLUSION

The relative longevity and stability of the Brezhnev regime has demonstrated that a collective leadership, or oligarchy, in the Soviet Union can maintain itself and operate effectively as a unified entity over an extended period of time. Much of its success can be attributed to the adoption by the leadership of a strategy of incrementalism, which has operated at two levels. On the level of leadership politics, Brezhnev and his Politburo colleagues observed the basic rule of avoiding, at least in public, fundamental issues that might reflect or cause disagreements about principle. The leaders tread a cautious path: there was a dearth of ideological formulations that might imply sharp and irreconcilable policy differences within the oligarchy. Furthermore, Brezhnev apparently played a role that provided the regime with a mechanism for mediating disputes; at the same time he delegated significant amounts of power to those individual members of the group with specialized competence.

A strategy of marginal incrementalism was also pursued in the policy realm. The Brezhnev leadership took a number of measured steps on the issues of party organization, economic development, state and public organizations, and ideology that emerged as an integrated, if limited, programme of modernization by striking a balance between continuity and innovation. The adoption of the concept of developed socialist society provided a basic ideological self-image of the regime and its society in terms of marginal incrementalism – an approach to change that starts with given successes and problems and formulates further policy on the basis of alternatives, potential effects, and results that differ only marginally from the existing situation. It is an approach that stresses an image of policy making as 'problem solving,' moving away from existing problems rather than striking radical new strategies to achieve ideological goals. The initial party and state reforms in 1964–1965 were legitimized in terms of a rejection of Khrushchev's allegedly radical reorganizations (i.e. his failure to adhere to the principles of marginal incrementalism) and in terms of a return to previous forms, but with some changes in the rules and procedures aimed at institutionalizing relationships and making the system more efficient. At the same time, the party leadership sanctioned the introduction of the concept of the scientific-technological revolution as a symbol of modernization, to give some direction to change. Yet, while modernization was a commonly accepted goal, its vagueness opened up the possibility of differing interpretations regarding techniques, criteria, indicators, and rates of modernization.

The party documents confirm that the Brezhnev leadership pursued a policy of adaptation combining security for certain basic, core principles and values while effecting limited change in form, style, substance, and scheduling aimed at making the components of the system more responsive to the requirements of a rapidly changing environment and simultaneously securing for the regime an acceptable degree of party control over the direction and rate of change. Reform under Brezhnev was determined, first, by the successes, commitments, and values of the past. The Brezhnev leadership worked within a number of self-imposed constraints and limitations that provided an element of continuity with previous Soviet regimes and the pre-revolutionary bolshevik heritage. The limiting parameters were determined primarily by the acceptance and incorporation into policy of certain commonly agreed upon principles which included the leading role of the party, the efficacy of central planning, and the territorial-branch production principle, the ideological orthodoxy and practical advantages of collective and state forms of economic activity, the basic mobilization functions of the state and public organizations, and certain basic social welfare goals associated with the ultimate attainment of communism.

Within the long-run and relatively immutable parameters there also developed a sense of agreement that the current phase of developed socialism required its own special forms and style in political, economic, and social life. This flexibility resulted in the incorporation of a number of principles into policies on the party, industry, agriculture, and society aimed at bringing the major institutions and relationships of Soviet society out of their transformationist stage and into a phase consistent with the imperatives of an advanced industrial nation. For the party, this meant changes like a greater emphasis on quality in recruitment, increased stability and security for personnel, a selective attempt to expel inactive and passive members, and an intensive campaign to increase responsiveness within the party apparatus through the introduction of techniques to institutionalize, routinize, and expedite party business procedures. In the sphere of industrial management, there was an initial attempt to deconcentrate decision-making power, giving it to enterprise managers and providing them with a new set of decision rules. When resistance to these changes proved too strong, there was a return to more traditional techniques of evoking compliance by widening the scope of those responsible for enterprise performance, reorganizing industry

according to larger integrated associations, intensifying the party's co-ordinating and supervisory role, and reactivating the mobilization and disciplin-
ary techniques available to ensure compliance. However, this conservative
swing was moderated by continuous recognition of many of the factors
underlying the original economic reform in 1965 – the need for improved
quality, efficiency, and productivity. Agricultural investment policy showed
the greatest degree of innovation. Brezhnev's basic commitment to a shift in
the balance of investment in favour of agriculture was pursued consistently,
although the impact was limited by a relatively conservative attitude towards
organizational change in the rural sector. State and public organizations
exhibited the least innovative change. However, even in this sector, there is
some evidence of an attempt to make these institutions (especially the soviets and trade unions) more responsive to the needs of their clients by
expanding their powers and operational independence in limited areas.

In the broad area of decision making, which cuts across the lines of
policy and the branches of the economy and state, a consistent pattern
emerges regarding style and procedures that distinguished the Brezhnev
regime. The criteria for sound decision making shifted away from the traditional emphasis on ideology and political experience. Under Brezhnev,
officials in party, state, and public organizations were exhorted to take a
'scientific' approach to decision making. This approach involved a series of
clearly defined stages and prescribed rules for decision making: the gathering
of a wide variety of evidence from administrators, specialists, and others
affected by the decision; collegial discussion of the evidence that may
involve debate and disagreement, as well as continual criticism and self-
criticism after the decision has been implemented; the arriving at decisions
that are realistic in terms of their assessment of the resources available,
limitations, and the goals; a gradual approach to decisions that often involves
controlled experimentation before the final decision is reached; and an
accounting of the needs and capabilities of the units which are to carry out
the decision and those which are affected by the decision. In brief, what
emerged was an image of decision making as a systemic process in which
feedback and responsiveness played key roles, epitomized by the concept of
'the scientific management of society.'

Politics in the Soviet Union under Brezhnev may be characterized as
an ongoing debate and struggle over a series of complex balances to be
struck between continuity and innovation and over the degree and direction
of reform. Positions taken in the debate and the course of debate and reform
were not always consistent and linear. It was not always possible to identify
individual leaders on a reformist-conservative spectrum across issue areas
and over time. For example, the dominant personality, Brezhnev, identified
strongly and personally with major reforms (agriculture), with conservative
positions (moral versus material incentives or discipline versus economic

levers), and as a force of moderation between the two extremes (at the December 1969 Central Committee Plenum). In addition, the balances were neither static nor linear in their development and the shifting balances in various policy spheres did not always parallel or reinforce each other. For example, the 1965 industrial reform had lost its momentum by 1969, but it was never completely rejected. The turn to intensive ideological methods did not gain its full momentum until the mid-1970s and even then it was tailored to meet the needs of a modern industrial society.

The moderate and incremental nature of political change under Brezhnev is evident from the results expressed in the resolutions and decisions of the CPSU since 1964. A compact was reached with regard to the basic shape and direction of policy and, for the most part, change took place within the context of these fundamental decisions. However, what is less evident and even obscured by the decisions is the process by which the decisions were reached. We can only deduce from the moderate, middle-of-the-road positions that were finally accepted that politics under Brezhnev must have involved a great deal of bargaining, trade-offs, shifting coalitions, and weighing of diverse evidence. From Brezhnev's career since 1964 and from the image of his leadership that emerged at the XXV Congress, it further appears that Brezhnev, himself, must have deliberately and willingly devoted much of his energies to acting as a broker and attempting to achieve and maintain a consensus on major issues of domestic policy in the Politburo and Central Committee.

D.V.S.

Documents

5.1
On Eliminating Unjustified Restrictions
on the Private Plots of Kolkhozniks,
Workers, and Employees*   27 October 1964

This decision, the first published by the new regime, indicated its strong and immediate concern for the agricultural sector. It signalled a change in attitude toward the private sector in agriculture which was to become part of a much broader set of policies dealing with organization and capital investments in the collective and state sectors. The decision was accompanied and followed by legislation restoring farm plots to their former size, reinstating norms for privately owned livestock that had been reduced under Khrushchev, facilitating livestock acquisition and feeding in the private sector, and improving the collective farm-market system that serves as the primary outlet for privately produced foodstuffs in the Soviet Union.

1   Union republic party central committees and councils of ministers are ordered to consider and solve the problem of removing the restrictions introduced in recent years on the production of agricultural output through personal subsidiary farming by kolkhozniks, workers, and employees (in rural, urban, and suburban zones), proceeding in this matter from the norms for keeping livestock and the dimensions for private plots in effect prior to the introduction of the indicated restrictions by the union republics.

In resolving these questions, there must be no relaxation in the struggle against social parasitism.

2   The USSR Ministry of Finance and the USSR Gosbank are to submit proposals within a month's time to the USSR Council of Ministers on procedures for granting credit to kolkhozniks, workers, and employees for the acquisition by them of cows and heifers.

Resheniia partii i pravitel'stva
po khoziaistvennym voprosam
v, 517

_____

*   Excerpt: document not published in full.

Plenum of the Central Committee   16 November 1964

The November 1964 Plenum of the Central Committee was the first held by the new leadership. The extent that party organization was a cause of Khrushchev's removal was indicated by the quick agreement of the oligarchy to rescind Khrushchev's bifurcation of the party apparatus of November 1962. N.V. Podgorny gave the major report on party reorganization to the plenum, suggesting that he was charged with party organizational matters within the Secretariat.

A *Pravda* editorial, which followed the Central Committee resolution on 18 November (*Current Digest of the Soviet Press* XVI, no. 45, 3–4, 16) identified the official reasons for the return to a territorial-production basis for party organization and outlined the major lines of party activity. Khrushchev was implicitly attacked through the rejection of 'endless reorganizations' that were detrimental to the cause and the suggestion that the proper leninist approach was a genuinely creative search for new and better organizational forms that reflected political and economic necessity and practical expediency. 'Failures and mistakes are inevitable when a scientific approach is replaced by subjectivism, harebrained scheming, arbitrary and hasty decisions.' The editorial suggested that the main reason for reverting to the territorial-branch production principle was to allow more effective party performance of certain duties associated with regional development and co-ordination. Several duties in particular were singled out: unified supervision of the development of a territory, province, or district; deployment and utilization of cadres more rationally; integrated co-ordination of industrial and agricultural life. The bifurcation of party organs had inhibited the efficient achievement of these tasks because it had resulted in an undesirable delimitation of the spheres of activity of industrial and rural party organizations. This had led to confusion in the functions, rights, and obligations of the party, soviet, and economic agencies and had forced party committees to replace economic agencies. As a result, administrative costs had increased and the district link had been seriously weakened. Cadres work had deteriorated. The ability of industrial centres to provide aid to the countryside had been reduced. In some cases, the influence of party bodies on production activity in the construction sector had been weakened.

Future party guidance of the economy was to be ensured by the party directing its attention towards technology and advanced experience, the solution of practical tasks, utilization of internal reserves, increasing production output, raising quality, and lowering costs. This activity was to be accompanied by the elimination of ostentatious ballyhoo and boasting, paper shuffling and large numbers of meetings, petty tutelage over economic bodies and incompetent interference in their activities, and administration by fiat and command. In other words, the party was to shift its techniques of leadership away from direct interference in the economic process and towards more proper party methods such as recruitment and socialization of cadres, supervision and verification of decision implementation, mass mobilization, and ideological work. While the redefinition of party functions contained in the Central Committee resolution and *Pravda* editorial may have made sense in terms of a theoretically rational division of functions and style of work between the party and state apparatus, it still did not resolve the traditional blurring of lines between party and state in practice. As is evidenced in many of the documents that follow, the old problems of party-state relations and administrative efficiency continued to plague the Soviet political system.

At the plenum P.G. Shelest and A.N. Shelepin were elected full members of the Presidium and P.N. Demichev was elected a candidate member. F.R. Kozlov was released from membership in the Secretariat and Presidium for reasons of health, and V.I. Poliakov was released as a secretary. Khrushchev's son-in-law, A.I. Adzhubei, was expelled from the Central Committee for 'mistakes committed in work.'

5.2
On the Unification of Industrial and
Agricultural Oblast and Krai Party Organizations   16 November 1964

1   To intensify the leading role of the party and its local organs in communist construction and to solve more successfully the tasks of the economic and cultural development of each oblast, krai, and republic, it is considered necessary that party organizations and their leading organs again be structured according to the territorial-production principle, this being a constituent part of the CPSU Rules adopted at the XXII Party Congress.

2   In oblasts and krais where party organizations have been divided into industrial and agricultural branches, unified oblast or krai party organizations are to be reconstituted, uniting all communists of the oblast and krai who work in both industrial and agricultural production.

In each krai or oblast party organization there is to be a single krai or oblast party committee.

3   It is recognized that it is necessary to reorganize the party committees of kolkhoz-sovkhoz production administrations into raion party committees responsible for the leadership of all party organizations, including those in industrial enterprises and construction projects located on the territory of the given raion.

The industrial-production (zonal) party committees that have been created on the territory of agricultural raions and in oblast and republic centres are abolished.

4   In all the krais and oblasts where unified krai and oblast party committees are being reconstituted party conferences are to be held in December 1964, to elect the appropriate party organs.

5   The procedures worked out and proposed by the Central Committee Presidium for unifying krai and oblast industrial and agricultural party organizations are approved. The Central Committee Presidium is charged with examining and deciding all organizational questions connected with the establishment of unified party organizations and their leading organs in krais and oblasts, and also with the reconstitution of unified soviet organs.

Pravda, 17 November 1964   *KPSS v rezoliutsiiakh* VIII, 495–6

Plenum of the Central Committee   24–26 March 1965

The Brezhnev regime made a major commitment to agricultural development that was closely associated with Brezhnev personally. Its approach to the agricultural issue was on two levels: organization and investment. The March 1965 Central Committee Plenum dealt primarily with the organizational aspects of agricultural reform. In his report to the meeting (*Current Digest of the Soviet Press* XVII, no. 12, 2–11), Brezhnev delivered a scathing indictment of Khrushchev's agricultural policies, suggesting that while the line adopted at the September 1953 Central Committee Plenum (4.2) had provided a correct course in the sphere of agriculture, the implementation of that line since 1959 had created serious shortfalls in agricultural growth rates and levels of production. He cited four causes to explain the failures: 'subjectivism' at the policy level, which resulted in mistakes in planning, pricing, financing, credit, and organization; insufficient and inefficient investment; failure to raise farming standards or increase land fertility; and short-comings in the work of party, soviet, and land agencies.

To rectify the economy's abysmal performance in agriculture, Brezhnev proposed basic reform of policy and administration in the system of state procurements and purchases by introducing long-run stability of prices and plans and by establishing pricing policies that encouraged the creation of approximately equal economic conditions for all agricultural units. The material and technical base of agriculture was to be expanded and improved through increased output, standardization, a rise in the quality, reliability, and durability of farm equipment, improved repair facilities, the availability of skilled specialists, etc. Scientific research was to be made more effective by freeing it from arbitrary administrative authority, increasing funding and incentives, and encouraging practical application of research results. Organization and administration of the collective and state-farm system was to be improved by promoting the development and prosperity of both forms of organization, eliminating management problems, improving financial and credit conditions, and the incentive system. Finally, party work in the countryside was to be made more effective.

Many of the problems identified by Brezhnev were dealt with in the mid-1960s through state plans, legislation, and directives. The Ministry of Agriculture (under the reappointed V.V. Matskevich) was returned to a central position in the planning of agricultural production. Farm managers were promised greater autonomy from central authorities in deciding exactly what to produce and how to produce it. All-encompassing campaigns that failed to account for local conditions were eliminated. Peasant and farm incomes were raised and the reward system was changed by abolishing the trudoden (workday unit). The agricultural pricing system was restructured to account for regional differences and encourage overfulfilment of plans. In general, prices of agricultural production were raised and prices of key agricultural inputs were decreased.

At the plenum, K.T. Mazurov was raised from candidate to full member of the Presidium and D.F. Ustinov was elected as a candidate member of the Presidium and secretary of the Central Committee. L.F. Ilyichev was removed from the Secretariat.

5.3
On Urgent Measures for the Continued Development
of Agriculture in the USSR   26 March 1965

... The continued development of the country's economy and a rise in the people's living standard demand that particular care be taken to ensure the continued advance of agricultural production.

The party has devoted steady attention to agriculture, and this is what made possible a significant expansion of the sown area and an increase in agricultural production.

However, the rate of growth of agriculture has been lagging in recent years. The plans for its development were not fulfilled. Crop yields have been rising slowly. During this time the production of meat, milk, and other products also increased insignificantly. All this has created certain difficulties for the country's economic development.

The fundamental reasons for the lag in agriculture were violations of the economic laws of the development of socialist production and of the principles of the personal material interest of kolkhozniks and sovkhoz workers in the advance of communal farming, the failure to strike a correct balance between public and private interests. Another significant factor was subjective leadership, which led to errors in planning, financing, and the supplying of credit to agriculture, as well as in pricing policy. There has been little capital investment in industrial and cultural-daily living construction; the material and technical base of agriculture was poorly consolidated. Great harm was done to kolkhoz and sovkhoz production by unfounded reorganizations of leading organs, which engendered an atmosphere of irresponsibility and nervousness in work.

There were serious short-comings in the organization of procurements and state purchases of agricultural products. The existing practice in procurements and state purchases of agricultural and livestock products fails to create the conditions necessary for the development of kolkhoz and sovkhoz production.

The needed measures have not been adopted for an advance in farming techniques, for increasing soil fertility, for the proper use of irrigated and reclaimed lands. Crops are sown at the wrong times on many farms. The rules of crop and livestock management are not always observed. Numerous stereotyped instructions on agricultural science, the maintenance and feeding of livestock, the arrangement of crop areas, and other matters were handed down from above to the kolkhozes and sovkhozes without considering local conditions. This hampered the initiative of leading personnel and specialists, as well as of all rural toilers, and prevented them from doing their jobs normally.

Other reasons for the backwardness of agriculture have been inadequate work with kolkhoz and sovkhoz cadres, an incorrect attitude toward specialists and a disregard for their knowledge and experience, poor use of the achievements of science and advanced practice.

The Central Committee plenum considers that the major task of party, soviet, and economic organs is to rectify, in a short time, the errors that have been made in agricultural leadership. The advance of kolkhoz and sovkhoz production is a vitally important task of communist construction. The efforts of the whole party and of the whole Soviet people must be directed towards its solution.

The CPSU Central Committee plenum resolves:

1   The measures for the further development of agriculture, worked out by the Central Committee Presidium and set forth in the report of Comrade L.I. Brezhnev, are approved. The CPSU Central Committee Presidium and the USSR Council of Ministers are directed to take appropriate decisions.

2   The Central Committee plenum considers that the successful implementation of the measures mapped out by the party for further consolidating the economy of the kolkhozes and sovkhozes and for increasing the personal material interest of the rural toilers in the results of their labour demands a radical improvement in the work of all party, soviet, economic, Komsomol, and trade union organizations. The principal and determining factor in their activity is daily concern for people, for the development of the economy of kolkhozes and sovkhozes, for increasing agricultural production, reducing costs, and ensuring the profitability of all branches of production.

It is necessary to reject decisively practices based on administration by injunction or by the mere issuance of orders and commands, on substitution for leaders and specialists in kolkhozes and sovkhozes; manifestations of showiness and ballyhoo are to be eradicated.

Efforts must be made to achieve active participation by the broad masses in the implementation of economic and political tasks, to ensure the correct selection, assignment, and training of cadres, and systematic supervision over the fulfilment of party decisions. Discipline must be strengthened in all links of the party and state apparatus, in all sectors of social production; the responsibility of each worker for his assigned task must be heightened.

Particular attention should be devoted to reinforcing and increasing the role of the primary party organizations of kolkhozes and sovkhozes. Raion party committees should rely on them in their daily work and help them to adjust their organizational, political, and educational activities with the masses.

3   The Central Committee plenum attributes special significance to the development of agricultural science. It is the duty of scientific workers to expand theoretical research, improve its scientific level and its productiveness, and give all possible assistance to kolkhozes and sovkhozes in the broad application of scientific achievements and advanced practice for the benefit of the further development of all branches of kolkhoz and sovkhoz production.

4   Party, soviet, and agricultural organs must strive for a decisive strengthening of the democratic bases of the kolkhoz system, for strict observance of the principles of artel administration and for extensive participation by kolkhozniks in solving the fundamental problems of kolkhoz production. Measures are to be taken for the further consolidation and safeguarding of public socialist property, for ensuring orderliness in the use of land and for ending incidents of land wastefulness.

It is considered necessary to start elaborating new Model Rules for the agricultural artel and to prepare for the Third All-Union Congress of Kolkhozniks ...

Pravda, 27 March 1965   *KPSS v rezoliutsiiakh* VIII, 502–5

5.4
On Serious Errors Committed by the Kharkov Oblast
Party Organization with Respect to the Admission of
Young Communists into the Party and their Education   20 July 1965

This resolution served as an open indicator of the struggle for political power that occurred after Khrushchev's removal from office. The choice of the Kharkov oblast party committee as the example of incorrect recruitment procedures and the naming of the party secretary, G.I. Vashchenko, in the public version of the document can be explained in terms of a direct attack on N.V. Podgorny. In the early 1950s Podgorny had been the first secretary of the Kharkov oblast party committee. He had maintained his contacts with Kharkov through 1963 as the second and then first secretary of the Ukrainian party organization. In the CPSU Secretariat since 1963 Podgorny had been Brezhnev's deputy for party organizational questions. In addition, a close Podgorny associate, V.N. Titov (who had succeeded Podgorny to the position of first secretary in Kharkov), had been since 1961 head of the Party Organs Department of the CPSU Central Committee and then the Central Committee secretary in charge of organizational work (i.e. cadres). Vashchenko had served as second secretary under Titov in Kharkov. Thus, an attack on party recruitment policy using Kharkov as the exemplary case was an attack on Podgorny and his protégés. Vashchenko was allowed to retain his position after admitting his mistakes. However, Titov was shortly removed from his position in the Secretariat and in December it was announced that Podgorny had been elected to the largely ceremonial position of Chairman of the Presidium of the Supreme Soviet. At the XXIII Congress, held in April 1966, Podgorny's absence from the list of Central Committee secretaries confirmed his removal from his power base (although he retained his Politburo seat until May 1977).

Having heard the report by Comrade G.I. Vashchenko, secretary of the Kharkov oblast committee of the Ukrainian Communist party, the CPSU Central Committee notes that serious short-comings and errors are tolerated in the work of the oblast party organizations in party admissions. Despite the provisions of the CPSU Rules and Programme calling for higher standards of admission into the party, many primary party organizations, raion and city party committees are concerned primarily with quantitative growth of the party ranks, frequently accepting persons for admission into the CPSU without carefully checking into their political, business, and moral qualities, forgetting that what is important for the party is not the admission of new members per se but filling its ranks with genuine fighters for the cause of communism. 'It is better,' as V.I. Lenin pointed out, 'for ten working people not to call themselves party members (real working people do not chase after titles!), than for one chatterbox to have the right and opportunity to be a party member.'

In their drive for quantity many city and raion party committees directly orient party organizations toward increasing the rate of admission to the party, often evaluate the state of their organizational and political-educational work primarily by the number of persons admitted to the CPSU, criticize party organizations not for short-comings and omissions in party organizational and mass political work but for growing too slowly or for taking in fewer new members than during the corresponding period of the previous year. The pressure of city and raion committees, and in some cases even of the oblast committee, on the party organizations, instigating them directly or indirectly to force the rate of admission into the party, leads to a situation where, in many party organizations, practically everyone who applies is admitted.

Violations of the Rules for admission into the party are tolerated and applications are examined only formally and in haste. CPSU members frequently write recommendations for people whom they hardly know, giving a non-objective description of their political, business, and moral qualities, and yet are not held responsible for this. The opinions of party groups are not always taken into consideration in deciding on admission to the party. As a rule, the primary party organizations, raion and city party committees do not discuss matters connected with errors of admission into the CPSU, do not evaluate them from the point of view of principle. As a result of these inexacting demands and inadequate verification, people make their way into the party who are unworthy of the lofty title of communist. Evidence of this is the increasing numbers of candidates in the oblast party organizations who have been expelled for various misdemeanours and violations of the CPSU rules.

In their guidance of party admissions some city and raion party committees do not always take into account concrete production conditions and features, issuing stereotyped directives on the composition of the new party membership to all party organizations. This leads to such abnormal situations as, for example, the presence of too few scholars, engineers, and technicians among the newly admitted party members of certain scientific institutions, and of too few workers among new party members in certain large production collectives.

The CPSU Central Committee notes that, in accepting a large number of new members and candidates into the ranks of the party, the party organizations, raion and city committees do not manifest sufficient concern for their education and ideological tempering, for increasing their vanguard role in production, for their activity in the struggle to implement party decisions, or for the personal responsibility of each communist for the situation in the sector where he is working. Many candidates and young party members know little about the fundamental principles and norms of party life, the statutory obligations of a communist, understand inadequately the domestic and foreign policy of the CPSU. Some young communists have no party assignments, are passive, and are losing their connection with the party organizations and even relinquish their membership in the party.

The education of party members and candidates is seriously harmed in many party organizations by violations of internal party democracy, by the disparagement of the role of party meetings as schools for training, by the inadequate development of criticism and self-criticism, and by a liberal attitude toward malicious violations of party and state discipline.

The CPSU Central Committee considers that the Kharkov oblast party committee is giving inadequate guidance to the work of city and raion party committees in the admission of young communists into the party and their education and has not taken the required timely measures to rectify the serious short-comings and errors that it has tolerated.

The CPSU Central Committee resolves:

1   The attention of the Kharkov oblast party committee must be directed to the serious short-comings in the work of the oblast party organization noted in this resolution. The oblast, city, and raion party committees are required to take measures ensuring undeviating observance of the requirements of the CPSU Rules on the admission of young communists into the party and their education.

2   The enthusiasm of many party organizations for quantitative growth in the party's ranks to the detriment of the quality of the newly admitted members is judged to be harmful and incompatible with leninist principles. The numerical growth of party organizations is not an end in itself but must proceed on the basis of day-to-day organizational and political-educational work among the broad masses of the toilers, promoting the consolidation of party organizations and strengthening their influence on the solution of economic and political tasks.

In selecting people for the party it must be borne in mind that the admission of even a few persons unworthy of the lofty title of communist is harmful to the party, chokes its ranks, lowers its authority, and weakens the fighting efficiency of party organizations.

3   In working to increase the ranks of the CPSU, the oblast party committee and the city and raion committees are ordered to be guided strictly by the requirements of the Rules and to ensure the individual selection of the most advanced and conscious workers, kolkhozniks, and representatives of the intelligentsia, particularly those occupied in decisive sectors of industrial and agricultural production, science and culture, and participating actively in communist construction.

4   The CPSU Central Committee directs the particular attention of the oblast, city and raion party committees, and all party organizations of the oblast to the need for strengthening the ideological education and party tempering of young communists. It is necessary to strive so that each young communist persistently masters marxist-leninist theory, actively participates in party and public life, serves as an example for the observance of the moral code of a builder of communism. Party organizations must inculcate in young communists a feeling of high party responsibility, irreconcilability to short-comings, actively help them develop within themselves the qualities of

true fighters for the cause of the party. They must decisively do away with the present lenience and liberalism in the attitude of members and candidates of the CPSU whose activities are incompatible with membership in the party.

The oblast, city and raion party committees and the primary party organizations must strengthen their leadership of Komsomol organizations, give them more active help in their work of communist education of young people, raise their responsibility for recommending the most worthy Komsomol members to the ranks of the party.

5   It is recommended that the oblast, city, and raion party committees discuss the condition of work in admitting young communists into the party and educating them at plenums of party committees and meetings of primary party organizations ...

Partiinaia zhizn', no. 15   *KPSS v rezoliutsiiakh* VIII, 511–14
(1965): 23–5

Plenum of the Central Committee   27–29 September 1965

Economic reform of the type approved by the September 1965 Central Committee Plenum was preceded by lengthy discussion and several experiments. As early as 1950 the economist, Evsei Liberman, had made rather tentative and cautious proposals to induce enterprises to strive for higher plans by introducing long-term norms of profitability as the basis for incentive payments and the drafting by enterprises of their own technical, production, and financial plans on the basis of assigned output and assortment targets. In the mid-1950s Liberman added to his reputation as an advocate of reform by writing a series of articles focusing on more effective use of khozraschet or economic accountability as a technique for assessing enterprise performance. However, these proposals were relatively conservative because they provided for highly differentiated norms of profitability by branch and industry and because of the way profitability was defined in relation to cost. The discussion was renewed in 1962 when Liberman presented his old ideas on establishing profitability norms and the preparation of plans by enterprises themselves. This time he provided a more complex and controversial definition of profitability as the relationship of profit to capital and by laying greater stress on the norms being applied not to individual producing units but to entire industrial branches and groups of enterprises in approximately the same natural and technical conditions so that comparisons of efficiency could be made within groups. The early

1960s also witnessed a number of limited experiments to test the feasibility and impact of new types of performance indicators and bonus systems.

After the change in leadership in October 1964, the move toward economic reform continued with additional support from the centre. There was an expansion of the experiments that had begun under Khrushchev. One of the new leaders, Kosygin, became a spokesman for the reform. Kosygin indicated in various public pronouncements that he was favourably disposed to the ideas of reforming performance indicators and expanding direct contacts between enterprises and that these changes should take place not only in the consumer goods sector. These were principles of administration that should be applied in other branches as well.

The importance of the present decision as a landmark in Soviet administrative policy was indicated by the expansion of the Central Committee meeting to include as participants oblast party committee first secretaries, chairmen of the councils of ministers of the union republics, second secretaries of the central committees of the union republic parties, chairmen of the USSR state committees, officials from the Secretariat and the USSR Council of Ministers, and editors-in-chief of the central newspapers. Kosygin delivered the main report on the reform (*Current Digest of the Soviet Press* XVII, no. 30, 3–15). The first part of his report dealt with a number of factors that were placing limits on the Soviet economy's ability to maintain high and stable growth rates. Pressures faced by the economy included the increased scale and complexity of the economy, an increased need to introduce scientific and technological advances into production, and a need to divert an ever-increasing share of investments into consumption. These pressures were compounded by a number of structural inefficiencies. Finally, administrative problems such as increasing administrative costs, restrictions on the rights and responsibilities of enterprises, formalism of economic accountability, and poor use of economic incentives were imposing further limitations on economic growth and efficiency.

Kosygin offered two specific kinds of solutions to overcome the problems of economic growth and administration in the Soviet Union. The first part of the reform required certain changes in planning and administrative processes. At the national level, there had to be improvements in planning and reforms in the pricing system. At the enterprise level, Kosygin advocated several changes on the input side: differential charges on capital, greater scope for enterprise management to manipulate labour resources, and an incentive system tied more closely to productivity. On the output side, Kosygin proposed the replacement of the multitude of performance indicators with two basic success indicators: profitability defined as the ratio of profits to fixed and working capital, and sales. Enterprise management was to be made more responsible for its actions through more extensive and systematic use of economic accountability, but was to be given more scope in deciding certain production questions. The second type of reform proposed in Kosygin's report dealt with a number of governmental and administrative reorganizations that would provide the organizational context of the reform. The most important of these was a rejection of Khrushchev's sovnarkhozes (4.16) and a return to the industrial-branch principle of government organization. At the same time Kosygin advocated retention of the territorial network of material-technical supply under a union republic state committee. At the intermediate level of the system Kosygin made mention of the need to develop production associations on a khozraschet basis as well as placing many glavki on the same type of economic accountability. The ministries were to refocus their efforts on broad policy issues, especially technological policy. In their relations with the enterprises under their jurisdiction they were to make wider use of economic levers and be more careful about defining the ministry's duties as well as exercising its rights vis-à-vis the enterprise.

The thrust of Kosygin's proposals was to maintain central prerogatives in planning and improve the planning process while at the same time decentralizing and simplifying the administrative component by strengthening and increasing the responsibility of intermediate structures such as production associations and providing an improved incentive system and performance indicators at the enterprise level. However, as was to be demonstrated in the implementation of the reform, such distinctions on paper are complicated in reality by conflicting political interests. Kosygin expressed a compromise between the centralizers who were to gain by having the central ministerial structure reinstated and the reformers who saw the critical component of the reform to be the new rights gained by enterprise managers. In the implementation stage, strong opposition to the decentralizing tendencies of the reform continued to operate and this required constant modification of the program (see 5.23, 5.25, 5.28). This course of events put extreme pressure on the local and primary party organizations, which were charged with the special responsibility of supervising the implementation of the reform.

At the plenum two personnel changes were announced. F.D. Kulakov was appointed to the Secretariat and V.N. Titov was relieved of his membership in the Secretariat in connection with his transfer to party work in Kazakhstan.

5.5
On Improving Industrial Management, Improving Planning, and Reinforcing Economic Incentives in Industrial Production   29 September 1965

... The important tasks that confront the Soviet economy in the sphere of raising the level and rates of industrial development, accelerating technical progress in all branches of the economy, and further raising the people's well-being, require the mobilization of all potentialities for the full utilization of existing industrial reserves and for the growth of national income. The most important of these include an increase in production efficiency, the growth of labour productivity, an increase in the return on capital investments and basic production funds, implementation of the strictest economy, the elimination of waste and non-productive expenditures, and the comprehensive development of the working people's creative initiatives in solving these tasks.

Great significance is attached to improving the planned direction of the economy and raising the scientific level of state planning. Economic plans must take account of the prospects for scientific and technological progress, provide for rapid introduction and mastery of the latest achievements of science and technology, and must be based on real and objective calculations. In the drawing up of plans it is necessary to observe the extremely important principles: strict regard for the economic laws of socialism, assurance of balance in the development of the economy, and obtaining maximum industrial production with minimum expenditures.

The Central Committee plenum notes that the existing management structure and methods of planning and economic incentives in industry do not correspond to present-day conditions and the level of development of productive forces.

A serious short-coming in the leadership of industry is the fact that administrative methods have prevailed to the detriment of economic methods. To a large extent economic accountability at enterprises bears a formal stamp; enterprises' rights in economic activities are limited.

The work of enterprises is regulated by a large number of plan indices, which limit the independence and initiative of enterprise collectives and reduce their responsibility for improving the organization of production. The system of material encouragement for industrial workers gives them little incentive to improve the overall results of the work of enterprises, to improve production profitability, and to improve the quality of industrial output.

The management of industry according to the territorial principle, while having somewhat broadened the possibilities for inter-branch specialization and co-operation in industrial production within the confines of economic regions, at the same time impeded the development of branch specialization and of rational production ties between enterprises located in different economic regions, made science remote from production, and led to splintered and multilevelled direction of the industrial branches and to a loss of operativeness in work.

In order to achieve a further development of industry and an increase in the effectiveness of social production, an acceleration of technical progress, an increase in the national income growth rates, and to assure on that basis a further upswing in the well-being of the Soviet people, it is necessary to improve planning methods, to strengthen economic stimulation of industrial production, and to increase the material interest of workers in improving results of the enterprises' work.

The Central Committee plenum considers it necessary to organize the management of industry according to branches of industry.

It is considered expedient to eliminate excessive regulation of enterprises' activities, to reduce the number of plan indices approved for enterprises from above, to provide them with the necessary means for developing and improving production, and to improve the utilization of such highly important economic levers as profit, price, bonus and credit.

Economic and planning agencies are required to show great flexibility and operativeness in the planning and management of production, ability to take account promptly of the changing economic situation, to manoeuvre resources, to tie production to the growing needs and demand of the population, to strengthen economic accountability, to introduce scientific and technical achievements quickly, and to find better ways of solving economic tasks in the concrete conditions of the enterprise.

The entire system for planning and directing production and for material encouragement must be directed toward securing high rates of development for social production and toward raising its effectiveness. A most important condition for achieving the indicated aims is the creation of an incentive on the part of enterprise collectives to work out higher plan targets, improve the utilization of production funds, the labour force, and material and financial resources, perfect technology and the organization of labour, and raise the profitability of production.

In broadening the economic independence of enterprises, the party and Soviet government will continue to conduct a unified policy in the sphere of planning the main trends in the development of production, technical progress, capital investments, prices, wages and finance.

The great significance of the proposed measures for improving the organization of management and strengthening economic methods of directing industry resides in the fact that they combine unified state planning with full economic accountability by the enterprises, centralized branch management with extensive republic and local economic initiative, and the principle of one-man management with an increased role for production collectives. At the same time, further expansion of democratic principles of management is assured and the economic preconditions are created for broader participation by the masses in the management of production and for their influencing the results of the enterprises' economic work. This system of economic management more fully corresponds to present-day requirements and will make it possible to utilize better the advantages of the socialist system.

The plenum approves the measures worked out by the Central Committee Presidium and set forth in the report by Comrade A.N. Kosygin, a member of the Central Committee Presidium and Chairman of the USSR Council of Ministers, for improving the management of industry, perfecting planning and strengthening economic stimulation of industrial production, and assigns to the Central Committee Presidium and the USSR Council of Ministers the task of taking decisions on these questions and of presenting for consideration by the USSR Supreme Soviet their proposals on the organs to be charged with the management of industry.

The plenum charges the Central Committee Presidium, the Council of Ministers, the central committees of the union republics, and the krai and oblast party committees quickly to resolve all organizational issues associated with the formation of union republic and all-union ministries, as well as organs of economic leadership at the localities, so that the normal work of industry can be ensured, questions of the utilization and placement of cadres from the abolished economic organizations can be decided correctly, and enterprises can be strengthened with highly qualified cadres. The newly created ministries and departments are to be staffed with highly qualified specialists and good organizers who are capable of conducting business according to state requirements.

The main task of the ministries, collectives of industrial enterprises, scientific research organizations, design and project organizations is considered to be ensurance of high rates of development and a rise in the effectiveness of industrial production, all-round growth of labour productivity, and optimal utilization of existing production funds. To achieve this, it is necessary to ensure in practice the wide economic application of the newest achievements of domestic and foreign science and technology, scientific organization of labour, improvement in the quality of production, strengthening of state and production discipline, and a rise in the responsibility of each worker for the task assigned to him.

The Central Committee plenum emphasizes that the ministries bear responsibility before the party, state, and Soviet people for the successful development of industry, its high technical level, for providing all branches of the economy with technically improved and highly productive machines, equipment, and instruments, and with high-quality raw materials and supplies, and for fuller satisfaction of the needs of the population for high-quality consumer goods.

The transition to the branch principle for the direction of industry and the strengthening of economic levers in the development of production raises even higher the role of party organizations of republics, krais, oblasts, cities, raions, enterprises, ministries, and departments in the struggle to assure high rates of economic development and increases their responsibility for the work of enterprises and economic organs in the fulfilment of economic plans and state targets. Party committees must – without taking over the functions of economic managers – concentrate their primary attention on organizational work, on the selection, assignment, and education of cadres, on supervising the implementation of party and government directives, and on strengthening the communist education of the working people.

Party organizations must constantly study the activity of enterprises and help economic managers to expose and eliminate short-comings, direct the efforts of the working people toward seeking out and putting to use all production reserves, and wage a resolute struggle against instances of both departmentalist and localist tendencies.

Party committees must achieve a profound and intelligent understanding of the economics of production, organize a resolute struggle for thrift and the economizing of monetary funds and material and labour resources, must make this a matter of concern for all the people, must arm cadres with economic knowledge and teach them to make proper use of economic levers to improve industrial production.

Party, trade union, and Komsomol organizations must strengthen their work of raising the communist consciousness of the working people, develop their creative activity, fight persistently to increase labour productivity, to strengthen labour and production discipline, and show more concern for improving workers' and employees' conditions of work and everyday life. It is necessary to improve the organization of socialist competition among the working people so that everything progressive that comes to light in production receives mass dissemination and application. Maximum use must be made of the possibilities offered by the new system of management for a further upswing in production and for material encouragement of enterprises and industrial workers who are doing good work.

Economic incentives for improving the productivity of social labour are a powerful means for moving a socialist economy toward communism. At the same time the party will continue in the future unswervingly to pursue the course of raising the communist consciousness of the working people and of inculcating a communist attitude toward labour. Only if each toiler displays consciousness, initiative, and creativity in his approach to his job, only if each person takes a careful and proprietary attitude toward public property is it possible to struggle for the building of a communist society. It is the duty of party organizations to develop moral incentives toward labour in every way and to create all the conditions for a flourishing of truly communist creativity on the part of the masses.

The plenum obliges party organizations to explain widely the essence of the decisions of the current plenum to industrial workers and all toilers, to focus all the energy of party, soviet, and economic cadres on the fulfilment of the measures worked out by the party and the state. In working out these measures, our party proceeded from the basic interests of the working class, all toilers of our country; it comprehensively considered the suggestions and wishes of male and female workers, engineers and technicians, scholars, party, soviet, trade union, and Komsomol organizations. ...

Pravda, 1 October 1965   *KPSS v rezoliutsiiakh* VIII, 516–22

Plenum of the Central Committee   6 December 1965

The December 1965 Central Committee Plenum dealt with two matters. Reports on the economic plan and budget for 1966 were given by the Chairman of Gosplan, N.K. Baibakov, and the Minister of Finance, V.F. Garbuzov. Brezhnev presented a concluding speech on the economic plan in which he focused on developments in the consumer sector, capital construction, and agriculture. In his speech Brezhnev made it clear that success in achieving the plan indicators would be determined by increases in labour productivity and improved management practices in conjunction with the new economic reform. He also stressed the importance the party placed on an improvement in the quality of production, especially in the consumer sector, and on the need for thrift and economy in production. Brezhnev emphasized two aspects of management in particular. First, he called for greater trust in managerial cadres and greater use of their experience. By this reference, he apparently meant that there was to be less interference in operational enterprise management by central ministries. The second aspect of managerial practices discussed by Brezhnev was the size of the administrative apparatus. He noted that when a small task arises there are requests to create a department or administration and then a main administration with additional staff and infrastructure. This tendency for any kind of work to require additional administrative staff and overhead was to stop.

The second major issue discussed at the December 1965 Central Committee Plenum dealt with one of the control organizations set up to counter administrative abuses such as those identified by Brezhnev. A decision was approved to reorganize the Party-State Control Committee into two separate hierarchies under the party and the state. This decision reversed Khrushchev's merger of the State Control Committee and the Party Control Committee which had been proposed at the November 1962 Central Committee Plenum (4.40) and brought into effect by a regulation of 18 January 1963. Under Khrushchev, the Committee of Party-State Control had combined the state control functions of supervising and verifying the performance of administrative officials in their capacity as state employees and the party control functions of supervising the administration of party discipline against party members who violated the party Rules. There had been historical precedents for both the combined and separate forms of control organization. Party and state control had been combined with the merger in 1923 at the Twelfth Party Congress of the People's Commissariat of Workers' and Peasants' Inspection (Rabkrin) and the Central Control Commission (2.35). Separate hierarchies for party and state control were re-established at the XVII Party Congress in February 1934, when Stalin abolished the joint Rabkrin–CCC and created two independent organizations: the state Commission of Soviet Control and the party Commission of Party Control (3.21).

The reform of the control organs can be interpreted in political, ideological, and administrative terms. The breakup of the potentially powerful Committee of Party-State Control undermined one of the power bases of Shelepin and was followed by his removal as head of the committee and as Deputy Chairman of the Council of Ministers. Thus, a relatively young member of the leadership, who had shown significant foreign policy initiatives in the previous thirteen months since his promotion to the party Presidium, was deprived of his control over the single institution that spanned party and government bureaucracies and possessed great potential power through its investigative functions. The political aspect was not referred to directly by Brezhnev in his report on the organs of party-state control (*Current Digest of the Soviet Press* XVII, no. 48, 3–4).

Brezhnev publicly legitimized the reorganization in ideological and administrative terms. Ideologically, the reform was explained as a further development and expansion of Soviet democracy, by transferring a properly 'public' duty to a people's organization, which could enlist the voluntary participation of the broad masses. What Brezhnev apparently had in mind was the placement of public inspection through the people's control organs into its proper perspective as one of several administrative devices available to the party and the state for carrying out the broad functions of supervision and verification. People's control was seen as a potentially useful, but limited, device in pushing economic reform and in combatting bureaucratism, red tape, mismanagement, and deception through guided populistic-participatory forms of activity. This was not meant to suggest that it would emerge as a substitute for the party's control responsibilities, either external over the economy or internal over the discipline of its members.

At the plenum, V.V. Shcherbitsky was elected as a candidate member of the Presidium and I.V. Kapitonov was elected to the Secretariat.

5.6
On the Reorganization of the
Organs of Party-State Control   6 December 1965

The CPSU Central Committee Plenum notes that the organs of party-state control have achieved substantial results in verifying the implementation of party and government decisions, in the struggle to advance the socialist economy, to reinforce state discipline, and to involve the broad masses of communists and non-party people in the work of supervision.

To involve the toilers widely in verification and supervision and to heighten their role in the functioning of control organs the Central Committee plenum *resolves*: the organs of party-state control are to be reorganized into organs of people's control, and these are to be one of the operational instruments of the party and government for the even broader involvement of the popular masses in the administration of state affairs, for ensuring systematic verification of the implementation of party and government directives by soviet, economic, and other organizations, for consolidating state discipline and socialist legality.

In accordance with this resolution the USSR Council of Ministers is to ratify the statute on the organs of people's control.

Pravda, 7 December 1965   *KPSS v rezoliutsiiakh* VIII, 559–60

XXIII Party Congress   29 March–8 April 1966

In the months immediately following Khrushchev's removal there were indications that the new leadership was committed to pursue a course of destalinization. By the spring of 1965, however, there were increasing signs that the political atmosphere was being influenced more strongly by conservative elements advocating a rehabilitation of Stalin. This tendency intensified through the remainder of 1965 and into 1966, thus providing the expectation that the XXIII Congress would be the scene of a formal announcement of a more conservative political line.

The proceedings of the XXIII Congress indicated that the leadership was still sharply split over the Stalin question and that no faction or coalition was able to generate enough support to impose its views. Brezhnev, who had publicly indicated some support for the rehabilitation of Stalin in earlier statements, opened his remarks in the Central Committee Report (*Current Soviet Policies* V (1973), 4–31) by referring to the fact that the success of the Soviet people in building communism in the recent past could be attributed to adherence to the line set down by the XX and XXII congresses which, of course, were known as bellweathers of destalinization. Only one other speaker at the congress made reference to the crucial Stalin issue. N.G. Yegorichev, First Secretary of the Moscow city committee, denounced recent attempts to look for elements of alleged stalinism in the country's political life for use in frightening the intelligentsia. He then went on to say that such an approach would not work and that the personality cult and violations of leninist norms of party life and of socialist legality had been decisively discarded by the party so that there would never be a return to this kind of past. Yegorichev then added, as a balance in his position, that this did not mean a total rejection of the past. There were temporary difficulties and individual failures that do not eclipse the achievements of the past. The weakness of Brezhnev's statement and the fence sitting of Yegorichev on the critical issue of Stalin suggested that the leadership was deadlocked at this point. This conclusion is reinforced by the failure of several leaders to address the congress (Suslov, Shelepin, Poliansky, Voronov, Mazurov) and by the absence of further discussion of the matter by any other speaker.

The leadership deadlock that necessitated compromise over the political issue of destalinization also affected the party's economic policy. One would normally expect the first congress of a new regime to act as a platform for the announcement of new directions. However, the resolution on the Central Committee Report was devoid of innovative approaches and policies. It was largely a reaffirmation of past economic successes and a promise for more of the same. Economic problems were attributed to poor administration, planning and leadership, and the tense international situation. To overcome some of these obstacles to economic efficiency the congress approved the approach adopted by the September 1965 Central Committee Plenum, and a new Five-Year Plan in which high and stable growth rates were to be achieved by improved efficiency, increased labour productivity, and wider use of scientific and technological achievements in production, as well as increased capital investments. An improved standard of living and a convergence of the rates of growth of the capital and consumer goods sectors were to result mainly from increased labour contributions to economic production.

The political component of the Central Committee Report and the changes in the party Rules reflected a concern for the development of more clearly defined procedures governing inner-party life and improved compliance with the procedures. In this regard, several principles were singled out for special mention: collective leadership, criticism and self-criticism, business efficiency in running the affairs of the party, and recruitment procedures. The party's societal functions were also to be regulated by adherence to more clearly defined principles setting rights and duties and establishing areas of jurisdiction and responsibility. The major party priority was to be implementation of the economic reforms. This was a wide mandate, but it was circumscribed by injunctions that party organizations avoid supplanting soviet and economic organs and assuming petty tutelage over them. Party organizations were exhorted to use compliance mechanisms appropriate to the party: selection, promotion and training of responsible officials; direction of the organization of supervision and verification of decisions; ideological work with the masses (agitation) and leading cadres (propaganda).

The congress was attended by 4620 voting delegates and 323 delegates who did not have voting rights. Kosygin delivered the report on the Five-Year Plan. There were several important personnel changes associated with the congress. A.I. Mikoyan and N.M. Shvernik were not re-elected to the Politburo and L.N. Efremov was dropped from candidate membership. A.Ia. Pelshe was elected as a full member of the Politburo and Chairman of the Party Control Committee. D.A. Kunayev and P.M. Masherov were elected candidate members of the Politburo. A.P. Kirilenko was elected as a secretary of the Central Committee. The Central Committee elected at the congress consisted of 195 full and 79 candidate members.

5.7
On the Report of the Central Committee   8 April 1966

Having heard and discussed the report by Comrade L.I. Brezhnev, First Secretary of the Central Committee of the CPSU, on the work of the Central Committee, the XXIII Congress of the CPSU resolves:

the political line and practical activity of the Central Committee is fully and completely approved;

the proposals and conclusions contained in the Report of the Central Committee are approved.

During the period under review, the party's activity was based on the line set forth at the XX and XXII congresses, and was directed at carrying out the Programme of the CPSU, at creating the material and technical base of communism, at further improving socialist social relations, and at the communist education of the toilers.

During this period major successes were achieved in economic and cultural development and in enhancing the material well-being of the people. The political foundations of Soviet society were consolidated: the alliance of the working class and the kolkhoz peasantry, the friendship of the peoples of the multinational Soviet Union, the solidarity of all the toilers around the CPSU. The CPSU ranks have been broadened, and its political and organizational role in Soviet society has been increased. The leninist principles of internal party life have become firmly entrenched in the party.

Guided by the teaching of Lenin, the party has improved the forms and methods of administering the economy, casting aside all that could not withstand the test of practice and was becoming a hindrance to our forward movement. Of fundamental significance for the activity of the party and for our society's continued movement along the road to communism was the October (1964) Plenum of the Central Committee of the CPSU ...

II

1   The Congress notes with satisfaction that, in the period under review, the working class, the kolkhoz peasantry, and the intelligentsia, in solving the historical tasks set out in the CPSU Programme, achieved substantial successes in economic and cultural development and in elevating the living standard of the Soviet people. As a result of the fulfilment of the Seven-Year Plan, an important step has been taken on the path to creating the material and technical base of communism.

A substantial increase in the volume of industrial production has been achieved. The major branches of the economy have been technically re-equipped. Power engineering, the chemical, oil, and gas industries, machine and instrument building have all been ensured rapid development. The production of foodstuffs, of manufactured consumer goods, and of articles for cultural and everyday use has increased considerably. The broad development of the productive activity of the toilers, the introduction of new machines and instruments, new techniques of mechanization, and automation into all branches of industrial production have made possible a substantial rise in labour productivity. The achievements of science and industry have facilitated the equipment of the Soviet Armed Forces with the most modern military technology so that the Soviet Army may be supplied with the most modern and powerful weaponry.

The Soviet share in world industrial production has increased. The Soviet Union has strengthened its positions and gained new victories in its economic competition with the principal capitalist countries. The past years have confirmed that in our country expanded reproduction at high and stable rates is an economic law of socialism.

The material standard of living of the toilers has improved. Important measures have been taken to standardize and elevate rates of pay in all branches of the economy. Taxes have been abolished or reduced for a substantial part of the toilers; benefits have been extended and pensions have been raised for a number of categories of the population; pensions have been instituted for kolkhozniks. The seven-hour working day has been introduced, and a six-hour day for certain categories of toilers. In the last seven years almost as much housing has been built as during the whole existence of Soviet power up to 1958.

Major successes have been achieved in cultural affairs, education, and health protection. During the last seven years the number of persons with higher and secondary education has increased almost one-and-a-half times, the number of scientific workers – more than two times.

The party's measures, especially after the October (1964) and subsequent plenums of the CPSU Central Committee, are promoting the rapid economic and cultural advance of all the union republics, an expansion of their

economic inter-relations and mutual assistance, and the further strengthening of the friendship of the peoples of the USSR. All this once again graphi-
cally demonstrates to the whole world that only socialism affords the peoples
reliable paths to their comprehensive development.

The Congress notes that, along with the great successes in socialist
economic development, the Seven-Year Plan was not fulfilled with respect to
some indices. The targets for the production of certain types of chemical
products, machinery, and fuel were underfulfilled. Agricultural production is
lagging, and this has had a negative impact on the growth rates of light industry and the food industry, has prevented the planned measures for raising the
living standard of the people from being carried out in full.

In recent years there has been a slight slackening in the growth rate of
production and of labour productivity. The effectiveness of the use of production funds and capital investments has declined. In many branches new
enterprises have not been brought into operation on schedule, and many of
those which were completed have not reached their projected output levels.
As a result, the growth rate of the national income has been less than that
projected by the Seven-Year Plan.

The reasons for these negative facts were short-comings in administration of the economy, underestimation of economic methods of leadership
and of economic accountability, incomplete use of material and moral incentives, certain miscalculations in planning, and a subjective approach to the
solution of many economic problems. The poor harvests in 1963 and 1965
had a negative impact on the development of the economy. It should also be
noted that as a consequence of the aggravation of the international situation,
there arose the need to divert additional funds to strengthening the defence
of the country.

2   The Congress fully approves the decisions of the March and September
(1965) plenums of the CPSU Central Committee which laid bare the reasons
for the short-comings in economic development and worked out a new
approach to leadership of the economy. The new system of economic management creates more favourable conditions for rational utilization of the
country's gigantic productive forces, for a rapid growth in the public welfare,
for a full revelation of the advantages of the socialist system.

The Congress places party, soviet, and economic organizations under
the obligation to implement consistently the principles of economic policy
worked out by the party that call for a combination of centralized branch
administration with an expansion of the rights of union republics, an enhancement of the role of economic methods in economic management, a radical
improvement in planning, an expansion of the economic independence and
initiative of enterprise collectives, and an increase in their material interest in
the results of their activity. The implementation of the new system of plan-

ning and economic incentives is one of the most important tasks of the forth-coming years.

Under the new conditions it is also necessary to devote increased attention to moral incentives in production, to strengthening labour discipline, to inculcating the attitude that labour is a patriotic duty and that each worker is personally responsible for the situation in his enterprise, construction project, or institution; maximum use must be made of the broad opportunities afforded for this purpose by the new system of economic incentives for production.

The Congress requires the industrial ministries to ensure more rapid application in production of the achievements of science and technology, the strengthening of ties between production enterprises and scientific-research and design organizations, and the comprehensive development of specialization and co-operation in production. Party and soviet organizations and economic organs must struggle resolutely to strengthen state discipline, to eradicate bureaucratic leadership methods, a narrowly departmental approach to affairs, and localism.

3   An important stage in the struggle of the party and the Soviet people to create the material and technical base of communism and to strengthen further the economic and defensive might of the country is the Five-Year Plan for developing the USSR economy from 1966 to 1970. The Congress views as the chief economic task of the Five-Year Plan a further significant growth of industry and high and stable rates of agricultural development – through comprehensive use of the achievements of science and technology, the industrial development of all social production, the heightening of its effectiveness and of labour productivity – and on this basis the achievement of a further substantial advance in the material and cultural living standard of the people.

In the new five-year period it is necessary to make better use of all existing opportunities for ensuring higher rates of growth of the country's economy. The productive forces created by the heroic labour of the Soviet people make it possible, together with the continued development of heavy industry, to develop more rapidly those branches of social production that directly satisfy the material and cultural demands of the toilers.

The Congress recognizes the necessity of ensuring during the new Five-Year Plan:

–   an increase over the previous five years in the rate of growth of social production, national income, and the real incomes of the urban and rural population;

–   a convergence of the rates of growth of the production of the means of production and the production of consumer goods;

–   the continued rapid development of industry, with electrical power

engineering, metallurgy, machine building, the chemical industry, and electronics growing at a more rapid rate;
–   a substantial increase in agricultural production;
–   an acceleration in scientific and technical progress and an increase in the effectiveness of social production;
–   the continued technical re-equipment of transportation and communication;
–   an increase in capital investments in the economy by about 1.5 times over the preceding five years, with state capital investments in agriculture to double; an enhancement of the effectiveness of capital investments and a substantial improvement in the basic proportions in the economy through more correct use of the material and financial means allocated to economic development;
–   a substantial development of construction, a growth in the capacities of the construction industry, a shortening of the time required to complete construction jobs and put installations into operation, an improvement in the quality of construction and assembly work, and a reduction in construction costs;
–   an improved distribution of production forces, the integrated development and economic specialization of the economies of union republics and economic regions; the accelerated economic development of the eastern regions of the country;
–   the further strengthening of economic ties with the fraternal socialist countries and the developing states; the development of mutually advantageous trade with capitalist countries.
4   The Congress attributes fundamental significance to developing agriculture on the basis of the system of economic measures worked out by the March (1965) Plenum of the CPSU Central Committee. The principal way to increase agricultural production is through the steady intensification of agriculture on a firm basis of the mechanization, electrification, and chemicalization of production, and also through the extensive development of land reclamation in areas with unfavourable natural conditions.

An increase in the output of grain remains an extremely important task of agriculture. The decisive condition for accelerating the growth rate of agriculture in general and the output of grain in particular is to raise the yield of each hectare of land in every possible way. To achieve this, large-scale measures must be carried out, both in the country as a whole, and on each kolkhoz and sovkhoz, to increase soil fertility and farming standards.

On the basis of an increase in the output of cultivated crops and a rise in the productivity of natural grazing lands, it is necessary to ensure significant progress of communal animal husbandry.

In the view of the Congress a further consolidation and development of both the kolkhoz and the sovkhoz forms of organizing the public sector of agriculture are needed if the plans elaborated for the growth of agricultural production are to be fulfilled. The significance of the sovkhozes, as model forms of the socialist rural economy, must be enhanced. The CPSU Central Committee is instructed to examine the question of forming kolkhoz-co-operative organs in raions, oblasts, krais, republics, and in the centre.

5 The Congress considers it necessary to ensure, during the forthcoming five-year period, the further advance of the material well-being of the people by raising the pay of workers and employees, and the incomes of kolkhoz members from the public sector, by establishing a guaranteed wage on all kolkhozes, by increasing cash payments and benefits from social funds, by further improving the pensions of workers, employees, and kolkhozniks, and by significantly improving the communal, daily living, and cultural services available to the population both in the city and in the village.

With the increased production of consumer goods and the accumulation of commodity and financial resources, measures will have to be adopted to lower state retail prices on certain foodstuffs and manufactured consumer goods, and above all on products for children.

The Congress sets as one of the most important tasks the further expansion of housing construction and construction for the cultural and everyday needs of the population in the city and the countryside.

In order to create better conditions for the work and leisure of the toilers, a working week with two days off (while maintaining the existing number of working hours in the week) is to be introduced gradually for workers and employees, as enterprises become ready to operate on the new schedule.

6 An extremely important task of party and economic organizations, of all workers in industry, transport, agriculture, and construction consists of ensuring that there are high rates of growth of labour productivity on the basis of the technical re-equipping of all branches of the economy, wide use of the experience of the leading production workers and innovators, and fuller use of existing reserves. The scientific organization of production and the application of the modern achievements of science and technology in the economy must create increasingly favourable conditions for the high labour productivity of all workers. It is necessary for economic organs and party organizations in enterprises persistently to follow a course of all-round mechanization of production processes, steady reduction of the share of manual labour, more rational use of manpower, wider application of the scientific organization of labour.

The Congress considers that party, soviet, economic, trade union, and Komsomol organs must focus their attention on increasing the effectiveness of production, especially on improving utilization of production funds and bringing newly completed enterprises and shops up to full production capacity more rapidly.

The Congress sets as one of the most urgent tasks a radical improvement in the quality of output and a lengthening of the service life of machines, ensuring their more reliable operation, since our industry has already achieved a technological maturity which permits it to ensure the production of machines, instruments, apparatuses, and other articles that completely meet the growing requirements of the economy and the world market in their technical and economic indices.

7   The Congress emphasizes that, under conditions when our country is building communism on a broad front, the comprehensive education of the new man and the continued development of popular education and culture acquire ever-increasing significance.

It is necessary to expand substantially the material base of culture, to ensure an improvement in all forms of cultural activity, to improve the content of the work of clubs, houses of culture, and libraries. Measures are to be taken to expand further the network of stadiums, sports facilities, and other installations, especially in kolkhozes and sovkhozes. This must be a matter for the entire party and all its organizations, soviets, trade unions, the Komsomol, and all working people's collectives in the city and in the countryside.

In this five-year period the transition to universal secondary education of young people will basically be completed. The quality and content of general, labour, and polytechnical instruction must meet contemporary requirements. Schools are assigned the duty of inculcating in children the principles of communist morality and of improving the aesthetic and physical training of the growing generation. The level of pedagogical science must be raised. It is necessary to strengthen the material base of schools, supply them with modern equipment, and strive for the rational and full utilization of the resources allocated for public education.

An increase in the general culture and technical literacy of the toilers is indissolubly connected with the continued development of higher and secondary specialized schools. At the present stage, their primary task is to elevate the quality of specialist training. Soviet specialists must be armed with marxist-leninist theory and have mastered knowledge at the level of the latest achievements of science and technology, must possess the necessary economic training, and must be able to provide skilful solutions for problems of scientific and technical progress, of the scientific organization of labour, and of the administration of production.

There must be fuller use of the press, radio, television, and the cinema for the formation of a marxist-leninist world view and for the political and cultural development of all Soviet people. Further improvement in the work of central and local newspapers and magazines must be achieved and publishing in the country is to be improved.

8   The Congress attributes great significance to the development of Soviet science, which is increasingly becoming a direct productive force of

society. The activity of our scientists must be directed at continuing to find solutions to pressing scientific problems of the present day, at accelerating scientific and technical progress in every way, at the most rapid application of the results of scientific research in the economy, at ensuring high rates of growth of labour productivity.

The major task of Soviet scholars in the social sciences is to work out problems of economics, philosophy and sociology, history, and law in close relationship with the practice of communist construction ...

III

1   The Communist Party of the Soviet Union came to the XXIII Congress united and fully armed with its rich experience in leading communist construction, in guiding the domestic and foreign policy of the country. The Communist Party of the Soviet Union is the leading and directing force of Soviet society. Armed with marxist-leninist teaching, it confidently leads the Soviet people along the road of communist construction, successfully fulfils its role of organizer and political leader of the whole Soviet people. The CPSU is linked by tight bonds of international solidarity with the fraternal marxist-leninist parties and revolutionary democratic forces.

The XXIII Congress notes with satisfaction that, expressing the will of the party, the Central Committee has resolutely followed a line of strict observance of leninist norms of party life and principles of collective leadership. In this connection the October and November (1964) plenums of the Central Committee were significant concerning matters of principle. The party corrected the mistakes associated with a subjective approach to the solution of important economic and political problems and those arising out of pointless reorganizations of the party, soviet, and economic apparatus.

2   The Congress approves the measures developed by the Central Committee for further improving the organizational activity of the party, for expanding ideological work among communists and toilers, for developing internal party democracy, and views their consistent implementation as essential. Criticism and self-criticism must also be further intensified. The development of internal party democracy presupposes a simultaneous comprehensive strengthening of party discipline, a heightening of the responsibility of communists for the state of affairs in their own organizations and in the party as a whole.

The Congress considers that the scientific approach, the collective spirit, and efficiency in the leadership of communist construction, and in the conduct of the domestic and foreign policy of the Soviet state, which have become firmly established in the working style of the Central Committee, should continue to remain the basis of all its activity.

3   The Congress notes that the growing authority of the CPSU intensifies the desire of Soviet people to link their lives with the party both ideologically

and organizationally and to enter its ranks. At the same time the Congress views as incorrect the trend, noted in certain party organizations, toward violating the principles of individual selection and lowering the requirements for entry into the CPSU. The Congress places all party organizations under the obligation to be more attentive to matters of party admission. Leading and conscious workers, kolkhozniks, and members of the intelligentsia, active participants in communist construction should be admitted into the ranks of the CPSU in strict compliance with the Party Rules. And workers must continue to occupy the leading position in the social composition of the party.

Concern for the purity of the party's ranks, concern that each communist bear with dignity the name of member of Lenin's party and warrant it, is a law of party life, of all party organizations. In the future as well, the party will continue to free itself of all unworthy members, of those who violate the CPSU Programme and Rules, who by their behaviour compromise the name of communist.

4   The Congress considers that the struggle for the successful fulfilment of the new Five-Year Plan for development of the economy must be at the centre of attention of all party organizations. Party organizations are called upon to ensure consistent implementation of the principles of socialist economic management, the new principles of planning and economic incentives in production, worked out by the March and September plenums of the CPSU Central Committee. At the same time, party organizations must use the organizational and educational methods which are properly theirs and not supplant soviet and economic organs or assume petty tutelage over them.

The Congress notes with satisfaction that the village raion party committees, having been restored as fully competent political organs, have again taken a firm position as militant and authoritative transmitters of CPSU policy in the countryside.

Enhancement of the fighting efficiency of all primary party organizations is of particular significance. Party committees must rely firmly upon them, help them in settling intra-party matters and in expanding their mass political activity among the toilers.

5   The Congress stresses that the mounting scale and complexity of the tasks of communist construction place increasingly stiff requirements on the selection, promotion, and training of cadres. Personnel promoted to leading positions must be devoted to the ideas of communism, must know their business well, and must be in continuous contact with the masses, capable of organizing them for performing the tasks before them. Young and energetic personnel must be promoted more boldly, and their energy must be properly combined with the experience of older cadres. The transition to the new system of socialist economic management obliges leading cadres to master methods of economic leadership.

6   The Congress attributes great significance to the correct organization of supervision and verification of the implementation of party and government decisions. Party organizations are called upon to direct the activity of the organs of people's control and to extend to them all possible assistance in their work. There must be an enhancement of the role of the Party Control Committee of the CPSU Central Committee, and of the party commissions of local party organs, in increasing the responsibility of communists for implementing the party's policy.

7   The Congress stresses the importance of further strengthening the Soviet state and of developing socialist democracy in every way. Particular importance is attached to enhancing the role of the Soviets of Working People's Deputies, so that they may make the fullest use of their powers in carrying out tasks of economic and cultural construction and in verifying implementation, and may display more initiative in resolving planning, financial, and land problems, and in guiding local industrial enterprises, and everyday social and cultural services for the population. The soviets are called upon to heighten the responsibility of executive organs, deputies, and officials before the people, are to liven up the work of their sessions, and submit to them a broader range of matters for their consideration.

The Congress considers that the role of the trade unions in resolving tasks of economic development must be enhanced and that their more active participation in working out state plans and in administering production must be ensured. The duty of the trade unions is to develop socialist competition even more broadly, to improve educational work among the toilers, and to be more concerned with organizing the work and the living conditions of workers and employees.

The Congress directs party organizations to devote particular attention to the communist education of Komsomol members and of all Soviet youth. The education of Komsomol members and of youth in the revolutionary, labour, and militant traditions of the Soviet people and the Communist Party is one of the most important tasks. It is necessary to continue to imbue young men and women with high ideological conviction and devotion to the cause of the party, love for the socialist homeland, readiness to defend it, a feeling of fraternal friendship for the toilers of the socialist countries, and international solidarity with all the exploited and oppressed. The participation of the Komsomol in economic and cultural construction, and the political life of the country needs to be intensified. The party nucleus in Komsomol organizations needs to be fortified and communists of Komsomol age – for whom this must be considered a very important party assignment – must be used more extensively for work in them.

8   The CPSU proceeds from the idea that further successes of communist construction depend in many respects upon the scope and level of the party's ideological and politicial work among the toilers. The effectiveness of the

party's ideological influence is indissolubly connected with all of its activity as the guiding force of Soviet society. The education of the toilers in the spirit of high political consciousness and of a communist attitude to labour must stand at the centre of ideological work. The paramount task of ideological work is to mobilize the efforts of the working class, the peasantry, and the intelligentsia for active struggle for fulfilment of the Five-Year Plan for development of the economy, for the building of communist society in our country.

The solidarity of the peoples of the Soviet Union in a single fraternal family is a great achievement of the Communist Party and Soviet power. The Congress directs all party committees to continue undeviatingly to implement a leninist nationality policy, to educate all Soviet people in the spirit of Soviet patriotism and respect for the best progressive national traditions of the peoples of the USSR, in the spirit of friendship with the peoples of all the fraternal socialist countries, with the toilers of the whole world, to conduct a persistent struggle against any manifestations of nationalism and chauvinism.

9   The Congress considers that an urgent task of party organizations is a serious improvement in the marxist-leninist education of party members, their ideological tempering, especially of young party members. High demands must be made on the ideological and political training of leading cadres. The whole system of party education must be raised up to the level of the tasks of the present stage of the building of communism. The Congress directs the party's ideological organs and the appropriate state institutions to effect a decisive improvement in the business of teaching marxism-leninism in institutions of higher learning and other educational institutions, to increase the ideological and theoretical level of instruction of university students, striving to ensure a close connection between this instruction and contemporary problems of social development, the most recent advances of science and technology.

The foundation of all the party's ideological work is propaganda of the ideas of marxism-leninism. The creative development of marxist-leninist theory on the basis of the experience of communist construction and the development of the world revolutionary movement, the struggle against all manifestations of bourgeois ideology are of the greatest significance for all of the party's activity.

10   The Congress attributes great significance to developing the literature and art of socialist realism. From creative workers the party expects new and significant works which will conquer by the profundity and honesty of their reflection of life, by the power of their ideological inspiration, by their high artistic skill, and which will actively help in the formation of the spiritual make-up of the builder of communism, will inculcate high moral qualities in Soviet people as well as devotion to communist ideals, a sense of good citizenship, Soviet patriotism, and socialist internationalism.

The role of the creative unions in consolidating the relationship between art and the life of the people, in heightening the social responsibility of Soviet artists for their creativity before society, in educating them in a spirit of faithfulness to the leninist principles of party spirit and feeling for the people must be enhanced.

11 The Congress directs party organizations to effect a serious improvement in their mass political work. The party's policy must be elucidated thoroughly and intelligibly, without avoiding acute problems; it is necessary to be tactful toward the demands and spiritual needs of the popular masses, to take into consideration the rising cultural and educational level of Soviet people. All political agitation must be based on information widely and systematically supplied to the population on the political, economic, and cultural life of the country and the international situation. It is necessary to ensure regular reports before the working people by party, state, economic and public figures on questions of the domestic and foreign policy of the state, the work of organs of party, government and public organizations, and also reports by leaders of local soviets, organs of popular education, public health, trade, and enterprises of communal economy and everyday services.

A consistent struggle must be waged against political apathy, against remnants of private-property mentality and petty-bourgeois attitudes, against manifestations of a nihilist attitude toward the ideals and achievements of socialism.

The Congress directs the attention of party organizations to the fact that the party is conducting its ideological work in conditions of a sharp class struggle between two opposing socio-political systems in the world arena. The interests of socialism and communism demand a heightening of the revolutionary vigilance of communists and of all Soviet people, an unmasking of the ideological diversions of imperialism against the Soviet Union and the other socialist countries ...

5.8
On Partial Changes in the Rules of the CPSU
[Revises Rules adopted 1961; see 4.34] 8 April 1966

The XXIII Congress of the Communist Party of the Soviet Union resolves to introduce the following changes in the CPSU Rules:

1 [Revises 4.34, art. 4] In order to improve further the qualitative composition of those admitted to the CPSU and to raise the responsibility of party organizations for the admission into the party of new members, it is established that:

a young people, up to the age of 23 inclusive, enter the party only through the Komsomol. Members of the Komsomol entering the CPSU must submit the recommendation of a district committee or a city committee of the Komsomol which is equivalent to the recommendation of one party member;

b those recommending applicants to the party must have party standing of not less than five years;

c a decision of the primary party organization on admission to the party is regarded adopted if not less than two-thirds of the party members attending the meeting have voted for it.

2   Proceeding from the tasks of further strengthening party discipline and raising the responsibility of communists for the fulfilment of the duties prescribed by the Rules:

a [Revises 4.34, preamble] a provision is added to the introductory section of the Rules that the party set itself free of individuals who violate the CPSU Programme, the Rules, and who by their behaviour compromise the lofty title of Communist;

b [Revises 4.34, art. 10] it is established that a decision of a primary party organization on the expulsion of a communist from the party takes effect after ratification by its district or city party committee.

c [Revises 4.34, art. 9] the transfer of a party member to the status of candidate as a party penalty is abolished.

3   In view of the proposals of many party organs and communists, and taking into account the fact that during party elections the composition of party commitees is regularly renewed with due regard for concrete local conditions and the businesslike and political qualities of personnel, and that the regulations on these questions did not justify themselves in practice, it is regarded as inexpedient to retain further in the CPSU Rules the provisions that determine the norms of renewal and turnover of the composition of party organs and secretaries of party organizations. In this connection article 25 is deleted from the Rules. An addition is made to article 24 that during elections of all party organs from the primary organizations to the CPSU Central Committee, the principle of the systematic renewal of their composition and continuity of leadership is to be observed.

4   [New art. 58] The section of the Rules concerning primary party organizations is supplemented with a new paragraph stipulating that party committees of primary party organizations numbering more than 1000 communists may, with the permission of the central committee of the communist party of a union republic, be granted the rights of a raion party committee on questions concerning admission to the CPSU, registration of party members and candidates, and scrutiny of the personal affairs of communists. Within these organizations, if necessary, party committees may be formed in shops, while the party organizations of production sections are granted the rights of a primary party organization. The party committees that are granted the rights of a raion party committee are elected for a term of two years.

5   Article 57 of the Rules is supplemented with a provision that in sovkhozes party committees may be established if there are 50 communists.

6   [Revises 4.34, art. 55] Taking into consideration organizations' suggestions that the CPSU Rules should determine in a more differentiated way the schedule for the convocation of meetings in primary party organizations, depending on the conditions of their work, structure, and size, it is established that in primary party organizations which have up to 300 members and where there are shop organizations, a general party meeting is to be held at least once every two months.

7   [Revises 4.34, art. 44] It is stipulated in the Rules that communist party congresses in all union republics are to be held at least once every four years.

8   [New article 40] Provisions are made in the Rules that in the period between party congresses the Central Committee may, when necessary, convoke an all-union party conference to discuss urgent questions of party policy while the central committees of communist parties of the union republics may convoke republic party conferences.

The procedure for conducting an all-union party conference is determined by the CPSU Central Committee, while that of republic party conferences, by the central committees of the communist parties of the union republics.

9   [Revises 4.34, art. 39] Provisions are made in the Rules that the CPSU Central Committee elect: a Politburo [this term was used from 1919 until Stalin replaced it with Presidium in 1952] for guiding the work of the party between plenums of the Central Committee; a Secretariat for guiding current work, mainly in the field of personnel selection and organizing verification of implementation. The Central Committee elects a General Secretary of the CPSU Central Committee.

The clause stipulating that the Central Committee create a CPSU Central Committee Bureau for the RSFSR, in article 39 of the Rules, is to be omitted.

10   The reference to economic councils in article 59 of the rules is to be omitted.

Pravda, 9 April 1966   *KPSS v rezoliutsiiakh* IX, 16–37

Plenum of the Central Committee   25–27 May 1966

The May 1966 Central Committee Plenum dealt with the technical aspects of Brezhnev's agricultural programme. Reports were delivered by the USSR

Minister of Land Reclamation and Water Resources, E.E. Alekseevsky, and the General Secretary of the party, Brezhnev. Alekseevsky's report (*Current Digest of the Soviet Press* XVIII, no. 22, 5–11) consisted of a series of proposals that had been made the previous year and had been elaborated in conjunction with the Ministry of Agriculture, the State Planning Committee, and the union republics. Additional experts were brought into the planning and decision making through conferences set up under the auspices of the Central Committee apparatus. From Alekseevsky's report it appears that there were real differences among the participants that led to substantial revisions in the proposals. The final report called for a whole series of measures to improve land fertility, undertake major land reclamation projects, employ extensive irrigation schemes in arid regions, direct major capital investments into water resource construction, improve the technology, capacity, and design of water resource construction, and raise the effectiveness of capital investments in reclamation construction.

As Brezhnev pointed out in his report to the plenum (*Current Digest of the Soviet Press* XVIII, no. 23, 3–8), the proposed agricultural programme indicated a significant turn in attitude towards agriculture, although he perhaps overstated his case by suggesting that 'we have all grounds for comparing it [the set of proposals for increasing and stabilizing agricultural yields] with any earlier important task, however great in scope, that our party has had to resolve in the sphere of agriculture.' Was Brezhnev comparing the new policy with the collectivization campaign from 1928–1933? In any case, he certainly was at pains to emphasize the change in direction for agricultural policy. He was also insistent on implicit comparison with Khrushchev's economically irrational agricultural campaigns, emphasizing that the new campaign was to be a long-range programme supported by heavy capital investments and reflecting real Soviet potentials.

Having established the scope of change in agricultural policy, Brezhnev also dealt with the financial and resource implications. He recognized that the policy could achieve success only if it was accompanied by a shift in the balance of capital investment in favour of agriculture and its subsidiary industries. The dilemma was posed in stark terms by Brezhnev, although he was not willing to admit publicly the difficulties involved: ... 'we had to work very seriously with the planning agencies so that, without slowing down the rates of development of the branches of heavy industry, and also taking into account the necessity for sharply advancing light industry and the food industry, we might at the same time find funds and material resources for agriculture in hitherto unprecedented amounts.' The declining growth rates of the Soviet economy in the past decade suggest that it was totally unrealistic or disingenuous of Brezhnev to suggest that the regime could attain all three sets of goals simultaneously.

5.9
On the Extensive Development of
Land Reclamation to Obtain High and
Stable Yields of Grain and Other Farm Crops 27 May 1966

Highly developed agriculture is an indispensible condition for a further upsurge of the entire socialist economy and a steady rise in the living standard of the Soviet people. That is why the XXIII Congress of the party, in determining the specific directions of communist construction at the present stage, has attributed paramount significance to the acceleration of the rates of agricultural development and the steady intensification of agriculture on the basis of the system of economic and organizational measures that were elaborated by the March and September (1965) plenums of the CPSU Central Committee.

Raising the yield of every hectare of land in every possible way is the basis for accelerated agricultural development in general and grain production in particular.

The plenum considers that the achieved level of the country's economic development makes it possible for these purposes to implement a complex of large-scale measures, both on a country-wide scale and on every kolkhoz and sovkhoz, for improving soil fertility and agricultural standards and for extensive land reclamation ...

The CPSU Central Committee Plenum resolves:

1   To approve measures for the extensive development of land reclamation to obtain high and stable yields of grain and other farm crops elaborated by the CPSU Central Committee Politburo and envisaging the following:

–   expansion in the next ten-year period of the area of irrigated land by 7–8 million hectares and of drained land by 15–16 million hectares, the total area of reclaimed land in the country to reach 37–39 million hectares in 1975;

–   improvements in the state of land reclamation of all land in regions of operating irrigation and drainage systems so that every hectare of these lands produces the maximum yield of agricultural products of high quality and with good economic indices;

–   considerable increase in the rates of progress of water resources work in the north Caucasus, southern areas of the Ukraine, Moldavia, Kazakhstan, in the lower reaches of the Amu Darya and in the Far East; advancement in the building of irrigation systems in the Volga Region; creation in these zones of large-scale production of grain, rice in particular, as well as of other agricultural products;

–   further development of land irrigation in the areas of Central Asia and the Trans-Caucasus;

–   the conducting of liming of all plough-land, meadows, and pastures that have acid soil in the non-chernozem belt;
–   the conducting of work during 1966–1970 to improve radically meadows and pasture-land over an area of 9 million hectares and supply pastures with water over an area of 50 million hectares;
–   the implementation of a system of measures to combat water and wind erosion of soil, where necessary the planting of shelter-belts and ravine afforestation, as well as the regrassing of eroded slopes, the building of anti-erosion structures and the afforestation of sands ...

The CPSU Central Committee Politburo and the USSR Council of Ministers are instructed to take the appropriate decisions.

The party, trade union, and Komsomol organizations, soviet, agricultural, and water resource bodies, leaders of ministries and departments, industrial enterprises, construction organizations, kolkhozes, and sovkhozes are required to take the necessary measures for unconditional fulfilment of these decisions.

2   The fulfilment of the programme mapped out by the party with respect to raising the fertility of soils, extensive land reclamation, planned and steady implementation of comprehensive mechanization, and electrification and chemicalization of agricultural production will make it possible to raise the productivity of all branches of agriculture and improve the material well-being of the Soviet people.

The task of party, soviet, agricultural, and water resource agencies is to organize and lead the struggle of the entire people to raise farming standards and the productivity of cultivated land, to put the land in exemplary order in all kolkhozes and sovkhozes, achieve high and stable yields on every hectare. Assistance must be offered to kolkhozes and sovkhozes in elaborating plans for specific measures to raise the fertility of soil and make effective use of every hectare of cultivated land.

The plenum considers it necessary to establish strict order when allocating parcels of land for industrial, construction, and other needs. When constructing various projects, it is necessary to use first of all the worst land or land that is unsuitable for agricultural purposes.

It is to be recognized as necessary that laws be adopted on the fundamental principles of land and water utilization, on the protection of cultivated land, and on raising responsibility for its utilization.

3   The CPSU Central Committee Plenum emphasizes that, in implementing the outlined programme for the extensive development of land-reclamation work, fuller use must be made of the economic measures that were worked out by the March and September [1965] plenums of the party Central Committee.

Questions of material incentives for workers engaged in operating irrigation and drainage systems and in cultivating high and stable yields on reclaimed land are gaining particular significance. The party, soviet, agricultural, and water resource bodies, and kolkhozes and sovkhozes must work out and implement measures to improve the organization, the fixing of output norms and remuneration for labour of workers engaged in farming on reclaimed land.

4   Along with the further strengthening of the material and technical base of agriculture in all the regions of the country, specific measures are to be carried out to equip specialized organizations, kolkhozes, and sovkhozes in the non-chernozem belt and in zones of irrigation farming with reclamation and excavation machinery and to supply them with the necessary quantities of mineral fertilizers, chemicals for plant protection, equipment, and building and other materials.

The implementation of the broad programme to reclaim land requires the supplying of agriculture with powerful tractors and a complex of highly productive excavation and construction machinery.

The CPSU Central Committee Plenum calls upon workers in industry, leaders of the industrial ministries and departments to do everything to fulfil and overfulfil plans concerning the provision of kolkhozes and sovkhozes, as well as water resource organizations, with the necessary high-quality machinery and equipment, fertilizers and toxic chemicals, various materials and other goods for production purposes.

The plenum recommends that the central committees of the union republic communist parties, the krai, oblast, city, and raion party committees, and primary party organizations take the necessary measures for the unconditional completion of orders for the countryside by industrial enterprises and building organizations.

5   In connection with the wide development of land-reclamation work, the CPSU Central Committee Plenum draws the attention of the USSR Gosplan, the USSR Ministry of Agriculture, the USSR Ministry of Land Reclamation and Water Resources, the USSR Academy of Sciences, the All-Union Academy of Agricultural Sciences named for V.I. Lenin and the appropriate scientific research, design, and construction institutes to the necessity of making timely and correct decisions on questions such as:

–   the establishment of priorities in carrying out land-reclamation measures, as well as the most effective use of capital investments for these purposes;

–   the implementation of land-reclamation construction on a scientific, technological, and industrial basis, in a single complex along with economic land-reclamation measures, not allowing delay between completion of construction projects and their agricultural utilization.

6   In carrying out the programme of land-reclamation measures to increase the production of grain and other agricultural products, an important role belongs to science. Scientists are called upon to expand considerably

theoretical and applied research in the area of land reclamation, to improve their effectiveness, to provide industry with substantiated recommendations for carrying out land-reclamation work in various zones of the country, and for introducing intensive farming on irrigated and drained land. Scientists are called upon to ensure the development of high-yielding varieties of agricultural crops and of those with high-standing power for reclaimed land. Engineers and designers must intensify work to create new highly productive and economical machinery for excavation and land reclamation.

The USSR Ministry of Agriculture the USSR Ministry of Land Reclamation and Water Resources, the USSR Gosplan, the USSR Academy of Sciences, and the Academy of Agricultural Sciences named for V.I. Lenin together with the union republic councils of ministers are instructed to work out economically substantiated proposals in the years 1966–68 on the directions for the further development of agriculture in the natural zones of the country for the next 10–15 years and present the proposals for consideration to the CPSU Central Committee and the USSR Council of Ministers by 1 January 1969 ...

Pravda, 18 May 1966   *KPSS v rezoliutsiiakh* IX, 106–11

5.10
On the Work of the Party Committee
of the Orekhov Cotton Combine
Named for K.I. Nikolaeva*   28 November 1966

The following decision contains the first elaboration of the party's new role at the enterprise level under the conditions of the economic reform approved at the September 1965 Central Committee Plenum. Heavy emphasis is placed on a wide range of techniques open to the party in educating labour and management into the attitudes and behaviour patterns considered appropriate in the new conditions. Stress is placed on educational programmes, personnel management, and supervision over the activities of other public organizations working within the combine. However, mention is also made of the party's joint responsibility with management for technical, economic, and output aspects of the combine's activity. No clear distinction is drawn in these matters between the responsibility of management and the party. In fact, the wording of the document suggests joint collective responsibility by management and the party committee.

*   Excerpt: document not published in full.

... As of the present January, the combine was the first in the cotton industry to be transferred to the new system of planning and economic stimulation of production ...

The party committee systematically considers questions connected with improving the activity and enhancing the organizing role of primary and shop party organizations and party groups. During the current year the party committee has discussed the work of party organizations with respect to the introduction of profit-and-loss accounting at the bleach and dye works, the profitability of output at the thread spinning mill, the utilization of fixed productive capital at weaving mill No. 1, the economic education of cadres, and the organizational role of party groups in implementing the decisions of the September Plenum of the CPSU Central Committee. Monthly seminars are conducted with the secretaries of primary and shop party organizations on exchanging experience and on the forms and methods of organizational and mass political work; quarterly seminars or instructional meetings are held with party groups; at these seminars and meetings, special attention is paid to the ability to work with people. Supervision over and verification of the implementation of adopted decisions has been improved; a wide circle of communists is attracted to this work. The fulfilment of previously adopted decisions and suggestions of a critical nature are reported to communists at monthly party meetings.

The improvement in the qualitative composition of party organizations' secretaries – more than two thirds of them already have a higher or secondary education – greatly contributes to enhancing the role of the party organizations at the factories and shops. Party groups, which are headed by the best communists and are organized at every very important production section, exert decisive influence over the fulfilment of production assignments, over the observance of the CPSU Rules by party members, and over the condition of labour discipline in collectives. Communists take the lead in all undertakings ... The leading role of communists, of which 80 per cent work directly in the shops and production sections, contributes to raising the authority of the party organization, its ranks being systematically reinforced with the best production workers, those who work in leading professions.

The party organizations of the factories widely involve permanent production meetings, voluntary bureaus for economic analysis, for fixing technical standards, and for labour organization, as well as groups of the people's control and Komsomol Projector posts in improving the state of affairs at the enterprise. The well-organized economic education of cadres also contributes to this goal. For the party aktiv, engineering and technical personnel, and deputy foremen, two-year economic schools, in which over 2500 people are studying, have been established. Economic conferences, seminars, and consultations are conducted for them. To improve their political knowledge, over 9000 people are studying in circles and schools where a great deal of attention is devoted to questions of economics and explaining the essence of the economic reform. Every factory sets up display stands, *Our Advances for 1966*, and, in the basic shops, 'economic corners' are organized that report on the results of profit-and-loss accounting activities of the shifts, brigades, and of the entire shop.

The party organization conducts significant work with respect to the political education of the toilers: in the shops, places of residence, and at workers' and youth hostels, lectures are systematically delivered and discussions on the most important issues of our country's domestic and international position are held. Over 2500 young workers study in schools for young workers, technical schools, and higher educational institutions. The combine's Palace of Culture operates a permanently functioning lecture agency dealing with today's urgent problems, a university of technical progress and advanced labour methods, and organizes thematic evenings to educate young workers in revolutionary and labour traditions.

At the same time, there are substantial short-comings in the work of the party committee of the Orekhov cotton combine.

The party committee and economic management of the combine are not yet sufficiently using the new conditions of planning and economic incentives to pull up lagging production sections, and to bring new equipment into production as rapidly as possible ...

The party committee is not sufficiently directing the attention of communists and of the engineering and technical personnel of the combine to renewing the assortment, improving the quality, and putting new kinds of fabric decoration into production. Technological discipline is often violated in decoration production, some produced fabrics have dingy colours, a high shrinkage, and are easily creased. In the output of low-grade products losses for the current year are 365 thousand rubles.

The party committee and the Komsomol committee have not succeeded in involving all Komsomol members in active work with respect to educating young people. There have been many incidents when labour discipline has been violated by young workers and Komsomol members; many of them do not hold their positions in production, and are slow in mastering their profession ...

The party and trade union committees are not making proper demands on the economic leadership of the combine and factories to improve the production and daily living conditions of the textile workers. The trade union committees are not sufficiently supervising the observance of labour legislation at the factories ...

The Orekhov-Zuev city committee of the party is not providing sufficient assistance to the combine's party committee in organizing work to utilize the available internal production reserves and improve the education of young workers; it is doing a weak job of raising the responsibility of leaders of soviet and economic organizations of the city for improving cultural and everyday services and local public utilities for those who work at the combine ...

The CPSU Central Committee resolves:

1   ... The party committee of the combine is ordered:

–   constantly to improve methods of guiding the primary and shop party organizations and party groups, raise their responsibility and organizational role for the education of the working people and for the state of affairs in production. Efforts are to be made so that every communist through his attitude to labour, his behaviour at work and in daily life, will have an active influence on raising the communist consciousness of the members of the collective;

–   to direct the attention of the trade union committees of the factories and combine toward the continued improvement of the organization of socialist competition, work conditions, and the daily life and leisure conditions of workers; intensification of supervision in resolving questions of setting labour and wage norms; the strict observance of labour legislation, and the rules and standards of production sanitation and safety measures. The initiative of trade union committees is to be raised in organizing public catering services, trade, and domestic services, and supervising the improvement of living conditions and providing working people with institutions for children;

–   to offer assistance to the combine's Komsomol organization in intensifying educational work with young workers and teen-agers, providing them with conditions to master their professions as soon as possible, and raise their general educational level ...

–   to raise the activeness of people's control groups in revealing and utilizing production reserves, quickly resolving questions raised by them, and organizing the exchange of work experience among groups ...

3   The economic leadership and the party committee of the combine must make fuller use of the advantages of the new system of planning and economic incentives in production for the further improvement of technical-economic results of economic activity and for creating and introducing a new assortment of fabrics that meet the growing demands of the Soviet people. The responsibility of engineering and technical personnel is to be raised for extremely rapid mastering of the production potential of newly installed equipment, for the mechanization of labour-intensive processes in basic and auxiliary production, for the introduction of the achievements of new technology and the scientific organization of labour, progressive technological processes, and for more rational utilization of raw materials and supplies ...

5   The Moscow oblast party committee and the Orekhov-Zuev city party committee are to provide assistance to the party organization of the Orekhov cotton combine to improve mass political and educational work in the collec-

tive and intensify supervision over the creation of the necessary production and living conditions, and over the course of construction and commissioning of residential buildings and children's institutions for people working at the combine ...

Partiinaia zhizn', no. 23   *KPSS v rezoliutsiiakh* IX, 150–6
(1966): 17–21

5.11
On Organizing Continuous Courses for
Retraining Party Leaders and Soviet Cadres*   27 December 1966

The party has always been concerned with the political socialization and training of its cadres. Since the early 1920s, networks of communist universities and higher schools have been set up to improve the political education and qualifications of party, state, and other cadres. In 1946, the system was reorganized, with the aim of greater centralization, standardization, and specialization of functions among the institutes (3.38). Research, the interpretation of the ideology, and its application to current developments have been conducted mainly by the Academy of Social Sciences and the Institute of Marxism-Leninism. The role of the Higher Party School and its subordinate network of institutes and courses has been primarily pedagogical. Its students have included a wide range of middle and lower level members of the political elite as well as 'opinion leaders' in the media.

As part of its campaign of 'trust in cadres' and in response to the rising educational level of cadres, the Brezhnev regime directed significant resources into expanded training and retraining programmes to equip party, state, trade union, and Komsomol officials with skills that would make them more efficient organizers and administrators. This necessitated a number of changes in the Higher Party School network (see 5.11, 5.19, 5.36, 5.44, 5.55). The network was expanded to include increased facilities for non-party cadres and a broad system of short retraining courses for party veterans who required upgrading of their qualifications to meet the changing demands of party work. The system also experienced a degree of operational decentralization, with many courses being conducted directly at enterprises, kolkhozes, sovkhozes, and scientific-research institutes. There was a serious effort to upgrade the quality of the programmes under Brezhnev. The traditionally ideologically oriented subjects continued to be taught. However, an increasing component of the curriculum focused on management-oriented subjects, partly by redefining older subjects

---

*   Excerpt: document not published in full.

such as scientific communism and party construction, but also by including new subjects such as applied sociology, economics, planning, and the practical implications of economic reforms. The courses increasingly stressed practical training and the development of the psychological and sociological dimensions of administration. In addition, attempts to upgrade the courses were made by improving the qualifications of the permanent staff, drawing on resources outside of the network, and differentiating programmes according to the profile and career patterns of the student body. Along with the attempt to upgrade the quality of the programmes, there was an attempt to raise their status by associating study in the network with academic achievement and professional qualifications. In 1972, provisions were made for the graduates of the Higher Party School to receive a certificate attesting that they met the minimum qualifications for a candidate's degree. In 1976, a structural reorganization occurred in which the permanently operating courses of the Higher Party School were transformed into an Institute for Raising the Qualifications of Leading Party and Soviet Cadres.

In accordance with the decisions of the XXIII Party Congress and in order to improve the qualifications and the ideological-theoretical training of leading personnel, the CPSU Central Committee has resolved that continuous one-month courses be organized, starting in February 1967, for retraining leading party and soviet cadres.

For secretaries and department heads of oblast and krai committees, and of the central committees of the union republic parties, for the first secretaries of party committees of large cities, editors of oblast, krai, and republic newspapers, the courses are organized on the basis of the Higher Party School of the Central Committee.

Inter-oblast, republic, and inter-republic courses are to be set up for secretaries of city and raion party committees, chairmen of city (or raion) executive committees, and for editors of city and raion newspapers on the basis of the local higher party schools, divisions, and study-consultation points of the Higher Party Correspondence School of the CPSU Central Committee in Moscow, Leningrad, Kiev, Minsk, Tashkent, Alma-Ata, Baku, Volgograd, Gorky, Irkutsk, Kuibyshev, Novosibirsk, Rostov, Sverdlovsk, and Khabarovsk.

The CPSU Central Committee has approved the model curricula for the courses and the thematic material for lectures and seminars. The course curriculum includes current problems in the history and policy of the CPSU, in marxist-leninist philosophy and scientific communism, in political economy, and in the international communist workers' and national liberation movement. The curriculum devotes considerable space to questions of party and soviet construction and practical guidance of the economy, science, and culture. It is proposed to organize the teaching of party and soviet construction on various levels, depending upon the composition of the participants. Leading personnel in the CPSU Central Committee, the ministries and departments, the central committees of the union republic parties, the oblast and krai committees, scholars and teachers in higher party schools, and institutions of higher education will be invited to lecture at the courses.

The Central Committee has directed the central committees of the communist parties of the Ukraine, Belorussia, Kazakhstan, Uzbekistan, Azerbaidzhan, the Moscow city party committee, the Leningrad, Volgograd, Gorky, Irkutsk, Kuibyshev, Novosibirsk, Rostov, and Sverdlovsk oblast party committees, the Khabarovsk krai party committee, the rector's office of the Higher Party School of the CPSU Central Committee, and the directors of higher party schools to make the necessary material and academic preparations for the courses and to select qualified lecturers and teachers.

The Party Organizational Affairs Section of the CPSU Central Committee will make the selection of participants for these courses jointly with the oblast and krai committees and the central committees of the union republic parties. While studying, participants will continue to draw salaries from their usual places of work; out-of-towners will receive stipends.

The Department for Science and Educational Institutions of the CPSU Central Committee will have responsibility for the scientific and methodological guidance of the courses.

Partiinaia zhizn', no. 2
(1967): 23

5.12
On the Work of the Central Committee of the
Estonian Communist Party with Leading Cadres*   30 January 1967

The September 1965 economic reform placed additional pressures on party organizations to ensure that managerial personnel and specialists were appropriately trained and placed. The following decision on the Estonian party organization's work with leading cadres identifies in some detail the expanded responsibilities that were assigned to party organizations in the personnel field.

The CPSU Central Committee notes that, in fulfilling the decisions of the party, the central committee of the Estonian Communist Party has been

---

*   Excerpt: document not published in full.

more attentive to cadre work and in recent years has taken a series of measures to strengthen party and soviet organs, and also certain sectors of the economy, through the appointment of qualified and knowledgeable personnel. The quality of leading cadres has improved; among them there are more industrial and agricultural specialists experienced in working with people. More than half of the party and soviet personnel have party political education. In the republic the number of economic and cultural specialists increases from year to year, and they are now almost three times as numerous as in bourgeois Estonia. Especially since the XXIII CPSU Congress, the party organizations have improved their work in the ideological tempering of cadres and raising their professional skills and economic knowledge ...

At the same time, the work of the central committee of the Estonian Communist Party with leading cadres does not yet fully meet the requirements of the XXIII CPSU Congress and the growing tasks of economic and cultural construction. Questions of the selection, promotion, and training of cadres are still not fundamental to the activity of many party committees.

Party and state organs are not always exacting in their selection of cadres, are hasty and undiscriminating. Personnel with little training and no initiative, who are poor organizers, are frequently advanced to responsible sectors, the consequence being a considerable turnover of cadres. Few who have passed through the school of party and soviet activity at the local level are promoted to positions in the central organs. There is insufficient concern for the promotion of women to leading positions.

There are serious short-comings in the selection of Komsomol cadres. Incompetents and even persons who just happen to be available are frequently appointed to Komsomol work. Many party organizations fail to devote the requisite attention to consolidating the party nucleus in the Komsomol, and the number of party members among the secretaries of primary Komsomol organizations is still insignificant. Some Komsomol organizations are functioning on a low level.

Now that a new system of planning and economic incentives is being introduced, and the rights and economic autonomy of enterprises are being expanded, the level of qualifications of the leading economic cadres, the level of their engineering, technical, and economic training, takes on special importance. However, at the present time many of the leaders of enterprises in the republic, many shop managers and their deputies, leaders of construction organizations, foremen in industry and construction are only practical workers, the overwhelming majority of whom are not studying anywhere. The economic services are understaffed.

Party and state organizations devote insufficient attention to the correct assignment and utilization of economic and cultural specialists.

There are serious omissions in ideological and educational work with cadres. Some leading personnel are not raising their ideological and theoretical knowledge, are not engaged in political work among the toilers. Some party committees are doing a poor job of instilling in cadres a lofty sense of responsibility for their assigned work, are not as exacting as they should be. Labour discipline is weak in some enterprises and at some construction sites. Some leaders have a callous attitude to people and violate labour legislation.

The central committee of the Estonian Communist Party is neglecting to instil in leading cadres a sufficiently implacable attitude toward various unhealthy manifestations in ideological matters. The role of creative unions in the ideological training of the artistic intelligentsia is hardly being intensified.

The short-comings in cadre work impair the level of party leadership of economic and cultural construction, prevent the fullest use being made of reserves in the republic's economy and of its opportunities for further development, have a negative impact on efforts to improve cultural and everyday services for the toilers. Although industry on the whole is coming along steadily, work is poorly organized in many enterprises, productive capacity and equipment are underutilized, and there is great waste. The increase in industrial production above the control figures for the Seven-Year Plan was obtained primarily by drawing additional labour into production. Although many workers are engaged in manual work in enterprises, sufficient attention is not devoted to the mechanization and automation of production processes. The productivity of the large- and medium-size refrigerator trawlers of the Estonian Fishing Administration is lower than for ships of the same size of other administrations fishing in the same regions. Every year the plan for the development of basic funds is unfulfilled. The construction plan was not fulfilled last year as well, and the number of uncompleted construction jobs increased. There are many unutilized reserves in agriculture.

The short-comings in the selection and training of leading cadres in the Estonian Republic are to be explained largely by the failure of the central committee of the Estonian Communist Party and of its bureau to be sufficiently exacting in requiring strict observance of leninist principles in cadre work by party, soviet, and economic organs, and by their failure to study and analyse these matters in depth. Some party committees are insufficiently concerned with developing criticism and self-criticism, tolerate serious short-comings in style and methods of work, and devote insufficient attention to supervising the implementation of party and government directives and of their own decisions.

The CPSU Central Committee resolves:

1   The Estonian Communist Party is obliged to eliminate the short-comings noted in this decision and to develop and implement practical measures for a radical improvement in work with leading cadres. As was demanded by the XXIII CPSU Congress, the selection and training of cadres should be treated as a matter affecting the whole party and the whole state.

Cadre work, the supervision and verification of the implementation of party and government decisions, must be fundamental to the activity of party committees in guiding economic and cultural construction ...

2   The central committee and the city and raion committees of the Communist Party of Estonia must be strictly guided by leninist principles in the selection of cadres, must study comprehensively and in depth the professional and political qualities of personnel as manifested in their practical activity. Comrades who have passed through the school of practical activity at the local level must be more actively promoted to leading work, at the same time ensuring a correct balance between experienced leaders and young, energetic personnel. And, while being more exacting, it is necessary at the same time to display more trust in cadres and perfect the style and methods of operation of party, soviet, and public organizations.

Party, soviet, and economic organs must devote serious attention to creating an effective cadre reserve. Promising personnel, whose qualities indicate the possibility of subsequent promotion to high positions, should be selected as deputy leaders. The responsibility of primary party organizations for cadre selection and assignment is to be increased, and their opinion on appointments is to be considered. Women are to be promoted more boldly to leading positions.

3   The CPSU Central Committee emphasizes that implementation of the new system of planning and economic production incentives demands that constant attention be given to appointing capable and qualified personnel to industrial enterprises, construction sites, kolkhozes, and sovkhozes. In view of the fact that a large number of the leading positions in many very important production sectors are filled by persons with practical training only, who do not possess the requisite engineering, technical, and economic background, it is suggested that party, soviet, and economic organs organize systematic study to improve the business skills of cadres. For this purpose broader use is to be made of correspondence and evening schools as well as a system of courses and seminars organized according to the principle of differentiation, depending upon the specific nature of the activity of the leading personnel. Concern for making more correct use of economic specialists in accordance with their knowledge and experience is to be intensified.

The efforts of leaders and specialists in enterprises, construction sites, kolkhozes, and sovkhozes are to be directed at improving the organization of labour and increasing production efficiency. Measures are to be taken to enhance the role of shop managers as leaders, making them fully responsible for the organizational, technical, and economic work of their collectives and granting them more autonomy in their work. The responsibility of foremen, work superintendents, brigade leaders, and farm managers of kolkhozes and sovkhozes for the training and education of workers and kolkhoz members is to be heightened. They must strive to become the organizers of profit-and-loss accounting in their sectors and must struggle actively to disclose and exploit the existing potentials for increased labour productivity at every workplace ...

4   The central committee of the Estonian Communist Party and the party committees must devote more attention to the selection and training of soviet and trade union cadres. They must heighten the responsibility of soviet organs for improving trade and the medical, communal, cultural, and everyday services of the population, for ensuring exemplary public order. They must be steadily concerned with the assignment of personnel with initiative to enterprises and to public service organizations.

They must enhance the role and significance of trade unions in strengthening labour discipline and in the wide involvement of the toilers in the administration of production. They must support the just demands of the trade unions upon economic leaders for strict observance of labour legislation and for improved labour protection and safety measures.

5   The CPSU Central Committee directs the attention of the central committee of the Estonian Communist Party to the existence of serious mistakes in selecting Komsomol cadres and directs it to take concrete steps to improve the activity of Komsomol organizations. The city and raion party committees and the primary party organizations must improve their work with Komsomol cadres and show constant concern for the need to reinforce the party nucleus in the Komsomol. They must offer daily assistance to Komsomol organizations in helping them involve young people actively in socio-political and production life, in training them in revolutionary, militant, and labour traditions, in the spirit of proletarian internationalism, communist moral principle, and a high sense of responsibility for the work with which they are entrusted ...

7   It is suggested that the central committee of the Estonian Communist Party conduct persistent and skilful propaganda of the ideas of proletarian internationalism and friendship of the peoples of the Soviet Union, the advantages of the socialist system, and the great social achievements of the Soviet people, and that it unmask the bourgeois way of life. It must involve scientific cadres more actively in elaborating the concrete problems of friendship among peoples and internationalism. It must struggle resolutely against any attempts to revive the remnants of nationalist prejudices in the consciousness of the toilers.

It must effect a radical improvement in ideological-educational work with the creative intelligentsia, seek to increase the activity of writers, artists, composers, and theatre and cinema personnel in producing works on a high ideological and artistic level, especially those dealing with the present day. In the creative unions it is necessary to establish an atmosphere of intolerance toward pseudo-innovationism, toward deviations from the principle of party spirit and socialist realism in literature and art. Party organizations must attract all strata of the intelligentsia to active educational work among the toilers, and especially young people.

Partiinaia zhizn', no. 6   *KPSS v rezoliutsiiakh* IX, 215–21
(1967): 8–12

5.13
On the Work of the 'Mikhailov' Sovkhoz Party
Committee in the Panin Raion of Voronezh Oblast   18 February 1967

The following document provides detailed instructions on the areas in which sovkhoz party organizations should be actively involved. Two aspects of the party's role are worth noting. First, the party committee is given responsibility for and the right to intervene in a wide range of daily operational and economic activities of the sovkhoz management. This document does little to settle the long-standing debate over the difference between party guidance (ruko-vodstvo) and state management (upravlenie). Second, the duties assigned to the party and the terminology used to describe party and management respon-sibilities are strikingly similar to parallel developments in the industrial sector. There appears to be a self-conscious attempt to treat the state farm as an inte-gral part of the industrial sector rather than as an agricultural producing unit with special needs reflecting rural conditions.

The CPSU Central Committee notes that, in its practical activity, the party committee of the 'Mikhailov' sovkhoz (Comrade Makarov, secretary of the party committee) is concentrating its attention on political and organizational work with people and mobilizing the collective for successful fulfilment of the decisions of the XXIII Party Congress, the decisions of the March (1965) and May (1966) plenums of the CPSU Central Committee. The party organi-zation is persistently developing initiative in its work, supporting creative activity of workers and employees in the struggle for the successful ful-filment of the Five-Year Plan, for a growth in production and in the economy of the farm, and is showing constant interest in improving the cultural and daily living conditions of the sovkhoz workers ...

The party committee conducts systematic work to enhance the role of shop party organizations in solving economic and political tasks, and takes concern for the correct placement of party forces. Three-fourths of the com-munists work directly on livestock sections of the farm, in brigades and workshops, setting examples of a communist attitude to one's job. Eight shop party organizations and seven party groups have been set up; the most experienced and prepared communists have been elected secretaries of these party organizations and party groups and training has been organized for them. This gives the party organization the opportunity to ensure its influence in all production sectors.

At party meetings, the most important problems of organizational, party, and ideological work are discussed, as well as the observance of the CPSU Rules by communists, introduction of scientific achievements and advanced experience into production, economy and thrift, improved quality of products, and better use of material and moral incentives. The party aktiv, specialists, and the sovkhoz leadership are extensively involved in preparing meetings. This enables the party committee and shop party organizations to deal more thoroughly with the essence of the problems discussed, and cultivates the communists' feeling of great responsibility for the state of affairs in their collective. At every party meeting the communists are informed of progress in the implementation of decisions.

After the XXIII CPSU Congress, the party organization activated its work in the ideological and political education of the working people. In the sovkhoz, lectures and reports are delivered regularly, discussions and political information meetings are held right in brigades and other production sections, dealing with the most important issues of domestic and international life. Leading personnel, specialists, and advanced production workers take an active part in mass political work. A great deal of attention is focused on the problems of improving marxist-leninist education for communists, Komsomol members, and those who are not party members. The sovkhoz has organized an extensive socialist competition among its departments, livestock sections, brigades, and links. The fulfilment of personal and collective obligations is checked systematically, the results are widely publicized, the best people are enrolled in the book of honour and are awarded diplomas, valuable presents, and passes to vacation and health resorts ...

The sovkhoz party organization devotes a great deal of attention to improving economic work. In the sovkhoz, specialization of departments and livestock sections is being implemented, as well as internal farm profit-and-loss accounting. The results of the profit-and-loss subdivisions are discussed monthly at permanently operating production meetings. Moral and material incentives are widely used, remuneration for work is carried out in accordance with work results, the quantity and quality of products ...

The party committee and management of the sovkhoz are enhancing the role and responsibility of specialists as organizers and technologists of production. They have started to study more thoroughly the farm's economy, as well as to elaborate and apply concrete measures to step up the production of agriculture and livestock products, to use more rationally every hectare of land, as well as material, financial, and labour resources ...

While noting the positive work of the party committee and of the entire sovkhoz collective, at the same time the CPSU Central Committee considers it necessary to direct the attention of the party organization to shortcomings and gaps in its work.

The party committee is still insufficiently directing the collective's efforts at making fuller use of the available internal reserves and potentials of the farm, at lowering the cost of production and eliminating unproductive expenses. The sovkhoz leadership and party committee do not always evaluate work results critically, and tolerate incidents of thriftlessness and backwardness of certain production sectors.

The sovkhoz yield capacity varies considerably. Behind the average farm indices are hidden sectors that are not fulfilling their plans ...

The management of the sovkhoz and the party committee are not devoting enough attention to raising the productivity of animal husbandry and to the mechanization of labour-intensive processes in livestock sections ...

The party committee is not yet giving enough assistance to primary party organizations to perfect internal party work; it is doing a poor job of generalizing the experience of practical activity of party groups and individual party organizations; it is not carrying out the necessary supervision over the timely fulfilment of party assignments by communists.

The party committee and the primary party organizations are giving altogether inadequate attention to the activity of the Komsomol organization and to enhancing the party's influence in the Komsomol. The Komsomol organization has a small membership; its work is conducted on a low level. Work in mass dissemination of culture, physical culture, and education is poorly set up for young people. The party committee and workers' committee are not showing the necessary concern for raising the standard of labour, for the organization of public services and amenities in population centres, or for the development of rationalization work. Incidents of a careless attitude to material values, violation of labour and production discipline have not yet been overcome in the collective.

The CPSU Central Committee resolves:

1   The party committee of the 'Mikhailov' sovkhoz is ordered to concentrate its attention on the further practical implementation of the decisions of the XXIII CPSU Congress, the March (1965) and May (1966) plenums of the CPSU Central Committee. The short-comings noted in its work are to be eliminated, forms and methods of its activity are to be improved constantly, the organizational role of primary party organizations and party groups is to be enhanced. Every member of the party is to be educated in the spirit of great responsibility for the successful solution of economic and political tasks, for the state of affairs both in his own party organizations and in the

party as a whole. Efforts are to be made to ensure that every communist is a militant implementor of party and government decisions, not only a good production worker, but also an active public figure, who is intolerant of short-comings in work and represents an example of high-principled nature, and strict observance of party and state discipline.

2   The chief task of the sovkhoz party organization is considered to be the mobilization of all workers to continue in every way to increase the farm's yield capacity for each hectare of land and productivity of animal husbandry, to increase the production of grain and other agricultural products, to make effective use of capital investments, and to strengthen the economy of the farm. The party organization must profoundly analyse economic indices in every branch, critically appraise achievements, expose short-comings with great exactingness, thoroughly study the farm's reserves and development perspective and carry out concrete practical measures so that the sovkhoz becomes a model socialist farm ...

3   The CPSU Central Committee emphasizes that, under today's conditions of the struggle to increase the effectiveness of agricultural production, problems of economic work acquire particular significance. The economic leadership and party organization of the sovkhoz are ordered to improve the organization and technology of production and to carry out a strict regime of economy. Concrete measures are to be developed and implemented to mechanize labour in animal husbandry, to lower the cost of production, and to raise the profitability of sovkhoz production. Initiative and innovation are to be developed in the work of specialists, collectives of every department, brigade, and link to improve economic indices. Sovkhoz cadres are to be taught how to utilize correctly economic levers for developing the public economy, how to manage it skilfully, and how to understand all production details with profound knowledge.

4   The party committee is ordered to take measures to improve mass political work, regularly to inform the sovkhoz workers on the political, economic, and cultural life of our country and on the international situation. The wide participation of the sovkhoz leadership and specialists in political work is to be ensured, as well as that of the entire rural intelligentsia, and advanced workers and production innovators. At the present time, all mass political work must be directed at the successful fulfilment of socialist obligations undertaken in honour of the Fiftieth Anniversary of the Great October Socialist Revolution, and for the further raising of the communist consciousness of the working people. It is necessary to enhance the significance of workers' meetings in the communist education of sovkhoz workers, to intensify the role of the public in the struggle with those who violate labour discipline and public order. In party studies, prime attention is to be concentrated on raising the quality and ideological content of the studies conducted,

and on inculcating in communists an organic need for independent and creative study of marxist-leninist theory and the policy of the CPSU.

5   The party committee is required to take measures to improve the activity of the Komsomol organization ...

More attention is to be given to the activity of the trade union organization, particularly in the development of socialist competition and the movement for communist labour, to ensure the wide participation of workers in considering plans, profit-and-loss assignments, and the results of their fulfilment. Assistance is to be provided to the workers' committee in improving public supervision over the correct use of output norms, measures for material stimulation, and the observance of labour legislation. The attention of the trade union organization and sovkhoz management is to be directed at intensifying concern for fuller satisfaction of the workers' and employees' cultural and everyday needs. There is to be steady improvement of the work of cafeterias, clubs, and medical and children's institutions.

6   The Panin raion party committee and the Voronezh oblast party committee are ordered to provide assistance to the party committee of the 'Mikhailov' sovkhoz in eliminating existing short-comings and fulfilling the present decision.

Partiinaia zhizn', no. 7   *KPSS v rezoliutsiiakh* IX, 226–32
(1967): 3–6

5.14
On the Work of the Omsk Oblast Party Committee of the CPSU*

11 May 1967

The local party organs were given overall responsibility for ensuring the implementation of the economic reforms adopted at the September 1965 Central Committee Plenum. This document starts by listing a wide range of shortcomings in the work of local party organs that were charged with supervising the smooth and rapid transfer to the new principles of planning and management in industry, construction, and agriculture. Administrative resistance at the local level is blamed on the failure of the local party organizations to enforce party discipline among members, to conduct work with cadres, to conduct the appropriate supervision and verification, criticism and self-criticism, ideological work, and to enhance the role and responsibility of the soviets, trade unions, and Komsomol organization. The bulk of the document included in this section focuses on the directives provided to local party organizations

*   Excerpt: document not published in full.

with the aim of improving their effectiveness in ensuring the implementation of the economic reform by the industrial ministries.

The CPSU Central Committee notes that after the October (1964) Central Committee Plenum and XXIII CPSU Congress, the Omsk oblast party committee improved its guidance over the oblast's political, economic, and cultural life. In the activity of the oblast committee and many raion party committees, there has been more businesslike efficiency, while internal party democracy, leninist norms of party life, and collective leadership have advanced further. Elements of bureaucratic administration are being done away with in practical actions and cadres now have more confidence and independence in deciding practical tasks. The life of primary party organizations has become more meaningful and versatile. Due to the admission of advanced workers, kolkhozniks, and intelligentsia, the primary party organizations have grown in number and have strengthened themselves organizationally; the responsibility of communists for the fulfilment of statutory duties has increased. Many party organizations have begun a more profound study of economics; their role and influence in collectives has been enhanced. The oblast committee, raion committees, and primary party organizations have intensified their attention towards the ideological preparation of communists and the education of the working people ...

The improvement in organizational and educational work contributes to enhancing the political and labour activity of the working people; it has a positive effect on the development of the economy and culture of the oblast, and on the fulfilment of the Five-Year-Plan targets ...

At the same time, the CPSU Central Committee notes that the activity of the Omsk oblast party committee does not totally meet the tasks set by the XXIII CPSU Congress and the March and September plenums of the Central Committee. The oblast party committee does not always critically analyse achieved results. In appraising the state of affairs in industry, construction, and agriculture, average indices are often accepted that cover up significant short-comings and gaps in the work of individual enterprises, construction sites, kolkhozes and sovkhozes ...

The oblast party committee and oblast executive committee do not show persistence in carrying out more correct and rational placement of productive forces. Industry is mainly concentrated in the city of Omsk, which leads to an unwarranted shift of the population from the oblast districts and to constant difficulties in hiring workers ...

Some raion party committees (the Tiukalin, Tevriz, and Poltav) are taking on functions that are not properly theirs. On many occasions they substitute for soviet and economic bodies in solving current problems and at the same time are not providing sufficient assistance to primary party organizations in improving internal party and mass political work, in enhancing their influence on production ...

The CPSU Central Committee views the short-comings in the work of the Omsk oblast party committee to be, to a considerable degree, the result of lack of attention of the oblast committee bureau and secretaries to organizational work in the localities, and of poor study and generalization of the work experience of raion party committees and primary party organizations.

The CPSU Central Committee resolves: ...

2   The CPSU Central Committee considers that the oblast committee and the Omsk city and raion party committees and party organizations at industrial and transport enterprises must focus their attention on the mobilization of workers, engineers, technicians, and employees to achieve high production effectiveness and a growth in labour productivity on the basis of putting into practice the achievements of science, engineering, progressive technology, and the extensive application of comprehensive mechanization and automation. At every enterprise, it is necessary to ensure the fullest use of production funds, the quickest achievement of designed capacities, high quality and technological level of products, the unconditional fulfilment of state plans and assignments with the least expenditures of materials and manpower. The party organizations must make efforts toward raising the standards of enterprises, toward the systematic improvement of labour organization, internal plant planning, and the wide application of profit-and-loss principles in the work of shops, shop subdivisions, installations, and brigades.

One of the most important tasks of party, soviet, economic, and all public organizations is to prepare for the transfer of enterprise collectives to a five-day work week.

3   The oblast party committee, the oblast executive committee, and agricultural organs of the oblast are ordered, on the basis of measures worked out by the March and May plenums of the CPSU Central Committee, to ensure high rates of growth of all branches of agricultural production, to concentrate the efforts of the kolkhozniks, sovkhoz workers, and specialists on gathering stable harvests of grain and other crop cultures. Efforts are to be made to introduce and master the correct crop rotation at every kolkhoz and sovkhoz ...

Party, soviet, and agricultural organs must develop independence in every possible way, support initiative and raise the responsibility of the leaders and specialists of kolkhozes and sovkhozes for the job assigned to them. Consistent efforts are to be made to improve economic work in agriculture; specialization of production is to be carried out consistently; the principles of profit-and-loss accounting and progressive forms of labour organization and remuneration are to be supplied more extensively; production funds are to be used more effectively; the profitability of production is to be raised on all kolkhozes and sovkhozes.

4   The oblast party committee, oblast executive committee, the Omsk city and raion party committees are to make a more profound study of construction problems and accomplish a more effective and rational utilization of capital investments. Higher demands are to be made on leaders of construction sites and party organizations for scheduled completion of projects under construction, improving the quality and lowering the costs of building and installation works, and strengthening the basis of the construction industry ... Daily concern is to be shown for the improvement of work conditions and cultural and everyday services for construction workers.

5   The CPSU Central Committee emphasizes that the further development of the economy and culture of the oblast is very much dependent on strengthening organizational and political work. The oblast party committee must constantly make efforts to improve the style and methods of work of party committees, take note of short-comings promptly and take measures to do away with them. Internal party democracy and leninist principles of collective leadership are to be observed strictly and developed consistently. The activity of party committee members is to be stepped up, and they are to be involved widely in working out party decisions and putting them into practice.

It is necessary to enhance the organizational role of primary party organizations in solving economic tasks and educating the working people. It should be taken into consideration that the realization of new economic management methods introduces substantial changes in the work of primary party organizations and requires them to study economics more thoroughly in order to mobilize collectives for the utilization of internal production reserves. Particular attention is to be paid to consolidating the activity of shop party organizations and party groups that are called upon to exert daily influence on the state of affairs directly in shops, brigades, departments, and livestock sections. Strict observance of the requirements of the CPSU Rules is to be ensured in every primary party organization, the role and significance of party meetings is to be enhanced, communists' proposals are to be considered carefully, and conditions are to be created for extensive criticism and self-criticism. Work with respect to the admission of new members into the party is to be improved, with the intention of further strengthening primary party organizations with advanced and conscientious workers, kolkhozniks, and representatives of the intelligentsia.

Systematic study by secretaries of primary shop party organizations and party groups is to be organized. They are to be informed regularly regarding the resolutions of the CPSU Central Committee and government and regarding the decisions of party committees. The significance of the staff of the oblast, city, and raion party committees is to be enhanced in studying and generalizing the practice of party work, instructing party personnel and improving inner-party information.

6   The oblast committee and the Omsk city and raion party committees are ordered to improve the selection and training of cadres, to show constant concern for reinforcing all sectors of party, soviet, and economic work with energetic people who are competent in their fields and enjoy authority with communists and those who are not party members. The unwarranted shifting of personnel is not to be tolerated. Cadres are to be educated in a spirit of high moral fibre, and principled Bolshevik nature, a critical attitude to the results of one's own work, efficiency, and a thoughtful attitude to people. Cadres are to be assisted in mastering marxist-leninist theory and acquiring experience in organizational and political work. The leaders of enterprises, construction sites, kolkhozes, and sovkhozes are constantly to improve their knowledge of the economy and their areas of specialization. Measures are to be taken to reduce labour turnover, and to secure and make correct use of specialists in production. Attention is to be paid to strengthening leading cadres and specialists at enterprises of light, foodstuffs, and local industries.

The organization of supervision and verification over the implementation of directives of the party, government, and local leadership is to be improved. Assistance is to be provided to the organs of people's control.

7   The oblast committee, the Omsk city and raion party committees, and party organizations are ordered to improve the organization of propaganda and mass political work, to make more active use of all means of ideological influence for the formation of the toilers' communist outlook and morals, for the cultivation of a conscientious attitude to one's job and to socialist property, exemplary discipline, and high responsibility for entrusted work.

The organized completion of studies in the system of party education is to be ensured and thorough preparation for the coming school year is to be carried out. Efforts are to be made to ensure that communists constantly raise their theoretical level and ideologically temper their character and mature as party political fighters. Work is to be intensified with propagandists and they are to be assisted in mastering the theory and methodology of propaganda.

Political agitation is to be improved in every possible way on the basis of widely and systematically organized information of the population. Agitators, lecturers, and politinformators are to be recruited from the best-trained leaders and specialists, who are capable of profoundly and intelligibly explaining questions dealing with the political, economic, and cultural life of the country and the international situation. The level of party guidance is to be raised with respect to newspapers, radio and television, and cultural and educational establishments; the effectiveness of newspaper reports is to be increased and those who do not react to signals and critical reports in newspapers are to be held strictly responsible.

8   The CPSU oblast committee and party committees are ordered to improve in every possible way their guidance over the soviets, trade unions, and Komsomol organizations, to develop their initiative and independence in solving assigned tasks ...

Partiinaia zhizn', no. 10   *KPSS v rezoliutsiiakh* IX, 270–9
(1967): 3–9

5.15
On Party Commissions of Oblast and Krai Party
Committees and Central Committees of
Union Republic Communist Parties   30 June 1967

1   In accordance with the resolution of the XXIII Party Congress, union republic party central committees and krai and oblast party committees are ordered to activate the work of party commissions of local party organs in increasing communists' responsibility for implementing party policy; they are also to enlist the party commissions in checking on the implementation of the CPSU Rules by party members and candidate members, and their observance of party and state discipline.

Party commissions are charged with:

–   studying and making a preliminary review of appeals from communists in order to prepare subsequent discussions of them at the bureaus of oblast and krai party committees and of union republic party central committees;

–   checking, together with the appropriate departments of party committees, letters and declarations concerning violations by party members and candidate members of the CPSU Programme and Rules, of party and state discipline, and also of party morality;

–   implementing supervision, together with the departments of organizational and party work, over the observance of the CPSU Rules during hearings on the personal affairs of communists in raion and city party committees and providing them with the necessary assistance in this work.

2   It is considered essential that the party commissions be put together from experienced cadres. Union republic party central committees and krai and oblast party committees are to consider the question of the possibility of increasing – at the expense of existing staffs – the number of party commission officials who are released from other duties.

3   Union republic party central committees and krai and oblast party committees are authorized to establish – within the limits of existing staffs – the position of full-time party commission chairman in city and raion party committees of major party organizations.

Spravochnik partiinogo
rabotnika VIII (1968), 297–8

5.16
On Measures for Further Developing the
Social Sciences and Enhancing their Role
in Communist Construction

14 August 1967

One of the themes symbolic of the Brezhnev regime's approach to administration was that things must be done 'scientifically.' A developed socialist society was to be characterized by 'scientific management of social processes' and by 'scientific decision making.' This approach meant an important re-evaluation of the status, scope, and functions of the social sciences. A 'scientific' approach to management and to decision making was interpreted to mean that decisions were to incorporate information gathered, processed, and analysed utilizing a variety of social science techniques. These techniques included the development of middle-range theories that are much more explicit and concrete than the generalizations normally associated with dialectical and historical materialism. They involved the use of various means for generating social science data, including sampling, interviews, and questionnaires. There was also more extensive use of computers for processing the data. All of this did not necessarily mean a growing autonomy for the social sciences as an independent academic discipline, although pressures certainly mounted in this direction. The main impact of the party's policy in the social sciences was to create a pool of experts and to train decision makers in the use of various types of social science techniques and information in order to improve the basis for decision making. As is indicated in the accompanying document, the party still reserved to itself the right to define areas of research and considered the strengthening of party guidance over research institutes to be an integral component in the development of social science.

... Measures conducted by the party to overcome the consequences of the cult of the personality, subjectivism, and voluntarism have had a favourable effect on the development of the social sciences. The October (1964) Plenum of the CPSU Central Committee and the XXIII CPSU Congress have shown the tremendous significance of theory in building communism at the present stage and have emphasized the necessity of scientific leadership of social development.

In recent years, more favourable conditions have been created for the development of the social sciences. The state and perspectives of research work in the field of philosophical, economic, historical, and other social sciences have been discussed in party organizations and collectives of scientists. Substantial changes have been introduced in plans of scientific research. New programmes have been worked out in social sciences for higher educational institutions and the preparation of standard textbooks is under way. Measures have been taken to improve the system of political education.

At the same time, the CPSU Central Committee considers that the enhanced tasks of communist construction and the ideological struggle taking place in the contemporary world require further development of theoretical conceptions, a more profound analysis of social development, and a new rise in the level of marxist-leninist education of cadres ...

The CPSU Central Committee resolves ...

3   The present stage of social development and the progress of scientific knowledge require that scientific research work in the social sciences be concentrated primarily in the following directions:

in the field of philosophical sciences – further elaboration of materialist dialectics, the theory of cognition and logic, methodological problems of the social, natural, and technical sciences; study of the dialectics of socialist society and the contradictions of contemporary capitalism, the correlation of objective and subjective factors of social development; the development of historical materialism as a general sociological theory, the development of empirical social research; elaboration of problems pertaining to the social structure of society, the improvement of socialist social relations and their transformation into communist relations; the drawing up of a methodology for scientifically predicting the development of social processes; research into the laws of social consciousness; theoretical elaboration of problems pertaining to the individual and the collective, society and the state, socialist humanism, ethics and aesthetics; research into problems of the organization, logic, and psychology of scientific creativity;

in the field of economic sciences – comprehensive disclosure of the laws and categories of the political economy of socialism and of the mechanism of their operation; research into economic problems of creating the material and technical base of communism and forming communist production relations; elaboration of scientific recommendations for carrying out the new principles of economic policy at the present stage, for raising the effectiveness of social production, and for rational distribution of productive forces and rational use of the country's labour resources; study of economic problems of technical progress; elaboration of the theory and methods of optimum planning and functioning of the socialist economy; problems of money-commodity relationships under socialism; the wide utilization of computer technology in planning and management; development of research in the economics of various branches of the economy; economic research in the field of demography; research on the forms and methods of economic co-operation among socialist countries, ways of strengthening the world system of socialism; the discovery of new phenomena in the economy of present-day capitalism; study of the socio-economic contradictions of imperialism, and of new forms of the imperialist struggle for the redivision of the world, etc.; study of the economic, social, and political problems of developing countries that have become free of colonial dependence;

in the field of scientific communism – elaboration of the leninist theory of the socialist revolution as applied to the present epoch; disclosure of the laws of development of the world revolutionary process, analysis of the class struggle of the international proletariat, problems of the national liberation movement, and the struggle against imperialism; elaboration of theoretical problems pertaining to the international communist movement in the present era; study of the problems of war and peace; thorough disclosure of the antagonistic contradictions between socialism and capitalism; comprehensive study of socio-political problems of the development of socialism and its transformation into communism; revelation of the social results of the scientific-technological revolution; study of the means and forms by which the conditions of labour, daily life, and the cultural development of the city and village can be drawn closer together and mental and physical work in production activity can be organically merged; working out of problems of the development of national relations; the elaboration of methods of scientific management of social processes; the analysis of the content and forms of work in communist education, the ways of overcoming private-ownership, religious, and other survivals in the consciousness and daily life of the toilers; research on the processes and problems of perfecting the state system and socialist democracy, cultivating patriotism and internationalism; study of the experience of socialist construction in other countries;

in the field of the history of the CPSU and other historical sciences – generalization of the experience of the CPSU in the struggle for the victory of the socialist revolution and the establishment of the dictatorship of the proletariat and in the struggle for carrying out the leninist plan for building socialism; study of the laws of party development and the growth of the party's leading role in communist construction, the activity of the CPSU in elaborating revolutionary theory and the strategy and tactics of the working class; study of the theory and practice of party construction, of the forms and methods of work in party organizations; elucidation of the struggle of the CPSU for the ideological and organizational unity of its ranks against anti-leninist groups and tendencies, for the unity of the international communist movement; disclosure of the decisive role of the masses of people in history, the struggle of the toilers against social and national oppression, the great liberating mission of the working class; depiction of the heroism of the Soviet people in defending the gains of the Great October Revolution in the struggle for socialist industrialization of the country, collectivization of agriculture and the cultural revolution, and in the rout of fascism in the years of the Great Patriotic War; generalization of the experience of strengthening the alliance between the working class and peasantry, friendship among peoples, the creation and development of the multinational Soviet state; study of the foreign policy of the USSR and international relations, the history of the international working and communist movement;

in the field of legal sciences – research on urgent problems of state construction and the development of socialist democracy; the working out of problems of the organization and activity of the Soviets of Working People's Deputies, of the scientific fundamentals of state administration, legal regulation of economic life and social relations; elaboration of measures for preventing and eliminating crime and other violations of law, strengthening legality, law, and order in the country; preparation of scientifically grounded recommendations for improving Soviet legislation; study of the experience of state and legal construction in foreign socialist countries; research on the state system of developing countries; unmasking the reactionary essence of the contemporary imperialist state and law; study of problems of international law.

The requirements of science and practice raise the necessity of organizing comprehensive research in all significant lines of development of the social sciences. Prime attention in scientific research is to be given to marxist-leninist methodology and to the principles of a class-party and concrete-historical approach to social phenomena.

One of the most important tasks of the social sciences is to wage a systematic offensive struggle against anti-communism, subject contemporary bourgeois philosophy, sociology, historiography, law, and economic theories of the apologists of capitalism to profound criticism; the falsifiers of marxist-leninist ideas are to be exposed, as well as those who falsify the history of the development of society and the communist and working-class movement; manifestations of 'right' and 'left' revisionism, national narrow-mindedness both in theory and in politics are to be repulsed decisively.

A more vivid exposition is to be given of the general international significance of marxism-leninism. The superiority of communist ideology over bourgeois ideology and the all-conquering force of the ideas of scientific communism are to be demonstrated by specific facts of world history and the experience of the socialist countries.

In the work of scientific research institutions on social sciences, it is necessary to make wider practice of comradely discussions on controversial or insufficiently clear questions.

4   The CPSU Central Committee has instructed the USSR Gosplan, the USSR Council of Ministers' State Committee on Science and Technology, the USSR Academy of Sciences and the USSR Ministry of Higher and Secondary Specialized Education to prepare and submit for the consideration of the CPSU Central Committee before 1 January 1968 proposals for fundamental improvement in the organization, planning, and financing of scientific research work in the area of the social sciences, with the following aims:

a to determine the real perspectives for fundamental and applied research on basic scientific questions, to direct major attention to the comprehensive elaboration of urgent problems of social development and the scientific-technological revolution; to enhance the role of scientific-research institutes in the social sciences in preparing scientifically based recommendations that are needed for working out the policy of the Communist Party and the Soviet state and for scientific bases of party propaganda;

   b to raise the quality and effectiveness of research, to reward bold scientific search, the conducting of fruitful discussions and conversations on urgent scientific questions; to conduct regularly summarizing conferences on various social sciences with the aim of determining the results of scientific research and working out scientific-theoretical recommendations; to improve the conditions for acquainting a wide public with the results of exploratory research and to ensure its prompt publication and creative discussion in scientific collectives; to strive for the correct combination of collective and individual forms of work, and of experienced cadres and young scientific successors;

   c to put in good order the existing network and structure of scientific research institutes with the aim of clarifying their specialization, and overcoming unwarranted parallelism, dispersion of forces and material resources; to bring the system of humanities institutes into accord with the requirements for developing science at the present stage and with the tasks of communist construction; to consider the delineation of new branches of the social sciences, the necessity of comprehensive elaboration of problems arising at the junctures of various social sciences, as well as at the junctures of the social and natural sciences; to take measures to improve the work of scientific institutes conducting applied social research and to ensure co-ordination of their activity; to provide for the possibility of creating in the appropriate scientific-research institutes and major institutes of higher learning specialized groups for operational elaboration of theoretical problems that have great political and economic significance;

   d in carrying out co-ordination of theoretical research in the sphere of the social sciences, the USSR Academy of Sciences is to give precision to current and long-run plans of scientific research work and is to strengthen its supervision over their implementation;

   e the USSR Gosplan, the USSR Council of Ministers' State Committee on Science and Technology, and the USSR Academy of Sciences are to strengthen the material base of social science institutes and are to create the conditions necessary for their fruitful scientific-research work.

5   The Institute of Marxism-Leninism of the CPSU Central Committee, as the centre for study of the ideological heritage of Marx–Engels–Lenin, is entrusted with co-ordination of all scientific research work in the area of the science of party history. The institute's chief attention is to be concentrated in the following directions: elaboration of urgent problems of the history of

the CPSU and party construction, scientific communism, history of the Comintern and the international communist movement; organization of scientific information in these directions.

In the next three months the leadership of the Institute of Marxism-Leninism is ordered to prepare and submit to the CPSU Central Committee proposals for appropriate changes in plans of work, structure, and staffs of the institute and its branches.

6   Measures are to be taken for further improving the theoretical preparation of leading cadres and the party's ideological personnel in the Academy of Social Sciences and the Higher Party School of the CPSU Central Committee, and in local party schools.

7   The USSR Academy of Sciences, the Institute of Marxism-Leninism, the Academy of Social Sciences, the Higher Party School, and the Institute of Social Sciences of the CPSU Central Committee are to ensure comprehensive study of the development of marxist thought abroad; constant contacts are to be maintained with scientific institutions of the socialist countries and fraternal communist parties; scientific research work is to be co-ordinated with them in the area of the social sciences and in working out forms and methods of offensive propaganda against anti-communist ideology; joint scientific conferences are to be held systematically on the most significant problems of marxist-leninist theory, socialist and communist construction, the world revolutionary movement and pressing questions of history.

8   With a view to radically improving the system of scientific information and to further expanding the documentary base of the social sciences, it is considered necessary that:

a   the USSR Council of Ministers' State Committee on Science and Technology, the Presidium of the USSR Academy of Sciences, and the Ministry of Higher and Secondary Specialized Education are to adopt measures to increase the volume and ensure the systematic reception of information materials, and to shorten the time for processing and improve the quality of information; they are to make information the property of a wide circle of scientific personnel and teachers; they are to prepare proposals on the organization of an Institute of Scientific Information in the Social Sciences;

b   the Institute of Marxism-Leninism of the CPSU Central Committee and the Main Archives Administration of the USSR Council of Ministers are to adopt measures to replenish and improve use of archive collections; there is to be wider publication of documentary materials on the history of the CPSU and Soviet society, including documents of the Communist Party and the Soviet government on industrialization of the country, collectivization of agriculture, cultural construction, the working out and implementation of the first five-year plans for the development of the economy of the USSR; they are to ensure the provision of state and party archives with modern technical means of photo- and microfilm-copying, with instruments for reading microfilms and with other means for reprinting and reproducing documentary materials in quantity.

c The Central Statistical Administration of the USSR Council of Ministers, together with the USSR Gosplan and the USSR Academy of Sciences, is to work out a scientifically based system of statistical data that are necessary for economic, sociological, demographic, and other scientific research; there is to be more statistical research based on sampling and applying the most modern methods of selecting statistical materials; publication of statistical data is to be expanded and specialized.

9 The central committees of the union republic communist parties, the krai, oblast, city, and raion party committees, the USSR Ministry of Higher and Secondary Specialized Education, other ministries and departments that are involved in preparing specialists, party organizations at teaching institutions, the rectors' offices of higher educational institutions, and the directors of technical schools are ordered to achieve a significant improvement in the teaching of the social sciences and strengthening the communist education of young students ...

10 The central committees of the union republic communist parties, the krai, oblast, city, and raion party committees, the USSR Ministry of Higher and Secondary Specialized Education, and the Presidium of the USSR Academy of Sciences are to do away with short-comings in the planning of training and in the distribution of scientific cadres, are to ensure an improvement in the qualitative composition of scientific personnel and teachers of social sciences, and a further rise in their ideological-theoretical level ...

14 The central committees of the union republic communist parties, and the krai, oblast, city, and raion party committees are to improve their guidance over party organizations of scientific-research institutes and teaching institutions, are to provide them with constant help in selecting, placing, and training cadres. Party organizations must devote more attention to the training of young scientific personnel and teachers in the social sciences ...

Pravda, 22 August 1967   *KPSS v rezolutsiiakh* IX, 342–57

5.17
On the Work of the Party Organizations
of Perm Oblast with Respect to
Guidance over the Trade Unions*   18 September 1967

The CPSU Central Committee notes that, in carrying out the decisions of the XXIII CPSU Congress, the party organizations of Perm oblast have

_____
*   Excerpt: document not published in full.

improved their guidance over the trade unions and activated their work in accomplishing practical tasks of economic and cultural construction. Many party committees have started to be more concerned with the selection, training, and education of trade union cadres; the committees are raising the responsibility of communists elected to trade union organs and are supporting the initiative and good undertakings of trade union organizations and their demands directed at improving the conditions of labour and daily life of workers and employees. The work of trade union organizations has taken on a more versatile and mass nature. Their role has risen in mobilizing production collectives to fulfil state plans and socialist obligations and in resolving problems pertaining to social and daily living conditions and the communist education of the toilers ...

At the same time the CPSU Central Committee notes that the level of guidance that the Perm oblast party organizations exercise over the trade unions does not totally meet the requirements of the XXIII CPSU Congress. The oblast, the Komi-Perm okrug, many city and raion party committees still fail to delve into the substance of the trade union organizations and do not make full use of the potentials of the trade unions as the most massive social organization in mobilizing the toilers to fulfil the tasks of economic and cultural construction ...

The short-comings in the Perm oblast party organization's guidance over trade unions are largely explained by the fact that the oblast committee of the CPSU fails to give the necessary attention to this important sector of work, and does not make proper demands on the okrug, city, and raion committees of the CPSU for the state of affairs in trade union organizations and for raising their role in the entire production, social, and political life of the oblast.

The CPSU Central Committee resolves:

1   The Perm oblast committee, the Komi-Perm okrug committee, and the city and raion committees of the party are ordered to do away with the short-comings noted in this decision, to raise the level of party guidance over the trade unions, to provide daily assistance to them, to make fuller use of the forces and potentials of the trade unions as schools of administration, schools of management, and schools of communism. The further intensification of the work of trade union organizations is to be secured in mobilizing the toilers for fulfilment of the decisions of the XXIII CPSU Congress and the Five-Year Plan for the development of the economy and for a worthy commemoration of the Fiftieth Anniversary of the Great October Socialist Revolution.

2   The oblast party organizations must constantly take concern in enhancing the role of the trade unions in developing the toilers' creative activity, involving them in production management, and improving the guidance of trade union organizations over socialist competition and the movement for

communist labour. It is necessary to direct the efforts of the competition participants to fulfilling state plans and socialist obligations at every enterprise, construction site, kolkhoz, and sovkhoz, to raising labour productivity, widely introducing advanced experience, making fuller use of available reserves, improving the quality of products, and to making economical use of raw materials, supplies, and energy resources. The activity of the toilers' creative associations is to be stepped up, a more massive involvement of workers and employees is to be achieved in the ranks of voters and rationalizers; the collaboration of personnel working in science and industry is to be developed and strengthened in every possible way.

It is necessary to ensure the active participation of trade union organizations in carrying out the economic reform, transferring collectives of toilers to a five-day work week, and to assist them in correctly organizing work under the new conditions. The trade union organizations need to occupy themselves more with questions of raising the economic effectiveness of production, the scientific organization of labour, as well as making fullest use of production capacities and rationally spending enterprise funds; they need to intensify control over the correct application of the systems of labour remuneration and awarding bonuses to workers, specialists, and employees; wider use is to be made of moral incentives. A struggle to raise production standards is to be conducted; the experience of the best collectives in this area is to be disseminated more energetically; efforts are to be made to establish model order at every enterprise.

3   The oblast party organizations must actively support the trade unions in making use of the rights granted to them of state supervision and public control over the observance of labour legislation, rules and standards of labour protection, and safety measures. One of the most important tasks of trade union committees and economic leaders is to conduct health improvement and preventive measures protecting people from occupational injuries and diseases, to introduce modern industrial safety techniques; to carry out the mechanization of heavy manual labour; to create normal sanitary conditions in production; to expand daily services and improve their operation.

The trade union organizations need to make more persistent efforts to fulfil plans for the construction and commissioning of residential houses, schools, children's and medical establishments, trade and public catering enterprises, to maintain exemplary order in dormitories and to do away with short-comings in medical services. Control is to be intensified over the organization of trade and public catering, with particular attention being paid to expanding the assortment and raising the quality of prepared food, and to the organization of public catering for evening and night shifts. A sharper reaction is to be given to incidents of an inattentive attitude of individual economic leaders towards satisfying the toilers' cultural and daily living needs; incidents of violation of the established order of distributing housing are not to be tolerated; correct use is to be made of state social insurance funds, passes to health resorts, holiday homes, and dispensaries.

4   The oblast, okrug, city, and raion committees of the CPSU and primary party organizations must enhance the role of the trade unions in educating the toilers and particularly young workers in a spirit of high ideological principles, socialist discipline and organization, and observance of the principles and standards of communist morale. Efforts are to be made to have every worker and employee raise his production qualification and general educational level, treat equipment and instruments carefully, and not tolerate short-comings in any area of production or daily life. Toilers are to be educated in the revolutionary and labour traditions of the working class and of their collective.

In connection with the transfer of enterprise collectives to a five-day work week with two free days, significant intensification of educational work among the toilers at their places of residence is to be ensured, and the activity of houses of culture, clubs, recreation and reading rooms, libraries, and sport installations is to be improved. Their material base is to be reinforced and expanded continually, a network of recreation centres, dispensaries, tourist and sport camps is to be developed, with fuller use being made of this potential by enterprises, construction sites, kolkhozes, and sovkhozes.

5   The oblast, okrug, city, and raion party committees, the primary party organizations, and party groups of the oblast trade union council and trade union committees must make efforts to improve the organizational activity of trade union organs, to perfect the forms and methods of their work, to develop trade union democracy, and to pay particular attention to activating the work of primary trade union organizations; they are not to act as substitutes for those organizations or permit petty tutelage; suggestions of trade union committees and organizations are to be considered attentively; trade unions are to be consulted in solving problems pertaining to production, labour, and the daily life of workers and employees.

It is necessary to enhance in every possible way the role of workers and production meetings as a very significant means of raising the political and production activity of the toilers, and involving them widely in economic management and improving control over production. The most important problems of the life and activity of enterprise collectives are to be discussed at workers' and production meetings. Control and organizational activity in carrying out the decisions of workers' and production meetings is to be intensified. Trade union organizations and economic leaders must improve the practice of concluding collective agreements, of mutual obligations of the administration and collective; timely reports on these activities are to be made to the toilers. At every enterprise, construction site, kolkhoz, and sovkhoz, conditions are to be created to develop criticism and self-criticism, and strictly hold those people responsible who do not respond to the criticism or reject it.

6   The CPSU Central Committee draws the attention of the oblast, okrug, city, and raion party committees to the necessity of radically improving the selection and training of trade union cadres. The party committees must recommend for election to trade union organs the best-prepared, authoritative organizers who show initiative and who have the ability to work with people. Practical assistance is to be rendered to trade union cadres in their ideological tempering, their mastering of the technology and economics of production, their acquiring the skills of organizational activity; the trade union aktiv is to be informed on a regular basis of the decisions of the party and government and of local party and soviet organs.

The party organizations need to strengthen the party nucleus in trade union committees, improve the practical activity of party groups in elected trade union organs, and raise the responsibility of communists for the state of affairs in trade union organizations. To justify the confidence placed in them and to ensure the successful accomplishment of tasks that face the trade unions at the present stage of communist construction must be a matter of party honour.

Partiinaia zhizn', no. 19   *KPSS v rezoliutsiiakh* IX, 374–80
(1967): 21–5

Plenum of the Central Committee   26 September 1967

The Brezhnev regime made a basic commitment to raising the living standards of the Soviet population. This commitment was a repeated theme of congress reports and resolutions. At the September 1967 Central Committee Plenum, Brezhnev made a number of wide-ranging promises for improved consumer welfare measures in conjunction with the annual draft plan and budget, noting that the growth rate for consumer goods was expected to outstrip the growth rate for other sectors of the economy. The Ninth Five-Year Plan, introduced at the XXIV Congress in March 1971, was the first in Soviet history in which planned growth in the Group B sector (light and consumer goods and agriculture) was to be greater than in the Group A sector (heavy industry).

There were several reasons for the shift in regime attitude and policy. The advances in social policy under Khrushchev had begun to create a climate of consumerism in which legitimate expectations for improved material well-being by the population kept increasing. In addition, the shift to material incentives associated with the 1965 economic reforms implicitly required more and better consumer goods and services as the reward for increased productivity and efficiency. As basic needs were increasingly satisfied, consumer tastes became more refined. Inventories of lower quality goods began to grow, as well as the savings of the Soviet consumer. There were also external factors at work. Increased contact with the West made certain strata of the Soviet population acutely aware of differences in living standards. Knowledge of Western levels of consumption became more widespread. The Soviet desire to establish a model of development for Third World countries may also have had some effect on the leadership's decision to improve the domestic consumption level.

Under Brezhnev, a series of social policies was introduced that had the effect of increasing disposable income available for the purchase of privately consumed goods. Minimum wages and the general level of wages increased. Improved old-age and disability benefits were instituted. The cash income and social welfare benefits of collective farmers increased substantially. While not keeping up with increases in the per capita disposable income (as reflected in growing savings and a flourishing 'second economy'), the regime made a number of efforts to increase investments so that the volume of consumer goods expanded and the product mix and quality improved in a number of key areas such as foods, personal goods and services, and consumer durables (especially private automobiles, housing, and appliances). In addition, the economic and administrative reforms introduced at the September 1965 Central Committee Plenum were first applied in the light industry sector with the aim of improving efficiency, quality, and responsiveness.

Despite the major investments and administrative reforms in the consumer goods sector, a number of serious problems were not solved by the Brezhnev regime. Large imports of grain were still required to satisfy consumer demand. The service and maintenance sectors lagged far behind the production sectors. The wholesale distribution and retail outlet networks continued to operate inefficiently. Consumers were still often faced with shortages while warehouses held overstocks of goods. Quality and product mix still failed to meet acceptable standards. Many of these problems reflected long-standing structural deficiencies in the light industry sector such as the lack of capital investment, lagging technology, lower wages, and the traditional low status accorded the production and distribution of consumer goods. Many of the administrative and economic reforms were undermined by resistance and obstruction (see 5.28). Large quantities of consumer goods continued to be manufactured as sidelines of heavy industrial enterprises. There was no market mechanism (or substitute) that allowed for the adjustment of production to shifting consumer tastes. Thus, while Brezhnev's policies dealt with some of the gross distortions in the consumer goods sector, they were not sufficiently radical to effect changes that could bring about a qualitative shift in the traditional relation between the heavy industrial and consumer goods sectors and within the consumer goods sector itself.

A.N. Shelepin, a conservative on domestic economic policy, was relieved of his position in the Central Committee Secretariat at the plenum.

5.18
On Measures for Further Raising the
Well-Being of the Soviet People   26 September 1967

Having heard the report of the General Secretary of the CPSU Central Committee, Comrade L.I. Brezhnev, on measures for further raising the wellbeing of the Soviet people in conjunction with the decisions of the XXIII Party Congress,
    The CPSU Central Committee Plenum resolves:
    To approve wholly and completely the measures for further raising the well-being of the Soviet people worked out by the CPSU Central Committee Politburo.

Pravda, 27 September 1967   *KPSS v rezoliutsiiakh* IX, 382

5.19
On Measures to Improve the Training and Retraining of
the Staffs of the Soviets of Working People's Deputies*   6 October 1967

The CPSU Central Committee has considered the question of measures to improve the training and retraining of the staffs of the Soviets of Working People's Deputies. The CPSU Central Committee has earmarked a number of measures aimed at improving the studies of soviet cadres. The resolution adopted by the CPSU Central Committee calls for a significant increase in the 1968–69 school year in the number of soviet personnel accepted for study at the Higher Party School of the CPSU Central Committee, as well as at the inter-oblast and republic higher party schools.

    Union republic party central committees and krai and oblast party committees are ordered to improve their selection of soviet staff personnel for study at higher party schools. Leading personnel of the supreme soviet presidiums and councils of ministers of union and autonomous republics and of krai and oblast soviet executive committees, and the chairmen of city and raion executive committees are to be sent to the Higher Party School of the CPSU Central Committee; senior staff on the apparatus of oblast and krai executive committees and chairmen, deputy chairmen, secretaries, and department heads at city (and raion) executive committees are to be sent to the inter-oblast and republic higher party schools.

    The CPSU Central Committee has recognized the need, in the study of soviet state construction and law at higher party schools, to focus attention on a profound mastery of the theses of marxism-leninism concerning the

* Excerpt: document not published in full.

role of the socialist state in the building of communism and the significance of the Soviets of Working People's Deputies in the life of society. More attention is to be devoted to problems of the scientific management of society and to questions of improving the work style and methods of the organs of soviet power. A comprehensive study is to be organized of the soviets' work experience in solving urgent tasks of economic and cultural construction and of the education of the broad masses of the working people.

It is anticipated that leading personnel from supreme soviet presidiums and councils of ministers of union and autonomous republics and from the executive committees of krai and oblast Soviets of Working People's Deputies will be enlisted in lecturing and conducting seminars at higher party schools.

Union republic party central committees and krai and oblast party committees are ordered to make better use of soviet and party schools for training and retraining the staffs of the Soviets of Working People's Deputies. Acceptance for study at soviet-party schools is to be granted to CPSU members from among the officials of city and raion soviet executive committees, the chairmen, deputy chairmen, and secretaries of village and settlement soviet executive committees, as well as deputies and those persons from among the aktiv of the local Soviets of Working People's Deputies who presumably will be advanced, subsequently, to work in the soviets. The Higher Party School of the CPSU Central Committee has been commissioned to develop for the soviet and party schools new study programmes on the fundamentals of soviet state construction and law.

The CPSU Central Committee has instructed the USSR Ministry of Higher and Secondary Specialized Education to open a faculty of soviet construction at the All-Union Correspondence Institute of Law; the course is to be based on a five-year study programme. Plans call for setting at 600 the number of persons to be accepted in the faculty in the first year. In selecting students for admission to this faculty, preference is to be given to persons making application for study at the recommendation of executive committees of krai, oblast, okrug, city, and raion Soviets of Working People's Deputies.

The Press Committee of the USSR Council of Ministers is ordered to increase the output of textbooks and study aids, reference works, books, and brochures dealing with questions of soviet construction, in order to give assistance to soviet cadres in their study and practical work.

Union republic party central committees and krai, oblast, city, and raion party committees are ordered to devote greater attention to the business of training and retraining the staffs of the Soviets of Working People's Deputies and to raising their ideological and theoretical level and their business qualifications. Broader use is to be made of seminars and conferences to exchange work experience. Theoretical and practical questions of soviet construction are to be elucidated more profoundly in the press, as is positive work experience of the soviets in the sphere of the economy and culture and in improving the forms and methods of organizational and mass work.

Pravda, 31 October 1967

Plenum of the Central Committee   9–10 April 1968

The April 1968 Central Committee Plenum was convened primarily to discuss foreign policy. From the published resolution there was obviously growing Politburo concern for developments in Eastern Europe (Czechoslovakia), the Far East (Vietnam), and the Middle East (the Arab–Israeli conflict). These sources of tension were all the more disturbing to the Kremlin leadership because they imposed severe limits on its pursuit of a policy of détente with the United States. Perhaps the most crucial developments at this time were the events in Czechoslovakia. The Soviet Union had convened a number of conferences of East European states to discuss the East European situation and apply pressure on the Dubcek regime to control and limit its internal reforms. The plenum resolution contained several ominous references suggesting that Soviet policy towards Czechoslovakia would take a hard line: a reaffirmation of the CPSU's readiness 'to do everything necessary for the steady political, economic, and defensive consolidation of the socialist commonwealth'; a warning of the dangers of West German revanchism and militarism, which increases 'the importance of joint action by the CPSU and the fraternal countries to increase the solidarity of the socialist countries ... for the struggle against West German imperialism'; and the emphasis given to the 'acute intensification of the ideological struggle between capitalism and socialism.'

The tense international situation had its impact on Soviet domestic policy. During early 1968 the trials of two Soviet dissidents (Ginzburg and Galanskov) were held. These two writers were charged with establishing links with a Russian émigré organization, harbouring songs of an anti-Soviet nature, and receiving anti-Soviet pamphlets from abroad. The resolution of the April 1968 Central Committee Plenum provided the general context for a continuation of this hard line towards dissident intellectuals in the Soviet Union and linked this policy with international events.

At the plenum the appointment of K.F. Katushev to the Secretariat was announced.

5.20
On the Pressing Problems of the International Situation
and the Struggle of the CPSU for the Solidarity of the
World Communist Movement   10 April 1968

... The plenum notes that the present stage of historical development is characterized by an acute intensification of the ideological struggle between capitalism and socialism. An entire, immense apparatus of anti-communist propaganda is presently aimed at weakening the unity of the socialist countries and of the international communist movement, alienating the leading forces of the day from one another, and attempting to subvert socialist society from within. Beset by serious upheavals and suffering major setbacks in domestic and foreign policy, imperialism, and American imperialism in particular, in addition to its adventures in the military and political sphere, is directing ever-greater efforts to a subversive political and ideological struggle against the socialist countries, against the communist movement and the entire democratic movement.

In these conditions, an implacable struggle against hostile ideology, resolute exposure of imperialist intrigues, education of CPSU members and all working people, and intensification of all the party's ideological activity assume particular importance and become one of the most important responsibilities of all party organizations. It is their duty to wage an offensive battle against bourgeois ideology and actively to resist attempts to drag views alien to the socialist ideology of Soviet society into individual works of literature and art and into other works. Party organizations must direct all available means of ideological education toward strengthening communist conviction and the sense of Soviet patriotism and proletarian internationalism in every communist and in every Soviet person, toward strengthening ideological steadfastness and the ability to resist all forms of bourgeois influence.

The carrying out of measures in connection with the 150th anniversary of K. Marx's birth and preparations for the centennial of the birth of V.I. Lenin should serve as a powerful stimulus for an upswing in ideological work and for widespread propaganda of the great ideas of marxism-leninism.

The ideological activity of party organizations is to be linked more closely with the tasks of increasing the labour and social activism of all working people and with the practical contribution of each Soviet person to the fulfilment of production assignments and to the successful completion of the Five-Year Plan.

The primary task of the party and of the entire Soviet people is the further strengthening of the political, economic, and defence power of the Motherland, and the comprehensive development of our society, which is opening the road to the victory of communism under the leadership of its leninist party.

The Central Committee plenum considers that the present-day international situation urgently requires active and united action on the part of all the forces of socialism, democracy, and national liberation. For its part, the CPSU will continue as before to conduct a policy of resolutely rebuffing imperialism and averting world war, a policy of strengthening the commonwealth of the socialist countries and of strengthening the solidarity of the communist movement and of all anti-imperialist forces.

Pravda, 11 April 1968   *KPSS v rezoliutsiiakh* IX, 421–4

5.21
On the Work of the Krasnoiarsk Krai Party Organization
with Respect to Guidance over the Komsomol*   8 May 1968

... the CPSU Central Committee considers that there are serious short-comings and gaps in the work of the krai, oblast, okrug, city, and raion party committees and primary party organizations with respect to their guidance over the Komsomol. In many party organizations, instructions of the XXIII CPSU Congress are poorly carried out in the area of improving the ideological training of young people, consolidating the party nucleus in Komsomol organizations and raising the responsibility of all communists for the state of affairs in the Komsomol. Some party committees and primary party organizations do not go deeply into the substance of the activity of Komsomol organizations, fail to provide concrete daily assistance to them, and on many occasions construct their work with young people without differentiation, without giving consideration to the interests and demands of various age and social categories of young men and women. The forms and methods of training often fail to meet the advanced general educational, political, and cultural standards of today's young people. The proper combination of their ideological and political training with satisfying their natural urge towards leisure and entertainment has not been accomplished ...

The krai committee of the CPSU fails to display proper exactingness towards party committees and primary party organizations for improving their guidance over the Komsomol; it has failed to raise sufficiently the responsibility of local soviets, economic bodies, trade unions, and other public organizations for training young people and improving their labour and daily life conditions.

The CPSU Central Committee resolves:

1   ... The implementation of the instructions of the XXIII CPSU Congress regarding the improvement of the rising generation's communist training is

* Excerpt: document not published in full.

to be ensured. It is important that the entire krai party organization, all the communists, and above all the leading cadres, work on a daily basis with young people and provide assistance to Komsomol organizations.

The chief task of the krai party and Komsomol organizations in working with young people must be to form the young people's marxist-leninist outlook, their class-consciousness, high ideological convictions, and intolerance of bourgeois ideology as well as to educate them in the spirit of devotion to the cause of the communist party, proletarian internationalism, friendship among peoples, and preparedness to defend the gains of the October Revolution ...

2   Party organizations must constantly improve the forms and methods of their guidance over the Komsomol so that they meet more fully the advanced general educational, political, and cultural level of young people and take into consideration the specific character of work with different groups of young people – workers, kolkhozniks, the intelligentsia, and university and school students. Measures are to be taken to raise the militant spirit of Komsomol organizations, encourage their useful undertakings, develop initiative and independent action, and consolidate discipline and organization in Komsomol ranks. The authority and influence of Komsomol organizations are to be raised with the broad masses of young people, more concern in the growth of the Komsomol ranks is to be displayed, and especially growth due to young workers, kolkhozniks, and specialists. Attention is to be paid to improving primary party organization guidance over the Komsomol, the responsibility of party bureaus and party groups is to be raised for training young people, and work is to be conducted on a regular basis in selecting the most active and best trained Komsomol members for the party.

3   The elimination of serious short-comings in selecting and training Komsomol cadres is considered to be one of the urgent tasks of the CPSU krai committee and party organizations. It is necessary to consolidate the party nucleus in Komsomol organizations, raise the responsibility of communists who have been elected to Komsomol committees, and consider the work of communists in the Komsomol as an extremely important party assignment. High turnover of cadres in the Komsomol is not to be allowed. The theoretical training and marxist-leninist tempering of Komsomol personnel and activists is to be improved in every possible way; they are to be trained in a spirit of principles, modesty, and efficiency. Leading party personnel must regularly inform the Komsomol aktiv of the most important issues of the domestic and foreign policies of the CPSU and the Soviet government, and transmit to them their experience of organizational and political work with the masses. Profound knowledge of the state of affairs in Komsomol organizations, comradely tactfulness, attention, and high exactingness must be an indispensible condition of party guidance over the Komsomol.

4   The party committees must raise the level of work in the area of Komsomol political enlightenment. Studies in groups and seminars must satisfy and develop the interest of young men and women in the revolutionary theory of marxism-leninism and in the problems of social and political life. The most experienced, prepared, and authoritative communists are to be directed into work as propagandists in the Komsomol political education network. Current, comprehensive information on the political, economic, and cultural life of the krai and the country and the international situation must become the most important means of ideological work with young people. It is necessary to try to get leading party, soviet, and economic personnel, as well as scholars, teachers, and cultural figures to make regular public appearances before young people. The entire ideological and educational work with young people must be connected with the practice of communist construction. It must be conducted intelligently and convincingly and take into consideration the interests and demands of various age and social categories of young men and women.

5   In work with respect to the labour education of the young generation, the CPSU krai committee and the party organizations must proceed from the idea that Komsomol members and young people are called upon to continue to make a great contribution to the carrying out of party and government decisions regarding accelerated rates of the development of the productive forces of the krai, and, together with the communists, come forth as pioneers of socialist competition and the movement for communist labour, and exhibit initiative and persistence in the struggle to accomplish the tasks of the Five-Year Plan by 7 November 1970.

The creative energy of Komsomol members and young people working at industrial and transportation enterprises, construction sites, scientific-research institutions, and drafting and designing organizations is to be directed at better utilizing production reserves, accelerating technological progress, raising labour productivity and the quality of manufactured production. The role of the kolkhoz and sovkhoz Komsomol organizations is to be enhanced in solving the tasks of the further expansion of agriculture and livestock breeding based on the implementation of an extensive programme of land reclamation, chemicalization, and comprehensive mechanization of agricultural production. Komsomol committees are to be involved more actively in improving the organization of labour in industry, construction, and agriculture, introducing the achievements of science, technology, and advanced experience into production, developing rationalization and invention, and raising the professional training of young men and women. Attention is to be paid to teaching young women who are kolkhoz members and sovkhoz workers, and especially those who graduated from secondary schools, the professions of agricultural mechanization experts. Participation of Komsomol committees is to be provided for in reviewing the results of socialist competition, awarding bonuses to workers and kolkhozniks, working out the conditions and checking the fulfilment of collective agreements, hiring and firing young people, and assigning places in hostels, kindergartens, and day nurseries.

6   The CPSU krai committee, party, trade union, Komsomol organizations, and economic leaders must display constant concern for consolidating cadres of young workers, kolkhozniks, and specialists, and for educating in them pride in their profession, respect for traditions of the collective, and love for their native krai. Particular attention is to be paid to strengthening labour discipline among Komsomol members and young people, cultivating in them feelings of intolerance to any display of laxity and of a careless attitude to labour. Meetings between young people and labour veterans, advanced workers and production innovators are to be held regularly. The honest labour of young men and women is to be encouraged in every possible way; those who have favourably proved themselves are to be promoted more boldly. Economic leaders are to be made strictly responsible for not taking all possible measures to create normal conditions of labour, daily life, and leisure for workers and specialists ...

7   In the course of building the material and technical base of communism, a rise in the scientific and technical education of young people becomes an issue of ever-greater importance and responsibility. The party, trade union, and Komsomol organizations must persistently involve young workers, kolkhozniks, and employees in evening and correspondence schools, technical and higher educational institutions, develop their interest in acquiring knowledge and in scientific and technical creativity. Efforts are to be made to create the necessary conditions for young people's studies and to take measures to strengthen the educational-material base of evening and correspondence educational institutions. The work of scientific and technical societies and scientific circles in educational institutions, enterprises, construction sites, kolkhozes, and sovkhozes is to be developed more extensively.

Party organizations and Komsomol committees must organize a truly massive movement of young people for mastering the achievements of modern science and technology.

8   Party committees must enhance the role and responsibility of party and Komsomol organizations and the staff of professors and teachers at educational institutions to improve further the teaching and training of young people. The level of teaching in socio-political and economic disciplines is to be raised, efforts are to be made so that the lectures, seminars, and lessons in these subjects provide answers to issues of the day and actively repulse bourgeois ideology. A struggle is to be conducted against attitudes of parasitism, lack of discipline, and a careless attitude to studies that have been displayed by some young people. Efforts are to be made so that graduates of higher and secondary specialized educational institutions are specialists who are highly

cultured and have a well-rounded education. Attention is to be paid to cultivating the preparedness of every student and pupil to labour honestly and conscientiously upon graduating in accordance with his acquired profession. Party and Komsomol organizations are to give more attention to the staffing of higher and secondary specialized educational institutions. Sending young people to higher educational institutions and technical schools with stipends from enterprises, kolkhozes, and sovkhozes is to be practised more extensively.

More concern is to be displayed in improving the work of the school, Komsomol, and Pioneer organizatons, and raising their authority and spreading their influence to all school children. The efforts of the Komsomol and Pioneer organizations are to be directed at cultivating the students' ideological convictions, their love for knowledge and labour, and high standards of behaviour. The selection of leading Pioneer cadres is to be improved, extracurricular educational work with students is to be conducted more actively, and the activity of children's non-school institutions is to be improved constantly.

9   In connection with the transfer to a five-day work week, party, trade union, and Komsomol organizations need to display particular concern for intelligent use of the toilers' free time. They must improve the organization of leisure and make it more useful for the health, cultural development, and training of young people. It is necessary to involve young men and women more actively in circles, clubs, and sport sections according to their interests and to develop tourism, raise the ideological and artistic level of amateur activities, and persistently to consolidate new traditions and rituals in everyday life. Cultural establishments and sport organizations are to be reinforced with qualified cadres who care for their work. Work must be conducted more extensively among young people at their place of residence. This calls for selecting capable organizers from the ranks of communists and active Komsomol members. The initiative of young men and women is to be encouraged and directed towards building and equipping the simplest sport installations in courtyard areas and hostels, equipping recreation and reading rooms, and establishing libraries.

10   The krai, oblast, okrug, and raion committees of the party must raise the responsibility of the executive committees of Soviets of Working People's Deputies, trade unions, and other public organizations for their work with respect to the communist training of the rising generation. It is necessary constantly to co-ordinate their activity and to strive to establish close working contacts and connections with Komsomol committees. Party organizations must extensively involve Komsomol members in the work of local soviets and in the management of kolkhozes, trade unions, and sport, cultural, and enlightenment organizations ...

Partiinaia zhizn', no. 10   *KPSS v rezoliutsiiakh* IX, 425–33
(1968): 3–7

5.22
On the Tasks, Structure, and Staff of the Institute of
Marxism-Leninsim of the CPSU Central Committee*   15 June 1968

... Resolutions of congresses, conferences, and plenums of the Central Committee have been prepared and published, as have the records of proceedings
and stenographic reports of the CPSU congresses. Scientific research is being
conducted on elaborating the ideological legacy of the classics of marxism-
leninism, the history of the Communist Party, and the history of the Civil
and Great Patriotic Wars of the Soviet Union. Substantial work has been
conducted by the branches of the Institute of Marxism-Leninism; the fourth
edition of *The Complete Works of V.I. Lenin* and selected works by K. Marx
and F. Engels have been translated into the languages of the peoples of the
USSR; essays on the history of the communist parties of the union republics
have been published as well as on the history of the Moscow, Leningrad, and
other party organizations of the country. Over 500 collections of documents
and research monographs on topical questions of the policy and history of
the CPSU have been issued.

In the decision of the Central Committee of the party, it is noted that,
at the present stage of communist construction, the Institute of Marxism-
Leninism, while continuing to collect and publish works by K. Marx, F.
Engels, and V.I. Lenin, and documents on the history of the CPSU, must also
direct its efforts at the creative elaboration of topical problems of marxist-
leninist theory, the history of the CPSU and party construction, scientific
communism, and the history of the international communist movement.
Together with other scientific institutions, the Institute must create fundamental generalizing works that should contain new scientifically grounded
conclusions and recommendations and be of profound theoretical and practical significance.

The CPSU Central Committee has determined the major directions in the
work of the Institute of Marxism-Leninism: publication, scientific research
and propaganda of the ideological legacy of Marx–Engels–Lenin, the elaboration of topical problems of the history of the CPSU, party construction,
scientific communism, the history of the international communist movement, and the exposure of anti-communist ideology ...

The Central Committee of the party has entrusted the Institute
of Marxism-Leninism with: the scientific-methodological guidance of its
branches – the institutes of party history of the central committees of the
communist parties of the union republics, the Moscow oblast committee and
Moscow city committee and the Leningrad oblast committee of the CPSU, the

---

*   Excerpt: document not published in full.

Museum of K. Marx and F. Engels, the Central Museum of V.I. Lenin and its branches; co-ordination of all scientific research work in the area of the science of party history; supervision over the publication of scientific papers and works of literature and art on the life and activity of the classics of marxism-leninism; providing scientific and methodological assistance to old bolsheviks in preparing and publishing their memoirs, while involving them in the discussion and study of questions relating to the history of the party.

In accordance with the tasks which have been entrusted to the Institute, the Central Committee of the party has approved the new structure and staff of the Institute of Marxism-Leninism and has ordered its board of directors to secure the staffing of the Institute with qualified scientific cadres who are capable of creatively solving the great and complicated tasks pertaining to the scientific elaboration of topical problems of the theory and practice of marxism-leninism.

Taking into consideration the necessity of enhancing the role of the branches of the Institute of Marxism-Leninism, the Central Committee of the party has commissioned the central committees of the communist parties of the union republics, the Moscow oblast committee and the Moscow city party committee, and the Leningrad oblast party committee to work out measures to improve the work of the institutes of party history – the branches of the Institute of Marxism-Leninism.

It has been recommended that the editorial staff of the journal *Voprosy istorii KPSS* concentrate its attention on providing thorough coverage of the ideological legacy of Marx–Engels–Lenin, topical problems of the history of the CPSU, party construction, the activity of the CPSU with respect to the guidance of communist construction, the history of the international communist movement, and on publishing materials to aid people studying the history of the CPSU, as well as material on source study and historiography and material opposing anti-communism and falsifiers of the history of the CPSU. A department dealing with party construction is to be set up in the journal.

The Institute of Marxism-Leninism and its branches are ordered to structure their work in close contact with the Academy of Social Sciences of the CPSU Central Committee and the Higher Party School of the CPSU Central Committee and to involve scholars of these institutions in conducting comprehensive scientific research.

By the decision of the CPSU Central Committee, the Institute of Marxism-Leninism is ordered to conduct all its scientific research work on the basis of strict observance of marxist-leninist methodology, the principle of party spirit, a concrete historical approach to social phenomena, wide utilization of the documentary base of the party and state archives, a decisive struggle with manifestations of subjectivism, and intolerance of bourgeois and reformist ideology, right-wing opportunism, and 'leftist' adventurism.

Partiinaia zhizn', no. 16
(1968): 20–1

5.23
On the Work of the Volgograd Oblast Committee
in the Selection, Assignment, and Training of
Management Cadres in Industry*   11 September 1968

The implementation of the economic reforms approved by the September 1965 Central Committee Plenum and affirmed at the XXIII Congress met strong resistance from administrative officials and workers. There were initial improvements in output indicators. However, these improvements were achieved primarily by utilizing readily accessible production reserves. Enterprise management was still resistant to fundamental changes in attitudes and behaviour that would ensure continuous and stable high levels of efficiency in enterprise operations. The economic reform required that management take the initiative in making rational decisions relating to technology, labour, and internal accounting practices. The evidence presented in this document and the resolution on the Rostov Oblast party committee (5.25) suggests that the declaration of intent and revised incentive system contained in the decisions of the September 1965 Central Committee Plenum were not sufficient to achieve the radical changes required at the enterprise level. However, the decisions of 1968 indicated that there was still hope that the local and primary party organizations could be mobilized to stimulate and direct the transformation of attitudes, behaviour, and skill levels of management and workers, as well as supervising the introduction of new technology and organization required to make the economic reforms more effective.

The cPSU Central Committee notes that the Volgograd oblast party committee, in executing the decisions of the XXIII cPSU Congress, is doing considerable work to improve the selection, assignment, and training of managerial cadres in industry. With the economic reform in progress, party committees have begun to devote more attention to questions of reinforcing various production sectors with capable organizers and competent specialists, particularly at enterprises of the chemical and petro-chemical industries that are

---

*   Excerpt: document not published in full.

being built in the oblast for the first time. Extensive measures are being carried out to raise the ideological and theoretical level and the business qualifications of cadres. Seminars, courses, and schools have been set up under the oblast, city, and raion party committees and at factories and plants, where enterprise management, specialists, and workers in the mass occupations study questions of economics and scientific organization of labour, and exchange work experience.

At the present time, many enterprises in the oblast have qualified, politically mature cadres capable of solving complex and responsible tasks concerning the continued development of production. All this has a positive influence on the work results of industry. In the past two-and-one-half years of the Five-Year Plan, total volume of output has grown 28 per cent and profit has grown by more than 50 per cent.

Nevertheless the CPSU Central Committee considers that the level of the Volgograd oblast party committee's work with managerial cadres at industrial enterprises still does not meet the requirements of the XXIII CPSU Congress. Certain city and raion party committees and party organizations at enterprises, in solving questions of the selection and assignment of cadres, fail to take adequate account of the knowledge and abilities of personnel and frequently permit important production sectors to be headed by people who lack the requisite technical education and economic knowledge. The middle level is undervalued in work with management cadres. Many shop heads and their deputies lack specialized education, while foremen and senior foremen lack occupational training.

The oblast, city, and raion party committees are not conducting systematic work with cadres at the many enterprises of the food, light, and local industries, and at industrial construction materials enterprises. Some of the directors and chief engineers at these enterprises do not have a higher education. Many people without specialized education are holding jobs as engineers and technicians. At the same time, the enterprises of these branches utilize only a third of the specialists in the oblast with the requisite credentials, while the rest are working in other branches of the economy.

The CPSU Central Committee calls the particular attention of party organizations in the oblast to the feeble job being done in creating a reserve of management cadres. The party committees are not making a profound study of specialists in their practical work and are not organizing planned study for them so they can master advanced management methods. Trained personnel with specialized education and extensive practical experience, and who have shown themselves to be capable organizers, are not being adequately used as a reserve for filling positions of greater responsibility. The absence of a reliable and constant reserve and – as a consequence thereof – the promotion of insufficiently qualified personnel to the management of enterprises is one of the reasons for the high rate of turnover among cadres.

The past two years have seen the replacement of one-fourth of the enterprise directors and chief engineers among those who fall within the oblast party committee nomenklatura.

In their work with cadres, the party committees are not showing adequate concern for the requirements of the economic reform and are doing a poor job of focusing the attention of managerial personnel at industrial enterprises on the need for mastering scientific methods of production management and the correct practical application of the laws of socialist production. Not enough is being demanded of managers who have not broken with the old methods of leadership, who strive to fulfil the plan at any price, and who do not conduct the necessary work of improving the organization of labour and mobilizing collectives for the solution of questions that are important for the development of production. Despite the high proportion of engineers and technicians in the oblast's industry, many of them are not being enlisted in solving the tasks of technical progress. Party organizations currently are not requiring that managerial staff put in order the business of correct utilization of specialists.

Certain party committees are not devoting constant attention to the marxist-leninist training of cadres and are doing a poor job of seeing to it that each manager raises his ideological and general educational level, personally participates in the education of the work force, shows concern for the satisfaction of workers' and employees' housing, cultural, and everyday needs, and is tactful and attentive toward their inquiries and proposals.

The CPSU Central Committee notes that short-comings in the selection, assignment, and training of cadres in the oblast are also a result of the fact that certain branch ministries have yet to draw the appropriate conclusions from the CPSU Central Committee Resolution, 'On the Work of the USSR Ministry of Power Engineering and Electrification With Managerial Cadres,' and have not taken the necessary steps to assure a fundamental improvement in this work.

Serious omissions in work with cadres and an insufficiently demanding attitude toward them on the part of party organs and ministries are one reason why there has been an increase from the 1965 level in the number of enterprises in Volgograd oblast that are not fulfilling their plans for overall output, labour productivity, reduction of the unit cost of production, and are not showing a profit. At a number of enterprises, production capacities are being mastered slowly and no resolute struggle is being waged to raise the technical level and quality of output and to strengthen socialist labour discipline; large, unproductive losses are being countenanced.

The CPSU Central Committee resolves:

1   The Volgograd oblast CPSU committee, city and raion party commitees, and primary party organizations are ordered to raise the level of their organizational and political work in the selection, assignment, and training of

managerial cadres at industrial enterprises in the oblast. They are to do away with the short-comings in work with cadres noted in this resolution.

In their practical work, the oblast's party committees must proceed from the fact that increased demands are made on managerial cadres in conditions of the widespread implementation of the economic reform and the broadening of enterprises' rights and independence. Managers must have a profound knowledge of technology, economics, and the principles of the scientific organization of labour; they must be capable of profound analysis of the results of economic activity and of correct practical application of moral and material incentives; they must establish the continual application to production of the latest achievements of science and technology and work out new management practices in their area of responsibility.

The oblast party organization must also have at the centre of its attention questions regarding the rational utilization of the labour of engineers and technicians and questions regarding the direction of their creative energies toward the achievement of technical progress; the procurement of internal production reserves and putting them to use, and the creation for specialists of the conditions necessary for fruitful work by introducing automation and organizational technology in the management of enterprises.

The fulfilment of the state plan by each enterprise is to be assured on the basis of a fundamental improvement in work with managerial cadres, through raising the technical and organizational level of existing production. There is to be an intensification of the organizational work of mobilizing the collectives of industrial enterprises for successful fulfilment of socialist obligations to meet Five-Year Plan targets ahead of schedule in honour of the centennial of V.I. Lenin's birth.

2   The oblast party committee, city and raion party committees, and primary party organizations at industrial enterprises are to organize planned work with cadre reserves, to be bolder about promoting to managerial positions both specialists and workers with organizational talent – those who have the necessary theoretical training and have been through extensive practical schooling in production work – and to arrange that those whose training is of a practical sort can get specialized education and improve their business qualifications.

The positive experience gained in working with cadres at the factories of the Sebriakov Cement Plant, the 'Red October' Metallurgical Plant, and other leading enterprises in the oblast is to be disseminated widely.

3   The oblast party committee and the appropriate branch ministries are ordered to take measures to reinforce enterprises with qualified managerial cadres, especially in light, food, and local industries and in the construction materials industry.

Attention is to be directed toward holding industrial cadres in their jobs, particularly middle-level managers: the heads of shops, installations, and sectors and their deputies, and also foremen and brigade leaders. The necessary conditions are to be created for a further rise in their theoretical and practical knowledge and greater concern is to be shown for improving their housing, cultural and everyday conditions. The political and business qualities of specialists are to be a subject of constant study; their assignment to sectors where they show their individual qualities to best advantage is to be facilitated.

4   The oblast, city, and raion party committees, guided by the decisions of the April and July (1968) plenums of the cpsu Central Committee, are ordered to raise the level of ideological work with managerial cadres in industrial enterprises. Efforts are to be made to improve the effectiveness of the organizational and political work that is conducted, ensuring the indissoluble connection of propaganda and agitation with concrete tasks facing industrial enterprise collectives. Managerial, engineering, and technical personnel are to be trained in a spirit of high ideological convictions and principles, and an attitude of intolerance to bourgeois ideology. Managers are to become more involved in propagandizing the ideas of marxism-leninism, in explaining the policy of the party and government, this work with the masses being considered the best school for training managers themselves. It is necessary that every manager in each area of production be an educator, develop the creative initiative of the working people, and actively encourage their participation in production management.

5   The oblast, city, and raion party committees are ordered to raise exactingness toward managerial cadres in industrial enterprises, to instil in them a feeling of great responsibility for solving production questions, to display concern that all managers persistently apply economic methods of management in practice. Their activity is to be directed at developing socialist competition and creating an atmosphere of comradely mutual assistance in collectives, and an attentive attitude to proposals by personnel. Labour legislation and collective agreements must be strictly observed by enterprise managers. Incidents of violation of state discipline are not to be allowed. The party committees are to intensify their control over the fulfilment of the decisions of the party and government and their own decisions ...

Partiinaia zhizn', no. 19   *KPSS v rezoliutsiiakh* IX, 468–73
(1968): 3–5

5.24
On the Work of the Dobrinka Raion
Party Committee of Lipetsk Oblast   **17 September 1968**

The cpsu Central Committee notes that the Dobrinka raion party committee, in implementing the decisions of the XXIII cpsu Congress, is conducting significant work in mobilizing the communists and all the toilers of the raion to carry out party policy in the countryside and is directing the efforts of the raion party organization at solving major problems of agricultural development and further improving the well-being and culture of rural toilers.

The raion committee is taking measures to increase the activeness of primary party organizations at kolkhozes and sovkhozes. Party committees have been set up at the majority of farms; the number of shop party organizations and party groups has increased, and the deployment of party forces has improved: at present about 90 per cent of communists engaged in agriculture are working directly in field-crop cultivation and animal husbandry. The raion party organization has started to devote more attention to work with leading kolkhoz and sovkhoz cadres, to enhancing the role of specialists as technologists and organizers of agricultural production. Of the 24 kolkhoz chairmen and sovkhoz directors, 22 are agricultural specialists. On the initiative of the raion committee, a plan to raise the qualifications of brigade-leaders, heads of livestock sections of the farms, and department managers has been worked out and is being put into practice. Over 300 kolkhoz members and sovkhoz workers are studying at correspondence and permanent agricultural educational institutions. Mass political work of party organizations is being directed at raising the labour activity of kolkhoz members and sovkhoz workers, developing socialist competition, and popularizing advanced experience.

The CPSU raion committee and the agricultural production administration have begun to deal more concretely with problems pertaining to improving economic work in kolkhozes and sovkhozes. Specialization of agricultural production is being carried out in the raion, six large specialized farms have been created where livestock complexes have been built with total mechanization of labour-intensive processes ...

At the same time, the CPSU Central Committee considers that the kolkhozes and sovkhozes of the Dobrinka raion, which have at their disposal fertile lands and enjoy favourable climatic conditions, have large reserves for further development of farming and animal husbandry and for raising the effectiveness of agricultural production. The raion party committee has failed to give a sufficiently critical evaluation of the state of affairs in the raion and to make a profound analysis of the situation at every farm, every sector of production, and tolerates the lagging behind of some kolkhozes and sovkhozes.

The necessary measures have not been taken in the raion to make the most rational and effective use of every hectare of land. On many farms the standards of farming are still low and the yield of agricultural crops grows too slowly ... The leaders of some farms take a one-sided approach to solving land reclamation tasks posed by the May Plenum of the Central Committee and they fail to take into consideration that the broad programme of land reclamation means not only irrigation and drainage but a whole complex of measures to raise soil fertility. In several kolkhozes and sovkhozes the productivity of livestock and fowl is low, breeding work is inadequate, and a stable fodder base for animal husbandry has not been created.

There are major short-comings in utilizing agricultural technology ...

The raion party committee and the agricultural production administration have not achieved effective utilization of production funds, capital investments, and labour resources on every kolkhoz and sovkhoz. Consequently, the economic indices of the work of several farms are still unsatisfactory, their profitability has increased not through lowering the cost of production, but mainly as a result of the rise in state purchase prices. Some kolkhozes have cut the amounts deducted for indivisible funds and allocate insignificant capital for purchasing agricultural machinery and equipment, for seed farming, improving livestock breeds, and other measures that provide for improvement of the economy, growth in the labour productivity, and a rise in the profits of farms.

There are incidents of the violation of collective farm democracy in the raion, the role of general meetings of kolkhozniks is minimized, members of artels do not always take part in solving important problems such as planning agricultural production, forming various funds, distributing income, and admitting new members to the kolkhoz.

The noted short-comings in agricultural development are explained primarily by the fact that the raion party committee has still not totally reorganized its work in light of the requirements of the XXIII CPSU Congress and has failed to denounce completely certain obsolete management methods. The raion committee is not sufficiently raising the responsibility of soviet and economic organizations, of the leaders of kolkhozes, sovkhozes enterprises, and institutions of the raion for entrusted affairs; it has not ensured that all leading cadres strictly observe party and state discipline. Instead of raising the responsibility of personnel who should immediately answer for sectors entrusted to them, the raion committee often tries to solve problems on its own, with its own personnel. This distracts party personnel from their organizational and political work with people, from the problems of practical assistance to party organizations, and from their supervision over the implementation of adopted decisions. The party organizations of a number of kolkhozes and sovkhozes fail to exercise deep influence over the development of agricultural production and do a poor job of exercising their right to control the activity of the administration.

In ideological and political work, local conditions and the growing demands of various categories of toilers are insufficiently taken into account. Party organizations fail to attribute proper significance to instilling in the population, and particularly in young people, a feeling of deep respect for agricultural labour and pride for the profession of agriculturist. In the raion there has been no persistent struggle for high standards of peasant daily life, no struggle against drunkenness, hooliganism, and religious survivals. Mass political work in remote settlements is not satisfactorily organized, many of the settlements do not have clubs and libraries, and films are seldom shown. The rural intelligentsia – teachers, doctors, and agricultural specialists – take an insignificant part in the ideological and political education of the toilers.

The CPSU Central Committee resolves:

1   The Dobrinka CPSU raion committee is ordered to do away with the short-comings noted in the present decision, to improve guidance over the economic and cultural life of the raion, and constantly to perfect organizational, ideological, and educational work with the masses.

It is considered that the basic task of the raion party organization is the mobilization of the toilers for successful fulfilment of the decisions of the XXIII Party Congress, as well as the decisions of the March and May plenums of the CPSU Central Committee and to ensure higher and more stable rates of agricultural production growth in all kolkhozes and sovkhozes. The socialist competition of agricultural workers for a worthy celebration of the 100th anniversary of Lenin's birth is to be headed by the raion party organization. The successful fulfilment of obligations that have been undertaken by the raion kolkhozes and sovkhozes is to be ensured with respect to increasing the production and the amount of field and animal husbandry products sold to the state during the rest of the five-year-plan period.

2   Taking into consideration the fact that consistent intensification of agriculture is the main way to increasing its production at the present stage, the raion party committee must concentrate the efforts of the party organizations, soviet and agricultural bodies, leaders of kolkhozes and sovkhozes, specialists and all working people in agriculture on implementation of the extensive programme for raising the standards of farming and animal husbandry on the basis of land reclamation, chemicalization, and comprehensive mechanization to achieve a further upsurge in agricultural production, a growth in labour productivity, and lower production costs. Particular attention is to be paid to increasing grain production by making rational use of agricultural land and raising the yield from every hectare of land in every possible way. Measures are to be taken to strengthen the fodder base, improve livestock breeds, and raise livestock productivity. Highly productive use of agricultural equipment and its correct storage is to be ensured.

Constant concern is to be taken in putting the newest achievements of agricultural science and advanced practice into production. On the basis of the experience of the best farms, specialization of production and scientific organization of labour are to be implemented persistently, and various forms of moral and material incentives for kolkhoz members and sovkhoz workers are to be applied skilfully. Profit-and-loss management is to be practised more extensively in farms, brigades, departments, and livestock sections and the profitability of all branches of agriculture is to be raised. In evaluating the activity of kolkhozes and sovkhozes, it is necessary to start first of all with the effectiveness of every hectare of farm land and every ruble of capital investment, as well as with the effectiveness of machinery and fertilizers.

3   The CPSU Central Committee emphasizes that now, when the party is accomplishing a most significant social task of overcoming the considerable differences between the city and village, the raion party organizations must devote a great deal of their activity to questions of improving the material and cultural conditions of the lives of the rural population, to radically reconstructing the village, its character, and daily life. It is necessary to carry out housing, cultural, and road construction by making more correct use of state capital investments, as well as the capital of kolkhozes and sovkhozes. Measures are to be taken to strengthen the production base of construction organizations and expand the production of local building materials.

4   The raion party committee must constantly perfect the forms and methods of its activity and ensure the further development of inner-party democracy and the principle of collective leadership. The role of plenums and the bureau of the raion committee is to be enhanced, and efforts are to be made to achieve active participation of all members of the raion committee in working out and implementing adopted decisions. The raion committee is to pay attention to the need for a more demanding and responsible approach to evaluating the results of its work and for extensive development of criticism and self-criticism in the work of the party organization.

In uniting and directing the activity of raion organizations, the raion committee must not exert tutelage over or usurp the functions of these organizations, but must develop their initiative and try to get them to bear full responsibility for the sectors of work entrusted to them. The organization of supervision and verification over the implementation of party and government directives must constantly be improved; leading cadres themselves – secretaries, bureau members, and heads of the raion party committee departments – are obliged to take care of this business.

5   The CPSU raion committee must show daily concern in the selection, placement and training of cadres. Efforts must be made to ensure that politically mature, ideologically stable, qualified, and authoritative personnel head all sectors of party, soviet, economic, cultural, and social activity. Trust and respect for cadres must be combined with high exactingness toward them.

The best prepared workers, kolkhozniks, and specialists, particularly from among young people who have proved themselves in practice, are to be promoted more actively to leading work. Women are to be promoted more boldly to party, soviet, and economic work in health, enlightenment, and cultural institutions; concern is to be taken for their political and professional growth. Attention is to be devoted to improving the qualitative composition of department managers, brigade leaders, and heads of livestock sections of kolkhozes and sovkhozes; measures are to be taken to strengthen cadres and raise their business skills. The preparation of tractor, combine, and machine operators at livestock farm sections, builders, electricians, and personnel in other professions is to be organized better. This work must be set up with consideration of both current and long-run needs. In mastering the profession of farm machine operators, more women are to be involved by creating the necessary production and cultural-everyday conditions for them.

6   One of the most significant duties of the raion committee is considered to be the further improvement of the activity of primary party organizations, the enhancement of their role in carrying out party policy in the countryside, and the intensification of organizational and political work directly with kolkhozniks, sovkhoz workers, and the rural intelligentsia. More assistance is to be given to shop party organizations and party groups that are called upon to exert their influence on the state of affairs directly in brigades, departments, and livestock sections. The practice of conducting party meetings is to be perfected as a very significant means of increasing the efficiency of party organizations. The activity of communists, their responsibility for the state of affairs in their organizations and collectives is to be raised, and efforts are to be made to ensure that every one of them is, in fact, an advanced person in production, social, and daily life, and serves as an example for his associates. A decisive end is to be put to existing incidents of lenience and liberalism with respect to members and candidate members of the party who violate the requirements of the CPSU Programme and Rules.

7   The party raion committee and primary party organizations are to pay more attention to questions of ideological work. They must raise exactingness toward communists in mastering marxist-leninist theory; leading cadres, the rural intelligentsia, and all party members are to be more actively involved in the ideological and political education of the population ...

The raion committee of the party is ordered to improve its guidance over the soviets, trade unions, and Komsomol organizations, and to intensify exactingness toward communists working in them ...

Pravda, 14 September 1968   *KPSS v rezoliutsiiakh* IX, 474–81

5.25
On the Work of the Rostov Oblast Party Committee
in Carrying Out the Decisions of the September (1965)
Plenum of the CPSU Central Committee on the
Introduction of New Management Methods   8 October 1968

In carrying out the decisions of the September (1965) Plenum and those of the XXIII Party Congress, the Rostov oblast party committee, the city and raion party committees, and primary party organizations are doing a considerable amount of work in introducing the new system of planning and economic incentives, in raising production efficiency and in improving economic management ...

At the same time, the CPSU Central Committee notes that the level of organizational work and moral training in many party organizations still does not satisfy present-day requirements and that the advantages of the new system of management are not being fully utilized. During the initial stage of work under the new system, the improvement in economic indices at many plants and factories has been achieved to a considerable degree through utilization of the most readily accessible reserves. At the same time, a feeble job is being done of adopting measures to assure stable, high rates of development for production – measures involving the technical re-equipping of enterprises and the introduction of advanced methods of labour organization. The oblast's industry is not systematically fulfilling its plans for the introduction of new technology and for the mechanization and automation of production processes; it is doing a slow job of raising the quality and technical level of goods being produced.

Many party organizations are doing a poor job of supervising the utilization of economic incentive funds and are not doing an adequate job of increasing the role of trade union organizations in the matter. At a number of enterprises very little money is being allocated from incentive funds for current bonuses to workers; people responsible for the incursion of losses are not being made to feel the weight of the ruble, and insufficient importance is being attached to the proper combining of moral and material work incentives. The fund for the development of production is not being utilized fully and is sometimes being spent for purposes other than those for which it is intended.

There are fundamental short-comings in economic work at enterprises; plans do not always take full account of existing reserves and at the majority of enterprises economic accountability is being applied only to the main shops. Of the 117 plants and factories that operated under the new system in 1967, 48 allowed the growth rate of labour productivity to lag behind the growth rate in average wages.

Party and trade union organizations are still doing an inadequate job of enlisting workers' active participation in the management of production. Little is being done to enlist workers and engineering and technical personnel in the discussion of current and long-range plans and in the working out of measures to improve the organization of production, the setting of labour norms, and the systems of material incentives. These questions are rarely put forward for discussion at meetings of workers and at production meetings. Sometimes no action is taken on critical remarks and proposals.

The oblast party committee, the city and raion party committees, and the primary party organizations are not availing themselves of all opportunities for improving the training of workers in the spirit of strict observance of socialist labour discipline. The frequency of unjustified absences, theft, and other violations of law is being reduced slowly. Labour turnover is high, and significant unproductive expenditures and losses of work time are still being tolerated. In 1967, four per cent of the enterprises working under the new system failed to fulfil their plans for total output sales; every tenth enterprise failed to fulfil its plan for profits and every fourth enterprise, for overall level of profitability. A number of enterprises did not meet their obligations for payments into the state budget.

The oblast party committee and the city and raion party committees are devoting little attention to enterprises that still have not made the switch-over to the new methods of planning and economic incentives and are doing an insufficient job of overseeing their preparations for work under the new system.

The CPSU Central Committee notes that the Ministry of Tractor and Agricultural Machine Construction and the RSFSR Ministries of Food, Meat, and Milk Industry are doing a poor job of giving guidance to enterprises in improving their activity under the new circumstances. The ministries fail to extend to enterprises the required assistance in perfecting economic work and the organization of production, allow violations of the rights granted to enterprises, and often change approved plan indicators.

The CPSU Central Committee resolves:

1   The Rostov oblast party committee, the city and raion party commit-tees and primary party organizations are ordered to ensure consistent intro-duction of the new system of planning and economic incentives on the basis of accumulated experience and of continued improvement in organiza-tional and mass political work. It is a most important task of the oblast party organization actively to enlist the broad masses of the working people in this work, to develop initiative in every way, and to mobilize their energies for uncovering and utilizing existing reserves to the fullest extent, for achieving higher rates for the growth of production and of labour productivity, for improving the quality of output, and for improving economies in raw and other materials. It is necessary to see to it that each and every worker makes a definite contribution of his own to improving the enterprise's overall work indices.

The oblast party committee and the city and raion party committees are to concentrate the attention of primary party organizations and of economic management on speeding up the introduction of new technology, on the scientific organization of labour and management, on improving the utiliza-tion of production funds, and on achieving design capacity as quickly as possible, keeping in mind that all these are basic factors for permanently increasing production efficiency and for continued growth in the material well-being of the working people. To these ends, fuller use is to be made of the funds for the development of production that have been created at enterprises, and of credits from the State Bank.

2   Reinforcing the role of economic methods in the management of production requires that party organizations improve the selection, assignment, and training of cadres. Placing trust in cadres and extending their independence in work must be combined with the setting of high standards for them and with increasing the responsibility of managerial, engineering, and technical personnel for work assigned. The oblast party committee and the city and raion party committees must organize the work of moral training and schooling for managerial cadres in such a way that they not only have a good command of advanced machinery and technology, but are also able to organize production in an economically competent fashion, and possess the qualities of political leadership necessary for making all workers conscious of the organic tie between the personal interests of the enterprise's individual workers and its collective, on the one hand, and the interests of society as a whole, on the other hand.

3   Party and trade union organizations and economic managers are ordered to make efforts to improve the effectiveness of material incentives, and to assure the working out and application of plant incentive systems that provide maximum incentives for workers, engineering and technical personnel, and employees to achieve the highest possible productivity, systems that promote the development of initiative and a creative approach to work and that can also be understood by all workers. Wider use must be made of bonuses for increasing labour productivity, for high quality of output, for economizing raw and other materials, and for applying to production the achievements of science and technology; the role of regular ongoing payment of bonuses to workers out of the material incentives funds is to be strengthened. Equalization of bonus payments and the payment of excess bonuses are not to be permitted. A worker's earnings should correspond to the results of his labour and his personal contribution to the overall results of the collective's activity. The growing role of material incentives in the development of production must be skilfully combined with moral incentives. Party organizations are ordered to step up their work of instilling in people a sense of proprietorship in production, a profound understanding of collective interests, and a communist attitude toward labour and socialist property.

4   The oblast party committee and city and raion party committees must make it a matter of daily concern to increase in every way the fighting capacities of party organizations and the vanguard role and authority of every communist in production. In the new conditions, primary party organizations must analyse knowledgeably the state of the economy, see the development of the enterprise in terms of the long range, seek out the paths for the most correct utilization of economic levers in order to increase production efficiency, improve the conduct of organizational work and moral training directly in shops, sectors, brigades, and workplaces. Enlarging enterprises'

rights and granting them greater independence must be combined with increased supervision over the administration's economic performance and with an increase in the role and responsibility of party organizations and of each individual communist for the state of production.

5   The oblast party organization is to assure further development of the socialist principles of enterprise management, principles that call for the broad participation by toilers in the management of production and for strengthening the principle of one-man management. It is to activate the work of the trade union organizations in introducing the new system of planning and economic incentives, in improving the organization of labour and wages, and in improving workers' and employees' conditions of work and everyday life. These questions must be discussed systematically at workers' meetings, at meetings of the aktiv, and at standing production conferences; conditions must be assured for creative discussion of these questions; there must be timely reaction to critical remarks and proposals from the working people and the latter must be regularly informed of the measures being adopted.

It is necessary to apply socialist competition still more extensively and to secure the active participation of all workers, engineering and technical personnel, and employees in carrying out the pledges made by enterprise collectives for fulfilling the Five-Year Plan ahead of schedule in honour of the centennial of V.I. Lenin's birth.

6   Ministries and departments are to improve their guidance of enterprises, improve the quality of planning, ensure stable annual plans and the timely elaboration of long-run plans, observe strictly the rights of enterprises, and extend assistance to enterprises in the introduction of economic accountability, in the technological improvement of production, and in strengthening the economic and technical services of qualified cadres ...

Partiinaia zhizn', no. 21   *KPSS v rezoliutsiiakh* IX, 495–500
(1968): 24–6

Plenum of the Central Committee   30–31 October 1968

By late 1968 the leadership had had an opportunity to assess the impact of its agricultural policy enunciated at the March 1965 and May 1966 Central Committee plenums. The proposed changes had been implemented but had not been entirely efficacious. Strong resistance to expected behaviour patterns still existed and was causing a severe drag on the efficiency and growth of the agricultural sector. In his lengthy report to the plenum (*Current Digest of the*

Soviet Press XX, no. 44, 3–8 and no. 45, 9–13), Brezhnev indicated a great deal of dissatisfaction with the changes occurring in the areas of chemicalization, land reclamation, mechanization, rural construction, animal husbandry, investment in material-technical supply, procurements, and income distribution. Failures in all these areas had resulted in shortfalls in gross output, as well as low growth rates in agricultural production and labour productivity. On the whole, these short-comings were attributed by Brezhnev to failures in administration by state agencies and weakness in supervision by party organizations. The ministries responsible for implementing the major land reclamation programmes and supplying agriculture inputs had not performed according to plan indicators. The middle-level management responsible for agricultural operations had not fully utilized the resources available and had not responded creatively to problems encountered in their jurisdictions.

Brezhnev's report and the subsequent resolution give us insight into a number of general limitations that prevented the regime from achieving its major policy goals in the agricultural sector. These limitations included ideological limits that prevent solutions dealing with and going beyond the collective forms of agriculture dominant in the Soviet Union; bureaucratic limits involving resistance to change by large, slow-moving hierarchies that can distort decisions through inaction; a planning process that simply does not have the capability of fully integrating all information and producing an acceptable plan within the parameters and time limits set down by the political leadership; political limits that dictate that established institutions such as the party not be ignored in any solution even though their role may not be clearly defined and may even be counter-productive; and, non-compliance at the base of the hierarchy in the form of resistance by individuals and production units to attempts to change and direct their behaviour patterns through economic levers and administrative controls.

5.26
On Progress in Implementing the Decisions of the
XXIII Congress and CPSU Central Committee Plenums
on Questions of Agriculture   31 October 1968

... In accordance with the decisions of the XXIII Congress and the March (1965) and May (1966) plenums of the CPSU Central Committee, significant measures are being carried out for further improving the country's agriculture. Its material and technical base has been strengthened. Industry has begun to produce more for the needs of the kolkhozes and sovkhozes in the way of tractors, automobiles, agricultural machinery, and mineral fertilizers. Work on land reclamation has been put on a broad footing. Of great significance was the transfer to the new policy of procuring agricultural products based on establishing firm plans and the material incentives for selling grain over and above the plan. In the countryside a number of social and economic measures have been carried out, monthly guaranteed pay for labour has been introduced in kolkhozes, pension provisions for kolkhozniks and sovkhoz workers have been improved ...

Along with the accomplishments in developing agriculture, there are short-comings and unresolved problems. The volume of production of a number of products and the growth of labour productivity in agriculture have not yet reached the level envisaged in the Directives of the XXIII CPSU Congress for the Five-Year Plan. In some oblasts, krais, and republics agricultural production growth rates are low, in a number of farms work is poorly conducted in raising the yields of grain and other crops, as well as increasing the productivity of animal husbandry. There still are cases where low quality seeds are used in sowing. A great deal of produce is lost due to the poor weed, insect, and disease control of plants and animals. Proper concern is not shown in accumulating and applying local fertilizers in the fields. Machinery is not used with the proper effectiveness. Plan targets in the area of land reclamation are not being fulfilled. On many kolkhozes and sovkhozes advanced methods of farm management and the best forms and methods of labour organization and production are introduced at too slow a pace; economic work is still poorly organized.

The prime costs of products are still high, particularly in animal husbandry; a campaign for economy and thrift has not been developed to the extent necessary. Despite growing receipts, in a number of kolkhozes not enough funds are allocated for the expansion of social production; there are unnecessary expenditures for the maintenance of the administrative and managerial apparatus and for other purposes.

The USSR Ministry of Agriculture, the All-Union Farm Machine Agency (Soiuzsel'khoztekhnika), the USSR Ministry for Land Reclamation and Water Resources, and their bodies in the localities still exhibit quite a few short-comings in their work. They fail to show due persistence in making the fullest use of reserves and potentials for kolkhoz and sovkhoz production. They do not always reach a timely resolution of many important problems concerning the development of farming and animal husbandry.

Considerable improvement is necessary in organizing the procurement and storage of agricultural products, and particularly that of vegetables and fruits.

There are essential short-comings in planning capital investments and material and technical resources for agriculture, as well as in the fulfilment by some industrial ministries of the targets established by the XXIII Congress and Central Committee plenums with respect to provisioning agriculture. Sluggishness is permitted in creating new types of machinery and in creating effective fertilizers and chemical agents for plant protection. The mastering of production of new agricultural machinery is delayed. The problem of supplying spare parts has not been resolved satisfactorily. There exists a lag in the development of industry for the processing of agricultural raw materials.

The Central Committee plenum notes that the source of insufficient growth rates of agricultural production lies in the still slow introduction of chemical processes, land reclamation and comprehensive mechanization, as well as the poor introduction of the latest achievements of science and advanced experience into agriculture.

The CPSU Central Committee plenum resolves:

1   The further steady implementation of the party policy and practical measures for developing agriculture, which have been elaborated by the XXIII Congress and the March and May plenums of the CPSU Central Committee, is considered to be a most significant task of party organizations, soviet, and economic bodies.

The plenum orders the central committees of the union republic communist parties, the krai, oblast, okrug, and raion party committees, the soviet organs, the USSR Ministry of Agriculture, the USSR Ministry for Land Reclamation and Water Resources, the All-Union Farm Machine Agency, and their bodies in the localities, the party organizations, and the leaders of kolkhozes and sovkhozes to take measures to do away with existing shortcomings in developing agriculture and to make better use of all kolkhoz and sovkhoz production reserves to ensure the fulfilment of the Five-Year-Plan targets.

2   The proposals on the basic directions and measures for further developing the agriculture of the USSR, which have been elaborated by the CPSU Central Committee Politburo and stated in the report of Comrade L.I. Brezhnev, are approved and recognized as being timely and meeting the requirements of communist construction.

The Central Committee plenum considers as a most important political task for the party and state as a whole the acceleration of the rates of agricultural development so that the present level of agricultural production in the country is surpassed as soon as possible. As before, attention must be focused on considerably increasing the production of grain and other agricultural crops on the basis of a sharp increase in yield capacity and comprehensive development of animal husbandry. It is necessary to show constant concern for improving the quality of products.

It is possible to achieve a high level of agricultural production only by placing kolkhoz and sovkhoz production, as well as branches which serve it, on a more powerful material and technical base. It is necessary to continue to equip agriculture with modern machinery, satisfy its requirements for mineral fertilizers and other chemical agents, and conduct land-reclamation work on a large scale.

The re-equipment of agriculture on a new technical base must constitute a most important direction in elaborating plans for the forthcoming Five-Year Plan. Economic plans are to provide for the funds and material and technical resources necessary for the fuller satisfaction of the growing needs of agriculture.

3   Considering the great significance of using chemistry in raising productivity of agricultural production, it is necessary in the coming years to accelerate substantially growth rates for the production of mineral fertilizers, effective chemical agents for plant protection, and products of microbiological synthesis ...

4   The USSR Ministry for Land Reclamation and Water Resources, the USSR Ministry of Agriculture, the All-Union Farm Machine Agency, party, soviet, agricultural, and water resources agencies are ordered to take all necessary measures for carrying out the programme of reclamation work that was approved by the CPSU Central Committee May Plenum ...

The Central Committee plenum supports the initiative of Komsomol organizations that have assumed patronage over the construction of most significant water resource units, and calls upon the Komsomol, our glorious young people, to take a still more active part in carrying out the broad programme of land reclamation.

The further accelerated development of the country's economy requires rational utilization of land, water, and energy resources ...

5   For the purposes of satisfying the requirements of agriculture for machinery used in comprehensive mechanization, it is considered necessary to ensure the further development of production capacities of tractor, agricultural, and land-reclamation machine building by widely reconstructing existing plants and building new plants, as well as by improving equipment, technological processes, and the organization of production and labour in these branches of machine building.

Measures are to be taken to improve designing, reduce the time necessary for creating and mastering the production of new, improved agricultural machinery. Greater responsibility is to be demanded of the ministries, departments and industrial enterprises, the USSR Gosplan, and the USSR Gossnab for the fulfilment of assignments for supplying agriculture with machines and spare parts, and for improving their quality, reliability, and durability.

6   The Central Committee plenum attaches great significance to improving construction in the countryside. It is necessary to strengthen construction and design organizations, raise the level of industrialization of rural construction, develop the production of local construction materials on a wide scale, substantially expand construction of production facilities in the countryside, as well as housing and cultural-everyday facilities. More attention is to be devoted to providing kolkhozes and sovkhozes with services and amenities, and water and gas supplies, and to road construction.

7   Taking into consideration the great importance to the economy of the quickest development of animal husbandry, of raising the productivity of livestock and poultry, reducing the production costs of meat, milk, and other products, the USSR Ministry of Agriculture is instructed, with the participation of local agencies, scholars, and specialists in animal husbandry to work out and bring to the CPSU Central Committee suggestions directed at significantly improving this branch of agriculture.

8   The Central Committee plenum considers it necessary to retain in the forthcoming five-year period the principle of fixed plans for the procurement of agricultural products. The fixed plan for grain procurement for the years 1971–75 is to be established at approximately the same volume as has been determined for the present five-year period; some adjustments are to be made when necessary for republics, krais, and oblasts ...

9   For the purposes of increasing the production and encouraging the sale of agricultural products by kolkhozes and sovkhozes over and above the fixed plan, it is recognized as necessary to extend the existing procedure for stimulating grain purchases over and above the plan to some other agricultural products.

The Central Committee Politburo and the USSR Council of Ministers are to work out specific measures on this question.

It is considered expedient to use part of the funds received by sovkhozes in the form of increments to the basic price for production over and above the plan, to award bonuses to sovkhoz workers, specialists, and farm managers.

10   Party, soviet, and agricultural bodies are to pay particular attention to improving economic work in kolkhozes and sovkhozes, further perfecting the organization and remuneration of labour, reducing costs of agricultural production, raising the profitability of all branches of kolkhoz and sovkhoz production and ensuring the all-round growth of labour productivity in agriculture.

11   The plenum instructs the Central Committee Politburo and the USSR Council of Ministers to carry out the necessary measures to do away with short-comings and improve the organization of procurement of agricultural products, develop industry that processes agricultural raw materials, and develop the refrigeration and warehouse industry to ensure the timely acceptance, processing, and storage of products and the fuller satisfaction of the working people's needs for products in all the country's zones.

12   The Central Committee plenum attaches particular significance to raising the effectiveness of scientific research as an indispensible condition for accelerating the rates of agricultural development ...

13   Party, soviet, and agricultural bodies are ordered to pay more attention to training agricultural specialists in higher and secondary educational institutions, to improving the qualifications of leading cadres of kolkhozes and sovkhozes, particularly brigade leaders, heads of livestock sections, and

department managers, as well as to retaining specialists in the countryside, and creating the necessary production and daily living conditions for them. There is to be improvement in the training and retraining of cadres in popular professions, especially machine operators. Advanced people in kolkhoz and sovkhoz production are to be promoted to leading positions in every possible way ...

Pravda, 1 November 1968   *KPSS v rezoliutsiiakh* IX, 501–9

5.27
On the Work of the Central Committee of the
Communist Party of Tadzhikistan in Implementing
the Decisions of the XXIII CPSU Congress*   17 December 1968

> The excerpts from the following document indicate the central authorities' continued concern for the effect of the national traditions of the Central Asian republics on Moscow's attempts to modernize attitudes and behaviour. The decision reflects particular concern for improving work with leadership cadres, and extending ideological work to counter the retention of certain popular and religious customs among the masses and to socialize local populations into attitudes that are consistent with a modern work ethic and with participation in the officially sponsored organizations and activities of the regime.

... In the activity of the central committee of the Communist Party of Tadzhikistan, the Gorno-Badakhshan oblast committee, and many city and raion committees, questions of the selection, placement, and training of leading cadres have not yet been given their proper place. On many occasions, persons lacking the necessary political and business qualities are promoted to important sectors. Supervision over the work of cadres is poorly carried out and this results in some leaders of enterprises, institutions, and departments losing their feeling of responsibility for entrusted work, violating party and state discipline, and failing to wage a decisive struggle against squandering and embezzlement of socialist property. In some individual cases, they take to the way of fraud and often distort data in reports to cover up their short-comings and create an outward show of a satisfactory state of affairs. Party committees often fail to give a principled evaluation of such phenomena and fail to speak openly with responsible personnel about their short-comings and errors in a party-like manner.

*   Excerpt: document not published in full.

The party organizations of the republic have not provided sufficient guidance in their ideological and educational work for the formation of a marxist-leninist outlook in all toilers or for raising their production and public activity. Atheistic propaganda has slackened recently and the activity of the clergy and religious sects has revived. A persistent struggle with survivals of the past in people's consciousness, in the way of life, and in family relations is not being conducted. This particularly applies to creating conditions for more active participation of women in public and cultural life. Phenomena are still preserved that are intolerable in a socialist society, such as giving minors in marriage, forced marriage, and the payment of bride-money. The proportion of women among communists is decreasing; their number has also decreased in the staff of raion and city party committees and secretaries of primary party organizations; few women are promoted to leading positions. The activity of many cultural institutions does not meet contemporary requirements. To this day a considerable portion of kishlaks do not have clubs, libraries, or facilities to show films. The special features of the republic, demands of various strata and groups of the population, and the need for more actively instilling traditions common to all Soviet peoples in the daily life of the Tadzhik people are not properly reflected in mass political work.

The CPSU Central Committee resolves ...

7   ... Taking into account the great political and economic significance of building up qualified worker cadres from the native population in basic occupations, the central committee of the Communist Party and the council of ministers of the Tadzhik SSR are ordered to develop and carry out measures to improve utilization of labour resources and to involve the local population more extensively in work in industry, construction, and other branches of the economy ...

8   ... Propaganda of the ideas of proletarian internationalism and friendship between peoples is to occupy the centre of attention of party, soviet, trade union, and Komsomol organizations, as is the consolidation of fraternal ties between the toilers of Tadzhikistan and all the peoples of the Soviet Union. As it has been pointed out in the Programme of the CPSU, the further strengthening of co-operation must continue to be promoted through voluntary study of the Russian language along with the native tongue, the former having become in fact the common language for communication between all the peoples of the USSR. While developing the best national traditions, it is necessary to contribute more actively to the consolidation of international traditions and those which are common to all Soviet peoples building communism.

Party committees, and state and public organizations must lead a persistent struggle against obsolete customs and traditions and they must not tolerate a spirit of conciliation and lack of principle toward survivals of the

religious or bai [rich Central Asian land owner] feudal past, any manifestation of the seclusion of women or incidents of infringement of their
rights. Women are to be involved more extensively in public and political
life, and favourable conditions are to be created for their daily life, work,
and studies ...

Partiinaia zhizn', no. 1   *KPSS v rezoliutsiiakh* IX, 512–20
(1969): 3–8

5.28

**On the Work Experience of the Party Committee of the
Shchekino Chemical Combine with Respect to Mobilizing
its Collective of Working People to Expand the Volume
of Production by Increasing Labour Productivity**   6 October 1969

The Shchekino Chemical Combine is a petro-chemical complex consisting of
approximately 21 industrial enterprises and 17 construction enterprises located
in the city of Shchekino in Tula oblast. A key unit in the chemical industry, it
had exhibited a number of difficulties characteristic of Soviet industry in general during the middle 1960s, especially failure to achieve plan targets due to
underemployment, inability to recruit qualified skilled workers, high labour
turnover, and problems with its material incentive system. A decision was
made to conduct a major experiment at the Shchekino Chemical Combine
beginning in late 1967. The basic aim of the experiment was to increase labour
productivity by giving the combine management the right to conduct an internal reorganization of the combine. Among the techniques available to the
management were the devising and introducing of progressive work norms,
the combining of jobs, the widening of servicing zones, the mechanization of
labour-intensive work, and the reorganization of the internal managerial structure of the combine. The key to the success of the experiment, and the most
contentious aspect of it, was the right granted to management to dismiss
inefficient or unnecessary workers while retaining the basic wage fund for
redistribution to retained staff in the form of incentives for improving qualifications, expanding duties, and increasing labour productivity. Thus, the
experiment had wide-ranging implications for a number of crucial issues in
Soviet industry, including the autonomy of enterprise management, differential pay rates, lay-offs, and unemployment. In many respects, the Shchekino
experiment embodied the essence of the administrative decentralization component of the economic reforms introduced at the September 1965 Central
Committee Plenum.

The apparent victory achieved by the proponents of the new economic
reform through Central Committee approval and wide dissemination of the

Shchekino experience was short-lived. At the December 1969 Central Committee Plenum, Brezhnev was to make a speech highly critical of economic
administration and calling for a much more conservative approach to improving labour productivity through greater emphasis on tight discipline and control. The prior approval of the Shchekino experiment may have acted as a
brake to slow the speed of the shift in the balance. However, it could not
indefinitely delay such a change in direction. By the late 1970s it appeared that
the Shchekino experiment had lost its momentum.

Part of the failure of the Shchekino experiment can be explained in terms of
institutional dynamics in the Soviet economy. During the first, successful stage
(until around 1970) the experiment was relatively self-contained. It involved
internal reorganization of the combine, mainly by shifting, reclassifying, and
dismissing personnel. However, the second stage of the experiment involved
modernization of the plant in order to achieve higher levels of productivity.
During this stage, the combine had to extend its external contacts and rely
increasingly upon other economic units over which it had no control and on
whom it depended for success. These outside agencies failed to meet their
obligations which, in turn, prevented the Shchekino combine from fulfilling its
plan indices. For example, the Ministry of Chemical Industries allegedly took
two years to confirm construction plans, made unreasonable demands for
reductions in managerial personnel, and continuously revised Shchekino production plans. Design plans, construction and installation work, modernization
processes, and equipment deliveries were all delayed and often incomplete,
thus interrupting current production and preventing the achievement of new
levels of efficiency. The authorities responsible for wage and norm setting did
not comply with the requirements of Shchekino, often improperly establishing
normatives for personnel and labour outlay and changing the conditions for
the use of wage savings. Finally, the local party organs apparently lowered the
priority of the experiment on their own agenda and thus ceased to act as a
strong advocate for its interests. As the experiment spread to other enterprises
by the early 1970s, evidence also arose of resistance on the enterprise level.
Some enterprises oversimplified the method, using it as a means of removing
from the organizational table underemployed workers, but failing to take the
supplementary crucial steps of technical and economic reorganization of the
plant. Old attitudes of directors held when it came to disclosing reserves. They
were still afraid (and justifiably so) of sudden plan changes. Some enterprise
managers and ministry officials abused the reform by manipulating norms and
wage funds so as to short-change the workers.

There seem to be two possible explanations for the eclipse of the Shchekino
experiment, one systemic and one political. To what extent was the failure
attributable simply to bureaucratic inertia and resistance to experimentation?
And, to what extent was it attributable to a conscious set of political decisions
by those who opposed its fundamental principles? The truth probably lies
somewhere between the two extremes, with the political opposition effectively

using the conservative characteristics of the administrative system to let the experiment die a slow and quiet death, which was possible in the 1970s because of the declining influence of the major patron of the experiment, A.N. Kosygin.

The CPSU Central Committee notes that the party organization of the Shchekino Chemical Combine is conducting significant organizational and political work in mobilizing its collective of working people to increase the volume of production while reducing the number of personnel by improving the organization of production, labour, and the wage system.

The main directions in work conducted by the collective of the combine to increase labour productivity are to work out and introduce progressive work norms, to combine professions, to widen servicing zones, to mechanize labour-intensive work, to simplify and improve the management structure of the enterprise and its production units, and to centralize and specialize factory services. At the combine, a system of material incentives has been created, and basic wage rates and fixed salary rates have been raised by using what is economized from wages due to reduction in personnel.

The party, trade union, and Komsomol organizations are conducting extensive educational and explanatory work among the working people in the collective, thus ensuring that the workers, engineering-technical personnel, and office employees have a profound understanding of the objectives, meaning, and significance of the tasks that have been set and ensuring that they actively participate in working out and implementing measures to accelerate the growth rates of labour productivity. Questions related to improving the effectiveness of production are submitted for discussion at workers' meetings and production conferences and at economic conferences.

On the party committee's initiative, commissions have been set up at the enterprise, in shop sections, and in production units to promote technical progress; innovators' councils and bureaus for economic analysis and norm setting have been organized; a university for technical and economic knowledge has been created; public reviews of production reserves are conducted. All this permits the wide enlistment of the working people in introducing progressive methods for labour organization and eliminating existing shortcomings. Propaganda of technical and economic knowledge has improved. Professional training and studies in the area of economics have been organized for personnel at the combine. More than 1000 toilers have mastered second trades and closely related professions and over 4000 workers have improved their qualifications. The party and trade union organizations have established strict control over the job placement of released workers, engineering-technical personnel, and office employees who are trained in new specialties and assigned to work at other shop sections at the combine or newly created production units.

The tangible, purposeful activity of the party organization and collective of the combine have produced results. In two years, labour productivity increased by 87 per cent and the volume of production output rose by more than 80 per cent, while at the same time the number of workers dropped by 870.

The work conducted at the Shchekino Chemical Combine is of great significance to the economy. Extensive utilization of the party committee's work experience opens great opportunities for making use of existing reserves to increase production output and increase labour productivity.

The CPSU Central Committee resolves:

1   The positive work experience of the party committee of the Shchekino Chemical Combine in mobilizing its collective of working people to increase labour productivity and expand the volume of production is approved.

The party committee and economic leadership of the combine are instructed to ensure a further increase in the effectiveness of production by paying particular attention to mechanization and automation, modernization of equipment, and improvement of technological processes.

2   It is recommended that the central committees of the union republic communist parties, the krai and oblast party committees, and the soviet, trade union, and Komsomol organizations extensively develop organizational and mass political work in mobilizing collectives of working people to make use of existing reserves for the growth of labour productivity and increasing production output with fewer workers.

It is considered expedient to hold a seminar for party and economic leaders to study the work experience of the party committee and collective of the Shchekino Chemical Combine.

3   Using the experience of the collective of working people at the Shchekino Chemical Combine and other experiences, USSR ministries and departments are instructed to organize the elaboration of measures to raise labour productivity and increase production output by improving the structure of production management, improving labour organization and norm setting, raising the qualifications of workers, and through the technical re-equipment of enterprises.

4   The editorial staff of the newspapers, *Pravda, Sovetskaia Rossiia, Trud, Sotsialisticheskaia industriia*, and *Ekonomicheskaia gazeta*, and of the magazine, *Partiinaia zhizn'*, and the Committee for Radio and Television Broadcasting of the USSR Council of Ministers are instructed to illuminate the positive work experience of party organizations and collectives of enterprises in increasing the output of industrial production through a growth in labour productivity and an increase in the effective utilization of industrial equipment.

5.29
On the Practice of Conducting Party Meetings in the Iaroslavl City Party Organization 3 November 1969

The CPSU Central Committee notes that the Iaroslavl city and raion party committees and primary party organizations, guided by the decisions of the XXIII CPSU Congress, have done definite work in raising the role of party meetings as organs of collective leadership and a school of political training for communists. The most significant questions pertaining to the life and activity of party organizations are considered and solved at the meetings. The results of plenums of the CPSU Central Committee and questions pertaining to the domestic and foreign policy of the party, economic and cultural development, and ideological work are discussed with great interest. At the meetings, communists define the concrete tasks of party organizations with respect to improving their guidance over economic work, implementing economic reform, accelerating rates of technical progress, and introducing scientific organization of labour and communist education of the working people. Recently, meetings have been taking place everywhere under the badge of mobilizing communists and collectives of toilers to fulfil plans and obligations for a worthy celebration of the 100th anniversary of V.I. Lenin's birth.

Within the city party organization a good practice has been established whereby the city and raion party committees and the committees and bureaus of primary party organizations regularly inform communists of their work at meetings. Reports by party members and candidate members on their fulfilment of the requirements of the CPSU Programme and Rules are heard regularly. All this raises the activity and responsibility of communists and has a positive effect on the activity of primary party organizations.

The communists and party organizations of Iaroslavl have been the initiators of many valuable patriotic undertakings, the dissemination of which has helped to achieve definite successes in the work of industry and construction.

At the same time, the CPSU Central Committee considers that there are major short-comings in the practice of preparing and conducting party meetings in the Iaroslavl city party organization. The period between convened meetings that is specified by the CPSU Rules is often violated. In many cases, meetings are held nominally and fail to exert the proper influence on the life and affairs of party organizations. Many meetings are held with only a small number of communists present, with an average of 75 per cent of party members and candidate members attending them. Some communists do not have the opportunity to attend meetings because almost no meetings are held for different shifts at enterprises with several shifts.

At party meetings insignificant and monotonous questions are often discussed which, for the most part, touch on current production work. At the same time, many important and pressing problems of how to advance production, raise its economic effectiveness, and improve organizational work are seldom discussed and not thoroughly enough. Few ideological and theoretical questions are put forward for consideration at meetings. Party meetings fail to promote sufficiently the leading role of communists or to mobilize them for the struggle against violations of state and labour discipline and public order, and against drunkenness, embezzlement of socialist property, squandering, and other anti-social phenomena.

The growing political maturity, general educational level, cultural and technical level, and needs of party members and candidate members are not sufficiently taken into consideration when party meetings are conducted. On some occasions, meetings are poorly prepared and conducted in a slapdash manner. Few rank-and-file communists are involved in direct participation in determining agenda, preparing meetings and working out decisions. No concern is shown in ensuring that more non-party workers and employees are present and take an active part in the discussion at open party meetings. As a result, there is no utilization of the fine potential for giving the non-party aktiv access to the work of party organizations, for drawing the toilers into participation in the administration of production and public affairs, and for further consolidating ties with the masses.

The effectiveness of party meetings is considerably reduced because the way questions are formulated is often neither businesslike nor principled and because a wide exchange of opinion fails to develop. In many organizations, a narrow circle of people speak at meetings, while a poor job is done of drawing into active discussion party members who are workers. For example, at the Iaroslavl Clothing Association 25 general party meetings have been held over the past three years and, of the 255 party members, 215 have not spoken even once. There are many incidents when the order of conducting meetings is regulated excessively. Instead of taking comradely counsel with communists at meetings, some leaders look upon meetings as a convenient place for criticism from above and for issuing current instructions.

Short-comings in the activity of enterprises and institutions and in their organizational and political work, and incidents of a careless attitude to business are not always subjected to principled party criticism in reports and speeches. At many meetings this is discussed in a general featureless form, and omissions in the work and errors of leaders are often presented as short-comings of the party organization and the collective as a whole. Proper exactingness is not always demanded of communists for the strict observance of party discipline and the moral code of a builder of communism.

The development of criticism and self-criticism is held back by the fact that party committees and leading personnel often do not sufficiently consider the opinion of communists and, at times, are inattentive to their remarks and proposals. Individual leaders react oversensitively to criticism and lack the tact and party courtesy to hear out their comrades. These intolerable phenomena do not always receive a principled evaluation on the part of party organizations and committees.

A serious short-coming is the fact that decisions of an unspecific, declarative nature are often adopted at meetings. Work with respect to fulfilling adopted decisions is conducted unsatisfactorily, and the proper exactingness in implementing decisions is lacking. Thus, over the course of a number of years, decisions were taken at the party meetings of the combine, 'Kransnyi Perekop,' on overcoming the technical lag in production and improving the work and daily living conditions of workers. However, neither the leadership of the enterprise nor the party committee, as should be, organized their fulfilment, and the situation remains without substantial changes. Short-comings in economic and political work are eliminated slowly because of poor organization and verification of the realization of adopted decisions. In industry, construction, and transportation, internal production reserves are far from being used to the full, large working-time losses and unproductive expenses are allowed, and a number of enterprises systematically fail to fulfil state plans. The number of violations of social order in the city is not being cut down.

The Iaroslavl city and raion party committees are doing an inadequate job of studying and generalizing the practice of party meetings and fail to provide sufficient assistance to primary party organizations in preparing and conducting party meetings. Sometimes party committees order party organizations to discuss the same questions repeatedly without adequate grounds and failing to take into account the specific nature and conditions of the activity of each party organization.

The CPSU Central Committee resolves:

1   The Iaroslavl city and raion party committees and primary party organizations are ordered to do away with the noted short-comings and ensure the further enhancement of the role of party meetings in carrying out the practical tasks of communist construction.

Party meetings are called upon to facilitate in every possible way the political and labour activity of party members, candidate members of the party, and all working people. They must be an effective means of mobilizing communists and non-party people for the implementation of the decisions of the XXIII CPSU Congress and party directives, and for the struggle to raise social production, strengthen socialist labour discipline, improve the ideological training of the masses, and provide the population with cultural and everyday services.

It is necessary to enhance the significance of party meetings, the highest organ of the primary party organization, and do everything possible to ensure that they exert a decisive influence on the further development of inner-party democracy and on the consolidation of the leninist principle of collectivity in work.

2   The party committees and primary party organizations are to pay special attention to the content of party meetings and raise their effectiveness. Questions of vital interest to the entire collective and of paramount importance for its activity should be brought up for consideration at meetings. Efforts are to be made to ensure that meetings become real schools of upbringing for communists, actively promote their political tempering, and raise their personal responsibility for the state of affairs in their organization and in the party as a whole. Every meeting must be an important event in the life of the party organization and favourably affect the improvement of all work.

It is necessary to prepare meetings thoroughly and take care that they are conducted in an organized manner and in an atmosphere of a free and businesslike exchange of opinions, high principles, and mutual exactingness. Rank-and-file communists, especially those who are workers, are to be enlisted more extensively in preparing and discussing questions, and all necessary conditions are to be created so that they speak more often at meetings and frankly share their thoughts.

3   The city and raion party committees and the bureaus of primary party organizations must ensure extensive development of criticism and self-criticism at party meetings, raise its effectiveness, and not avoid consideration of sensitive questions. Criticism must be used to eliminate and prevent errors and short-comings in work and to train cadres in the spirit of strict observance of party and state discipline and great responsibility for matters entrusted to them.

In all party organizations it is necessary to create an atmosphere where communists boldly expose short-comings and are certain that principled criticism and businesslike proposals will be accepted with good will and supported; incidents of a disrespectful attitude to speeches by participants at party meetings must be resolutely eradicated. Anyone who violates inner-party democracy or who suppresses criticism must be held strictly responsible in accordance with the CPSU Rules.

The party committees and bureaus of primary party organizations must regularly see to it that critical remarks and proposals are carried into effect and they must make timely reports to communists on this work. Remarks made to local party, soviet, economic, and other organs must be generalized and brought to their attention. The leaders of these organs must carefully consider all critical remarks and inform the primary organizations of measures undertaken with respect to them.

4   In order to raise the effectiveness of party meetings, it is necessary to strive for a situation in which concrete and well-grounded decisions are made

on questions that have been discussed. The organization and verification of the implementation of adopted decisions are to be improved radically and those who are to blame for failure to fulfil decisions are to be held strictly accountable. Every communist must take an active part in this work and show initiative and persistance in fulfilling collectively elaborated measures. At party meetings, the party committees and bureaus must regularly report on progress in implementing previously adopted decisions and proposals of communists.

5   The CPSU Central Committee has instructed the Iaroslavl oblast, city, and raion party committees to analyse systematically and to generalize the practice of preparing and conducting party meetings, to expose and eliminate existing short-comings promptly, and to raise exactingness towards primary organizations for the state of party discipline. The party secretaries, bureau members, and responsible officials of the oblast, city, and raion party committees are to provide more assistance in conducting party meetings and carrying out the decisions adopted by them; they are to deliver reports more often at meetings and participate personally in the work of party meetings.

It should constantly be borne in mind that all-round improvement in the practice of conducting party meetings is of great fundamental significance for the further enhancement of the level of all party work and the consolidation of leninist norms of party life. In this lies one of the most important conditions for the successful fulfilment of the instructions of the XXIII CPSU Congress on raising the fighting efficiency of primary party organizations.

6   The editorial staff of the newspapers, *Pravda*, *Sovetskaia Rossiia*, *Sotsialisticheskaia industriia*, *Sel'skaia zhizn'*, and of the journal, *Partiinaia zhizn'*, as well as the editorial staff of the republican, krai, oblast, city, and raion newspapers are ordered to publish systematically materials relating to party meetings and improve their coverage of the positive experience of party organizations in this matter ...

Pravda, 12 November 1969   *KPSS v rezoliutsiiakh* X, 101–6

5.30
On the Work of the Party Committee of the
USSR Ministry of Meat and Dairy Industry   3 February 1970

The December 1969 Central Committee Plenum was a critical juncture in the Brezhnev regime's economic policy. Unfortunately, the decisions of the plenum have never been published in the form of official resolutions, except for a brief, formal approval of Brezhnev's report and the activities of the Poliburo. However, we do have available excerpts from Brezhnev's report to the plenum as well as a number of follow-up resolutions spelling out details of the plenum's deliberations and decisions. The present resolution is the first such published resolution dealing with economic inefficiencies by pinpointing abuses and recommending corrective action.

According to Brezhnev, the major, objective circumstance confronting the economy was the fact that the economy had reached a new and higher level of development that prevented the working out of decisions in the old manner and required new methods and new solutions. While the new economic reform had produced overall good results, it had still not been able to cope with the question of economic efficiency in all its dimensions. In particular it had not given the regime the leverage to deal with the problems of full and rational utilization of existing production potentials, the science-technology-production link, and the lack of a parsimonious attitude towards resources. Brezhnev proposed to deal with these objective limitations to economic efficiency through a policy of speeding up the introduction of the advances of scientific and technological progress in production and through an improvement in the organization and management of the economy. He called for the improvement of planned management (especially at the ministerial level), improvements in Gosplan and the entire planning apparatus, and the development of a science of management (based on computer technology as well as marxism-leninism). Brezhnev also identified several subjective factors inhibiting the achievement of economic goals, referring specifically to short-comings in the work of individuals that must be criticized and eliminated. These short-comings involved the absence of a feeling of responsibility and incidents of violations of state discipline, the essence of which involved managers trying to carry out business clearly beyond their means and undertaking construction projects in the local interest and for which materials and labour resources had not been assigned. There also had been misinterpretations of central directives regarding construction priorities. The real problem, according to Brezhnev, lay in the evidence that these incidents of non-compliance with rules and norms by administrators were becoming regular patterns and widespread practices.

Brezhnev took the position of a moderate in offering a solution to the problems. He identified 'some comrades' who advocated a return to purely administrative methods of enforcing labour, party, and state discipline. Brezhnev rejected this proposal as a return to the old ways that would be counterproductive and even dangerous. His proposal was to pursue a policy of trust in cadres, creating a strong sense of responsibility among managers and an atmosphere of creative initiative and trust among workers. The solution involved adherence to the already elaborated principles defining the party's style and method of work. Cadres were to be held responsible through techniques such as criticism and self-criticism, the work of the people's control and the organs of party control, and by evaluating achievements and short-comings more objectively.

The present resolution is a detailed reflection of Brezhnev's position, dealing with administrative incompetence and abuse at the centre, both in the party and ministerial apparatus. It calls for improved supervision of the ministry by the party committee, improvements in the party committee's own internal activities, improvements in the ministry's internal organization and its relations with its operating units and with other ministries. Finally, all of this is to be ensured by improving the lines of communication between the ministry's party committee and the Central Committee apparatus. The thrust of the resolution's concern lies in the direction of identifying and defining areas of competence and jurisdiction in both the party and ministerial organizations, and ensuring that clear lines of responsibility and communication are established within and between the two administrative hierarchies.

The CPSU Central Committee notes that the party committee of the USSR Ministry of Meat and Dairy Industry, guided by the decisions of the XXIII Party Congress, has conducted definite work on training staff employees and mobilizing communists and the entire collective to accomplish the tasks of further developing the meat and dairy industry.

However, the level of organizational-party and ideological-political work within the apparatus lags considerably behind the requirements placed on ministry party organizations under present conditions. The party organization lacks clearness of purpose and fighting efficiency in its activity; an atmosphere of high mutual exactingness and intolerance of short-comings in work has not been created in the collective.

The party committee and party organizations of the administrations do not exert the necessary influence to improve the work of the ministry's apparatus, to strengthen discipline, and to raise the responsibility of its employees for implementing the directives of the party and government; they do not respond sharply to serious short-comings in their guidance of industry and fail to give the short-comings a principled party evaluation.

The ministry's apparatus does a poor job of ensuring the solution of basic problems of development confronting the meat and dairy industry; it fails to show daily concern in raising the economic effectiveness of production, accelerating scientific and technological progress, and extremely rapid mastering and full utilization of production capacities. In the past four years, the profitable recovery of outlay has declined by more than seven per cent. The number of enterprises failing to fulfil production plans has increased. The growth in wages has exceeded the growth in labour productivity. Plans for introducing new techniques and progressive technology, comprehensive mechanization and automation of production processes are not being fulfilled on an annual basis. Many enterprises are equipped with outdated machinery and equipment. At the same time, there are more than 100 million rubles of unassigned new equipment.

As a result of miscalculations and serious insufficiencies in planning, there is a lack of proper relationships with agricultural agencies, and existing potentials for raising output and improving the quality and assortment of meat and milk products are not being fully utilized. The central apparatus and ministerial agencies in the localities have failed to exert an active influence on the fulfilment and overfulfilment of plans for state purchases of livestock products. Development of a network of enterprises is not always carried out with consideration for the necessity of liquidating the imbalances that have formed in a number of districts of the country between the raw material base and the capacities of the processing industry.

In the ministry collective, work on mastering scientific methods for the management of industry has not been developed to account for the changing character of relationships with enterprises under the conditions of the economic reform. In many administrations and departments, formalistic and bureaucratic methods of leadership are tolerated. Instead of making a thorough analysis of the state of affairs in their branch of the economy or conducting active organizational work, many experienced specialists dissipate their energies on preparing general directives and instructions and all sorts of certificates, or on collecting a variety of information that is often unnecessary. This year alone more than forty thousand different directive letters and telegrams emanated from the ministry. Ministry officials often fail to visit the localities and fail to make an adequate study and generalize advanced experience; they also have failed to render necessary assistance to the ministries of union republics and enterprises in developing production. Ministry officials and heads of administrations and departments take business trips, for the most part, to participate in various types of meetings and conferences, and to present challenge banners to enterprises for the results of socialist competition ... The weak tie with subordinate organizations, party, and soviet organs results in the fact that many questions on industrial work in the ministry are considered without thorough knowledge of the actual state of affairs.

The party committee tolerates a situation whereby the ministry does not take necessary measures to improve and reduce the costs of the administrative apparatus and to eliminate parallelism and duplication in the activity of its different units. The functions of the administrations and divisions and the duties of personnel have not been clearly determined, giving rise to undefined responsibility and irresponsibility, hindering the operational solution of questions as a result of unnecessary agreements. There is no guarantee that party and government instructions will be carried out with respect to cutbacks in administrative and managerial personnel and in the ministerial system as a whole. In the past two years, personnel has increased by 13.6 per cent, while expenditures on maintenance have increased by 20.6 per cent.

Supervision and organization of the implementation of decisions of the board of the ministry, as well as orders and regulations, have been poorly set up in the ministry's administrative machinery. Time limits for completing state assignments are often violated. Some of the leading communists are really not engaged in checking on work done. Proper attention is not paid to work with letters and applications that have been received from the localities. A formalistic approach is often taken to considering proposals and complaints of the toilers and established time limits for their consideration are broken. Incidents of bureaucratic delay and a bureaucratic attitude to the requests of toilers are not strictly condemned by the party organization.

The party committee and party organization of the administration fail to exert an active influence on work with cadres in the apparatus; full use is not made of all possibilities for their creative growth and raising their professional qualifications. A significant portion of personnel pay no attention to technical literature for years on end and do not follow the achievements of national and foreign science and technology. Many administrative positions remain vacant for a long time. Systematic work is not being conducted to create a reserve of cadres. There are serious short-comings in the training of personnel. The party committee often displays liberalism and unscrupulousness and fails to provide an incisive political evaluation of incidents where some communists lose their feeling of responsibility for entrusted matters, and of violations of state discipline and incorrect behaviour.

There are substantial short-comings in the way inner-party work has been set up. Party meetings are sometimes held nominally and are of little use in raising the activity of all communists in accomplishing the tasks confronting the ministry. Criticism and self-criticism are developed poorly, often exhibiting a general featureless nature, and therefore appearing ineffective. Many decisions of the party committee and party meetings do not pose concrete tasks or define the personal responsibility of communists for their fulfilment. The party committee is not actively involving trade union and Komsomol organizations in work to improve the activity of the administrative apparatus of the ministry; it has also failed to provide daily guidance over them.

The party organizations of the administrations and the party committee are not sufficiently engaged in the ideological training of communists and administrative personnel, in moulding their profound communist conviction. With these ends in view, forms of party study such as problem seminars and theoretical conferences are poorly utilized. Mass political work in the collective comes essentially to the same thing as conducting ceremonial rallies and meetings in conjunction with revolutionary holidays, individual reports, and lectures.

Ministry officials inform the party aktiv and communists irregularly of the work of the ministry, the state of affairs in the branch of the economy, and progress in the fulfilment of plans and assignments; they also do not depend sufficiently on the party organization to improve the work of the administrative apparatus.

The CPSU Central Committee considers it inadmissable that the party committee fails to inform the Central Committee promptly of the shortcomings in the work of the ministry, as well as its individual employees, irrespective of the post held, as is required by the CPSU Rules.

The CPSU Central Committee resolves:

1   The party committee of the USSR Ministry of Meat and Dairy Industry is ordered to conduct a radical reorganization of the entire work of the party organization with due regard for the requirements put forward by the December (1969) Plenum of the CPSU Central Committee. The party committee and party organizations of the administrations are called upon to exert an active influence on the activity of the administrative apparatus, to educate employees in the spirit of great responsibility for entrusted affairs, and to strengthen party and state discipline in every possible way.

The attention of communists and all ministry personnel must be centred on the consistent implementation of measures to raise the economic effectiveness of production, to speed up rates of technological progress, and to make the fullest use of material and labour resources, and, on this basis, to increase the production of high-quality meat and dairy products that will provide for the growing needs of the population.

2   The party organization of the ministry must make persistent efforts to improve the style and methods of the work of administrations and departments, to introduce rational organization of labour, scientific processing and analysis of information, and the working out of well-grounded solutions to ensure that the administrative apparatus provides for effective and flexible guidance over its branch of the economy. In all its activity, the party organization must proceed from the fact that improvement of administration under today's conditions is an important reserve for the growth of social production and is of great political significance.

It is necessary to ensure that every employee systematically acquaint himself with the newest scientific recommendations pertaining to questions of administration and apply them skilfully in practice. With this end in view, all available potentials are to be utilized widely; scientific conferences dealing with problems of administration are to be conducted; the organization of labour in the administrative apparatus is to be reviewed.

The party committee and party organizations of the administrations must not tolerate any display of lack of organization, must decisively fight for efficient and co-ordinated work of all units of the administrative apparatus; it is necessary to see to it that there is exemplary order in the apparatus and that personnel at enterprises and institutions and toilers who turn to the ministry are received attentively and are provided with prompt, well-grounded answers to their requests, applications, complaints, and proposals.

3   Work is to be improved with respect to the selection, placement, and training of cadres in the ministry. Experienced, prepared specialists who are

competent in production affairs are to be promoted to the apparatus. A system to raise the professional qualifications of personnel and expand their knowledge in the area of economics and the technology of production is to be developed and implemented; advanced experience is to be studied.

The party committee and party organizations of the administrations are to make efforts to achieve a decisive improvement in all subdivisions of the apparatus for organizing supervision over the fulfilment of party and government directives; the personal responsibility of every leader for the state of verification of work is to be raised. The communists of the ministry are called upon to intensify the struggle for the absolute observance of state interests, a strict regime of economy, the preservation of socialist property, and against thriftlessness, squandering, narrow departmentalism, and localist tendencies. It is necessary to strengthen the ties of the ministry's administrative apparatus with collectives of enterprises and organizations, with local party, soviet, and economic organs, and with other central institutions and departments.

4   The party committee is ordered to improve its guidance over the party organizations of the administrations and to provide more practical assistance for them in their daily work. Pressing questions pertaining to production work and inner-party life, the training of cadres, and strengthening discipline are to be submitted for discussion to communists; effective measures are to be taken to do away with concrete instances of bureaucracy, punctiliousness, and a formalistic approach to business. It is necessary to listen keenly to the opinions and proposals of communists, to react to critical remarks in a party-like manner, and to adopt an irreconcilable attitude to feelings of complacency and placidity.

It is recommended that the party committee make wider use of forms of raising responsibility and strengthening discipline such as discussing at party meetings and meetings of the party committee communications and reports of communists on their fulfilment of official duties and the requirements of the CPSU Rules. The party organization may hear from any employee of the ministry on questions associated with the work of the administrative apparatus.

The role and responsibility of trade union and Komsomol organizations for the state of affairs in the collective is to be enhanced and the work of groups and posts of people's control is to be activated.

5   The party committee is ordered to take measures to improve ideological-upbringing work in the collective, to subject it to the interests of raising the political consciousness and responsibility of ministry employees, and to solving concrete questions of production. It should be kept in mind that a scientific approach to matters and the successful accomplishment of economic and political tasks are inconceivable without constantly mastering marxist-leninist theory and the historic experience of the CPSU and without

understanding the laws of communist construction. It is recommended that
the party committee organize thorough study for the personnel of the
administrative apparatus of the Theses of the CPSU Central Committee, 'In
Commemoration of the 100th Anniversary of the Birth of Vladimir Ilyich
Lenin.'

6   The central committees of the union republics and the Moscow CPSU
city committee are ordered to pay more attention to the party organizations
of the ministries and departments and to improve the generalization and
dissemination of their positive work experience. Study by the aktiv of ministry party organizations is to be organized and the aktiv is to be informed
systematically of the most significant party and government documents pertaining to questions of economic and cultural construction and the work of
the state administrative apparatus.

The adopted decision is to be discussed widely in party organizations of
ministries, departments, and soviet institutions ...

Partiinaia zhizn', no. 4   *KPSS v rezoliutsiiakh* X, 191–7
(1970): 3–6

Plenum of the Central Committee   2–3 July 1970

The tone of the July 1970 Central Committee's resolution was decidedly more
positive and optimistic than that of the previous Central Committee resolution
on agriculture (October 1968). Perhaps this is explained by the different purpose of the two resolutions rather than any real change in the circumstances of
agricultural production. The 1968 resolution was directed at past activity that
had produced impasses in agricultural production. Its purpose was to focus on
problems and their solutions. The 1970 resolution, in contrast, set the tone for
future planned development. By its nature it was less concerned with current
problems than with setting the goals and tempo of future activity in the coming
Five-Year Plan.

The continuation of the approach to agricultural development approved in
March 1965 and May 1966, despite the setbacks encountered by Soviet agriculture and the heavy capital costs associated with the policy, indicated the
strength of Brezhnev in determining agricultural policy. There was to be no
abandonment of the policy principles established in Brezhnev's earlier reports
and speeches, which emphasized that agricultural productivity and growth
depended largely on heavy infusions of capital for major land reclamation projects, fixed and operating capital, the development and production of chemical

fertilizers, and subsidiary industries both supplying and processing agricultural production. This was all to take place in the context of an organizational framework that provided for realistic planning of production and procurements, expanded research, and improved micro-management. In the forthcoming five-year period there was to be continued emphasis on substantial financial incentives for plan overfulfilment, expansion of inter-kolkhoz construction organizations, and extension of livestock farming on an industrial basis.

The 3 July plenum was followed 10 days later by a Central Committee plenum announcing the date of the next congress (March 1971) and the congress agenda (the major reports and rapporteurs).

5.31
The Immediate Tasks of the Party
in the Area of Agriculture   3 July 1970

... The CPSU Central Committee Plenum resolves:
1   The conclusions and proposals set out in the report by Comrade L.I. Brezhnev, General Secretary of the CPSU Central Committee, 'The Immediate Tasks of the Party in the Area of Agriculture' are approved.

A more rapid development of agriculture based on strengthening its material and technical base in every possible way is one of the major and high-priority tasks for the immediate future. It is necessary to make better use of land and machinery, to raise the effectiveness of social production in kolkhozes and sovkhozes, and to make efforts to accomplish a significant increase in labour productivity and a reduction in prime costs of agricultural products.
2   In the area of working the land, the CPSU Central Committee Plenum considers the organization of a nation-wide struggle to raise the yields of all agricultural crops and to ensure a steady increase in the production of grain, cotton, sugar beets, sunflowers, vegetables, potatoes, and other products to be a most important task. In the next five-year-plan period a substantial increase in the yield of grain crops in every kolkhoz and sovkhoz is necessary so that there is an increase over the country as a whole by no less than four centners per hectare. It is also important to increase the yield of industrial, feed, and other crops. With this end in view, a system of effective measures to raise the standards of farming – to raise soil fertility, to introduce highest yield varieties, to master crop rotation, and to eliminate harvest losses – is to be developed and carried out by the kolkhozes and sovkhozes.

The key problem still remains to increase grain production. In the next five-year-plan period, average annual gross yields are to total 195 million tons.

A stable, invariable plan for grain purchases is to be established for the years 1971–1975 at 60 million tons per year.

The principle of encouraging grain purchases over and above the plan that has been adopted at the March Plenum of the Central Committee is to be kept in force, and kolkhozes and sovkhozes are to be paid an extra 50 per cent over the basic purchase price for selling grain to the state in excess of the plan.

Party, soviet, and agricultural bodies are to take all measures to ensure that every kolkhoz and sovkhoz that is engaged in the production of commodity grain, every oblast, krai, and republic not only fulfils a stable plan, but also is able to sell the state a minimum of 35 per cent of grain over and above the plan in the next five-year-plan period.

State purchases of seed cotton, sugar beet, sunflower, flax fibre, vegetables, potatoes, fruits, berries, grapes, tea, and other agricultural products are to be increased considerably in the years 1971–1975.

3   The Central Committee plenum attributes particular significance to further increasing the production of livestock products ...

4   The plenum attaches great significance to correctly establishing plans of grain purchases and other agricultural products for kolkhozes and sovkhozes for all years of the next five-year-plan period. Stable purchase plans must be thoroughly substantiated, the potentials and natural and economic conditions of every farm and its specialization are to be given more consideration, as well as the delivery of new machinery and mineral fertilizers and the expansion of the area of reclaimed land.

The plenum calls the attention of agricultural, procurement, soviet, and party bodies, the party organizations, and leaders of the kolkhozes and sovkhozes to existing incidents of localistic tendencies and lack of discipline in fulfilling state plans for procuring agricultural products and requires that they decisively put an end to such phenomena. A stable plan for purchasing grain as well as other products is obligatory for all kolkhozes and sovkhozes. The plan must not be altered and it must be fulfilled. The fulfilment of state plans for the procurement of all agricultural and livestock products and active participation in above-plan sales of output are the foremost duty of the kolkhozes and sovkhozes.

5   The decision of the CPSU Central Committee Politburo is approved with respect to allocating the following in the new five-year-plan period for agricultural needs: 77.6 billion rubles of state capital investments in the area of production and housing construction, the construction of public amenities, and for purchases of machinery, including 45.9 billion rubles for construction and installation work.

In the process of implementing annual plans, the USSR Council of Ministers and the union republic councils of ministers are instructed to procure and allot additional means to develop agriculture.

6   By the end of the next five-year-plan period, the production of mineral fertilizers is to be brought to no less than 90 million tons; the production of chemical agents for plant protection is to be brought to 450 thousand tons.

The construction of new factories and the expansion of operating enterprises of the chemical and microbiological industries are provided. Deliveries of mineral fertilizers to agriculture in 1975 are to be brought up to a minimum of 72 million tons and food phosphates to 3 million tons.

The quality of mineral fertilizers is to be improved; deliveries of composite, highly concentrated solid fertilizers are to be increased; the output of special freight cars, conveyance vans, and packaging for mineral fertilizers is to be increased drastically; the construction of bases for storing fertilizers is to be expanded. Measures are to be taken to make better use of mineral and organic fertilizers in kolkhozes and sovkhozes and to raise the effectiveness of their utilization.

7   The Central Committee plenum emphasizes the great significance of developing land reclamation for the economy ...

8   The Central Committee plenum considers it necessary to ensure the further development of tractor, agricultural, and land-reclamation machine building within the next few years and to create in these branches of the economy additional production capacities in order to increase significantly the output of tractors, agricultural and land-reclamation machines, means of transport, and spare parts in the new five-year-plan period. All branches of industry must take an active part in accomplishing the tasks of technically re-equipping kolkhoz and sovkhoz production and increasing the output of machinery for agriculture ...

The USSR Gosplan and industrial ministries, directors and party organizations of factories are instructed to make use of all available capacities at their enterprises to increase output, through co-operation, of agricultural machines, aggregates, units, and spare parts.

Ministries and departments, scientific-research institutes and design offices are to take measures to produce improved agricultural machinery that is necessary to carry out comprehensive mechanization. The quality, reliability, and durability of the machines and mechanisms are to be improved significantly.

9   ... Special attention is to be paid to the mechanization of labour-intensive jobs in the area of animal husbandry; agriculture is to be supplied with the necessary machinery and mechanisms for this purpose.

Measures are to be taken to make highly productive use of tractors and agricultural machinery, to reinforce the repair base of the kolkhozes, sovkhozes, and All-Union Farm Machine Agency organizations, as well as automobile service stations.

Because of the great significance that is attached to stable machine operator cadres in the kolkhozes and sovkhozes, the USSR Council of Ministers is instructed to work out radical measures to hold these cadres in agriculture by creating highly productive labour conditions for them, intensifying their material and moral incentives, as well as improving their daily life.

10   In the forthcoming five-year-plan period, measures are to be carried out to expand considerably the capacities of industry that processes agricultural products and raw materials ...

11   Taking into consideration the fact that within the next few years a large programme of construction work is to be carried out in the countryside, measures are to be taken to strengthen the production base of the USSR Ministry of Agriculture so that, by the end of the next five-year-plan period, the enterprises and organizations of the ministry will have completed building and installation works in the countryside valued at not less than 5.5 billion rubles per year.

Other ministries are to be enlisted in sovkhoz and kolkhoz construction, the specific scope of their work being determined by subcontracting. Inter-kolkhoz construction organizations are to be strengthened in every possible way, and they are to be supplied with machinery, equipment, and necessary materials. Measures are to be carried out for a radical improvement of the designing of agricultural installations and to raise the quality of the designs. Capacities for producing building materials are to be built up in order to provide the ever-growing volume of rural construction.

12   The Central Committee plenum attaches great significance to the further development of scientific research in the area of agriculture, and expanding and strengthening the ties between science and kolkhoz and sovkhoz production ...

13   The CPSU Central Committee Plenum calls the attention of party organizations and all party and state cadres to the need to improve discipline, raise personal responsibility for entrusted matters, and ensure strict observance and execution of Soviet laws. For the toilers of the countryside, the observance of the Law on Land and the new Kolkhoz Rules are of special significance.

The plenum requires that the USSR Ministry of Agriculture, the USSR Ministry of Land Reclamation and Water Resources, the All-Union Farm Machine Agency, the USSR Ministry of Procurements, and their local agencies, party and soviet bodies, and all personnel carry on a decisive struggle against negligence and squandering in the use of land, state and kolkhoz capital, and any displays of localistic or parasitic tendencies. It is necessary to introduce steadily profit-and-loss acounting and to intensify supervision over the financial and business activity of kolkhozes and sovkhozes. An important role in this matter must be played by the trade union and Komsomol organizations, the village soviets, kolkhoz councils, and committees of people's control.

14   The Central Committee plenum emphasizes that the solution of major tasks in the area of agriculture requires great efforts on the part of the party and all party organizations, improvement in their level of organizational and political activity, and extensive development of the socialist competition of the toilers of the city and countryside.

The attention of rural party organizations must be centred on questions pertaining to raising the standards of farming and animal husbandry in kolkhozes and sovkhozes, introducing the achievements of science and advanced practice, making effective use of capital investments, land, machinery, fertilizers and other material, and financial resources, raising labour productivity and, on this basis, providing for a growth in production and the sale of all agricultural products to the state, and the further improvement of life in the countryside.

The party organizations of industrial enterprises and construction sites are called upon to keep the timely fulfilment of agricultural tasks under their steady supervision, to seek out additional reserves and sources for increasing deliveries of machinery, equipment, fertilizers, construction, and other materials to the countryside, and to promote actively the introduction of the latest machinery into agricultural production ...

Pravda, 4 July 1970   *KPSS v rezoliutsiiakh* X, 280–8

5.32
On the Work of the Party Committee of the
Institute of Physics Named for P.N. Lebedev
of the USSR Academy of Sciences*   25 September 1970

The CPSU Central Committee has discussed the report on the work of the party committee of the Institute of Physics named for P.N. Lebedev of the USSR Academy of Sciences (FIAN). The ensuing decision notes that the party organization of the institute, guided by the decisions of the XXIII Party Congress and the plenums of the CPSU Central Committee, is conducting significant organizational and political work with respect to training scientific, engineering, and technical personnel and is directing their efforts to work out fundamental scientific problems of great importance to technological progress in the economy and strengthening the defence capacity of the country ...

The party organization is waging a persistent struggle to enhance the leading role of communists in scientific and public life; it is conducting significant work with respect to the political education of the entire collective of the institute. The majority of scientific workers are studying in the party education network. Methodological seminars, general institute theoretical conferences, and symposia on philosophical problems of the natural sciences in which prominent scientists play a leading role are taking on great significance in marxist-leninist education.

---

*   Excerpt: document not published in full.

At the same time the CPSU Central Committee has noted that there are substantial short-comings in the work of the party committee with respect to training the scientific and engineering intelligentsia. A genuinely creative atmosphere is not created in all laboratories. Quite a number of scientists are working on insignificant themes with no long-range perspective. Some scientists lack a sufficiently developed feeling of responsibility for the results of scientific labour. Proper attention is not paid to the rational deployment of scientific cadres.

The party committee does not sufficiently analyse the state of ideological and political work in the collective of the institute and takes little concern in improving it. In a number of scientific subdivisions the political education network is organized without differentiated consideration for the theoretical training of the staff. In the institute political information does not always satisfy the needs of the collective in its effectiveness and content.

FIAN scholars have not established regular contacts with collectives of workers; they are not sufficiently involved in disseminating and popularizing scientific knowledge; little work is done in the way of advancing and publishing papers on philosophical problems of the natural sciences; the necessary persistence is not displayed in the struggle against the unscientific idealist concepts of bourgeois scientists.

Party meetings have not been fully utilized in the party organization as the most important and tested form of training communists. Open party meetings are seldom held. The party committee fails to attribute the proper attention to consolidating the lower party organizations and party groups.

The party committee does not provide sufficient direction for the activity of the Komsomol organization. Problems pertaining to work with young people are rarely included in the discussion at party meetings and meetings of the party committee and party bureaus of the laboratories and departments. Scientists of the older generation and the leaders of departments and laboratories are not sufficiently drawn into work with young people.

The CPSU Central Committee has ordered the party committee of the Institute of Physics of the USSR Academy of Sciences to do away with the noted short-comings. The work of the party organization is to be directed at further raising the responsibility of communists and all staff members of the institute for high scientific standards of the research that is being conducted and for accelerated scientific and technological progress. The efforts of the institute's collective are to be focused on advancing fundamental research in the most significant areas of physics. FIAN, as the leading physics institute, must take concern for the advancement of new emerging areas of physics in the country. Efforts are to be made to achieve greater effectiveness of scientific research, make use of obtained results in practice, and constantly improve the forms of administering the activity of the collective. Socialist competition for a worthy welcome of the XXIV CPSU Congress is to be developed widely.

The further improvement of ideological and educational work in the collective is considered one of the major tasks of the party organization. The scientific and engineering intelligentsia are to develop a need to study the theory of marxism-leninism and apply it creatively in their scientific and public work. A marxist-leninist understanding of political, social, economic, and philosophical problems of the present time and laws of scientific development are to be propagandized systematically among scientists, and an intolerant attitude to the ideological concepts of anti-communism and revisionism is to be taught.

The CPSU Central Committee has ordered the party committee to take measures to improve its work with respect to the selection, placement, and training of scientific cadres by ensuring a correct combination of scientists of the older generation with young people of science. More young talented scientists are to be promoted to leading scientific work by providing the conditions for their creative growth and drawing them into active scientific, organizational, and public work. The formation of an atmosphere of creative inquiry, good organization, and mutual exactingness and responsibility in the collective are to be promoted more persistently. In the process of their work, scientists are to be trained in the best traditions of the institute and of Soviet science.

The party committee is ordered to improve its guidance over party organizations of laboratories and departments, to strengthen party organizations, and to conduct systematic work on the admission to the party of authoritative scientists and young specialists from the ranks of the Komsomol who have proved themselves in their scientific work and public life. Efforts are to be made to ensure the leading role of communists in science and their active participation in educational work. Reports by communists on their fulfilment of statutory duties and party assignments are to be practised more extensively.

It is recommended that the party committee intensify its guidance over the institute's Komsomol organization, make a more profound study of the needs and mood of young people, and support their useful initiative in every possible way. The best features characteristic of the Soviet intelligentsia are to be instilled in every young scientist: ideological conviction, Soviet patriotism, diligence, and high moral qualities. The role and responsibility of leaders of departments and laboratories and prominent scientists for the ideological and political training of young people is to be enhanced. Young, pioneering communists are to be drawn into the work of the Komsomol organization to a greater extent ...

The Central Committee has expressed confidence that communists and all non-party scientists in one of the largest institutes of the USSR Academy of Sciences will continue in the future to work persistently on the most significant problems in the area of physics, contribute to scientific and technological progress and to the development of the productive forces of our socialist Motherland, and do everything possible to ensure that the Soviet school of physicists occupies a consistent leading position in world physics.

Partiinaia zhizn', no. 21
(1970): 8–10

5.33
On Measures for Further Improving the Work of
Raion and City Soviets of Working People's Deputies*   12 March 1971

The CPSU Central Committee has considered the question of measures for further improving the work of raion and city Soviets of Working People's Deputies.

The decision adopted by the CPSU Central Committee points out that the present period of communist construction places new and higher demands on the activity of raion and city Soviets of Working People's Deputies, which are the key link in the state bodies that ensure practical implementation of party and state policy in the localities.

By carrying out the instructions of the CPSU Programme and the decisions of the XXIII Party Congress, raion and city soviets have appreciably stepped up their activity, improved their work with the masses, and increased attention to questions connected with the communist training of the toilers. The responsibility of soviets for the development of social production, guidance of the local economy, and fulfilment of plans for social and cultural construction has increased. Soviets have begun to devote more attention to questions of the improvement of domestic services for the population and provision of public services and amenities in cities and rural areas.

In the activity of raion and city soviets, democratic principles have received further development. Sessions of soviets have become more significant and the most essential questions pertaining to the life of raions and cities are solved at the sessions. Ties have been consolidated between the deputies and the voters. Greater regularity has been achieved in the reporting of executive committees, their departments and administrations to the soviets and the population.

At the same time, the CPSU Central Committee has noted that raion and city soviets still do not make full use of their rights and opportunities for improving service to the population and for comprehensive development of the economies of raions and cities; they have failed to show due persistence in solving problems of economic construction connected with implementing the economic reform. The soviets do not yet sufficiently co-ordinate the

---

*   Excerpt: document not published in full.

work of enterprises and organizations that are subordinate to different branches of state administration in the area of housing and communal construction, the construction of social, cultural, and everyday facilities, and the production of consumer goods.

A considerable proportion of enterprises in local industry, domestic services, municipal services, trade, and other enterprises and organizations within the territory of raions and cities primarily serve the population of these areas. However, many of these enterprises and organizations are directly subordinated to krai and oblast bodies and to republic ministries and departments. This lowers the responsibility of raion and city soviets for the state of affairs within their territory, ties down their initiative in solving problems of local economic development and improving the provision of the population with services.

Raion soviets in many rural raions are doing a poor job of directing the work of kolkhozes and sovkhozes at making fuller use of reserves to increase the production and amount of field cultivation and animal husbandry products sold to the state, lowering unit costs, and raising labour productivity. In a number of locations, soviets do not show the necessary initiative and persistence in further improving the daily life of agricultural workers and retaining cadres of machine operators and specialists in rural areas. Proper supervision over the financial and economic work of kolkhozes and sovkhozes is not ensured, and the struggle against manifestations of lack of discipline and mismanagement is conducted poorly. The transformation of production administrations into agricultural administrations subordinate to the executive committees of raions and the adoption of new kolkhoz regulations create every condition for a decisive improvement in the work of raion soviets in guiding agriculture and eliminating existing short-comings.

The constant growth of the city population presents ever-higher demands on the work of city soviets in developing housing and the municipal economy. Nevertheless, many city soviets are not directly involved with the maintenance, repair, and organization of most of the state housing space available, approximately two-thirds of which belongs to enterprises, institutions, and organizations.

Housing construction plans, and particularly plans for social and cultural facilities, which are carried out by ministries and departments, are frequently underfulfilled, while city and raion soviets and their executive committees tolerate such a state of affairs and fail to put an end to manifestations of departmental narrow-mindedness in this matter. The practice of pooling by soviets of the resources of industrial enterprises, kolkhozes, sovkhozes, and other organizations allocated for housing, social and cultural, and municipal construction has failed to take sufficient root. At the same time there are incidents where soviet executive committees have made decisions that oblige enterprises, economic organizations, and kolkhozes to bear large non-repayable expenses for local needs, thus evading the legislation in force.

Under the conditions of the rapid development of large cities, the work of raion Soviets of Working People's Deputies within the cities is of great significance. However, in many cities the rights of raion soviets are unjustifiably curtailed, there is no clear dividing line between the competence of raion and city soviets. Raion soviets in cities still fail to exert substantial influence on the solution of problems relating to the organization of daily services, trade, and public catering and do not take part sufficiently in considering questions of importance to the entire city.

There are serious omissions in the organizational work of raion and city soviets. There are quite a few incidents when questions included for consideration by soviets have been discussed superficially, without serious criticism of short-comings. In the practice of raion and city soviets one still comes across elements of formalism; the work of a soviet frequently is evaluated by the number of various types of measures, meetings, and conferences, rather than by results achieved in the economic, social, and cultural fields.

Many soviets exercise insufficient supervision over the observance of legislation, are not conducting a proper struggle with violations of state discipline, and are doing a poor job of raising the responsibility of officials for the duties entrusted to them. Necessary measures are not taken to improve the work of the apparatus of executive committees of soviets, their departments and administrations; the principles of scientific organization of administrative work are introduced slowly.

The CPSU Central Committee decision notes that the overcoming of deficiencies in the work of raion and city soviets and a further improvement in the style and methods of their work are connected with the necessity to improve party guidance over soviet bodies. In the practice of raion and city party committees, there are still many cases of petty tutelage over soviets and of the usurpation of their functions, and party decisions are often made on issues that are totally within the jurisdiction of soviets. Some party committees give instructions to economic managers, disregarding soviets and those soviet bodies to which economic managers are subordinate.

Such a practice does not meet the principles of party guidance over soviets and ties down the initiative of soviet personnel. Individual party committees devote little attention to the questions of selecting, placing, and training of soviet cadres, and they poorly supervise the activity of communists in soviet bodies. In some raion and city soviets, the level of work of party groups is still too low.

The CPSU Central Committee has ordered the central committees of the union republics, and the krai, oblast, okrug, raion, and city party committees to take the necessary measures for further improving the work and enhancing the role of raion and city Soviets of Working People's Deputies which, as the plenipotentiary bodies of state power, are called upon to solve within their territory all problems of local significance, as well as to co-ordinate and supervise within their limits of competence the work of all enterprises and organizations, irrespective of their departmental subordination.

The decision of the Central Committee orders raion and city soviets to ensure the elaboration and carrying out of a complex of specific measures in every raion and city directed at improving the work of local industry, enterprises providing the population's everyday services, schools, hospitals, children's institutions, clubs, cinemas, stores, cafeterias, housing and municipal, repair and construction, and other enterprises, and organizations of raion and city subordination.

It is recognized as necessary that the enterprises, institutions, and organizations that chiefly serve the population of a given raion or city are also to be transferred to raion and city subordination.

Raion and city soviets must devote more attention to questions of the comprehensive development of raion and city economies, to the correct specialization and siting of industrial and agricultural enterprises, as well as to making maximum use of local resources for the expansion of production and raising its effectiveness, to stepping up their work with respect to providing assistance to enterprises and economic organizations in carrying out the principles of the economic reform, and to intensifying supervision over their observance of the requirements of legislation.

With a view to involving enterprises and organizations more actively in the development of raion and city economies and to raising the material interest of local soviets in the results of the work of enterprises and organizations situated within their territory, it is recognized as necessary to ensure that part of the profits of enterprises and economic organizations of republic, krai, and oblast subordination be transferred to the budgets of raions and cities. The USSR Council of Ministers and the councils of ministers of union republics will determine the amounts and procedure for transferring the above-mentioned deductions to the budgets of raions and cities and also will take other necessary measures to reinforce the financial base of raion and city budgets, expand the sources of financing, and increase the means that are left at the disposal of raion and city Soviets of Working People's Deputies.

The CPSU Central Committee has pointed out that one of the most important tasks of raion Soviets of Working People's Deputies is the fulfilment of the broad programme outlined by the party for the accelerated development of agriculture on the basis of an all-round consolidation of its material and technical base, for an improvement in the protection and utilization of land, utilization of machinery, fertilizers and fodder, for an enhancement of the effectiveness of social production in kolkhozes and sovkhozes, for provision of a considerable increase in labour productivity and a reduction in the unit costs of agricultural products, and for introduction of the achievements of science and advanced experience into production. Raion soviets and their executive committees must take an active part in working out plans for the development of agricultural production, ensure supervision over the work of kolkhozes, sovkhozes, and other agricultural enterprises with respect to their meeting plan targets and overfulfilling them in the area of selling grain, meat, milk, and other agricultural products, observing the requirements of legislation, carrying out the rules of kolkhozes and the principles of inner-kolkhoz democracy. The raion soviets must wage a decisive struggle against mismanagement and squandering in the utilization of land, state and kolkhoz resources, and manifestations of localistic and parasitic tendencies.

It is recommended that raion and city soviets step up their activity in co-ordinating the work of all enterprises, institutions, and organizations situated within their territory that are responsible for housing and municipal construction, the construction of social, cultural and everyday facilities, the production of consumer goods and local building materials; they are also to step up their activity in elaborating and carrying out other measures connected with providing services for the population in the raion and city as well as for pooling the resources of enterprises, institutions, and organizations allocated for these purposes. In this, the decision of the Central Committee emphasizes that the creation of good conditions for the labour, daily life, and leisure of the Soviet people is an important social task of the soviets, the fulfilment of which shall promote the further increase of social labour productivity, the retention of cadres in production, and a steady improvement in the communist training of toilers.

With a view to improving the operation and preservation of housing space, provision is made for a further transfer to local soviets of the state housing space available that belongs to enterprises, organizations, and institutions in cities and settlements, as well as facilities of the municipal economy that serve the population of these cities and settlements.* The appropriate state bodies are entrusted with working out conditions and establishing deadlines for the gradual transfer of departmental housing space and facilities of the municipal economy to local soviets, while at the same time consolidating the material, repair, and construction base of the executive committees of the soviets.

Great significance is attributed to intensifying state supervision by soviets over the fulfilment of plans for housing and municipal construction and the construction of social, cultural, and everyday facilities, which is carried out by ministries and departments, as well as supervision over the

---

*   The document in *KPSS v rezoliutsiiakh* ends at this point. The extended version of the document appears in *Pravda*.

quality and balanced nature of construction, over the observance of general city plans for building up other population centres. Attention is directed to the fact that wider practice should be made of the fulfilment by executive committees of the raion and city soviets of responsibilities as initiators of orders regarding these types of construction; supervision is to be improved on the part of soviets over the state of affairs and correct operation of departmental housing space and municipal economy facilities.

It is recommended that the councils of ministers of the union republics take measures to improve the work of raion soviets in cities, grant them broader independence in solving the basic problems of serving the raion population, organizing everyday services, trade and public catering, cultural and enlightenment work, and ensure their active participation in considering and solving questions of importance to cities as a whole.

As the party Central Committee has noted, raion and city Soviets of Working People's Deputies should provide for the further comprehensive improvement of their educational work among the population, keeping in mind that the raising of cultural standards of the people, their educational level, and the molding of the New Man – the active builder of communism – is one of the most significant tasks of the Soviet state.

A great deal of attention is to be devoted to improving the organization of the work of raion and city soviets on the basis of strict observance of the principles of socialist democracy, constant expansion of the participation of the masses in the activity of the soviets, and raising the level of guidance over voluntary bodies. It is pointed out that the significance of the sessions of soviets is to be enhanced further to ensure that every deputy in fact takes an active part in solving pressing problems, and also exposes short-comings boldly and in a principled manner, develops criticism, and introduces suggestions on ways to improve the work of the soviet and its subordinate bodies.

One of the important tasks of soviets is to ensure the further intensification of publicity in their work; efforts are to be made to ensure that the voters and population of every raion and city are constantly informed of the state of all the practical work of the soviet and take an active part in the measures it conducts. With this end in view, it is necessary to ensure regular presentations by leading personnel of executive committees, their departments and administrations, by the chairmen and members of standing committees, and by all deputies before the population, in the press, over radio and television. There must be wider dissemination of the practice of submitting the most important problems of the life of raions and cities for discussion by working people at enterprises, institutions, and organizations as well as at citizens' places of residence. The soviets must attentively study the demands of the population, listen to the suggestions of working people, and take appropriate measures to implement them.

The CPSU Central Committee has pointed out that it is necessary steadily to develop the activity and raise the responsibility of deputies who are the plenipotentiary representatives of the toilers in the bodies of state power. Deputies must make efforts to achieve the fulfilment of instructions from electors, inform them of the state of affairs in their electoral district, of the difficulties that arise in economic and cultural construction and how they are overcome. All state bodies and officials must take an attentive attitude to the proposals of deputies and provide assistance to deputies in every possible way in fulfilling their duties.

It is necessary to raise the responsibility of raion and city soviets for the strictest observance and implementation of Soviet laws, bearing in mind that the consolidation of socialist legality is an integral part of the development of Soviet democracy, of the perfection of the work of state bodies, and of the protection of the rights and interests of citizens. The soviets, their executive committees, standing commissions, and deputies, must be intolerant toward any violation of legislation, fight against bureaucratic manifestations, and strive for the correct and prompt resolution of proposals, applications, and complaints of toilers, and ensure an improvement in legal propaganda.

In the decision of the CPSU Central Committee it is stated that the presidiums of the supreme soviets and the councils of ministers of the union republics are called upon to improve their guidance over the work of local soviets and their executive and administrative bodies. The presidiums of the supreme soviets of union republics must conduct systematic work to enhance the role of soviets in solving questions of state, economic, and cultural construction, make a more profound and comprehensive study of positive experience, generalize and disseminate it, take concern for improving the organizational mass work of local soviets, supervise their observance of the requirements of legislation and democratic principles in their organization and activity. The councils of ministers of the union republics must devote more attention to the work of executive committees of local soviets, their departments and administrations in concrete sectors of economic, social, and cultural construction, perfect the style and methods of work of executive and administrative bodies, offer daily assistance to them in fulfilling economic plans, devote more attention to questions of scientific organization of administrative labour, and ensure consolidation of the material and financial base of executive committees of local soviets.

The decision of the CPSU Central Committee obliges raion and city party committees to show daily concern for enhancing the role and authority of soviets, to support and develop their independence and initiative so that soviets bear full responsibility for the solution of questions that fall within their competence. It is necessary to reinforce soviets with worthy, qualified cadres, to train communists and all personnel of soviet bodies in the spirit of great responsibility for affairs entrusted to them, to strive for their absolute observance of party and state discipline, and to ensure all-round intensification of the influence of party groups in soviets. Raion and city party committees must decisively put an end to incidents of a liberal attitude toward those communists – economic leaders – who disregard the decisions of soviets and evade fulfilment of their assignments.

The CPSU Central Committee has emphasized that, in being guided by leninist principles, party organizations must always bear in mind that the population often judges the entire policy of the Soviet state and its democratic nature by the level of the work of the soviets and that everything that is connected with the soviets and Soviet power has been and will remain the cause of the entire party.

Proposals have been approved on adopting appropriate all-union and republican legislative acts that determine the rights and duties of raion and city Soviets of Working People's Deputies, and raion soviets within the cities, as well as proposals for consolidating the material and financial base of the executive committees of these soviets.

Pravda, 14 March 1971　　　　　　　　　　　*KPSS v rezoliutsiiakh* X, 331–6

XXIV Party Congress　　　　　　　　30 March–9 April 1971

The XXIV CPSU Congress met a year later than planned – a fact which contravened the party Rules, meant that the congress would not coincide with the centenary of Lenin's birth, and meant that it had to be postponed after Brezhnev had announced publicly that it would be held in 1970. These circumstances suggest that there were many unresolved issues among the leadership. The lengthy and unexplained delay in convening the congress indicated that the change in course in industrial management policy debated and announced at the December 1969 Central Committee Plenum had not yet been resolved. The leadership was still split on the shift that was to occur in the direction of discipline, direction, control, and centralization as opposed to a continuation of the course established in 1965 stressing decentralized administration.

The decisions of the congress reflected the continuing impasse and resulted in only incremental changes in the party's approach to economic administration. There were some indications of a tightening of party supervision, such as the announcement of the exchange of party documents, the extension of the rights of control to primary party organizations in a wide range of research and service institutions, and the extension of this same right of control to party organizations in ministries, state committees, and other government departments. However, this obvious strengthening of the party's direct role in administration and management was counterbalanced by the announcement to move ahead more rapidly with the formation of production associations. These forms of industrial organization are intermediate co-ordinative structures that often span the jurisdiction of a number of local party organizations. Consequently, the party had to sacrifice some of its direct political supervision and its own co-ordinative powers for the sake of the economic efficiencies attributed to integrated administrative organization on a level between the ministry and the enterprise.

The balance of power within the Politburo was another issue that caused the delay of the XXIV Congress. The congress was used to announce the expansion of the Politburo by including four new full members, raising its total membership to an unusually large fifteen. The background of the new recruits indicated some advantage for Brezhnev. Three of the four new members (Kulakov, Kunayev, and Shcherbitsky) were known to be close supporters of Brezhnev. In addition, their positions reinforced the relative weight of the party apparatus in the Politburo. A second indicator of the instability of the leadership's relations was the unusual discrepancy between the initial announcement of the Politburo membership on radio, which provided an ordered ranking of the Politburo members, and the follow-up in the press the next day, which provided only an alphabetical ranking. The radio announcement involved an ordered ranking of the members as follows: Brezhnev, Podgorny, Kosygin, Suslov, Kirilenko, Pelshe, Mazurov, Poliansky, Shelest, Voronov, Shelepin, Grishin, Kunayev, Shcherbitsky, and Kulakov. This ranking suggested a number of interesting points. Brezhnev was ranked first. However, Kosygin was dropped to the third position behind Podgorny. Shelepin was dropped to last place among the old Politburo members, maintaining a position only ahead of the four new members. One new member, Kulakov, was elected to his position without previous candidate membership in the Politburo. No new candidate members were elected to replace the three who had been promoted to full membership.

The XXIV Congress was attended by 4740 voting delegates and 223 non-voting delegates who heard major reports from Brezhnev (Central Committee) and Kosygin (Five-Year Plan). The congress elected a Central Committee of 241 full and 155 candidate members.

5.34
On the Report of the Central Committee   9 April 1971

Having heard and discussed the Report by Comrade L.I. Brezhnev, General Secretary of the CPSU Central Committee, on the work of the CPSU Central

Committee, the XXIV Congress of the Communist Party of the Soviet Union resolves:

the political line and practical activity of the cpsu *Central Committee are fully and completely approved;*

the proposals and conclusions contained in the Report of the cpsu *Central Committee are approved.*

The Congress proposes that all party organizations be guided by the provisions of the report in their practical activity.

The XXIV Congress notes with satisfaction that, as a result of the steady and persistent struggle for fulfilment of the cpsu Programme and the tasks set by the XXIII Congress, great successes have been achieved in the building of communism. An important accomplishment of the period under review is that the further development of the economy and the strengthening of the defence capacity of the country have been combined with a considerable growth in the well-being of the working people in the city and the countryside. Socialist social relations and Soviet democracy have developed successfully. The moral and political unity of the workers, kolkhozniks, and intelligentsia, and the fraternal friendship between the peoples of the ussr have become even stronger.

The period under review was marked by a further enhancement of the leading role of the Communist Party in the life of Soviet society. The Soviet people wholeheartedly and unanimously support the party's domestic and foreign policies ...

II

1   In the period under review, the party firmly implemented the XXIII Congress Directives for the development of the country's economy. Much work has been done by the Central Committee to improve guidance of the economy. The Congress takes great satisfaction in noting that, thanks to the selfless labour of the working class, kolkhoz peasantry, intelligentsia, and all working people, a new significant step has been taken in creating the material and technical base of communism, raising the well-being of the people, and increasing the country's power.

The basic targets of the Five-Year Plan for the development of the economy in the years 1966–1970 have been successfully achieved. The scope of the economy has grown significantly and its qualitative indices have improved. A significantly accelerated growth of the national income and productivity of social labour have been reached, the volume of industrial production has increased one-and-a-half-fold, and the rates of growth in the production of the means of production and of consumer goods have drawn closer together, while sectors determining scientific and technological progress in the economy have developed at priority rates.

Significant successes in the advancement of agriculture are an important result of the activity of the party and the people. A substantial increase has been achieved in the production of grain, cotton, meat, milk, and other crop and livestock products. The economy of the kolkhozes and sovkhozes has been strengthened, significant measures have been carried out to supply agricultural production with material and technical facilities and to provide economic incentives.

In the eighth five-year-plan period a broad programme for capital construction was carried out. The country's economic potential has risen significantly; the basic productive assets of the economy have been modernized. All modes of transport and communication have received further development.

Progress has been made in the [territorial] distribution of productive forces; all of the union republics have experienced successful development of their economies.

Favourable conditions have been created for the further expansion of the entire economy of the country.

The past five-year period has been of importance in accomplishing social tasks. Plan targets for the growth of the real incomes of the population, the wages of workers and office employees, and remuneration for kolkhozniks' labour have been overfulfilled. Social consumption funds have grown. Great successes have been achieved in the development of popular education, culture, and health services. The turnover of state and co-operative trade has increased considerably. The majority of workers and office employees have now switched over to a five-day work week with two days off; the minimum vacation time has been lengthened. Housing conditions and communal and everyday services for Soviet people have been improved.

The Congress notes that there have been short-comings along with the major successes in the development of the USSR economy. Plan targets have not been fully reached in the area of commissioning new production capacities, time periods are still too long in building new production facilities and putting them into operation. The planned production level has not been reached for several important categories of industrial and agricultural production, and not all enterprises have utilized existing opportunities to accelerate technical progress, boost labour productivity, improve the quality of products, and reduce costs of production.

Party, soviet, economic, trade union, and Komsomol bodies must take all the necessary measures to do away with the above-mentioned deficiencies and direct the toilers' efforts at achieving a further quick increase in social production, and at successfully fulfilling the XXIV CPSU Congress Directives for the Ninth Five-Year Plan and annual economic plans.

2   The Congress fully approves the tasks set out in the Report for the economic development of the country in the forthcoming period and it instructs the party's Central Committee, all party organizations, and all communists to strive persistently for their fulfilment.

The ninth five-year-plan period must become an important stage in the struggle of the party and the people for the further advancement of Soviet society on the path to communism, in building its material and technical basis, and in strengthening of the country's economic and defence power. The chief task of the five-year period is to provide a significant rise in the material and cultural level of the life of the people on the basis of high rates of development of socialist production, a rise in its effectiveness, scientific and technological progress, and accelerated growth in labour productivity.

The Congress fully approves the projected broad programme of social measures for the ninth five-year-plan period aimed at growth in the well-being of all strata of the population, the growing together of the living standards of the urban and rural population, the creation of more favourable conditions for labour and leisure, for the all-round development of the talents and creative activity of the Soviet people, and for the upbringing of the rising generation.

For these purposes, the Congress views as necessary in the ninth five-year-plan period:

– to raise the real incomes of the population, mainly by effecting a further increase in the payment for labour – the wages and salaries of workers and office employees, and the incomes of kolkhozniks from the communal sector. To increase minimum wage rates and the basic wage and salary rates of middle-bracket earners; to raise zonal allowances in eastern and northern regions of the country;

– to provide for further growth of social consumption funds, channelling the money in these funds into further improvement of the material situation of large families and low-income families, families of women working in production; improvement of public health services, development of the system of education and the upbringing of the rising generation; increases in pensions as well as student stipends;

– to increase significantly the production of manufactured goods and foodstuffs for the population, to improve their quality, widen their assortment, and develop the service industries;

– to expand housing construction and the construction of community, cultural, and everyday facilities, especially in eastern regions; to create the necessary conditions for the labour, leisure, and physical education of working people. To improve the sanitary condition of cities and workers' settlements; to intensify the protection of nature, to use natural resources rationally.

The Congress emphasizes that the continued steady increase of material production, its effectiveness, and the productivity of social labour are an indispensable condition for carrying out the planned measures to enhance the well-being of the Soviet people.

The Communist Party's course to raise the well-being of the people will not only determine the main task of the Ninth Five-Year Plan, but will also determine the general orientation of the long-term economic development of the country. The increased economic potential and the requirements for the development of the economy make possible and necessary a more thorough turn in the economy toward solving the diverse tasks connected with promoting the people's well-being. The Congress considers that our cadres – economic, soviet, trade union, and party – both in the centre and the localities, must display the greatest degree of exactingness and responsibility in all matters concerning the living conditions of the Soviet people.

3   In the ninth five-year-plan period, the Congress views it necessary to ensure high rates of growth and proportional development in all sectors of the economy, to increase considerably the national income – the source of growth of social production and of enhancing the well-being of the people – to improve the distribution of productive forces, to develop the economy of all union republics, and to exploit more rapidly the rich natural resources of the country's eastern regions.

The fundamental task facing industry is to widen and improve the industrial base of the socialist economy, to satisfy more fully the vital needs of the Soviet people. In this connection, it is necessary to provide for changes in the structure of industrial production, to ensure higher rates of development of the production of consumer goods and of those sectors that facilitate the acceleration of technological progress.

In the future, high rates are to be developed in heavy industry – the basis of extended reproduction, technical rearmament of the economy, and the defence capacity of the Soviet state. Heavy industry must significantly increase the output of the means of production to develop agriculture, light industry, and the food and service industries, as well as to increase systematically the production of cultural, everyday, and household goods.

The Congress attaches paramount importance to capital construction and to raising the effectiveness of capital investments. In planning capital construction, it is necessary to secure a concentration of capital investments, to reduce the number of projects under construction at the same time, to co-ordinate construction programmes with available resources and possibilities. It is necessary to shorten construction schedules decisively, to concentrate the basic forces and means on completing projects already started, to give more attention to reconstruction of enterprises and to modernization of production. As previously, the industrial basis of construction also is to be developed.

The further enhancement of the economic effectiveness of the economy must be aided by improving the system of foreign economic, scientific, and technical ties. The Congress attaches great significance to their development.

The Congress directs the attention of party, soviet, and economic bodies to the fact that, under the conditions of a large-scale economy and complicated ties in the economy, the significance of sectors that service the production process, especially transport and communications, increases. The work of these branches needs to be improved so that they more fully satisfy the growing needs of the country; it is also necessary to improve material and technical supplies.

4   One of the most important tasks in the new five-year-plan period is considered to be to increase significantly the production of agricultural products, to ensure fuller satisfaction of the population's growing requirements for foodstuffs, and industry's requirements for raw materials. The Congress approves the broad integrated programme worked out by the CPSU Central Committee for agricultural development, for its comprehensive intensification, and for strengthening its material and technical base.

Particular attention must be paid to boosting grain production and to the further advancement of livestock farming. It is necessary to provide for a general increase in crop yields throughout the country, to strengthen the feed base for animal husbandry and step up its productivity on the basis of accelerated mechanization of agricultural production, expanded chemicalization and land reclamation, as well as improved exploitation of land, machinery, and of all the material and labour resources on kolkhozes and sovkhozes.

In agricultural production, specialization is to be deepened, production is to be concentrated to a greater extent, the system of production and technical service of kolkhozes and sovkhozes is to be improved, and inter-kolkhoz and state-kolkhoz production associations are to be developed. All rural construction is to be improved decisively.

The Congress considers that the upsurge of agriculture is a nationwide issue and calls upon party, soviet, trade union, and Komsomol organizations, on toilers in kolkhozes and sovkhozes and in industry to carry out steadily the party's projected programme of rapid agricultural development.

5   The Congress attaches particular significance to increasing the production of foodstuffs and manufactured goods, expanding public utilities and everyday services to ensure satisfying the growing purchasing power of the population, and considers it necessary to allot larger capital investments for these purposes. In accomplishing this task, state retail prices for consumer goods must remain stable and the prices of some goods must be reduced as more of them are produced and the necessary resources accumulate.

The organization of trade and public catering in cities and rural areas must be improved, customer demand is to be studied constantly, more operational efficiency is to be displayed in utilizing commodity stocks, the production base of trade is to be strengthened, up-to-date service methods are to be utilized, and consumer service standards are to be raised. In accomplishing these tasks, it is important to make use of locally available resources.

6   For the successful implementation of the projected economic and social tasks, the Congress considers it necessary to raise the effectiveness of social production in every way and to make efforts to accelerate labour productivity rates in all branches of the economy.

The task is to improve the structure of the economy, increase production output per unit of fixed capital, increase the return on invested funds, reduce material and labour outlays, and improve the quality of products in every possible way. It is necessary to carry on a decisive struggle against mismanagement, squandering, and extravagance, to improve labour organization, to take measures to improve qualifications and retain cadres, and to utilize every minute of working time productively.

The decisive condition in raising the effectiveness of social production is to accelerate scientific and technological progress. Fundamental scientific research must be expanded, fuller use is to be made of the achievements of science and technology, the re-equipping of all branches of the economy is to be carried out steadily and according to plan on the basis of modern, highly productive machinery, the time period for developing and deploying new machinery and progressive technology is to be reduced in every possible way, and advanced domestic and foreign experience is to be applied more actively.

In accomplishing these tasks, great responsibility rests with USSR Gosplan, the USSR Council of Ministers' State Committee for Science and Technology, the ministries, the USSR Academy of Sciences, and with all scientific-research and design institutions.

The Congress considers that questions regarding the acceleration of scientific and technological progress must constantly be in the focus of attention of the central committees of the communist parties of the union republics, the krai, oblast, city, and raion party committees, party, soviet, economic, trade union, and Komsomol organizations, collectives and enterprises, kolkhozes and sovkhozes.

7   The Congress recognizes that it is necessary to continue the course designed to improve the administration of the economy and to improve planning. It is necessary to improve the scientific grounding and balance of plans, to combine optimal branch and territorial planning, to ensure comprehensive planning and the resolution of major economic problems. The responsibility of cadres for the fulfilment of state plans and assignments is to be enhanced.

Material and moral incentives are to be utilized to a great extent to advance production, accelerate scientific and technological progress, raise labour productivity, and improve the quality of products; economic levers are to be used more efficiently to achieve fuller mobilization of reserves and for the economic development of expedient direct contacts between enterprises. The transfer to the new system of planning and economic incentives for enterprises is to be completed in all branches of material production, research and design organizations, and service sectors, and there is to be steady work on the further development and extension of this system. In this connection, profound tasks face economic science.

It is also necessary to continue to concentrate production by creating production and science-production associations and combines that must become the basic profit-and-loss units in social production in the long run. The structure of the administrative-managerial apparatus is to be improved and superfluous subdivisions in it are to be reduced; organizational techniques and computer technology, automated systems, and scientific methods of administration and planning are to be applied more widely.

At the present stage of communist construction, with its high rates of scientific and technological progress, the Congress considers education in economics to be of paramount significance for all cadres and the broad masses of the working people.

The scope and nature of the economic tasks posed by the party dictate the necessity of seriously raising the level of all economic work. The ever broader involvement of the working people in the management of production remains a central task ...

III

1   The Congress notes that important social changes are taking place in the process of building communism under the conditions created by the development of the scientific-technological revolution and profound shifts in the economics and nature of labour. The level of professional training and skill of workers and peasants are increasing, as well as their levels of education and culture; work and daily living conditions in the city and countryside are gradually drawing together; the intelligentsia, and especially the scientific and technological intelligentsia, is increasing in number. The unity of Soviet society is becoming stronger on the basis of the socialist interests and communist ideals of the working class.

The Congress views an extremely important task of the party's social policy to be the steady translation into reality of the leading role of the working class, the strengthening of the union between the working class and peasantry, and the consolidation of the workers, kolkhozniks, intelligentsia, and all Soviet people in their joint labour.

2   The Congress notes that the recent past is marked by all-round progress and a further drawing together of all nationalities and national groups in our country. The outstanding achievements of the peoples of the USSR are the result of their united labour and of the consistent implementation of the nationality policy of the CPSU. In the process of socialist construction, a new historic community of people has taken shape – that of the Soviet people.

Proceeding from the common interests of the Soviet state, and also considering the conditions of development in each constituent republic, it is necessary in the future to follow without deviation the leninist course for the strengthening of the Union of Soviet Socialist Republics, consistently striving for the further blossoming of all the socialist nations and their gradual drawing together.

The Congress attributes great significance to the upbringing of all the working people in the spirit of Soviet patriotism, pride for their socialist Motherland and for the great achievements of the Soviet people, in the spirit of internationalism, intolerance towards manifestations of nationalism, chauvinism, and national groups.

3   The Congress emphasizes that the struggle to build communism is inseparable from the all-round development of socialist democracy, the strengthening of the Soviet state, and improving the entire system of the political organization of society.

As a result of measures taken by the party, the Soviets of Working People's Deputies have become more active and diversified, their supervision over the state of affairs in basic sectors of economic and cultural construction has intensified. The Congress considers that the soviets must exercise their functions more fully and exert effective influence on the development of the economy and culture and on the enhancement of the people's welfare and that they must be more persistent in dealing with questions of the social and everyday services of the population and the preservation of public order. The principle of accountability of executive organs to representative organs is to be put into practice more consistently, the authority and activity of deputies is to be raised, as is their responsibility to the voters. With these ends in view, the Congress considers it expedient to define legislatively the status, authority, and rights of soviet deputies at all levels, as well as the obligations of officials in relation to deputies.

An important task is to improve accuracy, co-ordination, and culture in the work of the state apparatus and of all administrative organs. In every institution an attitude of consideration must be developed to the needs and concerns of the working people and there must be goodwill and respect for man. It is necessary to continue to strengthen socialist legality and to improve the work of the militia, procurator's office, and courts. Party organizations, trade unions, and the Komsomol must strive for the strictest observance of the law by all citizens and officials, and for a rise in the level of the legal upbringing of the working people. The work of people's control must be improved, and care must be taken that the leninist ideas on constant and effective supervision by the broad masses are steadily put into practice.

While noting the great significance of the trade unions as the most massive organization of the working people, the Congress views it necessary to continue to improve their work in the future. The party will continue to see to it that the trade unions successfully fulfil their role as a school of communism. The trade unions are called upon to intensify their work in further developing the country's economy, still more actively involve working people in production management and the administration of social affairs, improve the organization of socialist competition, and instil a communist attitude to labour. One of the fundamental tasks of the trade unions is concern for the legitimate interests of the workers and of all working people, concern for improving their work and everyday living conditions, strengthening supervision over the observance of labour legislation, the rules and standards of labour protection and safety measures, and concern over improved organization of the cultural and health recreation of the working people.

Under present conditions, the role and significance of the Komsomol are growing ever greater as the reserve and closest assistant of the party in the communist upbringing of the rising generation and the building of a new society. The central task of the Komsomol is to socialize young people in the spirit of communist ideological conviction, Soviet patriotism, internationalism, efficient organization, and discipline, to conduct active propaganda of the achievements and advantages of the socialist system among young people, and to see that every young person becomes an active builder of the new society. The Komsomol must better utilize the opportunities provided to it for involving young men and women in extensive participation in public life and in state, economic, and cultural construction. The party nucleus in Komsomol organizations must continue to be strengthened in the future.

4   The Congress notes with satisfaction that the party and its Central Committee are constantly maintaining at the centre of their attention questions of military construction and strengthening the power and combat efficiency of the Soviet Armed Forces. The comprehensive enhancement of the defence might of our Motherland and education of the Soviet people in the spirit of great vigilance and constant readiness to defend the great achievements of socialism must continue in the future to be one of the most important tasks of the party and the people.

5   The Congress notes that, during the period under review, party organizations have conducted constant work in educating the Soviet people in the spirit of communist consciousness.

The Congress emphasizes that the formation of the working people's marxist-leninist outlook and of their high ideological and political qualities and norms of communist morality will continue to be the central task of the ideological work of party organizations.

The main emphasis in the ideological work of the party is propaganda of the ideas of marxism and leninism and an uncompromising offensive struggle against bourgeois and revisionist ideology.

One of the most important components of ideological and political work is the moulding of a communist attitude to labour and public property, the development of the creative activity of the working people, and the strengthening of conscious discipline and organization.

An object of constant attention for the party, trade union, and Komsomol organizations must be the development of socialist competition of the working people as an effective method for economic construction and for strengthening socialist relations among people. While improving the forms of material incentives, it is necessary to enhance the significance of moral incentives in every possible way, to surround exemplary workers with honour and glory, and to disseminate their valuable experience.

Labour production collectives play an important role in social and political life and in the communist education of the working people. The collective's concern for each worker, its attention to his needs, mutual assistance and exactingness – these are all inherent features in our way of life that need to be strengthened and developed. Public opinion is to be directed more resolutely to the struggle against violations of labour discipline, money-grubbing, parasitism, embezzlement, bribery, and drunkenness. It is necessary to continue to struggle against all survivals of the past in the people's minds and deeds. This requires the constant attention of the party and of all our society's politically conscious forces.

6   The Congress views as an important task the further improvement of the entire system of education in accordance with the requirements of the development of the economy, science, and culture, and the scientific-technological revolution.

In the new five-year-plan period, the complete transfer of young people to universal secondary education is to be ensured, measures are to be taken for a further expansion of the material basis of schools providing general education, the quality of teaching is to be raised, and pupils are to be prepared more actively and purposefully for socially useful labour.

It is necessary to continue to develop vocational-technical education, and to expand in every possible way the network of vocation-technical schools that provide secondary education.

In the area of higher and secondary specialized education, it is necessary to expand the training of cadres in new and promising fields of science and technology, to arm better young specialists with modern knowledge, with the experience of organizational, social, and political work, and with the ability to apply acquired knowledge in practice.

The entire business of the education and upbringing of young people must serve the purpose of moulding in the rising generation communist convictions and morality, and boundless devotion to the socialist Motherland.

7   The Congress emphasizes that one of the main factors in the successful accomplishment of the tasks of building communism is the development of Soviet science. While extending scientific research on a broad front, it is necessary to concentrate the efforts of scientists on solving the most important problems, to strengthen the connection between science and the practice of communist construction, and to accelerate the application of its achievements in the economy. It is necessary to enhance in every possible way the effectiveness of the work of institutes, departments, and laboratories, to strive for a genuinely creative situation, an atmosphere of fruitful discussion, and mutual exactingness of scientists in every scientific collective.

Interaction among scientists working in the fields of natural, technical, and social sciences must be strengthened.

8   The Congress notes the growing role of literature and art in the creation of the spiritual wealth of socialist society. The Soviet people are interested in the creation of such works in which reality is correctly reflected and communist ideas are affirmed with great artistic force. Party policy in questions of literature and art proceeds from the leninist principles of party spirit and kinship with the people. The party stands for a variety and wealth of forms and styles elaborated on the basis of socialist realism. It greatly values the talent of the artist, the communist ideological direction of his creativity, and intolerance to anything that impedes our progress. It is necessary that our literary and art criticism actively pursue the party line, take a strong principled stand, combining high standards with tact and regard for the creators of artistic values.

The Congress considers that unions of writers, cinematographers, artists, composers, theatrical workers, and architects be called upon to show daily attention to the creative problems of developing literature and art, to raise the ideological and theoretical level and professional skill of their members, to cultivate a strong sense of responsibility in literary and artistic people for their work before society, and to strengthen in all possible ways co-operation between creative workers and production collectives.

9   The Congress emphasizes the growing significance of the party's propaganda and mass agitation work. The task is to do away with all existing short-comings in this area, to make propaganda of communist ideals and of the specific tasks of our construction more active and purposeful. In the immediate future, one of the central tasks of party ideological work must be to give the working people a profound explanation of the decisions and materials of the XXIV CPSU Congress.

The Congress attributes great significance to further improvement in the work of the press, radio, and television. Party organizations must make skilful use of the media of mass information and propaganda, must show concern for the effectiveness and efficiency of their work and for raising the political maturity and skill of journalist and propaganda cadres.

IV

1   In summing up the path that has been covered and defining the tasks for the future, the Congress takes satisfaction in noting that, under the leadership of the Central Committee, the party firmly follows a leninist course and honourably fulfils its role as the political leader of the working class, the working people, and of the entire Soviet people.

Practice has fully confirmed the correctness and vital force of the positions of the XXIII Congress on the main issues of party construction. Through their consistent implementation, the party has further strengthened its ranks, enhanced its influence in all sectors of communist construction, and consolidated its ties with the masses. Recent reports and elections in the party have shown with new force that the CPSU has come to the XXIV Congress as a monolithic party, closely rallied around its Central Committee and enriched with new experience in political and organizational work.

The Congress emphasizes that the successful implementation of the political line and concrete programme of work for the next five-year period will require the mobilization of all the strength of the party and the people. It is necessary to continue in the future to enhance the leading role of the party in every possible way and to strive for the further consolidation of the unity of views and actions of all communists and of all Soviet people.

2   The period under review is characterized by a further growth in party ranks and an improvement in its qualitative composition. Party organizations are consistently carrying out the XXIII Congress' instructions providing for working class predominance in the social structure of the party. More than half of the new members admitted into the party are workers. We should continue to be guided by this situation in the future as well; it fully corresponds to the nature of our party and to the place and role of the working class in Soviet society.

The improvement of the qualitative composition of the party's ranks and the education of communists must remain one of the party's most important tasks. It is necessary to continue to reinforce the party's ranks with worthy representatives of the working class, kolkhoz peasantry, and intelligentsia on the basis of strict individual selection.

3   The Congress notes that the Central Committee is consistently pursuing a course for the further development of inner-party democracy, observance of leninist norms of party life, and intensification of the activity of communists. In the party, election and accountability of leading organs and the principle of collective leadership are consistently being realized. Questions of the party's activity are discussed and decided on a wide democratic basis. Party committees have become more attentive to critical comments

and suggestions of communists and have intensified supervision over their implementation. The responsibility of communists has grown for the state of affairs in their organizations and in the party as a whole.

The Congress emphasizes that steadfast observance of the leninist principle of democratic centralism must in the future continue to be the immutable law of party life, as the decisive condition of its strength and ability to act. In every party organization, active participation of all communists must be ensured in discussing, elaborating, and carrying out party decisions; principled criticism and self-criticism, that tested method of removing short-comings and improving work, must be advanced. It is necessary to continue to improve inner-party information, to use it more fully as an important instrument of leadership and as a means of upbringing and control.

The strength of the CPSU lies in the high ideological conviction, activity, and dedication of its members; the party will not tolerate passivity, indifference, and political apathy. Every communist must be a conscious political fighter and always and everywhere carry the lofty title of member of the leninist party with dignity. In developing the activeness of communists, it is necessary to enhance their responsibility for the fulfilment of the requirements of the Programme and Rules of the CPSU, hold strictly responsible those who discredit the lofty title of party member by their deeds and violate party and state discipline. The Committee on Party Control of the CPSU Central Committee and party commissions of local party organs are called upon to play a serious role here.

Considering that the term of validity of party membership cards has expired, the Congress commissions the Central Committee to conduct an exchange of party documents, subordinating this important organizational-political measure to the tasks of further strengthening the party and raising the activeness and discipline of communists.

4   The Congress considers it necessary to improve party leadership over all sectors of communist construction and to raise the level of organizational and political work among the masses.

In accordance with the established practice of planning the economy for five-year periods, it is recognized as expedient to convene regular congresses of the CPSU and congresses of the union republic communist parties once every five years. It is established that krai, oblast, okrug, city, and raion party conferences, and report-and-election meetings and conferences in primary party organizations that have a party committee, are to be held twice in the five-year period between congresses.

In the interests of further enhancing the role of party organizations in the implementation of party policy, the Congress finds it necessary to grant the primary party organizations at scientific-research institutes, educational institutions, and cultural and medical institutions the same right as those of primary party organizations in production regarding supervision over the activity of the administration. In view of their specific character, party organizations of central and local soviet and economic institutions and departments must increase their supervision over the activity of the apparatus in fulfilling party and government directives.

5   The Congress notes that raising the level of leadership over all aspects of society's life and raising the level of organizational and political work among the masses is inseparably linked with improvement in the selection, placement, and upbringing of cadres. The party attributes paramount significance to a situation where all sectors of party, state, economic, cultural-upbringing and public work are headed by politically mature, knowledgeable, capable organizers. The great and complex tasks that confront the party and the country urgently require that leading cadres thoroughly master contemporary techniques of administration, possess a feeling for the new, see long-range prospects for development, are capable of finding the most effective ways to solve problems as they arise and applying the knowledge and experience of others. Party policy on cadres must in the future continue to be directed towards combining the promotion of young promising functionaries with regard for veteran cadres and the utmost use of their experience and knowledge.

The Congress considers that the trust and respect for personnel, which has been firmly established in recent years and combined with principled exactingness towards them, must continue to permeate all work with cadres. It is necessary to increase the responsibility of cadres for work assigned and to take necessary measures against those who violate discipline, draw no conclusions from criticism, or behave incorrectly. Every functionary must remember that socialist discipline is uniform and obligatory for all.

While positively evaluating the work that has been done in recent years in creating a system to train and retrain leading cadres, the Congress views improvement of this system as necessary. To keep abreast of life, all our cadres must constantly study, raise their ideological and theoretical level, and master the achievements of science and advanced practice.

6   The Congress notes that the period under review is characterized by an activation of the ideological and theoretical activity of the party and an improvement in marxist-leninist upbringing of communists.

Profound generalizations of experience in building socialism and communism and of the experience of the world revolutionary movement are presented in the decisions of Central Committee plenums and party documents in commemoration of the 50th anniversary of the Great October Socialist Revolution, the 100th anniversary of V.I. Lenin's birth, and the 150th anniversaries of the birth of Marx and Engels.

The party's theoretical thought has been enriched with new conclusions and propositions on important issues such as ways of creating the material-technical basis of communism, raising the effectiveness of production, forms of management of the economy, and agrarian policy. Together with the fraternal parties, fundamental problems of developing the world system of socialism were elaborated and new phenomena in the development of contemporary capitalism have been studied.

Much attention has been allotted to the development of teaching on the party and on its leading role in the building of socialism and communism. The CPSU has waged an offensive struggle against anti-communist ideology and various bourgeois and revisionist conceptions.

The vigorous theoretical activity of the party has facilitated the further consolidation of the ideological unity of our society and the growth of the authority of marxism-leninism on the international scene.

The Congress considers that the creative development and propaganda of marxist-leninist teaching, the struggle against attempts to revise it, must in the future remain at the centre of attention of the party's ideological work. The party's theoretical forces must be directed to further elaboration of pressing problems of contemporary social development and, first of all, problems of communist construction.

The Congress instructs party organizations to increase attention to the marxist-leninist education of communists, to the training of cadres on the basis of profound mastery of marxism-leninism, and the views elaborated by the party on the fundamental problems of our time. It is necessary to continue to improve the existing system of party study, to overcome decisively elements of formalism in party study, consistently striving to increase its influence on the growth of the political consciousness and activeness of communists.

Party organizations must show constant concern for propaganda cadres and create the best conditions for their effective activity ...

5.35
On Partial Changes in the Rules of the CPSU
[Revises Rules adopted 1961; see 4.34]   9 April 1971

The XXIV Congress of the Communist Party of the Soviet Union resolves:
1   [Revises 4.34, art. 31, 44, 57] To establish that:

a regular congresses of the Communist Party of the Soviet Union are convened by the Central Committee at least once every five years;

b regular congresses of the communist parties of the union republics are convened by the central committees of the communist parties at least once every five years;

c regular krai, oblast, okrug, city, and raion party conferences are convened by corresponding party committees twice in the five-year period between congresses of the CPSU, i.e. once every two-to-three years;

d report-and-election meetings (conferences) in primary party organizations that have party committees are conducted once every two-to-three years in accordance with the schedules for holding raion and city party conferences. For all other primary party organizations, as well as for shop party organizations, report-and-election meetings are conducted annually.

2   [Revises 4.34, art. 53, 57, 59] For the purpose of further increasing the responsibility and activeness of primary party organizations in implementing party policy and raising the level of their organizational and upbringing work in working people's collectives:

a   to extend the provision in the CPSU Rules on the right to supervise the activity of the administration to the primary party organizations of all design organizations, design bureaus, scientific-research institutes, educational institutions, cultural-enlightenment, medical, and other institutions and organizations whose administrative functions do not extend beyond their collectives.

With regard to party organizations of ministries, state committees, and other central and local soviet and economic institutions and departments, it is determined that they exercise supervision over the work of the apparatus in implementing party and government directives and in the observance of Soviet laws.

b   to establish that, when necessary and with the permission of an oblast or krai committee or the central committee of the communist party of a union republic, primary party organizations may be created in the framework of several enterprises that constitute an industrial association and are located, as a rule, on the territory of one raion or several raions of one city.

c   to allow oblast and krai committees and the central committees of union republics to form, in individual cases, within party organizations numbering over 500 communists, party committees at large shops, and to grant the rights of primary party organizations to production sections of the primary party organization ...

Pravda, 10 April 1971

KPSS v rezoliutsiiakh X, 342–64, 432–3

5.36
On Measures to Improve the System of
Courses for Training and Retraining
Leading Party and Soviet Cadres*   10 August 1971

... In accordance with the instructions of the XXIV CPSU Congress on improving the system of courses for retraining leading party and soviet

---

*   Excerpt: document not published in full.

cadres, the CPSU Central Committee has resolved to base the work of regularly operating courses for the study of current problems of marxist-leninist theory and the policy of the CPSU on a close connection with the practice of communist construction and the tasks posed by the Congress. It has been proposed that familiarization of students with the fundamentals of scientific management of the economy and the latest achievements in science, technology, and culture be organized. For this purpose, it has been recommended that studies be conducted directly at leading enterprises, kolkhozes, sovkhozes, scientific-research institutions, and organizations.

The length of the courses at the Higher Party School of the CPSU Central Committee has been established at forty days; at other courses it is to be up to one month.

The CPSU Central Committee has approved the curriculum of the courses and a model plan of lectures and seminars. The central committees of the union republic communist parties and the krai and oblast party committees are permitted to introduce necessary changes in the curriculum in consideration of the student constituency. The rector's office of the Higher Party School of the CPSU Central Committee is instructed to work out the curriculum for courses by 1 October.

The CPSU Central Committee has recommended that the central committees of the union republic communist parties and the krai and oblast party committees determine the organizations, institutions, enterprises, kolkhozes, and sovkhozes where students are to study the advanced experience and practice of party and soviet work. Measures are to be taken to improve the staff of lecturers and seminar leaders by using leading party and soviet personnel, prominent scientists, and the best qualified teachers of higher educational institutions.

The CPSU Central Committee has considered it necessary that secretaries of the central committees of the union republic communist parties and of the krai and oblast party committees, leading personnel of the councils of ministers of the republics and of the oblast (or krai) executive committees, and leaders of central and republican institutions and organizations, ministries and their departments regularly address the courses on questions of the theory and practice of party and soviet construction and their experience in guidance over the economy and culture.

Co-ordination of all the educational and methodological work in the system of courses for retraining party and soviet cadres is entrusted to the Higher Party School of the CPSU Central Committee. For these purposes, an educational and methodological council is to be created on the base of the Higher Party School of the CPSU Central Committee from the staff of course leaders, party personnel, and experienced teachers. The inter-oblast and republican higher party schools are responsible for the methodological guidance of local courses within their zones.

The CPSU Central Committee has approved the schedule for the courses at the Higher Party School of the CPSU Central Committee for the year 1971/72. It has been recommended that the central committees of the union republic communist parties and the krai and oblast party committees work out plans for retraining cadres at local courses; the structuring of courses is to be carried out with consideration for the students' profile. Party and soviet personnel must be acquainted with the dates of study of the courses and the curricula and subject-matter of the seminars so that they can prepare for the studies in good time and work out the appropriate reports and materials.

It has been recognized as necessary to organize planned work to improve the qualifications of staff teachers in the courses. The rector's office of the Higher Party School of the CPSU Central Committee and the directors of higher party schools are to conduct regular seminars and consultations for teachers on the most significant themes of the curriculum, especially on questions of the scientific management of the economy and party and soviet construction.

It has been recommended that the central committees of the union republic communist parties and the krai and oblast party committees make fuller use for the retraining courses of the educational base of houses of political enlightenment and their accumulated experience of scientific and methodological work.

The CPSU Central Committee has entrusted the Higher Party School of the CPSU Central Committee with responsibility for training, while responsibility for publication of educational and methodological materials and visual aids for the course curriculum is assigned to the Press Committee of the USSR Council of Ministers and Politizdat ...

Partiinaia zhizn', no. 18
(1971): 9–14

5.37
On Further Improving the Organization
of Socialist Competition   31 August 1971

... The CPSU Central Committee resolves:
1   Further development of the initiative and creative activeness of the masses and deployment of nation-wide socialist competition for the success-ful implementation of the decisions of the XXIV CPSU Congress and ful-filment of economic plans and assignments are considered to be extremely important tasks for party, soviet, trade union, and Komsomol organizations and economic leaders.

Under the conditions of the scientific-technological revolution, socialist competition is called upon to play a qualitatively new role in the development of the economy and the upbringing of the working people. The main direction of socialist competition must be mobilization of the working people for the utmost increase in labour productivity and the effectiveness of social production – a reduction in labour outlays, rational utilization and savings of resources, raw materials, and supplies, improvement in the quality of products, better use of production assets and capital investments. It is necessary to support the initiative of collectives in every way in increasing the output of high-quality industrial and agricultural products and durable consumer goods in accordance with the requirements of the economy and the growing demand of the population.

The CPSU Central Committee emphasizes the necessity of raising, in every possible way, the activeness of the working people in accelerating scientific and technological progress. Persistent efforts need to be made to establish an atmosphere of mass creativity and intolerance toward technical and scientific conservatism and stagnation. Competition must facilitate an improvement in the scientific organization of labour as an indispensable condition for the creation of a genuinely creative spirit of struggle for high work indicators.

The efforts of personnel in industrial enterprises, transport and construction, scientific research, design and drafting organizations must be directed at reducing the time necessary for developing and introducing new machinery and advanced technology, as well as at effective reconstruction of operating enterprises, acceleration of the designing and commissioning of new production capacities, comprehensive rationalization of production and its integrated mechanization and automation, modernization of equipment, improvement of the organization of labour, production, and management, and the ensuring of precise, well-ordered and rhythmic work at enterprises.

Agricultural workers must persistently struggle for an increase in production and a reduction in the unit costs of output, an increase in the yield capacity of agricultural crops and the productivity of animal husbandry, an improvement in the quality of products, an increase in the production and procurement of fodder, a strengthening of the material and technical base of kolkhozes and sovkhozes, an acceleration of the rates of electrification and chemicalization of production and land reclamation, and improved use of machinery and labour resources.

In the area of services, socialist competition must be directed at the transformation of services into an industrial branch of the economy, at raising the standards of service to the population, and at providing the fullest satisfaction of the requirements of the Soviet people.

2   The CPSU Central Committee orders party, soviet, trade union, Komsomol, and economic bodies steadily to develop democratic principles of

socialist competition as a creative affair of the working people themselves, decisively to do away with elements of formalism and bureaucratic distortions in the practice of organizing and guiding competition, to enhance in every possible way the role of labour collectives in solving questions of competition, steadily to carry into effect the leninist principles of its organization: publicity, comparability of results, and the opportunity of repeating practical experience. In developing competition, it is important to apply incentives correctly and it is especially necessary to pay more attention to moral incentives that are increasingly becoming the major force for our progress in conditions of communist construction.

It is necessary to use socialist competition in full measure for intensifying the people's education in the spirit of a communist attitude to labour and public property, for further developing initiative, increasing the production and social activeness of workers, kolkhozniks, and employees, for drawing the working people into production management to a greater extent, for instilling high moral qualities, and for strengthening relations of co-operation and comradely mutual assistance, discipline, and good organization.

Love for one's collective, a feeling of responsibility for the honour of the trademark of one's factory and of one's professional pride are to be instilled in every working person ...

3   ... There is to be wider dissemination of the development of individual and collective creative plans, competition by professions, the movement for workers to operate several machines siimultaneously, patronage of experienced workers and kolkhozniks over young workers, skill contests, public reviews of production reserves, and personal records of what one has economized. Contract principles in socialist competition are to be developed in every possible way; competition is to be expanded among workers, kolkhozniks, brigades, collectives of similar and closely related enterprises connected through co-operative deliveries, among construction, installation, and transport organizations, industrial associations and firms, as well as among scientific research, drafting, and design organizations; a differentiated approach is to be taken towards organizing competition among various categories of working people.

The practice of working out and adopting socialist pledges is to be improved. Socialist pledges of collectives must be formed by proceeding from the goals and tasks that confront enterprises and branches during a given plan period for production development, and they must include the individual pledges and proposals of workers, kolkhozniks, engineering and technical personnel and employees, reflect their initiative and experience, and induce the working people to work creatively and make the best use of available reserves and opportunities. There is to be condemnation of the practice whereby individual leaders of enterprises, ministries, and departments conceal considerable reserves and potentials, fail to include them in plans, and subsequently take on higher pledges; this practice creates definite difficulties in planning and in material and technical supply, and leads to adverse consequences in the people's upbringing. When comparing competition results of various collectives, it is necessary above all to consider the intensity of the adopted and fulfilled plans, as well as the level of production outlays.

4   The CPSU Central Committee draws the attention of party, trade union and soviet bodies, ministries and departments to the necessity of enhancing the role and responsibility of economic leaders, engineering and technical personnel, and agricultural specialists for organizing socialist competition.

Economic leaders must create the necessary organizational, technical, and economic conditions for highly productive labour, conditions that allow for every working person to fulfil his adopted pledges and to show his abilities to the fullest. It is important to notice in time and support everything new that is engendered by the creative work of the masses, to take effective measures for dissemination of the achievements of the advanced and best collectives, and constantly to take concern in raising the level of professional training of workers, kolkhozniks, and employees.

Engineers, technicians, and economists at enterprises, and specialists in kolkhozes and sovkhozes are called upon to take an active part in procuring and using production reserves, providing technical and economic substantiation of pledges taken by participants in competition, improving the organization of every workplace, facilitating development of the technical creativity of workers and kolkhozniks in every possible way, as well as in introducing their proposals in production and fulfilling socialist pledges. They must direct their efforts at the technical improvement of production, at studying and introducing all that is advanced in the area of machinery and technology, and labour and production organization in both domestic and foreign practice, as well as developing and carrying out measures for improving all economic indices of the work of industrial enterprises, kolkhozes, and sovkhozes.

5   The central committees of the union republic communist parties, the krai, oblast, city, and raion party committees, and the primary party organizations are to ensure the communists' vanguard role in socialist competition, to make fuller use of the right to control the activity of the administration in improving the organization of competition, to direct it at developing the many forms of political work in the masses, and to enhance the role of the trade unions in organizing and guiding socialist competition.

The trade unions are called upon to develop the creative activeness of the working people, to improve and enrich the forms and methods of socialist competition, and to raise its effectiveness. Questions concerning the organization of competition, the movement for a communist attitude to labour, the dissemination of advanced experience, scientific, technical, and economic knowledge, the development of rationalization and innovative activity among the working people, and improvement in the work of scientific and technical societies must be at the centre of attention of every trade union organization and must be discussed systematically at meetings of workers and kolkhozniks.

A most important task of the Komsomol, together with the trade unions, is to draw the broad masses of young people, especially Komsomol members, into the competition and the movement for a communist attitude to labour, to raise the creative activeness of young men and women, to instil in them a love for labour and a zealous attitude to public property, to enhance the role of young workers, kolkhozniks, and specialists in accelerating technological progress and introducing the scientific organization of labour, to develop the aspirations of young people to master economic knowledge, improve professional skill, master modern machines and mechanisms, and to improve the patronage of Komsomol organizations over shock construction sites, animal husbandry, enterprises of the light and food industry, trade, and the sphere of services ...

Pravda, 5 September 1971   *KPSS v rezoliutsiiakh* x, 488–97

5.38
On Improving the Economic Education
of the Working People   31 August 1971

At the present stage of communist construction, with its high rates of scientific and technological progress and qualitative changes in the economics of production and nature of labour, there is a steady growth in the requirements made on economic education for cadres and the broad masses of the working people. Training in economics is an important condition for raising the scientific level of management, raising the initiative and activeness of the working people in managing production, and implementing the programme for the development of the economy outlined by the XXIV CPSU Congress.

Party, trade union, and state bodies have devoted more attention to economic education in recent years. Many leading personnel, specialists in the economy, workers, kolkhozniks, and employees are mastering economic knowledge in various systems to improve production qualifications; about 14 million people are studying in the party education system, schools for communist labour, and people's universities. The admission of students in economics specialization has more than doubled in higher and secondary specialized educational institutions. Fuller coverage is being given to the problems and experience of socialist management by the press, radio, and television.

At the same time, the scope and content of economic study do not yet meet the requirements of the XXIV CPSU Congress.

Some leading personnel in ministries and departments, enterprises, sovkhozes and kolkhozes, and especially the heads of shops and departments, foremen, brigade and link leaders do not possess sufficient skills in economic analysis of managerial activity and they cannot always substantiate decisions that have been taken and evaluate work results from the positions of the economic effectiveness of production.

Higher schools still fail to satisfy the requirements of the economy for economists with a profound knowledge of production economics, as well as of the scientific organization of labour and management, and who have mastered to perfection contemporary computer technology and methods and can apply them in economic calculations.

Many workers, employees and kolkhozniks are not involved in studies in economics and are poorly informed of the state of affairs in the shop, enterprise, branch of economy, or the economy as a whole. Propaganda of the economic theory and policy of the CPSU is often divorced from the concrete tasks of production development, while on many occasions a one-sided interest is taken in the organizational and technical side of the activity of labour collectives without delving into the social and political experience of management. Not all personnel have developed a state approach to accomplishing production tasks or a feeling of responsibility for the fulfilment of plans and pledges, as well as intolerance to mismanagement and violations of labour discipline ...

The underestimation of economic education adversely affects the level of management and administration, as well as the effectiveness of social production and the state of the toilers' economic education.

Attaching great significance to the economic education and training of cadres and the broad toiling masses in the development of their creative activeness to implement the decisions of the XXIV Party Congress, the CPSU Central Committee resolves:

1   The central committees of the union republic communist parties, the krai and oblast party committees, the All-Union Central Trade Union Council, the Central Committee of the All-Union Leninist Communist Youth League, the ministries and their departments, party organizations and leaders of enterprises, associations and kolkhozes are ordered to take measures for the radical improvement of the economic education of cadres, engineers, technicians, and specialists in all branches of the economy, and the broad masses of the workers and kolkhozniks.

Study of the party's economic policy worked out at the XXIV Congress, of the laws governing the economic development of society, of leninist

principles and methods of management, and of the economics and organization of production will lay the basis for economic education.

Economic education of the working people must be closely tied to the
organization of all economic work at enterprises, in associations, in sovkhozes
and kolkhozes and it must facilitate a rise in the level of management and the
successful fulfilment of the targets of the ninth five-year-plan period. It is
necessary to subordinate economic studies to the development of the creative activeness of the working people in the struggle for a further increase in
production efficiency and to instilling in every worker a communist attitude
to labour and socialist property. It is necessary to ensure the combination of
economics instruction with the application of acquired knowledge in practice
and the extensive involvement of all working people in solving questions of
the economic life of labour collectives. It is necessary to view training in
economics as a mandatory, important aspect of the qualifications of every
worker.

2   Party, trade union, Komsomol, state, and economic bodies are obliged
to ensure a high level of content in the economic education of:
–   managerial cadres and specialists in the economy – in the area of
marxist-leninist economic theory and the economic policy of the party, the
contemporary science and practice of production management, and improving the methods of training and organizing people;
–   workers, employees and kolkhozniks – on questions of the party's economic policy, the fundamentals of economic knowledge and the scientific
organization of labour and production, and the practice of economic activity
at enterprises and kolkhozes ...

Pravda, 16 September 1971   *KPSS v rezoliutsiiakh* X, 498–505

5.39
On Literary and Art Criticism   21 January 1972

The publication of the Central Committtee's Resolution, 'On Literary and Art
Criticism,' signaled the beginning of a campaign to tighten the limits of socialist
realism. The immediate purpose of the resolution was to mobilize literary criticism more effectively as a means for shaping and directing literary activity.
Articles and editorials followed, calling for greater party involvement in educating, selecting, and placing cadres and heightening their ideological awareness,
ensuring that critical works were aimed at a mass audience, and publicizing
Russian literature abroad. A plenary session of the Board of the USSR Writers'
Union, held in early 1972 (*Current Digest of the Soviet Press* XXIV, no. 4, 3–6),
provided the public forum for elaborating the directions of criticism and gener-

alizing them for other creative media. Among the changes urged for all creative arts were: an end to the tendency toward 'deheroization,' especially in the areas of labour achievements and military feats; portrayal of the positive hero in a non-stereotyped fashion; more attention to class content and to the social context of writing, especially social processes and social relations associated with the scientific-technological revolution; less 'poeticizing' of traditional qualities, fewer religious images and more emphasis on the formation of new socialist qualities; more emphasis on revolutionary-democratic traditions and socialist thought; intensification of the struggle against alien ideological and aesthetic concepts. One of the concrete results of the resolution was the publication, beginning in 1973, of two new journals devoted exclusively to literary criticism, *Literaturnoe obozrenie* (*Literary Review*) and *V mire knig* (*In the World of Books*).

The CPSU Central Committee notes that party committees, cultural institutions, unions of creative artists and press organs are directing their active efforts toward fulfilling the instructions of the XXIV CPSU Congress on raising the level of literary and art criticism. The tasks of criticism are discussed at congresses, plenums, and meetings of the artistic intelligentsia. More interesting articles are now being printed that are imbued with concern for the further development of the art of socialist realism.

However, criticism still does not fully meet the requirements that are determined by the growing role of artistic culture in communist construction. The processes of the development of Soviet literature and art, and of the mutual enrichment of the cultures of the socialist nations and their coming closer together lack profound analysis. Many articles, surveys, and reviews are superficial in character, are distinguished by a low philosophical and aesthetic level, and are indicative of an inability to correlate art with actual life. In criticism there is still evidence of an attitude of conciliation towards ideological and artistic deficiencies, subjectivism, and of partiality to friends and associates. At times, materials are published that give an incorrect picture of the history of Soviet and pre-revolutionary art and are biased in assessing certain artists and works. Criticism is still not sufficiently active and consistent in consolidating the revolutionary, humanist ideals of the art of socialist realism and unmasking the reactionary essence of bourgeois 'mass culture' and decadent tendencies, as well as in the struggle with various non-marxist views about literature and art and revisionist aesthetic concepts.

Party committees, ministries, departments, and unions of creative artists have not yet ensured proper supervision over work in the area of criticism and bibliography of their subordinate press organs, publishing houses, and appropriate editorial offices in the television and radio network; poor use is made of the mass media for purposeful ideological and aesthetic education of the toilers and for propaganda of the best accomplishments of multi-national Soviet art.

Editorial offices of a number of newspapers and magazines are not always demanding with respect to the ideological and theoretical level of critical articles. There are substantial short-comings in the practice of reviewing. On many occasions, published reviews are one-sided in nature, contain groundless compliments, come to a cursory exposition of the content of a work, and fail to give any idea of a work's real significance and value. In general, many books, performances, films, art exhibitions, musical compositions, and concert programmes are left beyond the field of vision of criticism. Leading specialists in the area of marxist-leninist aesthetics, the theory and history of art, and masters of Soviet culture are poorly recruited for work in the press; editorial offices have failed to devote the proper attention to the variety of genres and clarity of critical materials.

The leading organs of the unions of creative artists seldom organize collective discussions of urgent problems of artistic work; they are slow in reorganizing the work of commissions and councils in the area of criticism. There is no daily concern shown for the ideological upbringing and professional training of critics, for creating an atmosphere of high exactingness among personnel in literature and art, and in forming a correct attitude toward criticism.

Short-comings in literary and art criticism are conditioned, to a large extent, by a shortage of qualified cadres. At the same time, necessary conditions have not been created in universities and higher educational institutions in the humanities for the specialization of undergraduate and graduate students in the field of criticism; this work has not been organized satisfactorily in educational institutions specializing in literature and art.

Serious short-comings in the organization of scientific research work adversely affect the development of criticism, as do the departmental isolation of scientific and creative cadres and the lack of proper co-ordination in the work of scientific institutions.

Considering the important role of literary and art criticism in the development of Soviet literature and art, the CPSU Central Committee resolves:

1   To call the attention of the central committees of union republic communist parties, krai and oblast party committees, ministries and departments, unions of creative artists, leaders of press organs, publishing houses, television, and radio to the necessity of raising the ideological and theoretical level of literary and art criticism, its activeness and principled nature in conducting the party line in the area of creative work.

It is the duty of criticism to give a profound analysis of phenomena, tendencies, and patterns of the contemporary art process, to promote the consolidation of the leninist principles of party-mindedness and kinship with the people in every possible way, to struggle for a high ideological and aesthetic level of Soviet art, and consistently to oppose bourgeois ideology. Literary and art criticism is called upon to facilitate the expansion of the artist's ideological views and to perfect his skills. In developing the traditions of marxist-leninist aesthetics, Soviet literary and art criticism must combine accuracy of ideological evaluation and profoundness of social analysis with aesthetic exactingness and a careful attitude to talent and to fruitful creative search ...

Pravda, 25 January 1972   *KPSS v rezoliutsiiakh* XI, 29–33

5.40
On Preparations for the Fiftieth Anniversary of the
Formation of the Union of Soviet Socialist Republics   21 February 1972

The celebration of the fiftieth anniversary of the USSR on 30 December 1972 was signaled early in the year by a lengthy Central Committee resolution outlining the national and international significance of the anniversary and calling on all party, soviet, and public organizations to undertake the appropriate political education programs, socialist competitions, and other activities. This document is the only one of the Brezhnev period that deals extensively with the theme of the multinational composition of the Soviet Union and relates it to the concept of 'developed socialism.' The anniversary was chosen as an occasion to confirm publicly and officially the historical unity of the nationalities of the Soviet Union on the basis of a voluntary and democratic association 'headed by the working class under the leadership of the Communist Party.' The current stage of national development was placed in historical context by elaborating on the meaning of developed socialism from the perspective of the multinational Soviet state – national integration of the economies of the separate republics, elimination of national and class antagonisms, the unified nature of the federal state system, widespread mobilization of all nationalities for participation in socialist construction, and ideological unity. The extent to which the regime was bent on pursuing a course of national unity through industrialization and Russification is evident in the explicit inclusion of two indicators: the remark that practical experience has convinced the country's peoples of the material pay-offs connected with national unity; and, the voluntary choice of Russian as the common working language of the country.

... In preparing for the fiftieth anniversary of the formation of the USSR, the Communist Party and the Soviet people recall with legitimate pride the path of

heroic victories and achievements that they have traversed. The Soviet Union approaches this important jubilee with great achievements in all areas of life.

The fraternal friendship of the working people of all nationalities plays an important role in these achievements. It is the unity of all the country's forces and resources that made it possible for the Soviet people in a very short historical period to liquidate the economic and cultural backwardness inherited from tsarism and capitalism, to carry out the industrialization of the country, the socialist transformation of agriculture and a genuine cultural revolution, to build socialism and transform the USSR into a mighty, highly developed power, and to launch the construction of a communist society. Due to the unity of the state, our Soviet Motherland was able to create its invincible defensive power that reliably ensures the freedom and independence of its peoples and the conditions for their peaceful creative labour.

Through many years of practical experience, all the peoples of the country have become convinced of the rich rewards that come from being united in the Union of Soviet Socialist Republics and the vast opportunities that this affords for the future.

Concentration of material means and efforts and the selfless mutual assistance of the Soviet peoples have made it possible to create a highly developed industry and large-scale mechanized agriculture in all the republics. Compared with 1922, the year when the USSR was formed, there has been a more than one hundred-fold increase in the national income of the country. Numerous industrial and cultural centres and well-equipped cities and villages have grown up on what had been feudal and semi-feudal outlying districts of tsarist Russia.

Deep qualitative changes have taken place in the socio-political life of Soviet society: exploitation and the exploiter classes, unemployment and illiteracy have all been liquidated; the alliance between the workers and the peasants has become stronger. Socialist nations have been formed, the social, ideological, and political unity of the Soviet people has been established. National cadres have been trained and the people's culture, socialist in content and national in form, is flourishing. Works of literature and art, and scientific works are created, and newspapers and magazines are published on an unprecedented scale in the languages of the peoples of the USSR.

The comprehensive development of the languages of all the socialist nations and nationalities of the Soviet Union is an important result of the successful resolution of the nationalities problem in our country. In the Soviet period, over forty peoples previously without their own written language have acquired a scientifically developed written language and now have developed literary languages. All the nations and nationalities of the USSR have voluntarily chosen the Russian language as a common language for communication and collaboration between the nationalities. It has become a powerful vehicle for communications between and cohesion of the Soviet peoples, a means of giving access to the best achievements of Soviet and world culture.

The equalization and enhancement of the levels of economic, social, political, and cultural development were an important factor in the rapid and all-round progress of all the republics of the USSR. With fraternal unity, the constructive energy, creative abilities, and talents of all the nationalities and peoples of the Soviet state have flourished to an exceptional degree.

The RSFSR, the Ukrainian SSR, the Belorussian SSR, the Uzbek SSR, the Kazakh SSR, the Georgian SSR, the Azerbaidzhan SSR, the Lithuanian SSR, the Moldavian SSR, the Latvian SSR, the Kirgiz SSR, the Tadzhik SSR, the Armenian SSR, the Turkmen SSR, and the Estonian SSR are approaching the fiftieth anniversary of their indestructible union in their prime. More than one hundred nations and nationalities are working in our country shoulder to shoulder, creating a communist society. Every Soviet person, regardless of his nationality, above all takes pride in being a citizen of the great Union of Soviet Socialist Republics.

The CPSU Central Committee notes with satisfaction that the party organizations of all the union and autonomous republics, autonomous oblasts, and national okrugs play a vanguard role in accomplishing the leninist nationality policy, and in strengthening the friendship of peoples. They always stand out as the militant detachments of our party, carrying high the banner of Soviet patriotism and socialist internationalism and marching at the head of the toiling masses in their struggle for the implementation of the principles of scientific communism.

The heroic efforts of the Soviet people have been duly crowned by the building in the USSR of a developed socialist society in which:
–   a high level of development of the all-union economy has been attained – an interrelated economic complex that includes the economies of the republics and develops in accordance with a unified state plan in the interests of the country as a whole and each individual republic;
–   class and national antagonism has been eliminated. Society as a whole and each nation and nationality have the same type of social structure consisting of the working class, the kolkhoz peasantry, and the toiling intelligentsia;
–   the all-round development of union statehood and national statehood of the republics has been ensured on the basis of the principles of democratic centralism, socialist federalism, and Soviet socialist democracy;
–   the necessary conditions for the active participation of the working people of all nationalities in developing science, technology, and culture have been created. The flourishing, drawing together, and mutual enrichment of the cultures of the socialist nationalities and nations have become a regular pattern in spiritual life;
–   marxist-leninist ideology, socialist internationalism, and friendship of

peoples have been established, the process of exchange of material and spiritual values and cadres proceeds intensively, and mutual influence and internationalization of the entire tenor of life of the peoples in a variety of forms is intensifying. Today the working people in every republic constitute a multinational collective in which national features are organically connected with international socialist features, as well as features and traditions common to the entire Soviet Union.

In the years of building socialism and communism in the USSR, a new historical community of people has arisen – the Soviet people. It was formed on the basis of social ownership of the means of production, on the unity of economic, social, political, and cultural life, marxist-leninist ideology, and the interests and communist ideals of the working class. Soviet man has developed remarkable features: devotion to the cause of communism, socialist patriotism and internationalism; a high level of labour and socio-political activity; intolerance of exploitation and oppression, nationalist and racial prejudices; class solidarity with the working people of all countries. Generations of genuine internationalists have grown – selfless fighters for communism. In the USSR the necessary material and spiritual conditions have been created for further growth of the creative abilities of every Soviet person and for the all-round development of one's personality.

The experience of building the Soviet multinational state has brilliantly confirmed the following conclusions of marxism-leninism:

–   that the nationality question can be consistently resolved only on the basis of the socialist transformation of society;

–   that, unlike formal bourgeois democracy, which proclaims national equality but never practices it, socialist democracy guarantees equal rights and opportunities for nations and creates the conditions for solving nationality problems with due regard for the vital interests of the toilers of various nationalities;

–   that the closest unity, the all-round flourishing and steady drawing together of all nations and peoples of the land of the Soviets are determined by the nature of our system and are an objective pattern in the development of socialism;

–   that a union of socialist republics is the most viable and perfect form of structure for a multinational state which harmoniously combines the interests of the entire society with the interests of each nation.

Thus, marxist-leninist teaching on the nationality question has passed the test of practice and the leninist nationality policy has scored a complete victory.

In marking the glorious jubilee of the Soviet Union, we must follow the leninist tradition of our party – summing up the results of the past and turning above all to the tasks of today and tomorrow.

In the conditions of communist construction, the development of national relations proceeds along the line of the all-round consolidation and improvement of the voluntary union of socialist nationalities. The Report of the CPSU Central Committee to the XXIV Congress notes that 'In past years, under the guidance of the party, new steps have been made toward the all-round development of each of the fraternal Soviet republics, toward further gradual drawing together of the nations and nationalities of our country. This drawing together is taking place in conditions of attentive consideration for special national features and for the development of socialist national cultures. Constant consideration for both the common interests of our Union as a whole and the interests of each of its constituent republics – this is the essence of the policy of the party in this question.'

In the course of communist construction, the significance of the USSR as an historically completely proven state form of the joint struggle of free peoples for the programme goals of the party and for communist ideals is growing. The concerted efforts of the working people of all republics and economic regions, of personnel in all branches of the economy and culture, and of multinational labour collectives are especially necessary for the success of this struggle. The resolution of gigantic problems such as the creation of the material and technical basis of communism and communist productive forces, the comprehensive intensification of social production, the organic combination of the achievements of the contemporary scientific-technological revolution with the advantages of the socialist planned economic system, ensurance of the further enhancement of the material and cultural levels of the working people and the formation of the New Man – the resolution of all these requires the concentration of the entire might of the multinational Soviet state, the potentialities of which are determined by the wealth and diversity of its resources, and by the well-co-ordinated actions and good organization of all the people ...

Pravda, 22 February 1972   *KPSS v rezoliutsiiakh* XI, 46–63

5.41
On the Organizational and Political Work
of the Tbilisi City Committee of the
Communist Party of Georgia in Fulfilling
the Decisions of the XXIV CPSU Congress*   22 February 1972

The apparently mild criticism leveled at the work of the local party organs in the Georgian Republic in this document obscured the seriousness of the situation as it was perceived by Moscow. The directive resulted in widespread reper-

*   Excerpt: document not published in full.

cussions throughout the entire republic and also contained implications for local party organs in other republics. (For example, within six months, a Central Committee Resolution, 'On Marxist-Leninist Study and the Economic Education of Leading Cadres in the Tashkent City Party Organization,' ominously warned that the Tashkent city party committee had not drawn the necessary conclusions from the Tbilisi resolution and was not sufficiently taking into consideration the special characteristics and tasks of the party organization of a republic capital city. See *Voprosy ideologicheskoi raboty*, 2nd ed., Moscow 1973, 365–73.) The Georgian case is certainly an extreme one because of the traditional reputation of Georgians for their independence and defiance of central directives. However, the present resolution resulted in unusually elaborate public discussions, personnel changes, and other visible activities in response to the centre's demand for compliance. It thus provides us with an excellent opportunity to examine some of the meanings implicit in general signals found in many resolutions in this volume such as injunctions 'to improve organizational and political work,' 'to eliminate short-comings,' 'to raise the level of leadership,' 'to improve or intensify work,' 'to take effective measures,' 'to ensure undeviating observance,' 'to show daily concern,' 'to improve guidance,' 'to enhance the role,' etc.

The resolution led to a series of party meetings during the course of which the local leadership reiterated and detailed the charges in the resolution and confirmed its responsibility for the lax state of affairs in Georgia. This exercise in 'criticism and self-criticism' led to admissions of irregularities, crimes, and deviations in three broad areas. The general charge of plan underfulfillment and problems in the economic sphere produced evidence of a lengthy series of economic crimes on a massive republic-wide scale. A number of outright criminal activities were revealed, including bribery, embezzlement, theft, speculation, appropriating state property and/or private use of state property, unauthorized and illegal construction of houses and dachas, manufacture and use of narcotics, defrauding of consumers, extortion, favouritism, parochialism, cronyism, careerism, nepotism, corruption, graft, and forgery. In addition, a number of crimes relating to negligence or simulation in plan fulfilment were revealed, including systematic plan underfulfilment, poor output quality, improper norm setting, supply breakdowns, unwarranted plan reduction, hiding of low growth rates, voluntarism and subjectivism in personnel policy, mutual backscratching and toadyism. In the course of these revelations several important patterns became evident. First, the charges were not made in the usual general and impersonal manner. Individuals were named and held responsible for their actions and those of their subordinates. Furthermore, as the revelations continued over time, the idea emerged that the economic crimes in Georgia were not simply incidents of individuals acting in isolation. They were being systematically perpetrated by groups or networks and the scale of crime often reached hundreds of thousands and even millions of rubles.

At one stage it was suggested at a central committee plenum of the Georgian Communist Party that the republic was run by a number of political bosses and political machines, with certain leaders dividing the republic into spheres of influence, assuming patronage over entire districts, cities, and party organizations, and promoting their protégés (*Current Digest of the Soviet Press* XXV, no. 13, 5). Finally, although the crimes took place in the state sector, the party was directly implicated on two levels. Many of those responsible for criminal activities were party members, often holding responsible party posts in addition to their state posts. In addition, the party as an organization was seen to be implicated in criminal activity, at least as a willing accomplice, through its lax cadre policy (continuing to promote personnel who were known to be engaged in criminal activity), its failure to supervise and inspect, its acquiescence, and through individual party officials who participated willingly in the criminal activities. This was not simply an administrative-organizational issue; it was a political issue.

A second broad area that came under scrutiny as a result of the resolution was a variety of anti-social or socially unacceptable forms of behaviour. This was a more fuzzy area than the economic crimes because the types of activities identified were not always illegal. Sometimes they encompassed personal characteristics or behaviour that countered the regime's officially designated sets of norms and standards and at times they were activities which, while themselves not illegal, were conducive to the perpetration of illegal acts. Again, the tone of the discussion and the multitude of cases suggested that these were widespread and deeply rooted phenomena in the Georgian Republic. They included drunkenness, hooliganism, parasitism, observance of religious customs and rituals, wakes and weddings attended by large crowds and becoming drunken brawls (often involving violence and murder), unprincipled pragmatism, localism, buddyism, favouritism, egoism, individualism, religious prejudice, superstition, blood feuds, a cult of money and of the 'golden calf,' money-grubbing, and a cult of gain. A major concern of the discussion was the degree of party acceptance of these activities and the active pursuit of them by numbers of responsible party officials.

The third major area of concern in the aftermath of the Central Committee resolution was the ideological sphere. Here again, a wide variety of charges were laid, the most serious among them dealing with various manifestations of Georgian nationalism and traditions. A number of unreliable elements were attacked among the writers, historians, social scientists, and officials who were accused of deviations involving nationalist and chauvinist tendencies such as propagating nationalism and nationalistic prejudices, downgrading the Soviet Union (i.e. the Russian influence) and the working class (i.e. the party) in Georgian development, failing to devote sufficient attention to the 'internationalist upbringing' of the working class (especially youth and the intelligentsia), replacing feelings of Soviet national pride by national conceit and excessive stress on the uniqueness of Georgia's developmental path, and favouring the indigenous nationality in filling posts. A number of charges were laid against workers in the ideological field who had failed to eradicate survivals of the past in people's minds and behaviour, failed to combat an infatuation with antiquity and idealization of antiquity, and failed to deal properly with manifestations of petit-bourgeois ideology and morals and remnants of private-ownership psychology. Several 'political' deviations were also identified, including trotskyism, right-wing opportunism, and revisionism, as well as the general absence of a class approach in socio-political writing.

The extensive exercise in 'criticism and self-criticism' in which the Georgian Communist Party indulged was more than the routine generalized and impersonal procedure so dominant in party organizations. It had widespread repercussions in personnel policy throughout the party and state organizations and extended into the courts. The Georgian party organization experienced a series of sanctions ranging from reprimands to demotions and dismissals for the responsible personnel and, in many cases, the laying of criminal charges. The seriousness of the business was indicated by the removal of the republic party first secretary, V.P. Mzhavanadze, and his replacement by the former head of the Georgian security police, E.A. Shevardnadze. The purge then ranged all the way from the republic secretariat through the city and raion party organizations to the primary party organizations. The state administration also suffered major shake-ups from the Chairman of the Presidium of the Georgian Republic Supreme Soviet, ministers and deputy ministers through heads of main administrations, and down to enterprise directors and individual workers and employees who were exploiting the system. While all sectors of the economy were affected, the trade network and the higher educational system were singled out for the extremities of the abuses taking place in them.

Having heard the report of the first secretary of the Tbilisi city party committee, comrade O.I. Lolashvili, the CPSU Central Committee notes that the city party organization is conducting significant work in mobilizing communists and all the toilers to put the decisions of the XXIV CPSU Congress into practice ...

Nevertheless, the CPSU Central Committee considers that the level of organizational and political work of the Tbilisi city party committee and of its guidance over economic and cultural construction still does not fully meet the requirements of the XXIV CPSU Congress and the tasks that the city party organization is called upon to accomplish.

The city party committee has failed to consider sufficiently the specific nature of its leadership of the capital's party organization and it does not always keep in its field of vision extremely important sectors of work that are significant not only for the city, but also for the republic as a whole. In political and organizational work, proper use is not made of all possibilities available to the party organization of a republic centre – the existence of a numerous detachment of the working class, scientific, technical, and creative intelligentsia, highly qualified, experienced cadres, a developed industrial base, and a network of cultural institutions. In a number of cases, the city committee fails to notice essential short-comings in its work behind overall satisfactory indices and fails to take the necessary measures to do away with the short-comings; little attention is devoted to organizing and verifying the implementation of party and government directives ...

The CPSU Central Committee resolves:

1   The Tbilisi city party committee must do away with the short-comings noted in the current resolution. The further intensification of the organizational and political work of the city party organization is to be ensured in the practical implementation of the decisions of the XXIV CPSU Congress. The forms and methods of the activity of the city and raion party committees and of the primary party organizations are to be perfected constantly.

2   The city and raion party committees and primary party organizations must develop the labour and political activeness of the masses in every possible way, improve the organization and raise the effectiveness of socialist competition for the successful fulfilment of the targets of the Ninth Five-Year Plan, state plans, and pledges accepted by the working people of Tbilisi for the year 1972. The responsibility of leading engineering and technical personnel for the fulfilment of plan assignments according to all indicators by every enterprise, shop, production section, and brigade is to be raised. It is necessary to work out and steadily to put into practice at every enterprise concrete measures for raising the effectiveness of production on the basis of accelerating technological progress, raising labour productivity, improving the quality of manufactured products, and a more rational utilization of available capacities, labour, and material resources. A decisive struggle is to be waged against departmental narrow-mindedness and manifestations of localist tendencies. Party supervision in the area of the economy is to be intensified and a party approach in solving economic problems is to be ensured.

3   An urgent task of the city party organization is considered to be the achievement of a radical improvement in the business of capital construction. Necessary measures are to be taken to eliminate the lag in the construction of production capacities, residential houses, municipal enterprises, and enterprises for trade, cultural, and everyday services. They are to ensure that construction units are commissioned on time, that the quality of construction is improved, and that construction materials are used economically ...

4   The CPSU Central Committee especially directs the attention of the city and raion party committees, the executive committees of the city and raion Soviets of Working People's Deputies, and of party and trade union organizations to carry out effective measures to improve trade and public catering, municipal and everyday services, and the population's medical service.

5   The city party committee is ordered to raise the level of its leadership of party organizations at scientific-research and design institutes, educational and cultural-enlightenment institutions. Efforts are to be made to concentrate scientific research on the most important problems of scientific and technological progress and on developing fundamental sciences; the effectiveness of the work conducted by institutes, university departments, and laboratories is to be raised; an atmosphere of creativity and mutual exactingness is to be formed in every scientific collective. Personnel in science, literature, and the arts are to be trained in a spirit of great responsibility to society for their work; their ties with production collectives are to be strengthened.

Educational and upbringing work is to be improved in higher, secondary specialized and vocational-technical institutions, and general educational schools. A more extensive influx of young workers and peasants into higher educational institutions and technical schools is to be ensured; complete and prompt filling of places in vocational-technical schools is to be accomplished with eighth- and tenth-grade graduates of secondary schools. More attention is to be paid to questions of the professional orientation of school children.

6   The city and raion party committees and primary party organizations must significantly improve their ideological work, actively direct it at moulding the toilers' marxist-leninist outlook and the high moral features necessary to a builder of communism; the decisions of the XXIV CPSU Congress and the November (1971) Plenum of the CPSU Central Committee are to be propagandized widely. The meaning and grandeur of the tasks of the Ninth Five-Year Plan are to be explained to all the working people, as well as the significance of the fulfilment of these tasks for strengthening the economic and defence might of our Motherland and for raising the living standard of the population. The heart of all mass political work must become the proposition that, in the long run, the fulfilment of the Five-Year Plan will depend on the activeness, creative attitude to work, and persistent labour of every worker. The economic education of cadres and the broad toiling masses is to be improved. There is to be an elevation of the role of the press, radio, and television in solving the tasks of social and economic development and communist training posed by the Congress.

Work is to be intensified in educating the toilers in the spirit of fraternal friendship between the peoples of the USSR, Soviet patriotism, and socialist internationalism. In the course of preparations for the 50th anniversary of the formation of the USSR, the triumph of the leninist nationality policy is to be revealed in detail, as well as the historical significance of uniting the Soviet republics in a single multinational socialist state, the patterns of development of the socialist nations and their drawing together, and the achievements of the Soviet people in communist construction.

7   The Tbilisi city committee, party, soviet, trade union, and Komsomol organizations, organs of people's control, court, procurator's office, and the

militia of the city are required to take effective measures to intensify the struggle against embezzlement of socialist property, bribery, speculation, parasitism, and misuse of office in trade and domestic services. Constant political work is to be conducted to overcome survivals of private property and other negative phenomena; all means are to be used to cultivate in people an intolerant attitude to views and behaviour alien to our society. The role of labour collectives is to be elevated in the struggle with survivals of the past, and violations of law and order and the rules of socialist communal life.

8   The city and raion party committees are to ensure undeviating observance of the leninist principles of selection, placement, and training of cadres in the city party organization and are constantly to see to it that all sectors of party, soviet, and economic work are headed by politically trained, competent, and capable organizers. Efforts are to be made to ensure that every leader persistently masters contemporary methods of guidance, demonstrates efficiency and businesslike character in work, and organically combines the qualities of an organizer and educator. It is necessary to develop in personnel a feeling for the new and the ability to give a critical evaluation of what has been achieved. Exactingness and personal responsibility of leading cadres of all ranks are to be enhanced for entrusted work, and personnel are to be made strictly responsible for violating party and state discipline and abusing their official position.

9   One of the most important tasks of the city party organization is considered to be the undeviating observance of leninist norms of party life, the steady development of inner-party democracy, and principled criticism and self-criticism. It is necessary to elevate the role of raion party committees as organs of political leadership. Constant attention is to be given to questions of raising and improving the qualitative composition of party ranks, to the ideological and political education of communists, and to raising their activeness and responsibility for the fulfilment of the requirements of the CPSU Programme and Rules. The city and raion party committees are to show daily concern in intensifying the fighting efficiency of primary and shop party organizations and party groups, and strengthening their influence over all spheres of the life and activity of labour collectives. Efforts are to be made to ensure that primary party organizations correctly and with utmost effectiveness exercise the right granted to them by the CPSU Rules to supervise the activity of the administration and the work of the administrative apparatus of institutions and departments in their fulfilment of party and government directives.

10   The Tbilisi city and raion party committees must improve their guidance over the toilers' mass organizations. The role of city and raion Soviets of Working People's Deputies is to be enhanced, as is their influence on the further development of the city's economy, on improving the social and cultural services of the population, and on strengthening the protection of public order. The authority and activeness of deputies is to be enhanced, as

well as their responsibility before the voters. Trade union work is to be improved in involving the toilers more extensively in production management, organizing socialist competition, exercising supervision over the observance of labour legislation, and improving the work and daily life conditions of workers and employees. The activity of Komsomol organizations must be scrutinized thoroughly from day to day, and they are to be helped in doing a better job of accomplishing the task of providing for communist education of young men and women, taking into account the specific nature of various groups of young people. The party nucleus in the Komsomol is to be consolidated further; the work of party members and candidate members in Komsomol organizations is considered to be an important party assignment.

Pravda, 6 March 1972   *KPSS v rezoliutsiiakh* XI, 67–74

5.42
On Measures for Intensifying the Struggle
against Drunkenness and Alcoholism*   16 May 1972

This resolution signaled an intensification of the ongoing campaign against one of the major social and industrial problems in the Soviet Union. The thrust of the current campaign was to be in two directions: a propaganda drive focusing on the harm that alcoholism does to people's physical and emotional well-being and a program of constructive alternatives to alcoholism as a social activity. These programmes were part of an overall campaign conducted by the regime against alcoholism that included attempts to mobilize peer and public pressures against drunkenness, the promulgation of legislation to deal with the problem, the extension of compulsory treatment, and attempts to manipulate prices and accessibility to alcohol. However, with traditional attitudes towards the illegal production of alcohol and its widespread consumption, compounded by the pressures of an urban industrial environment with relative scarcities of consumer goods and services, it is unlikely that the limited approach of the Brezhnev regime will have a significant impact on drinking patterns in the Soviet Union.

**
...

2   The central committees of union republic communist parties, krai, oblast, city and raion party committees, and primary party organizations are

---

*   Excerpt: document not published in full.
**   Part of the document is omitted in the original.

ordered to conduct a decisive and persistent struggle against drunkenness and alcoholism, to work out concrete measures for the extensive development of mass political, cultural, and educational work in collectives and among the population at their places of residence, for intensifying anti-alcohol propaganda, and for raising the effectiveness of public and administrative pressure on persons who abuse alcohol ...

Pravda, 13 June 1972   *KPSS v rezoliutsiiakh* XI, 89–90

Plenum of the Central Committee   19 May 1972

The issue of an exchange of party documents was first made public by Brezhnev in his Central Committee Report to the XXIV Congress. At that time he noted that the last exchange of party documents had taken place seventeen years earlier and that the period of validity of the party cards issued in 1954 had expired. In his report Brezhnev stressed that an exchange of party documents had as its aim the strengthening of the party through an increase in the activeness and discipline of party members. Brezhnev's recommendation and its goals were embodied in the congress resolution on the Central Committee Report.

There are a number of indicators that the leadership was split over the significance that should be attached to the exchange of documents. It was a full year before the Central Committee met to act on the congress decision and to announce details of the exchange. The main report to the plenum on the exchange of party documents was delivered by I.V. Kapitonov, a member of the Secretariat. According to the communique issued in conjunction with the plenum, no Politburo member spoke on the issue, although this was later contradicted by a reference in a *Pravda* editorial to remarks attributed to Brezhnev at the plenum. Furthermore, the communique noted simply that 'the plenum adopted an appropriate resolution on this issue,' avoiding the usual form indicating unanimity of Central Committee decisions. The decision, itself, indicated a further year's delay in the actual implementation of the exchange. These circumstances suggested an inability of the leadership to come to firm agreement over the purposes, scope and procedures of the exchange.

An editorial in *Pravda* on 24 June (*Current Digest of the Soviet Press* XXIV, no. 25, 1–4), more than a month after the Central Committee plenum, gives us some insight into the nature of the differences over the exchange of documents. There appeared to be three positions in the party leadership. One extreme saw the exchange as a purge in the traditional sense with strong political overtones, if not a complete return to the party purges of the 1930s aimed at the removal of alien class elements. At the other extreme were those who took the position that the exchange was to be conducted as a purely technical procedure, involving only the replacement of old party cards with new ones. Apparently, a moderate group, headed by Brezhnev, was able to bridge the gap between the two extremes and had won the day by the last week in June. The position of this group was embodied in a statement attributed to Brezhnev at the plenum that 'it [the exchange of party documents] must not be reduced to a purely technical operation, while at the same time it should be borne in mind that this is not a party purge.'

The success of the compromise can be attributed to its definition of the 'political' dimension of the exchange, which emphasized goals that were probably acceptable to a broad spectrum within the party. The exchange was to incorporate a political component, but the meaning of 'political' was sharply limited to administrative and organizational activity. The political goal of the exchange of party documents was to be a strengthening of the party by intensifying the participation, initiative, and discipline of party members and their vanguard role in building communism. It was to be a review of the party's forces and a strict, exacting check-up aimed at improving the party's efficiency as an administrative and supervisory agency, especially in the economy, culture, and its own internal operation.

The substance of the May 1972 Central Committee resolution and the follow-up resolutions of February 1973 and January 1975 (5.47) tended to reflect and reinforce the moderate position of Brezhnev. As the exchange of party documents got underway after 1 March 1973, it became clear that the purpose of the exercise was to enhance the party's ability to carry out its leadership tasks in the economic, cultural, and political sectors, to conduct ideological, educational, and organizational work among the masses, and to improve its own internal organization. The procedures for conducting the exchange were clearly defined and, if one is to believe the published reports, rigorously adhered to in order to protect party members against arbitrary and unfounded expulsions and to provide an important organizational experience for those conducting the exchange.

One personnel change was announced at the plenum, the election of the Secretariat's B.N. Ponomarev as a candidate member of the Politburo.

5.43
On the Exchange of Party Documents   19 May 1972

In accordance with the decision of the XXIV Party Congress, the cpsu Central Committee Plenum resolves that:

1   In the years 1973–74, an exchange of party documents of cpsu members is to be conducted. All necessary preparatory work is to be done before that time.

The exchange of party documents is to be carried out as an important organizational-political measure, subordinated to the tasks of further consolidating the party and raising the activeness and discipline of communists. It must facilitate an improvement in the activity of all party organizations and an intensification of their work in fulfilling the tasks of economic and cultural construction posed by the XXIV CPSU Congress. The exchange of party documents must be used to the utmost for the further activization of inner-party life, for improving methods of party leadership, and for raising the level of ideological, educational, and organizational work among the masses.

Party organizations must make efforts to ensure that all communists strictly observe the requirements of the Programme and Rules of the CPSU, actually fulfil their vanguard role in production and in social and political life, take a conscientious attitude to party assignments, constantly master marxist-leninist theory, and serve as a model of observance of Soviet laws, the norms of communist morality, and rules for socialist communal life.

2   It is established that all party membership cards and record cards of the 1954 form are subject to exchange. An exchange of candidate membership cards is not to be carried out in view of the fact that candidate members of the party will receive the new party documents upon their admission as members to the CPSU. From the moment party documents are to be exchanged, all those admitted as candidate members are to be given candidate membership cards of the new form.

3   The exchange of party cards of CPSU members is to be carried out according to a strictly individual procedure, directly in the raion and city party committees and in political departments where communists are permanently registered. The exchange is to be conducted by the secretaries of raion and city party committees and by heads and deputy heads of political departments; they are to bear personal responsibility before the CPSU Central Committee for the correct issuance of party membership cards.

Taking into consideration the large amount of work to be done, permission will be granted to enlist bureau members in verifying entries in party documents; in the largest city and raion party organizations, members of the city and raion party committees may also be enlisted with the permission of the central committees of the union republic communist parties.

During the period when party membership cards are to be exchanged, the right to sign party documents of communists is to be granted, along with the first secretaries, to other raion and city party committee secretaries, as well. New party membership cards are to be presented to communists by the secretaries of the raion and oblast committees and, in the largest raion and city party organizations, the presentation of party membership cards may also be conducted by members of the bureaus of raion and city committees.

4   The leadership of the exchange of party documents in the oblasts, krais, and republics is to be made the responsibility of the oblast and krai committees and the central committees of the union republic communist

parties; in the party organizations of the Soviet Army and Navy, border-guard troops and other party organizations, it is to be the responsibility of the political administration and the appropriate political departments.

It is viewed as necessary to discuss the tasks of party organizations in connection with the exchange of party documents at plenums of the central committees of the union republic communist parties, krai, oblast, okrug, city, and raion party committees, and at meetings of communists in primary party organizations.

Pravda, 20 May 1972   *KPSS v rezoliutsiiakh* XI, 92–3

5.44
On Measures for Improving the Training of
Party and Soviet Cadres in the Higher Party School
of the CPSU Central Committee*   1 September 1972

... the Higher Party School of the CPSU Central Committee occupies an important place in the system of training and retraining leading party and soviet cadres. Many of its graduates have been promoted to responsible sectors of party, soviet, and state work and are coping successfully with their assigned tasks. The Higher Party School provides scientific and methodological assistance to republic and inter-oblast higher party schools, soviet-party schools, and permanent courses. Scientific ties between the Higher Party School and party educational institutions in other socialist countries have been expanded** ...

Proceeding from the instructions of the XXIV CPSU Congress on the need for a further improvement in the training of leading party and soviet cadres, the CPSU Central Committee resolves:

1   The rector's office and party committee of the Higher Party School of the CPSU Central Committee are ordered to concentrate the efforts of the Higher Party School on training leading party and soviet cadres who master marxist-leninist theory, are able to apply it creatively in their practical activity, and have a good knowledge of contemporary problems of communist construction. Efforts are to be made to ensure that students steadily master the leninist art of leadership of the masses, cultivate in themselves a feeling for the new and an ability to connect the solution of current problems with long-range social development, and conduct an uncompromising struggle with bourgeois ideology and revisionism.

---

*   Excerpt: document not published in full.
**   Part of the document is omitted in the original.

The educational process is to be based on thorough study of marxism-leninism, the historic experience of the CPSU, the party's current strategic and tactical positions, leninist principles and methods of party and state leadership, the processes of the transformation of socialism into communism, the development of the scientific and technological revolution, and the utilization of objective economic laws in planning and managing the economy.

A course is to be introduced into the school's curriculum entitled 'The Fundamentals of Scientific Management of the Socialist Economy' and more attention is to be devoted to studying the theory and practice of party and soviet construction, the scientific fundamentals of party propaganda, social psychology and pedagogy in party work, and questions of cultural construction.

It is considered necessary to rework the curriculum and direct its contents at a broad range of problems of contemporary social development, at the creative study of the experience of the CPSU in guiding communist construction, and at forming and developing qualities in students that every party and soviet worker should possess ...

3   The role and responsibility of departments for ensuring a high ideological and theoretical level in the training and retraining of party and soviet cadres is to be raised.

To carry out instructional, scientific, and methodological work, the school is to have the following departments: history of the CPSU, marxist-leninist philosophy, political economy, scientific communism, party construction, soviet state construction and law, soviet economy and the fundamentals of scientific management of the economy, the international communist workers' and national liberation movement, journalism, Russian language and literature, and foreign languages. It is planned that the departments will have instructional-methodological offices and laboratories for generalizing party work experience and economic management** ...

4   The rector's office of the Higher Party School has been commissioned to implement measures to improve practical training. Study is to be organized of the experience of the work of party organizations and soviet bodies by the students, as well as their study of the application of modern methods of managing the economy, and the latest achievements in science, technology, and culture; provisions are to be made for studies in computer centres, at leading enterprises, on kolkhozes and sovkhozes, and, where necessary, in scientific-research institutes.

5   The term of study in the Higher Party School of the CPSU Central Committee remains two years. For the purposes of the students' more profound training in the various areas of party and soviet work, options are to be pro-

**   Part of the document is omitted in the original.

vided during the last six months, taking into consideration the subsequent employment of the school's graduates. It has been established that students complete a course project on the problems of party guidance over economic and cultural construction, organizational and ideological work, and that they pass state examinations in the history of the CPSU, dialectical and historical materialism, and political economy.

Graduates of the Higher Party School will be given a diploma indicating that they have received higher party political education, as well as an appropriate certificate indicating that they meet the minimum qualifications for a candidate's degree in philosophy, economics and history ...

7   The Higher Party School of the CPSU Central Committee is commissioned to provide systematic assistance to local party educational institutions in instructional, methodological, and scientific work ...

10   The party committee of the Higher Party School of the CPSU Central Committee must elevate the role of party organizations and party groups in the life of the school and raise the personal responsibility of communists for the state of their exactingness in the selection of candidates, for the state of teaching, scientific, and upbringing work ...

Kommunist, no. 16 (1972):   *KPSS v rezoliutsiiakh* XI, 160–3
3–5

5.45
On Conducting Report-and-Election Meetings
and Party Conferences*   3 October 1973

This resolution signaled the first time that report-and-election meetings were to be held in primary party organizations according to the change in Party Rules approved by the XXIV Party Congress. From the description of the focus of the meetings (production and labour mobilization) and the attendant publicity to be given to the proceedings, it appears that their purpose was essentially to generate widespread enthusiasm for the regime's immediate goals rather than to hold party officials responsible to the membership or to discuss problems in an open and frank manner.

In accord with the CPSU statutes, reports and elections have begun in party organizations. The present report-and-election campaign is taking place in an atmosphere of nation-wide struggle for the implementation of the historic decisions of the XXIV Congress of the party ...

*   Excerpt: document not published in full.

In the course of implementing the decisions of the Congress, the leading role of the CPSU in communist construction has become ever greater. The party and all party organizations have been enriched with new experience in guiding the various sides of economic and social life. Party ranks have become stronger and there has been a noticeable growth in the creative activeness of communists. To a great extent, this is being facilitated by the exchange of party documents now being conducted.

The significance of the forthcoming report-and-election conferences in raion, city, okrug, oblast, and krai party organizations is determined by the fact that they will be held for the first time after the XXIV Congress and are called upon to exert a serious influence on the entire course of subsequent work in accomplishing the tasks confronting the party.

The CPSU Central committee resolves:

1 ... ** Taking into consideration the proposals of the central committees of union republic communist parties and of the krai and oblast party committees, regular report-and-election raion, city, and okrug party conferences are to take place in December 1973–January 1974, while oblast and krai conferences are to be held in January to early March 1974. Before the beginning of the raion and city conferences, reports and elections are to be complete in primary party organizations.

2 At the report-and-election meetings and conferences, it is necessary to give a comprehensive analysis and summing up of the results of work in fulfilling the decisions of the XXIV Congress and the subsequent resolutions of the CPSU Central Committee. They are to be conducted under the badge of elevating the role and responsibility of party organizations for the practical implementation of the economic and social policy of the party, the further development of productive forces, science and culture, and a rise in the material well-being of the working people.

The preparation and conduct of reports and elections must become an important stage in the struggle for the unconditional fulfilment of state plans and pledges undertaken for the third and decisive year of the five-year-plan period in industry, agriculture, capital construction and other branches, and for the fulfilment of the entire Five-Year Plan ahead of schedule. The energies of party organizations are to be directed at an even broader development of socialist competition and at developing and carrying out counter-plans of labour collectives for 1974.

The meetings and conferences are called upon actively to facilitate the mobilization of communists and all toilers for raising the effectiveness of social production in every possible way, accelerating scientific-technological progress, improving the quality of products, and perfecting methods of management and administration. It is necessary to pay special attention to doing away with existing short-comings, making use of unused reserves at every

** Part of the document is omitted in the original.

enterprise, construction site, kolkhoz, and sovkhoz. At the meetings and conferences, questions of securing the preservation of socialist property and the observance of state and labour discipline and Soviet legality must receive appropriate representation.

3   The central committees of the union republic communist parties and the krai, oblast, okrug, city, and raion party committees are to ensure that report-and-election party meetings and conferences are conducted in an atmosphere of businesslike, principled discussion of the work of every party organization on the basis of widely developed criticism and self-criticism. Questions of the practice of party guidance over economic and cultural construction must be considered thoroughly, as well as the intensification of supervision and verification of the implementation of party and government directives, raising the responsibility of cadres for assigned tasks, and perfecting party political and organizational work.

In the course of the report-and-election campaign, experience of work conducted in connection with the exchange of party documents is to be generalized in order to ensure that fullest use is made of this important organizational-political measure for improving the activity of party organizations, developing the initiative and activeness of communists, and strengthening party discipline.

4   At the meetings and conferences, it is necessary to discuss thoroughly questions of the ideological and political work of party organizations, the marxist-leninist education of communists, and the training of the toilers in a spirit of high consciousness, Soviet patriotism, socialist internationalism, implacability to bourgeois ideology, and strict observance of the norms of communist morality. Concrete measures are to be determined for raising the level of ideological and political work with the masses in accordance with the requirements of the present stage of communist construction and the international activity of the party and Soviet state ...

6   The central committees of the union republic communist parties and the krai and oblast party committees must exercise constant guidance over the preparation and conduct of report-and-election party meetings and conferences. Strict observance of leninist norms of party life is to be ensured. Efforts are to be made to accomplish further improvement in the qualitative composition of party organs by electing to them the best prepared, politically active, and authoritative communists ...**

The CPSU Central committee emphasizes that party organs must attentively take criticism into consideration, promptly consider the proposals and remarks of communists, and take effective measures for their realization.

**   Part of the document is omitted in the original.

The course of the report-and-election meetings and conferences is to be covered widely in the central and local press, by radio and television.

Partiinaia zhizn', no. 20   *KPSS v rezoliutsiiakh* XI, 332–5
(1973): 3–5

5.46
On the Work of the Moscow Higher Technical College,
Named for N.E. Bauman, and the Saratov State
University, Named for N.G. Chernyshevsky,
in Raising the Ideological-Theoretical
Level of Social Science Teaching   5 June 1974

... There are substantial short-comings and omissions in the work of the party committees, rectors' offices, and departments of the Moscow Higher Technical College and Saratov University in improving social science teaching.

The necessary attention is not devoted to the quality of lectures that determine the content and ideological-political orientation of the entire educational process. In a number of cases, teachers fail to ensure a profound, vivid, and intelligible presentation of the material when lecturing. Important questions of theory and practice, the history of the Communist Party and the socialist state are sometimes presented superficially, without proper argumentation and scientific generalizations. Criticism of modern bourgeois theories, reformism, and revisionism is carried out with insufficient sharpness and persuasion and does not always take into consideration the special features of the present stage of the ideological struggle.

At seminars, many teachers fail to create an atmosphere of creative discussion of topical questions of marxist-leninist theory, thus lowering the activeness of students and failing to facilitate their independent thinking. At times, students do not receive convincing answers to questions that concern them. Study of theoretical problems is poorly related to life, to the practice of communist construction, and to inculcating a class approach in evaluating events and phenomena of contemporary social life.

The serious short-comings in lectures and seminars are above all a result of the weak teaching-methodology work of the departments which, as the basic units, are called upon to ensure the unity of instruction and upbringing in all forms of the educational process. The cinema, television, and other modern technical educational media and visual aids are not utilized in teaching the social sciences.

Many graduates do not receive sufficient training in a number of present-day problems in the philosophical and economic sciences that are important for the practical activity of young specialists. At the Moscow Higher Technical College there is no fundamental study by students of the ways and methods of organically combining the achievements of the scientific-technological revolution with the advantages of the socialist economic system and the character and patterns of its development. The political economy department in some natural science faculties of Saratov University fails to focus attention on questions of raising the effectiveness of socialist production.

Questions concerning the formation of communist morality and ethics in young people and problems of labour training and intolerance to everything that opposes the Soviet way of life are not properly reflected in social science teaching. There are still cases of a careless attitude to studies and violations of public order among the students.

In the departments, integrated research has not been organized on problems of developed socialist society, on questions concerning social science methodology and teaching methods, and also on the forms and methods of ideological work.

The rectors' offices, party committees, and department heads make serious mistakes in their work with teaching cadres. When selecting lecturers, they do not properly consider the leninist instruction that the ideological-political orientation of lectures and their content are determined 'completely and exclusively by the staff of lecturers.' The correct combination of experienced and young teachers is not ensured. Competitions to fill vacant positions and certification of scientific and pedagogical cadres are carried out formally. In the departments of political economy and philosophy of Saratov University more than half of the teachers do not have a basic higher education in their given specialities.

There are substantial short-comings in work on selecting students for graduate school. At the Moscow Higher Technical College, most of the graduate students in the social science departments fail to cope with plans for scientific work and are poorly prepared for pedagogical activity.

The party committee and rector's office of Saratov University are not sufficiently increasing the responsibility of party organizations and social science department heads for the ideological-theoretical level of teaching in the socio-economic disciplines and for upgrading the qualifications of teachers and they are not devoting the necessary attention to the housing and daily living conditions of students. For a long time, the academic council of the university failed to examine and analyse the activity of the social science departments.

The CPSU Central Committee resolves:

1   The party committees and rectors' offices of the Moscow Higher Technical College and Saratov State University are ordered to do away with existing short-comings in their instructional-upbringing and scientific activity.

Further improvement in the system of marxist-leninist education and the formation of the communist outlook of young specialists is to be ensured. Social science teachers are called upon to tie theory closer to the practice of communist construction and to the present political and organizational work of the party. Persistent efforts are to be made to ensure that every graduate of a higher school creatively master marxist-leninist theory and constantly strive to augment and deepen his knowledge and apply it in life, have communist convictions, possess high moral qualities, be an ardent patriot and internationalist, and a consistent fighter against bourgeois ideology and for the implementation of the policy of the Communist Party ...

Pravda, 24 June 1974   *KPSS v rezoliutsiiakh* XI, 405–11

5.47
On the Results of the Exchange of Party Documents*   31 January 1975

The CPSU Central Committee takes into consideration reports by the central committees of union republic communist parties, the krai and oblast party committees and political organs to the effect that all party organizations have completed the exchange of party documents in the established time period ...**

The exchange of party documents has been carried out as an important organizational-political measure in total accordance with the decisions of the XXIV Party Congress, the May (1972) Plenum of the CPSU Central Committee, and the instructions of Comrade L.I. Brezhnev, General Secretary of the CPSU Central Committee, on questions of party construction. The exchange has shown the infinite devotion of communists to the ideals of leninism, and the invincible unity and monolithic solidarity of the party around its Central Committee.

The chief result of the exchange of party documents consists in the fact that our party has become enriched with new experience of organizational and political work, it has strengthened its ranks and consolidated its ties with the masses, and its role as the guiding and directing force of Soviet society in the struggle for communism has grown greater.

The presentation of party membership cards of the new form, which are the same for party organizations of all republics and bear the image of the founder and leader of the CPSU, Vladimir Ilyich Lenin, and his words: 'The party is the mind, honour, and conscience of our epoch,' evokes in communists a feeling of legitimate pride and great responsibility for their membership in the great leninist party of internationalists.

---

*   Excerpt: document not published in full.
**   Part of the document is omitted in the original.

The exchange of party documents has been a genuine review of party forces and a strict verification of how every party organization and every communist carries out in practice the decisions of the XXIV CPSU Congress. It has promoted greater fighting efficiency of party organizations and a significant growth in the labour, public, and political activeness of communists. The mobilizing force of party organizations and the vanguard role of communists are convincingly shown in the struggle for the fulfilment and over-fulfilment of the targets of the Ninth Five-Year Plan for further development of industry, construction, transport, and communications, for an increase in the production and procurement of agricultural products, and for a rise in the level of the people's well-being. Army communists serve as an example in the fulfilment of their military duty.

In the course of preparing and carrying out the exchange of party documents, positive processes that are taking place in the life of party organizations under the influence of the decisions of the XXIV CPSU Congress have received further development. The principle of democratic centralism has been practised more fully, inner-party democracy has been expanded, the role of party meetings and plenums of party committees has been enhanced, criticism and self-criticism have become more objective. The activeness of communists and their responsibility for the affairs of their party organizations and the party as a whole have grown. The attention of party organizations towards questions of the ideological training and marxist-leninist education of party members and candidate members has shown a marked increase.

Party organizations have significantly intensified individual work with party members and candidate members. Interviews with communists, as well as reports by them at sessions of party bureaus, party committees, and party meetings on their fulfilment of statutory duties and production work, study, and participation in public life have been effective means in this. All this enables party organizations to evaluate more fully the contribution of each communist to the common cause, to distribute party assignments more correctly, and to strive for a higher level of party work.

An important result of the work connected with the preparation and implementation of the exchange of party documents has been an increase in the mutual exactingness of communists ...**

Along with raising exactingness towards communists, party organizations have intensified their regulatory influence on the growth of their ranks and are making efforts to ensure that the admission of new reinforcements to the party ensures a further growth in the fighting efficiency of party organizations. A line to ensure that the leading place in the social composition of the party belongs to the working class is being consistently implemented. More concern is shown in selecting as party members young workers, kolkhozniks, and students, above all Komsomol members, as well as women.

**   Part of the document is omitted in the original.

While noting the great principled significance of the experience accumulated in the course of exchanging party documents for further consolidating and developing the party, at the same time the CPSU Central Committee emphasizes that individual party committees have not made full use of the possibilities created as a result of the exchange to step up inner-party life in every party organization ...**

The CPSU Central Committee resolves:

1   The central committees of the union republic communist parties, the krai, oblast, okrug, city, and raion party committees, the Main Political Administration of the Soviet Army and Navy, and political organs are instructed to carry out a thorough and self-critical analysis and generalization of the results of the exchange of party documents. Positive experience is to be consolidated and used extensively, measures are to be taken to do away with short-comings and, on this basis, the further improvement of party work is to be ensured.

It is also necessary to continue to consolidate party organizations in the organizational and ideological-political respects, constantly to elevate the title and significance of member of the CPSU, to develop the activeness, and raise the discipline of communists in every possible way. Efforts are to be made to affirm a genuinely party style of leadership and management and to intensify the supervision and verification of the actual implementation of the directives of the party and the decisions of party organizations. The development of principled criticism and self-criticism is to be ensured in every organization as a tested method of correcting short-comings and raising the responsibility of all personnel for entrusted matters.

Every party organization must focus its activity on questions pertaining to the mobilization of communists and all toilers to implement the decisions of the XXIV CPSU Congress and the tasks posed by the December (1974) Central Committee Plenum, the Appeal of the CPSU Central Committee to the party and the Soviet people, and resolutions on developing socialist competition for the successful fulfilment of the State Plan for Developing the Economy of the USSR for the year 1975 and the tasks of the Ninth Five-Year Plan as a whole. The lofty duty of communists is to continue to be in the vanguard of socialist competition, the movement for a communist attitude to labour, and to set an example of conscientiousness and creative initiative in production and in public and political life.

Special attention is to be paid to further increasing the fighting efficiency of primary party organizations as the decisive condition for intensifying party influence over all sectors of economic and cultural construction. The central committees of the communist parties, the krai, oblast, city, and raion party committees, and political organs are called upon to ensure differentiated guidance of primary party organizations, taking into consideration

**   Part of the document is omitted in the original.

the concrete conditions of their activity. Attention is to be focused on questions of the placement of party members and candidate members in production and in the sphere of science and culture. More concern must be shown for the training and instruction of the secretaries of primary and shop party organizations and party group organizers and in providing them with practical assistance in their work.

2   Party committees, political organs, and primary party organizations are instructed to use examples of the heroic history of the CPSU and concrete facts of its everyday multifaceted activity to instil in every communist the lofty qualities of a political fighter of the party. Fuller use is to be made for these purposes of party meetings where questions are to be discussed that trouble party members and candidate members, businesslike principled proposals and useful initiatives are to be supported, and cases of a disrespectful attitude to the opinions of communists are to be eliminated decisively. Forms of individual work with party members and candidate members that have proved themselves in the period of the exchange of party documents are to be perfected.

Party organizations must show unabated concern for the marxist-leninist training of communists, efforts are to be made to ensure that every member and candidate member of the party constantly raises his ideological-political level, and the necessary assistance is to be offered to them in this matter. The state of political training is to be evaluated according to its influence on the work and behaviour of communists.

In every party organization there must be an atmosphere of intolerance to any kind of negative phenomena. It is necessary to continue to raise the demands made on communists for strict fulfilment of the provisions of the CPSU Programme and Rules ...**

3   Party committees and political organs must continue to ensure the proper procedure with respect to the personal registration of communists and the handling of party housekeeping, considering this as an important factor for improving organization and strengthening discipline in the party. They have been instructed to strive for strict observance of the established procedures for transferring communists from one organization to another.

Pravda, 7 February 1975   *KPSS v rezoliutsiiakh* XI, 514–7

5.48
On the State of Criticism and Self-Criticism in the
Party Organization of Tambov Oblast   12 February 1975

The CPSU Central Committee notes that the Tambov oblast party organization, in fulfilling the decisions of the XXIV CPSU Congress, has done certain

----

**   Part of the document is omitted in the original.

work to improve guidance over economic and cultural construction and the communist education of the working people. However, the results achieved could have been significantly better had the CPSU oblast, city, and raion committees made fuller use of the party's tested method of criticism and self-criticism in doing away with existing short-comings and raising the responsibility of cadres for their assigned tasks.

Industry and agriculture in the oblast are developing much more slowly than projected by the Five-Year Plan. Every year the programme for capital construction is disrupted and poor use is made of reserves to raise the effectiveness of production. There are still high losses associated with management, turnover of cadres, violations of labour discipline, and theft of socialist property. These and other short-comings often do not receive an objective evaluation and are not subjected to principled criticism in party bodies and primary party organizations.

The CPSU oblast committee fails to serve as an example of self-critical analysis of its own work and state of affairs; it does little to teach the city and raion party committees and primary party organizations to do so. Proper exactingness is not required of cadres who fail to ensure the fulfilment of economic plans and assignments. A liberal attitude is taken towards personnel who violate party and state discipline and misuse their office. Many party committees, to the detriment of vital organizational work, concentrate their main efforts on preparing and adopting a large number of decisions and on conducting meetings and conferences. In their reports at plenums and party meetings, the positive sides of their activity are emphasized; as a rule, criticism is impersonal, is reduced to listing unsatisfactory indices, and fails to expose short-comings in the methods of work of party, soviet and economic bodies, and specific persons. This has an effect on the nature of speeches which, in a number of cases, fail to go beyond reports of the speaker's own activity and reports of accomplishments.

Criticism from below is developing poorly. In recent years, the plenums of the oblast committee and the Inzhavino, Umet, and Zherdevka raion committees have made essentially no criticism of their bureaus, secretaries, or departments, despite short-comings in their work. The activeness of communists is often reduced due to the fact that the party committees do a poor job of informing communists of their work and permit excessive regimentation in conducting plenums and party meetings. Not enough attention is paid to developing criticism and self-criticism in labour collectives, at trade union, Komsomol, and workers' meetings, and at regular production meetings.

Party organs fail to respond sharply enough to cases of an incorrect attitude to criticism. Some personnel agree verbally with rebukes but do nothing to rectify the short-comings. In the Tambov and Michurinsk city and Kirsanov raion party organizations, there have been cases of criticism being suppressed and persecution of those who voice criticism, yet the officials responsible for this were not promptly made answerable for it.

In the oblast newspaper, *Tambovskaia pravda*, and in the city and raion newspapers, critical articles, correspondence, and letters of the working people on questions of production development, upbringing work, and the activity of the party organizations and leading cadres are rarely printed. Many publications lack concreteness and persuasive argumentation. Party committees do not take adequate concern for the effectiveness of press material and often fail to respond to critical materials printed in newspapers.

The CPSU Central Committee resolves:

1   The CPSU oblast, city and raion committees and primary party organizations are ordered to do away with the noted short-comings and to ensure fulfilment of the instructions of the XXIV CPSU Congress and the requirements of the CPSU Rules on the all-round development of criticism and self-criticism.

The CPSU Central Committee emphasizes that, under present conditions, in connection with the growth in the scope and complexity of the tasks of communist construction that are being solved, the transfer to intensive methods of management and the turn toward qualitative indicators in all spheres of activity, criticism, and self-criticism take on ever greater significance as a means for raising the level of organizational, ideological, and educational work. As comrade L.I. Brezhnev points out, a thorough and self-critical analysis of both our accomplishments and our existing problems and short-comings is a necessary precondition for further progress. Extensive development of principled criticism and self-criticism is a sign of the political health of a party organization, its correct understanding of its duty to the party and the people.

Criticism and self-criticism must encourage the mobilization of communists and all working people in the oblast to carry out the decisions of the party congresses and plenums of the CPSU Central Committee, to fulfil and overfulfil state plans, to reveal and utilize more fully reserves for raising production effectiveness, to accelerate scientific and technological progress, and to develop the activeness of the masses in the competition for increasing the output of higher quality products with smaller outlays. It is necessary to analyse critically the state of affairs at every enterprise, construction site, kolkhoz, and sovkhoz that falls behind and to map out and implement concrete measures that ensure fulfilment of plans and socialist pledges. The introduction and mastering of new capacities, particularly in the chemical, light, and food industries, is to be accelerated. High growth rates are to be achieved in all branches of agriculture, backwardness is to be done away with in the production and procurement of sugar beets, sunflowers, potatoes, vegetables, and more persistent work is to be conducted to intensify specialization of farming and animal husbandry. Serious short-comings are to be eliminated in housing construction and in providing the population with cultural and everyday services.

2   The Tambov CPSU oblast, city, and raion committees are ordered to make fuller use of the method of criticism and self-criticism in educating cadres, organically combine trust and respect for people with principled exactingness towards them for their assigned tasks and for the observance of party and state discipline. There must be decisive opposition to the tendency of some leaders to cover up, by citing objective reasons, their failure to meet plan targets and their mistakes in organizational and educational work. High moral qualities, socialist initiative, intolerance of stagnation and inertia are to be instilled in all personnel. One must criticize not only those who make mistakes, but also those who fail to use every opportunity to develop production and who show no initiative.

It is important that the example of a correct attitude to criticism come from leaders. Principle in the posing of questions, the creation of the conditions for frank criticism from below, and the effectiveness of measures taken in response to criticism all depend primarily on them.

3   Guided by leninist norms of party life, the CPSU oblast, city, and raion committees must ensure active participation by all communists in discussing, working out, and implementing party decisions. Party members are to be better informed regarding the activity of party committees. Constant care must be taken that plenums and party meetings proceed in a businesslike manner, in an atmosphere of high exactingness by communists to each other and to elected party bodies, and that the most urgent questions are included for discussion. Reports at the plenums of the Tambov oblast committee and of many city and raion party committees must be more principled and self-critical.

With a view to raising the effectiveness of criticism, party committees have been ordered to establish strict supervision over the prompt elimination of disclosed short-comings and the causes of negative phenomena. It is necessary to put an end to incidents of suppressed criticism and to correct and, if required, punish – up to and including removal from their posts – personnel who fail to respond properly to criticism, interpret just rebukes leveled at them as undermining their authority, place personal self-esteem above public interests, and take vengeance on comrades who criticize them. At the same time, demagogy and slander must not be allowed to substitute for criticism. As V.I. Lenin pointed out, it is necessary to ensure that criticism be 'comradely, direct, and free of diplomacy and petty considerations.'* Its value is determined not by harshness of expression, but by the veracity, conclusiveness, and social significance of the questions it raises.

4   The CPSU oblast, city and raion committees, and primary party organizations are ordered constantly to improve their style and methods of activity and try to establish everywhere a truly party approach and party style in their

*   V.I. Lenin, *Polnoe sobranie sochinenii*, vol. 15, p. 245.

guidance of economic and cultural construction. They must subject to principled criticism everything that impedes this goal: bureaucratism, red tape, localist tendencies, and habits involving outdated techniques and methods of work. Particular attention is to be paid to ensuring that verification of the implementation of party and state directives and their own decisions is effective and systematic.

Measures are to be taken for the further development of criticism and self-criticism in soviet, economic, trade union, and Komsomol organizations of the oblast. Ties with the masses are to be consolidated systematically, the people's needs and attitudes are to be studied, and an attentive attitude on the part of all leaders with respect to the statements and letters of the working people is to be ensured.

5   The party committees are ordered constantly to show concern for the enhancement of the role of the press and other media of mass information in developing criticism and self-criticism. When propagandizing advanced experience, the oblast, city, and raion newspapers must expose shortcomings in work more thoroughly, analyse the causes of short-comings, and make efforts to ensure that critical material relates to issues of the day, reflects an understanding of the issues in question, and contains principled conclusions. Worker and rural correspondents are to be drawn more actively into discussing urgent problems of the life of the oblast in the press. Existing cases of formal answers and the scornful attitude of some personnel to press warnings must receive a sharper response.

Pravda, 28 February 1975   *KPSS v rezoliutsiiakh* XI, 531–5

5.49
On the Work Experience of the Party Organizations and Collectives of Advanced Industrial Enterprises in L'vov Oblast in Developing and Implementing a Comprehensive System to Control Quality of Output*   8 August 1975

The theme of quality control has grown increasingly relevant to the party's assessment of the production process. In the resolution on the Central Committee Report adopted by the XXIV Congress, quality was identified along with scientific-technological progress and labour productivity as essential components of economic development. At the XXV Congress, Brezhnev was to advance the theme that the Tenth Five-Year Plan be called 'the Five-Year Plan of efficiency and quality.' The present resolution signaled the implementation

*   Excerpt: document not published in full.

of a nation-wide campaign aimed at improving, stabilizing, and co-ordinating quality control in production. On the basis of a number of limited experiments at the local level, a unified approach to quality control was to be developed in each locality. The experience in setting standards, applying them, and co-ordinating quality control at the local level was to be generalized by all-union state agencies, which were then to work out the basic principles for a state-wide quality control system. The ultimate aim was to set up a network incorporating a number of standardized criteria and procedures to ensure quality control through the regulation of the several stages of production at the plant level by applying all-union norms that were supervised by each ministry (branch) and by local party organs (territorial).

... Advanced plants in the city of L'vov have developed and are actively implementing a comprehensive system of quality control. The experience that has been accumulated and proved its value in the work of the industrial enterprises of Saratov, Moscow, Leningrad, Sverdlovsk, Gorky, Iaroslavl, and Kremenchuk has been incorporated into this system. Further creative development of this experience has made it possible to implement a unified approach to solving the problem of raising quality on a planned basis and to combine branch and territorial techniques of quality control ...

The L'vov oblast party organization is conducting active work for the extensive study and dissemination of the experience of advanced associations and enterprises that have attained high indicators of quality in their output. Under the oblast, city, and raion party committees there are operating voluntary commissions to check the quality of output and technical-economic councils, which work out concrete proposals to eliminate existing short-comings on the basis of analysis of the work of industrial enterprises. They provide assistance to the enterprises in disseminating advanced experience.

The party organizations of the enterprises are persistently engaged in educating the working people in the spirit of a communist attitude to labour and raising their sense of responsibility for the quality of output. They regularly organize technical conferences, 'Quality Days,' public reviews, contests, and make extensive use of the factory press and radio for these purposes ...

The CPSU Central Committee resolves:

1   To approve the work experience of the party organizations and collectives of advanced industrial enterprises of the L'vov oblast in developing and implementing a comprehensive system of product quality control ...

2   To recommend that the central committees of the union republic communist parties, the krai and oblast party committees, the State Committee

for Standards of the USSR Council of Ministers, ministries and departments organize study of the work experience of the L'vov oblast party organizations and collectives of advanced enterprises in planning and ensuring steady growth in the quality of output on the basis of enterprise standards and that they take measures to use this experience more extensively in industry.

3   The USSR State Committee for Standards, together with the State Committee for Science and Technology of the USSR Council of Ministers and the USSR Gosplan are instructed to generalize the accumulated experience of the application of the L'vov, Saratov, Iaroslavl, and other systems of product quality control and, on this basis, they are instructed to work out the basic principles for a unified system of state quality control ... They are also to prepare proposals for the introduction of standard technological processes, equipment, instruments, and means of mechanization in the economy based on the complex of standards of a unified system for technological preparation of production ...

4   ... It is recommended that the USSR ministries and departments consider this question at meetings of the boards of ministries with the participation of the leaders of enterprises, scientific-research institutes, draft and design organizations ...

Pravda, 15 August 1975   *KPSS v rezoliutsiiakh*, XII, 35–9

5.50
On Party Guidance over the Organs of
People's Control in the Latvian SSR*   12 August 1975

This resolution on the party's guidance over the organs of people's control in the Latvian Republic indicated an interest on the part of the Brezhnev regime in redefining and reinvigorating the role of people's control agencies responsible for supervision over the state administrative apparatus. The organs of people's control were to be upgraded from their eclipsed status since the December 1965 Central Committee Plenum. However, they were not simply to regain their status as a symbol of the transition to communism through increased participation of the broad working masses in the process of communist administration. Performance was to be evaluated primarily by pragmatic, efficiency-oriented criteria rather than populistic images. Greater stress was to be placed on the results of supervision and verification rather than on the educational benefits accruing to participants at the rank-and-file level. The organs of people's control were also to tighten up their own internal organiza-

*   Excerpt: document not published in full.

tion, identify priorities, focus attention, and channel efforts and co-ordinate them with similar activities of the Komsomol and soviets. In brief, the organs of people's control were to undergo a process of professionalization characterized by improved internal operations, clearer definition of goals and jurisdiction, and improved co-ordination of activities with other state and public agencies. All of this was to be done under the close guidance and supervision of the local party organs.

The CPSU Central Committee notes that, owing to increased attention and assistance on the part of the central committee of the Latvian Communist Party and of the republic's party organizations following the XXIV Party Congress, the organs of people's control of the Latvian SSR have become stronger in their organization and have considerably improved their work in verifying the implementation of party and government directives and in strengthening state discipline. Of great significance in this matter were the decisions of the December (1973 and 1974) plenums of the CPSU Central Committee and the instructions of Comrade L.I. Brezhnev on intensifying supervision and verification of the implementation of directives. The committees, groups, and posts of people's control are actively assisting party and state bodies in implementing the economic and social policy of the party and in accomplishing economic tasks.

In guidance over the organs of people's control, the party committees attach important significance to the selection and training of cadres. In the republic, 35 of the 41 chairmen of committees of people's control have been elected members of party bureaus of city and raion party committees; almost half of the members of the committees of people's control are deputies of soviets; about 90 per cent of group leaders are deputy secretaries or bureau members of primary party organizations.

At the same time, the CPSU Central Committee considers that the central committee of the Latvian Communist Party, the city and raion committees, and the primary party organizations are not yet making full use of the potentials of organs of people's control to intensify verification of work done in all sectors of economic and cultural construction; they have not made efforts to ensure organic unity in verification, prevention, and correction of short-comings in their activity throughout the republic.

Many party organizations fail to scrutinize thoroughly the work of the organs of people's control and fail to take into consideration their specific character; they do an insufficient job of directing the attention of committees, groups, and posts [of people's control] toward the struggle to improve the qualitative indices of the work of enterprises and organizations and to raise the effectiveness of social production. In the republic, individual branches of the economy fluctuate in their work, some enterprises and organizations fail to cope with their targets in production volume and growth of labour productivity. In many kolkhozes and sovkhozes the yield capacity of fields and the productivity of livestock increase slowly and development of the fodder base has been permitted to lag seriously. In the economy, non-productive expenditures are still high; squandering and embezzlement, deceit and distortion of data are permitted ... At the same time committees and groups of people's control fail to show the necessary persistence and principle in overcoming the noted short-comings and do not provide systematic supervision over the state of executive discipline in ministries, departments, organizations, and institutions; on many occasions incidents of bureaucratism and red tape are accepted.

The still-low effectiveness of supervision must be noted. In a number of cases, the verifications conducted by the organs of people's control are superficial and lack effectiveness. The activity of many committees and groups often is limited to a statement of exposed short-comings and negligence; they often disperse their forces, fail to complete work that has been started, and get carried away with the quantitative aspect, forgetting that the effectiveness of supervision is determined not by the number of verifications and adopted decisions, but by real results and improvement of matters.

The republic, city, and raion committees of people's control are not yet closely connected with their groups and posts and, for this reason, they do not always possess comprehensive and objective information on the state of affairs at enterprises, institutions, and organizations. The results of the activity of the groups and posts are at times weakened because conditions necessary in their work are not created; often their proposals and recommendations fail to receive proper support from the administration and economic leaders, while party organizations accept such a state of affairs. This leads to lower activity of some groups and posts and to a lack of interest on the part of many people's inspectors in the work assigned to them; a significant proportion of inspectors are formally listed on paper, but, in essence, do not work. Close ties between the organs of people's control and trade union and Komsomol organizations have not been truly established.

The CPSU Central Committee resolves:

1   The central committee of the Latvian Communist Party and the city and raion party committees are ordered to do away with the short-comings noted in the current resolution, to ensure a comprehensive improvement in guidance over organs of people's control, to scrutinize more thoroughly the essence of their activity, and to provide more assistance in their work. Exactingness towards the organs of people's control is to be intensified for fulfilment of the tasks confronting them. In this, party organizations must take fuller consideration of their character and specific nature as one of the important forms of socialist democracy; efforts are to be made to ensure that lenin-

ist principles of organizing mass, permanently operating, effective, and open supervision is strictly implemented everywhere.

A very important task of people's inspectors is the struggle for the fulfilment and overfulfilment of assignments of the final year of the five-year-plan period and of the socialist pledges accepted by labour collectives, and for a worthy welcome for the XXV CPSU Congress, thereby creating a sound basis for successful work in the tenth five-year-plan period.

2   It is necessary that the central committee of the Communist Party, the council of ministers of the republic, the city and raion party committees, and the primary party organizations continue to strengthen the organs of people's control organizationally, to perfect the methods of their practical activity, to generalize and disseminate their positive experience. Efforts are to be made to ensure that every committee of people's control becomes a truly exemplary, highly authoritative body. Particular attention is to be paid to guidance over groups and posts of people's control that operate directly in the very midst of the masses and constitute the foundation of the people's control.

Party and soviet bodies are to examine regularly the reports of committees and groups of the people's control on the results of verifications, on the observance of legality in economic activity, and on the establishment of departmental supervision. The leaders of ministries and departments, enterprises and organizations must eliminate the short-comings revealed by people's inspectors without delay.

3   The CPSU Central Committee demands that party and soviet bodies of the republic and economic leaders take a more attentive attitude to people's inspectors. Constant concern is to be taken to ensure that those who are elected as people's inspectors are principled comrades, demanding of themselves and uncompromising, people who, as Lenin expressed, 'shall not say a word contrary to their consciences' when it concerns the defence of state and public interests. It is necessary to enhance their authority in every possible way, to encourage them for conscientiously fulfilling their honourable public duty, to protect their honour and personal dignity. Officials who permit suppression of criticism, covering up of short-comings, or persecution of people's inspectors are to be held strictly accountable.

The responsibility of people's inspectors before the labour collectives that elect them is to be raised. It is considered expedient to ensure that the groups and posts of people's control inform collectives of working people at least once a year of their activity and their fulfilment of the instructions given to them.

4   The committee of people's control of the Latvian SSR is to take concrete measures designed to perfect the entire practice of supervision and raise its effectiveness. Efforts of the people's inspectors are to be concentrated on verification of the most important and pressing questions; they are not to disperse their efforts; they are to ensure unity of verification with organiza-

tion of the implementation of decisions. In the organs of people's control it is necessary that all materials be examined in a detailed and qualified way and that substantiated and concrete decisions and recommendations be worked out.

There must be high principle and a businesslike nature at the base of the work of organs of people's control. By their entire activity, the organs of people's control are called upon to maintain a truly party approach to matters, actively to shape public opinion against existing short-comings, decisively to struggle against inertia and stagnation, to oppose anything that goes against the interests of the state and the people and any attempts to act by evading the law, no matter what the source. In the struggle to safeguard socialist property against incidents of mismanagement and squandering and various types of violations, fuller use is to be made of the rights granted to committees and groups by the statute on the organs of people's control in the USSR.

5   The central committee of the Latvian Communist Party, the city and raion party committees, and the republic's committee of people's control are to devote more attention to publicity of supervision as an important means of raising its effectiveness. For these purposes, more extensive use is to be made of the mass media, of party, trade union, and Komsomol meetings, sessions of soviets, branch conferences, and meetings of activists.

The editorial offices of newspapers, radio, and television have been instructed to provide more profound and substantive coverage of the activity of organs of people's control and to present a vivid picture of the activists of public supervision.

6   The CPSU Central Committee calls attention to the fact that various departments of the republic conduct too many verifications and reviews of all types of enterprises, kolkhozes, and institutions, distracting personnel from fulfilling their immediate duties and lowering their responsibility for work assigned to them.

The central committee of the Communist Party and the council of ministers of the Latvian SSR are instructed to bring the necessary order into this business and to eliminate parallelism and duplication in conducting verifications. Measures are to be taken to consolidate ties between the work of organs of people's control, standing commissions of Soviets of Working People's Deputies, the 'Komsomol searchlight,' commissions, and trade union organizations.

7   The USSR People's Control Committee is to devote more attention to the work of organs of people's control in the localities, to improve direction of their activity, to provide more practical assistance, and to raise the activeness of people's inspectors in fulfilling party and government directives.

Partiiinaia zhizn', no. 17   *KPSS v rezoliutsiiakh* XII, 40–4
(1975): 5–7

XXV Party Congress   24 February–3 March 1976

The XXV Congress proceedings broke with the pattern that had been established under Brezhnev in two important ways. First, there was no lengthy and detailed resolution on the Central Committee Report. This change had the effect of raising the status of Brezhnev's report to that approaching a formal congress resolution. Second, the XXV Congress was noted for an unprecedented outburst of praise for the General Secretary. At no previous congress since Stalin's death had any Soviet leader been the subject of such an outpouring of personal adulation.

In his report to the congress (*Current Soviet Policies* VII (1976), 4–31), Brezhnev presented a sober analysis of the achievements of the Ninth Five-Year Plan and the prospects for the next plan period, starting from the position that, unless structural limitations on economic growth could be overcome, the Soviet economy would suffer. This led Brezhnev to argue that the economy must undergo significant changes in the areas of labour productivity, efficiency, quality, investment policy, and planning. Five sets of policy areas were identified as crucial to determining the success of the party's economic programme: an acceleration of scientific and technological progress; continuation of Brezhnev's agricultural programme of capital investments, along with organizational reform to reduce unit costs through concentration and specialization of production on the basis of inter-farm co-operation and agro-industrial integration; significant improvements in consumer goods production and distribution, mainly through a change in attitude of those responsible for light industry and better use of the industry's existing reserves; greater use of foreign economic relations to advance the Soviet economy; and, an improvement in economic management.

Several aspects of Brezhnev's report on the party are worth noting. First, there were no proposals for substantial change in the party's structures or procedures. The keynote was continuity with the principles established at the XX Congress in 1956 and reaffirmed with the removal of Khrushchev in October 1964. Within this context of institutional stability and continuity Brezhnev re-emphasized the messages of Central Committee decisions issued since 1964, including the need to stress quality in recruitment, routine and publicity in the conduct of party business, and responsiveness of leadership. Third, while taking note that there was no alarming situation in the party with respect to the fulfilment of decisions or the state of criticism and self-criticism, Brezhnev went on to make the point that steadfast adherence to a leninist style in work was essential for the successful activity of the party. He then suggested that this might include the possibility of improving the forms and methods of party work on a scientific basis: '... there is nothing immutable about either the party itself or the nature of its activity.' However, no specific indications were provided by Brezhnev as to the general direction these changes might take or the specific adaptations that party organizations might have to cope with in the immediate future.

Brezhnev's remarks in the area of ideological work were suggestive of a tighter policy, but again, specific recommendations were lacking. In contrast to the flexibility expected of party form and activity, Brezhnev started with 'the immutability of the theoretical propositions and principles that express the essence of marxism-leninism.' Research in the social sciences was a necessary contribution to the development of socialist society, but Brezhnev warned that 'the creative comparison of views should be based on our common marxist-leninist platform. It is important that the principles of party spirit in science be consistently observed ...' In an extremely strong statement on the subject, Brezhnev warned that détente had intensified the ideological confrontation between the imperialist and socialist systems and that in this struggle between the two world views 'there can be no place for neutralism and compromise. Here we need a high level of political vigilance, vigorous, efficient, and persuasive propaganda work, and a timely rebuff to hostile ideological sabotage.' This language is reminiscent of the April 1968 Central Committee Plenum. According to Brezhnev, the situation called for a tightening of policy and controls in a number of areas affecting ideological work.

Finally, Brezhnev's position on the state was ambiguous, suggesting an attempt at balancing differing views. There were several indicators in Brezhnev's report of a 'law and order' approach to the state: reinforcement of the role and status of the soviets; a call for the issuance of a code of laws of the Soviet state with the express purpose of increasing the stability of the entire structure of law and order; improvement in the activities and cadres of the militia, procurators' offices, courts, and judicial agencies so that they could protect Soviet legality, the interests of Soviet society and the rights of citizens; conducting of all work of the state security agencies under the party's guidance and unremitting control, with the support of the broad masses of the working people, and on the basis of strict observance of constitutional norms and socialist legality; and, the preparation of a new draft constitution. In contrast to the 'law and order' theme were a number of indicators that an element of arbitrariness was still to persist: the continuing role of ideological considerations in determining the direction of literature and art; praise for the state security agencies and the notation that their activities were organized in accordance with requirements stemming from the international situation, which had previously been described in terms of an ideological confrontation requiring a high level of political vigilance and a rebuff to hostile ideological sabotage; and, Brezhnev's commitment to a position of political relativism in recalling 'Lenin's words to the effect that in our society everything that serves the interests of the construction of communism is moral' and in drawing the conclusion from these words that 'for us that which serves the interests of the people, the interests of communist construction, is democratic.'

A total of 4998 delegates attended the congress. No delegates with consultative rights were elected, a break with tradition dating back to before the revolution. The congress followed the pattern of the two previous congresses in receiving the Central Committee Report from Brezhnev and the Report on the Five-Year Plan from Kosygin. The congress elected a Central Committee of 287 full and 139 candidate members. Several changes in personnel were announced: D.S. Poliansky was dropped from the Politburo; D.F. Ustinov and G.V. Romanov were promoted to full membership in the Politburo; G.A. Aliyev was promoted to candidate member; K.U. Chernenko and M.V. Zimianin were promoted to the Secretariat.

5.51
On the Report of Comrade L.I. Brezhnev: Report of the CPSU Central Committee and the Party's Immediate Tasks in the Sphere of Domestic and Foreign Policy   1 March 1976

Having heard and discussed the report of the General Secretary of the CPSU Central Committee, Comrade L.I. Brezhnev, the Report of the CPSU Central Committee and the Immediate Tasks of the Party in the Sphere of Domestic and Foreign Policy, the XXV Congress of the Communist Party of the Soviet Union resolves:

1   Wholly and completely to approve the political line and practical activity of the Central Committee of the party.

2   To approve the Report of the CPSU Central Committee and to recommend that all party organizations be guided in their work by the propositions and tasks set forth by Comrade L.I. Brezhnev in the Report of the CPSU Central Committee.

Pravda, 2 March 1976   *KPSS v rezoliutsiiakh* XII, 83

5.52
On the Further Development of Specialization and Concentration of Agricultural Production on the Basis of Inter-farm Co-operation and Agro-Industrial Integration   28 May 1976

The early 1970's saw the introduction in Soviet industry of a nation-wide campaign to reorganize the industrial sector according to a network of intermediate level structures known as associations (obedineniia). The principles of inter-enterprise co-ordination developed in this process soon came to be applied in a number of experiments in the agricultural sector as well. Inter-kolkhoz associations had been formed as early as the late 1950's on a local level. However, their development was sporadic and uneven, a reflection of the failure to develop a national policy on the issue and of the differential degree of commitment to them on the part of regional political leaders. At the XXV Party Congress in 1976, Brezhnev raised the question of inter-farm associations to a high-level policy matter by remarking in his Central Committee Report that 'the experience of Moldavia, a number of Russian Federation provinces, the Ukraine, Belorussia, and some other republics indicates that great possibilities for the rapid growth of production volume, a sizable rise in labour productivity, and a reduction of unit costs can be found in the specialization and concentration of production on the basis of inter-farm co-operation and agro-industrial integration. Hence, this course must be pursued more vigorously' (*Current Soviet Policies* VII (1976) 19–20).

Inter-farm associations were to be developed for ideological and economic reasons. On the ideological level, it was suggested that the formation of agricultural associations had emerged as a logical and necessary stage in the evolution of collective forms of property in the direction of the purer state form of ownership. The conditions for this stage had matured and must be exploited to achieve a new and higher level of agricultural organization. The associations, which would bring state and collective farms closer together through co-operative endeavours and which would bring the city and countryside together through the industrialization of agricultural activities, were seen as a proper mechanism in achieving the ultimate goals of full socialist ownership of the agricultural means of production through state ownership and the elimination of essential differences between urban and rural ways of life. The more compelling reason for the introduction of inter-farm associations in agricultural organizations at this time lay in the regime's desire to improve efficiency in the agricultural sector. The major organizational and investment policies that the regime introduced in 1965 and 1966 had still not accomplished their desired effect by raising agricultural efficiency and productivity to required and stable levels. The inter-farm associations represented an attempt to restructure management and reorganize agriculture to take advantage of certain economies of production: economies associated with vertical integration of supplies for agricultural production, agricultural production itself, and the processing of certain agricultural outputs (e.g. reduction of storage and transportation losses and costs); more rational utilization of the rural labour force by close siting of agricultural and processing enterprises; a more effective balance between centralized and decentralized agricultural decision making by consolidating local decision-making units and giving them greater autonomy in some areas; and, a more rational approach to agricultural concentration and specialization through the consolidation of middle-level management in fewer decision-making units, pooling financial and material resources, and possibly allowing for some limited working out of intermediate prices of agricultural products at the association level, which would give the farms some flexibility in adjusting their output mix to maximize their incomes.

1   The CPSU Central Committee, having discussed the proposals submitted by Comrade L.I. Brezhnev, General Secretary, on the further development of specialization and concentration of agricultural production on the
basis of inter-farm co-operation and agro-industrial integration and on
improving the forms of agricultural management in the country, considers
that implementation of these important measures approved by the XXV CPSU
Congress has become an urgent necessity and will have great political, economic, and social significance.

The Communist Party, our state, and the entire Soviet people are making great efforts to ensure reliable growth in agricultural production. The
March (1965) and following plenums of the CPSU Central Committee worked
out a broad, comprehensive programme for an upswing in agriculture that
was developed by the XXIV and XXV party congresses. The basic elements
of this programme are: creation of stable economic conditions ensuring
expanded reproduction in kolkhozes and sovkhozes; consistent implementation of the course for intensification; introduction of contemporary achievements of scientific-technological progress; consolidation of the material and
technical base; comprehensive mechanization and chemicalization of agriculture; extensive land reclamation; observance of the leninist principle of
material incentives; a correct combination of public, collective, and private
interests; a system of social measures aimed at a considerable rise in the
standard of living of rural workers ...

3   Despite the positive results achieved in agriculture in recent years, its
level, economic indices, and production growth rates of its most important
products, the CPSU Central Committee notes that our growing requirements
do not correspond to existing potentials. If this branch is to achieve the
advanced goals opened by modern science and technology, the tasks of
intensifying agriculture and improving its efficiency must be given top priority. One of the main ways to resolve this task is to specialize and concentrate
agricultural production and transfer it to a modern industrial base. The
potentials found here are enormous ...

Now that our agriculture has grown significantly stronger and its material base is becoming more solid, the multibranch character and inadequate
concentration of production in kolkhozes and sovkhozes hinder the development of industrialization in agriculture and animal husbandry, lower the
efficiency of expenditures and, in essence, are becoming a drag on economic
progress and, hence, on scientific-technological progress in this area. The
state is allocating large capital investments for the production of new equipment and mineral fertilizers and construction of land-reclamation systems, is
supplying kolkhozes and sovkhozes with tractors, combines, and other
machinery on an ever-greater scale, yet labour expenditures are decreasing
slowly and the unit costs of the most important agricultural products remain
essentially at the same level.

On multibranch farms, agricultural commodity output, and particularly in animal husbandry, is dispersed in many cases over small brigades and livestock sections, resulting in a scattering of funds and material resources, a hindering of comprehensive mechanization and the introduction of new progressive technologies, and a lowering of profitability.

In a number of oblasts, krais, and republics, attempts have been made to accomplish the task of raising the effectiveness of agricultural production only by amalgamating existing brigades and livestock sections without conducting specialization with an accounting of natural and economic conditions and without radical changes in production organization and technology. However, such an approach, like the consolidation of kolkhozes and sovkhozes conducted in the past, does not overcome the major short-comings inherent in multibranch farming.

Further development of productive forces objectively requires a new approach in principle to organizing agricultural production, its more thorough specialization, the combining of the efforts of farms for the purpose of making extensive use of the achievements of scientific-technological progress. Science and contemporary practice confirm that this is a reliable way to make rational use of land, labour, machinery, and other factors that intensify and, on this basis, accelerate the growth of output and improve the efficiency of agricultural production. The advantages and positive influence of inter-farm specialization and concentration on the economy is evident in the numerous examples of the work of large livestock farms, complexes, and other inter-farm enterprises in the Moldavian ssr, the Belorussian ssr, the Ukrainian ssr, Krasnodarsk Krai, the Mari assr, Voronezh and Penza oblasts, and a number of other oblasts and republics. At present, there are approximately 6000 inter-farm specialized associations, organizations, and enterprises operating in the country. As experience shows, outlays of labour on production per unit of output are 2.5 to 3 times lower and unit costs are 1.5 to 2 times lower than on non-specialized farms. An ever-increasing number of kolkhozes and sovkhozes are entering into inter-farm co-operation. This process has active support among kolkhozniks and workers on sovkhozes.

The cpsu Central Committee considers that specialization and concentration of agricultural production on the basis of extensive co-operation and its transfer to a modern industrial base is the main direction for the further development of socialist agriculture and a new stage in the practical implementation of the ideas of the leninist co-operative plan under the conditions of developed socialism.

Compared to the period of collectivization when small individual peasant farms with their primitive means of production were unified in co-operatives, today's process of agricultural concentration is characterized above all by the combined efforts of kolkhozes and sovkhozes for the purpose of creating large industrial-type enterprises producing for large markets by more thorough specialization of all farms, by the emergence and development of new forms of inter-branch ties, and by radical changes in the structure and nature of production. Inter-farm co-operation expands the scope and possibilities of kolkhoz and sovkhoz production and raises the level of its concentration without excessively enlarging farms or forming unmanageable ones. All this facilitates the increased production of agricultural products and the accomplishment of a major social task: to raise the level of socialization of kolkhoz production, improve social relations, bring the two forms of socialist ownership closer together, and gradually eliminate the essential differences between the city and the countryside. Such a qualitatively new stage in the creative application of leninist teaching on co-operation in the practice of communist construction is a historical law, has matured objectively, and cannot be ignored or bypassed. As Comrade L.I. Brezhnev, General Secretary of the CPSU Central Committee, emphasized at the XXV Party Congress, it is necessary to pursue the course of specialization and concentration more actively. Our organizational work, planning, and utilization of economic levers must facilitate this progressive process in every possible way. The key to raising the effectiveness of agricultural production lies in more thorough specialization and concentration ...

4   Specialization and concentration of agricultural production is a many-sided process. The country consists of large specialized zones for the commodity output of grain, cotton, sugar beet, vegetables, fruits and grapes, tea, citrus crops, fiber flax, milk, and wool. It is necessary to continue to intensify zonal specialization. Planning and agricultural agencies must improve it in every possible way, striving for the rational utilization of land and favourable natural, climatic, and economic conditions in every district of the country to obtain more agricultural products and reduce expenditures.

In recent years, state specialized enterprises producing individual types of agricultural products have received considerable development. Poultry farms, large complexes producing pork, beef, and milk, vegetable farms, and hot-house combines are being set up around cities and industrial centres. They are developing on an industrial basis, have high labour productivity, and their contribution will grow steadily in providing the country with agricultural products.

At the same time, the task of supplying the country with necessary products to a fuller extent requires rational utilization of the enormous potentials of all kolkhozes and sovkhozes through all-round co-operation, specialization, and concentration of their production. This process arises and develops in the course of economic co-operation between kolkhozes, sovkhozes, and other state enterprises for the purpose of organizing the production of individual types of products on a modern technological basis with the use of industrial methods and progressive technologies, this often being beyond the power of and disadvantageous to an individual farm, even a large or economically strong one.

More thorough specialization and concentration on the basis of inter-farm co-operation creates for every kolkhoz and sovkhoz, large or small, and with different economic levels, equal possibilities for a consistent transfer to highly intensive specialized production, for a steady strengthening and development of socialized farming, and for ensuring high rates of expanded reproduction.

While noting that in many republics, krais, and oblasts only the first steps have been taken in specialization and concentration on the basis of inter-farm co-operation, that it is still in its initial stage, and that it is developing through adaptation to the existing system of planning, financing, material-technical supplies, and management of agricultural production, the CPSU considers it necessary to give this process – which to a great extent determines the future of our agriculture – a planned character.

Party, soviet, and economic bodies are ordered to facilitate in every possible way the specialization and concentration of agricultural production on the basis of extensive co-operation and to create the necessary conditions for this. Fuller use is to be made of existing experience in agriculture, as well as in industry, relating to specialization, concentration, and co-operation of enterprises and the organization of production and science-production associations.

5   The CPSU Central Committee draws the attention of party, soviet, and agricultural agencies to the necessity of a differentiated approach to and stage-by-stage resolution of all questions related to the practical introduction of specialization and concentration of production on the basis of inter-farm co-operation and agro-industrial integration.

In the first stage, on the basis of inter-farm co-operation, pooling of finances, material-technical resources, and manpower, kolkhozes and sovkhozes possess the possibility of creating large specialized inter-kolkhoz, inter-sovkhoz, kolkhoz-sovkhoz, sovkhoz-kolkhoz, and other state-kolkhoz enterprises and associations of an industrial type for the production of meat, milk, eggs, wool, combined and other kinds of fodder, for pedigreed stock breeding, seed growing, gardening, and vegetable growing, for storing and initial processing of agricultural products, for agro-chemical servicing, joint utilization of machinery and transport, construction and land-reclamation work, forestry, and production of building materials and other materials.

By creating large specialized enterprises on an inter-farm basis, the co-operative members are able to concentrate their efforts on developing the production of grain, industrial crops and other branches that will become more specialized on these farms.

It is necessary for the state to provide all possible assistance by working out draft projects and supplying machinery, equipment, and other material resources to kolkhozes and sovkhozes that enter co-operatives and are ready to allocate their funds for this purpose.

Scientific-technological progress and the organization of large specialized enterprises and associations in agriculture ensure favourable preconditions for further development of agro-industrial integration, an organic fusion of agricultural production with industry, and the creation in the country of an extensive network of agro-industrial enterprises and associations that have a great future. This process must be accompanied by further deepening of the division of labour among farms, a still higher level of specialization and co-operation, and the establishment of direct contacts between agriculture and industry. As a result, conditions will be created for bringing kolkhoz-co-operative property closer to state property and their merging into general public property in the future.

The ripening of economic conditions and the accumulation of experience in inter-farm co-operation and agro-industrial integration in the interests of accelerated agricultural development and its greater effectiveness do not take place simultaneously in different districts of the country and different branches of production. In a number of republics, krais, and oblasts, parallel to the process of specialization and concentration on the basis of inter-farm co-operation, agro-industrial integration is already developing successfully, even today; there is effective operation of enterprises and associations in which production, storage, and industrial processing are organically combined, for example, in the case of fruits, grapes, vegetables, and some other types of agricultural products. Stages in the development of inter-farm co-operation and agro-industrial integration in different zones may take place consecutively or simultaneously. The time period and rates for carrying out this work must be specified with consideration for local possibilities and features ...

6   The CPSU Central Committee considers it necessary to emphasize that, when conducting work in specializing and concentrating agricultural production on the basis of inter-farm co-operation and agro-industrial integration, the following principles that have been tested in the practice of socialist construction in the countryside must be strictly observed:

–   the voluntary nature of joint co-operation between kolkhozes, sovkhozes and other enterprises;

–   a scientific approach to the selection of organizational forms, directions, and sequencing in conducting specialization and concentration of farms, with consideration for their production structure and economy, the peculiar features of the branches of production and accumulated experience;

–   preservation of the economic independence of kolkhozes, sovkhozes, and other enterprises and organizations entering into inter-farm and agro-industrial associations;

–   democratic centralism in organizing the management of the production activity of associations;

–   the material interests of the farms, as well as kolkhozniks and workers on sovkhozes and in other enterprises, in developing and raising the effectiveness of social production of the association as a whole and every enterprise individually;

– the accomplishment of the main objective of specialization and concentration – a considerable increase in the production of agricultural products and amounts sold to the state, improvement in the quality of agricultural products, a growth in labour productivity, and a reduction in expenditures.

Inter-farm, agro-industrial specialized production associations (inter-kolkhoz, inter-sovkhoz, kolkhoz-state, and state-kolkhoz) are created with consideration for territorial and branch criteria.

As a rule, production associations are organized within the boundaries of an administrative district according to the territorial-branch criterion. In this case, the farms create, in co-operative conditions, large specialized inter-farm enterprises, determine the directions of specialization in the production of commodity output for each kolkhoz and sovkhoz, and jointly carry out measures to transfer all branches of agricultural production over to an industrial base within the framework of the association.

Production associations based on the branch criterion are created according to the volume of production and location of farms specializing in a given type of production within the framework of a single or several administrative districts, or within an entire oblast, krai, or republic. Science-production associations are organized according to this criterion for selection and seed growing, pedigreed stock breeding, developing progressive industrial technologies for farming and animal husbandry, and producing individual types of specialized products and other products.

A significant number of sovkhozes and kolkhozes, especially in Kazakhstan, Siberia, the northern Caucasus, the Urals, and the Volga Region have large areas of arable land. In these places, reserves for intra-farm specialization and concentration often are still not used in optimal amounts on an industrial basis in the farms themselves. But, even on such kolkhozes and sovkhozes it is necessary, along with the intensification of co-operation of profit-and-loss intra-farm subdivisions and the consolidation of production ties among them, to make fuller use of the large possibilities opened by inter-farm specialization and concentration of production.

Co-operation in the sphere of production services, as well as in the non-productive sphere of creating joint health protection and cultural-everyday facilities must receive wide development.

7   The CPSU Central Committee commissions the communist party central committees and the councils of ministers of the union republics, the krai and oblast party committees, the councils of ministers of the autonomous republics, the executive committees of krais and oblasts, the USSR Gosplan, the USSR Ministry of Agriculture, kolkhoz councils, the USSR Ministry of Food Industry, the USSR Ministry of Meat and Milk Industry, the USSR Ministry of Light Industry and their local agencies, with the participation of scholars, leaders, and specialists in agriculture and the processing industry and the broad enlistment of kolkhozniks and workers on sovkhozes and other enterprises, to work out concrete, scientifically substantiated, long-range plans for carrying out specialization and concentration on the basis of inter-farm co-operation and agro-industrial integration, taking into account local conditions and potentials as well as existing practical experience. In doing so, there is to be no haste, skipping of stages, or carrying things to extremes. It is necessary to conduct this business in a rational and economically knowledgeable manner, taking into account all aspects and consequences of the work being done ...

... It is especially necessary to warn about the impermissibility of gigantomania, the construction of economically unfounded super-large enterprises for production of meat, milk, and other products ...

The CPSU Central Committee calls attention to the fact that specialization and concentration on the basis of inter-farm co-operation and agro-industrial integration, the transformation of agricultural production to an industrial base is not a one-time measure but a lengthy process designed for the long term and tied to specific economic conditions and the level of development of productive forces. The pace of conducting this work will depend, in significant measure, on how purposefully and effectively kolkhozes, sovkhozes, and other enterprises utilize their own funds, as well as state capital investments and material-technical resources allocated in accordance with economic plans. The task consists in striving to achieve the greatest results from invested funds, not dissipating resources, directing them above all to the reconstruction of livestock sections and other operating units, and ensuring the rational combination of new construction with the reconstruction of existing production facilities.

The CPSU Central Committee warns party, soviet, and economic organizations against any 'decreeing' from above of specialization and co-operation and the imposition of forms of production organization and management that are not tested by science and practice. It is also necessary to curb resolutely all attempts to impede this process, to mark time, and to approach the business from a departmental or localistic perspective ...

Pravda, 2 June 1976   *KPSS v rezoliutsiiakh* XII, 274–88

5.53
On the Tasks of Party Studies in Light of
the Decisions of the XXV CPSU Congress   12 June 1976

... The CPSU Central Committee resolves:

1   The central committees of the union republic communist parties, the oblast, okrug, city and raion party committees, and primary party organizations, proceeding from the decisions of the XXV CPSU Congress, are to carry out practical measures for further development of the marxist-leninist education of communists and non-party people, for enriching the content of study, and for raising its theoretical level. Particular attention is drawn:

–   to thorough assimilation of the fundamental principles of marxism-leninism as a unified international teaching, the historical experience of the CPSU, the creative contribution to theory contained in the decisions of the latest CPSU congresses and Central Committee plenums, in the speeches of Comrade L.I Brezhnev, General Secretary of the CPSU Central Committee, and other party leaders, and in documents of the international communist movement;

–   to study of the theory and policy of the party in their organic unity, in close connection with the practice of communist construction, the international activity of the CPSU, and the ideological struggle;

–   to the transformation of acquired knowledge into a person's active, living position and a guide to action in solving urgent problems in the development of our society.

Study of the report by Comrade L.I. Brezhnev, 'The Report of the CPSU Central Committee and the Immediate Tasks of the Party in the Sphere of Domestic and Foreign Policy,' 'Basic Directions for the Development of the USSR Economy for the Years 1976–1980,' and other materials of the XXV CPSU Congress is considered to be the main task of party study and mass propaganda in the forthcoming period, this being viewed as a prerequisite for steadfast implementation of the Congress decisions.

2   For the purposes of a thorough study of the materials of the XXV Party Congress, courses shall be introduced in 1976–1978 dealing with pressing questions of the theory and policy of the CPSU that have been worked out by the Congress. Appropriate textbooks for the primary and intermediate levels in the system of party education are to be prepared ...

3   The CPSU Central Committee emphasizes that, with the current educational level of Soviet people and with the presence of the necessary literature and powerful information media, political self-education takes on ever-greater significance as the basic method of learning revolutionary theory. In the course of training, more extensive use is to be made of active forms and methods of lessons such as theoretical conferences, seminars, discussions,

practical assignments, preparation of essays, and the conducting of socio-political analysis.

It is necessary to implement steadily a differentiated approach to the organization of marxist-leninist education; the principle of voluntary choice in selecting the subject and forms of study is to be observed strictly. At the same time, supervision must be intensified over the work of communists in enhancing their ideological and theoretical level; incidents of an abstract elucidative and narrowly utilitarian approach to political and economic studies must be eliminated. Efforts are to be made to ensure that all communists, and above all the leadership, systematically combine work on raising their ideological-theoretical level with their active participation in the communist education of the working people.

4   Taking into consideration existing positive experience, it is recommended that party committees develop universities of marxism-leninism as one of the effective forms of raising the ideological-theoretical level of active communists and non-party people, leading personnel, ideological cadres, and for preparing propagandists and politinformators. The central committees of the union republic communist parties and the krai and oblast party committees are permitted, where expedient, to transform universities of marxism-leninism of the city party committees of the republic capitals, and krai and oblast centres into universities of marxism-leninism of the central committees of the union republic communist parties (in union republics without oblasts), krai, or oblast party committees; these universities are to be subordinated to houses of political enlightenment. In such cases, other universities located within the territory of a republic, krai, or oblast are to be transformed into university branches working under the guidance of the appropriate city or raion party committee.

5   The central committees of the union republic communist parties, the krai and oblast party committees, the central committees of the All-Union Leninist Communist Youth League and the All-Union Central Council of Trade Unions, the board of directors of the All-Union Society 'Znanie,' ministries and departments are to take concrete measures for further improvement in the theoretical level and effectiveness of the following mass forms for the study of marxism-leninism: Komsomol political education, economic education for the working people, schools for communist labour, and people's universities; it is to be ensured that their role is enhanced in the ideological, political, patriotic, international, labour, and moral upbringing of Soviet people and in inculcating in every toiler high responsibility for entrusted affairs and for the quality of his work.

6   Party committees are to increase attention to work with propagandists, being guided strictly in this matter by leninist instructions on a careful attitude to propaganda cadres and the importance of constantly replenishing their knowledge and improving their skills.

Care is to be ensured in the selection of propagandists; their theoretical and methodological studies, their political awareness, and the exchange of work experience are to be improved. Conditions are to be created for the creative work of propagandists and they are to be involved in explaining and solving the problems of the economic and social development of collectives. The work of propagandists is to be considered a most important party assignment and their noble labour is to be encouraged.

Measures are to be taken to improve the activity of houses and offices of political enlightenment and to reinforce them with qualified cadres ...

Pravda, 12 June 1976   *KPSS v rezoliutsiiakh* XII, 289–93

5.54
On Progress by the Georgian Party Organization in
Implementing the Decisions of the CPSU Central
Committee Regarding the Organizational and Political
Work of the Tbilisi City Party Committee   24 June 1976

As with the initial resolution on the organizational and political work of the Tbilisi party organization (5.41), the language of this follow-up document tended to obscure the full import of its message. The previous three years had been a period of intense activity in Georgia aimed at cleaning up some of the excesses of criminal activity in the republic. For example, the bland reference to the improvement in the admissions procedures and composition of the student body in higher educational institutions referred, at least in part, to the revelation that the former rector of the Tbilisi Medical Institute, P. Gelbakhiani, had instituted a system whereby 'his' applicants were guaranteed admission to the institute before taking entrance exams. This had involved large-scale bribes of hundreds of thousands of rubles for a whole network of examiners and instructors under Gelbakhiani. As a result of Gelbakhiani's system, over 90 per cent of entering students came from middle-class families, largely highly placed officials who were able to offer the necessary bribes.

Two components of the Georgian campaign that are only hinted at in the document are the extent of Moscow's direct interference in Georgian affairs in the previous three years and the continuing resistance exerted by local officials. The degree of direct interference by the central authorities was brought out in a remark by E.A. Shevardnadze, First Secretary of the Georgian Communist Party, at the 35th conference of the Tbilisi city party organization in early 1974. Discussing the implementation of the resolution, he noted that 'we thank the CPSU Central Committee, the Politburo, and Comrade L.I. Brezhnev personally for their genuine party and paternal concern for the development of Georgia's economy' (*Current Digest of the Soviet Press* XXVI, no. 8, 1–4). Reporting to the congress of the Georgian Communist Party in January 1976, Shevardnadze noted in a similar vein that, since the adoption of the resolution on the Tbilisi party organization, 'the Georgian Communist Party, *under the leadership of the CPSU Central Committee*, decisively strengthened party and state discipline ...' (*Current Digest of the Soviet Press* XXVIII, no. 4, 6–9; editor's emphasis). Despite the centre's direct intervention in Georgian affairs, there was also evidence of continuing resistance to the campaign. In late 1974, Shevardnadze reported to a plenum of the central committee of the Georgian Communist Party that 'the situation remains alarming in many sectors of our national economy; in some places, the heavy burden of the old mistakes still jeopardizes the fulfilment of the Ninth Five-Year Plan assignments ...' (*Current Digest of the Soviet Press* XXVI, no. 46, 1–7, 27). In mid-1976, the Georgian Minister of Internal Affairs, K. Ketiladze, reported that crimes committed for personal gain and crimes of office were still numerous despite attempts to implement the Central Committee resolution. In a particularly frank revelation of the dynamics of the situation, he noted that 'the sharpers, money-grubbers and bribe-takers are in no hurry to surrender their positions. Regrouping, carefully camouflaging themselves, resorting to more refined methods and moving from the branches of the economy in which they have traditionally operated to others, the plunderers continue to conduct their dirty business' (*Current Digest of the Soviet Press* XXVIII, no. 19, 12–13). The campaign produced a number of additional unintended reactions. Reports indicated that there were attempts by the guilty to cover up investigations. The situation produced a large number of anonymous letters, presumably written by those who hoped to gain through the denunciation of their superiors and who tried to protect themselves by denouncing honest officials. There were reported attempts at blackmail and extortion. Finally, in the course of the investigations it was revealed that the police and the courts were subject to corruption so that legal and judicial sanctions were not systematically enforced. Apparently, the central leadership must have concurred with the critical assessment that the Georgian leadership gave of its own performance. At the XXV CPSU Congress in March 1976, Shevardnadze was overlooked and G.A. Aliyev, First Secretary of the Azerbaidzhan party organization was awarded the 'Caucasus seat' in the Politburo (which had become vacant with Mzhavanadze's removal in 1972) with his promotion to candidate member.

...

3 The Central Committee emphasizes that the positive changes taking place in the economic and cultural life of the Georgian SSR are the result of a significant improvement in the style and methods of party leadership, in consolidating the ideological-political and organizational unity of the republic

party organization, and in strengthening its ties with the masses. The central committee of the communist party of the republic has waged a decisive struggle for strict observance of the leninist principles of selecting, placing, and training cadres. Many sectors of party, state, and economic life have been reinforced with politically mature and morally stable cadres who are devoted to the cause of the party. In solving cadre questions, the principle of collegiality is being confirmed and, in doing so, party organs are taking into consideration the opinion of party members and collectives of working people. This makes it possible to avoid errors that existed until recently in evaluating personnel, promoting them on the basis of personal loyalty, family, or friendship ties. More concern is shown for the growth of the ideological-political and business level of leading cadres and more demands are placed on them for the results of their work in entrusted sectors and in educating people.

The significance of plenums of party committees and party meetings as bodies of collective leadership, schools for training cadres and all communists has grown. On the basis of further development of inner-party democracy, comradely criticism and self-criticism, the activity, discipline, and responsibility of communists for the state of affairs at enterprises, in kolkhozes, sovkhozes, organizations, and institutions is increasing.

Party committees are improving the organization and verification of the fulfilment of party directives and their own decisions and are raising the level of information available to communists and non-party people in economic and political questions, thus facilitating the further development of supervision over the creativity of leading bodies and cadres on the part of the broad masses. Party committees regularly inform party organizations and all communists of their work. The central committee of the [Georgian] Communist Party reported at all oblast, city, and raion party conferences on progress in implementing decisions regarding the Tbilisi city party committee, while the Tbilisi city committee reported at the meetings of primary party organizations. Work has improved in considering and implementing proposals and critical remarks coming from communists and letters and requests of the working people.

The CPSU Central Committee instructs the central committee of the Georgian Communist Party to ensure further enhancement of the level of organizational-party work in light of the instructions of the XXV CPSU Congress. Party committees must continue to show tireless concern for raising the fighting efficiency of primary party organizations and the unity and purity of their ranks and make efforts to ensure that every communist possesses the qualities of a political fighter, worthily performs the vanguard role in production and public life, and sets an example in his daily life. Work is to be continued on improving the qualitative composition of leading cadres; they are to be taught the leninist style of work and an approach to solving all questions from party positions and general state interests; they are to fight against existing manifestations of bureaucracy, irresponsibility, lack of discipline, and a contemptuous attitude to the demands and needs of the working people. Criticism and self-criticism are to be developed in every possible way, efforts are to be made to ensure that a self-critical analysis of both achievements and existing short-comings are the basis of the activity of every party committee, every leading staff member, every communist. State discipline is to be strengthened, cadres are to be educated in the spirit of absolute fulfilment of economic plans in all sectors, by all collectives, and for all indicators. Work is to be improved with cadre reserves and their theoretical and professional training is to be improved. It is necessary to improve the style and method of party, soviet, and economic work, approach its evaluation not by the number of meetings conducted and decisions adopted, but by real results, by how high the level of organizational work is and how efficiently supervision is set up. The effectiveness of party guidance over the soviets, trade union, and Komsomol organizations is to be raised, the activeness and responsibility of communists working in these bodies is to be raised, socialist democracy is to be developed steadily, law and order and socialist legality are to be strengthened ...

4   ... The republic party organization is conducting comprehensive work in moulding the communist ideological conviction, high political consciousness, and social and labour activeness of communists and Komsomol members, workers and collective farmers, the intelligentsia and young people, and leading cadres in creating a healthy moral-political atmosphere in every labour collective and in the republic as a whole. In accordance with the decision of the CPSU Central Committee on the Tbilisi city party committee, the party, trade union, and Komsomol organizations of Georgia are improving the education of people in the spirit of communist morality, Soviet patriotism, friendship among the peoples of the USSR, in the spirit of a conscientious attitude to labour and to public property, socialist discipline and responsibility for the common cause. An uncompromising struggle is being waged against relapses into philistine, petit-bourgeois psychology, nationalist manifestations that are still sometimes encountered, money-grubbing, outdated harmful customs, manners, and religious prejudices.

Concrete measures are being taken to intensify ideological-educational work with representatives of all the nationalities inhabiting Georgia and to enlist them in active labour, social, and political life. More attention is now paid to questions regarding the development of the economy and culture of the Abkhaz and Adzhar autonomous republics and the South Ossetian autonomous oblast.

In the matter of ideological-political and moral education, the role of the mass information media, creative unions, cultural, and art institutions has increased appreciably. Writers, artists, composers, and theatre and cinema personnel of the Georgian ssr are making a worthy contribution to the further development of literature and art that are socialist in content, international in spirit, and national in form. In recent years, a number of talented works have been created in which a profound analysis of contemporary social phenomena is given from party positions and the heroic spirit and enthusiasm of labour achievements and the active civic position and high moral qualities of working people are glorified.

Specific steps have been taken in the direction of further improving the public education system. Serious short-comings taking place in the admission of students to higher educational institutions and vocational schools are being overcome. There has been a noticeable improvement in the composition of the student body, in which the number of workers and kolkhozniks has almost doubled and the proportion of young men and women entering studies from production and from the ranks of the Soviet Army has grown. More attention is now being paid to improving the quality of professional training and to the upbringing of students and pupils. Along with the labour semester, all higher educational institutions and vocational schools have introduced practical training in socio-political work in the course of which future specialists acquire the skills of ideological-upbringing work with people.

Party organizations are taking serious steps to strengthen socialist legality. The broad masses of the working people are being enlisted in the struggle against anti-social manifestations and prejudices of the past and the role of labour collectives is increasing. In the cities and raions, law and order centres and clubs for teenagers are being set up, the activity of the comrades' courts and the people's militia is improving, thus facilitating a decline in law violations.

The cpsu Central Committee, however, considers that this is only a beginning in the big job that lies ahead in conducting the ideological and political education of communists and all working people. The growing activeness of the republic party organization in conducting ideological work creates good opportunities for the more successful accomplishment of the tasks posed in this area by the XXV cpsu Congress. In ensuring the further enhancement of the level of ideological-upbringing work, party committees must work out long-range comprehensive plans for ideological-political, labour, and moral education and must strive to ensure more thorough co-ordination of the efforts of all ideological institutions and all the forces and media of propaganda and agitation in accomplishing the socio-economic tasks of the tenth five-year-plan period and in forming the New Man. In improving ideological work, it is necessary to eliminate more persistently the elements of formalism, isolation from life, and other short-comings that have been tolerated in this work. It is necessary to continue an active struggle against the infiltration of bourgeois ideology, to oppose decisively private property tendencies and remnants of the past in the consciousness and behaviour of people ...

Pravda, 27 June 1976   *KPSS v rezoliutsiiakh* XII, 299–306

5.55
On Further Improving the System for Raising the Ideological-Theoretical Level and Professional Qualifications of Leading Party and Soviet Cadres   17 August 1976

... For the purpose of further improving the system for raising the ideo-logical-theoretical level and professional qualifications of leading party and soviet cadres, the CPSU Central Committee resolves:

1   To transform the permanently operating courses at the Higher Party School of the CPSU Central Committee into the Institute for Raising the Qualifications of Leading Party and Soviet Cadres and to organize studies in the Institute for leading personnel in party and soviet organs at the republic, krai, and oblast level.

The Institute must become the leading educational and scientific-methodological centre in the entire system for raising the qualifications of cadres and ensure that its work is on a high theoretical level in accordance with the instructions of the XXV CPSU Congress.

2   The permanently operating courses for retraining cadres in the Higher Party School of the central committee of the Ukrainian Communist Party, in the Leningrad, Alma-Alta, Baku, Gorky, Minsk, Novosibirsk, Rostov, Sara-tov, Sverdlovsk, Tashkent, and Khabarovsk higher party schools and in the Correspondence Higher Party School of the CPSU Central Committee are to be transformed into permanently operating inter-oblast, republic, and inter-republic courses for raising the qualifications of party and soviet personnel.

At these courses, studies will be concentrated for leading personnel at the city and raion level, as well as officials of the apparatus of party and soviet organs at the republic, krai, and oblast level.

3   Measures are to be taken to improve the work of republic, krai, and oblast courses for raising the qualifications of party and soviet personnel. Studies are to be organized in local courses for secretaries of primary party organizations, officials at the city and raion level, and chairmen of village and settlement soviets who are to be relieved of their responsibilities when attending these courses.

4   The basis for the work of the Institute and courses for raising the qualifications of leading party and soviet cadres is to be the study of pressing problems of marxist-leninist theory and the practice of communist construc-tion in light of the tasks put forward in the speech, 'Report of the CPSU Cen-

tral Committee and the Immediate Tasks of the Party in the Sphere of Domestic and Foreign Policy,' by Comrade L.I. Brezhnev, General Secretary of the CPSU Central Committee, and in his other reports and speeches.

In the courses, key problems of the development of the Soviet economy must be covered extensively, as well as problems of accelerating scientific-technological progress and improving the effectiveness of social production and the quality of work, and problems of the foreign policy activity of the CPSU and modern world development and the revolutionary process. More attention is to be paid to studying questions of party construction, the organizational and ideological-educational work of the party, leninist norms of party life and principles of party leadership, and to the activity of state and public organizations ...

5   ... The duration of studies in the Institute for Raising the Qualifications of Leading Party and Soviet Cadres has been set at a period of one to one-and-a-half months, at inter-oblast, republic, and inter-republic courses in higher party schools studies are to take one month, and at local courses they are to last three-to-four weeks, depending on the nature of the work of the students, their theoretical training and experience ...

8   It is established that leading party and soviet personnel will raise their knowledge in the Institute and courses once every period between CPSU congresses. Along with this, it is considered expedient for the departments of the CPSU Central Committee to conduct seminars once every two-to-three years for secretaries and department chiefs of the central committees of the union republic communist parties, the krai and oblast party committees, and other party personnel on pressing problems of the work of party organs and on generalizing work experience of party organizations in implementing party decisions ...

9   For the purpose of improving the training of primary party organization secretaries who are not relieved of their responsibilities when attending courses, the central committees of the union republic communist parties and the krai and oblast party committees are permitted to conduct seven-to-ten-day seminars, when needed, based on oblast, krai, and republic courses and using funds allocated for this purpose from the party budget ...

Partiinaia zhizn', no. 18   *KPSS v rezoliutsiiakh* XII, 337–41
(1976): 12–15

5.56
On Work with Creative Young People   12 October 1976

... The growing role of literature and the arts in communist construction and the tasks posed by the XXV CPSU Congress in the sphere of ideological work

require the further intensification of attention to the professional and ideological training of creative young people by party, state, and public organizations.

There still exist serious short-comings in work with young writers,
cinematographers, artists, composers, and actors. In some post-secondary
institutions and colleges in the arts not all the necessary measures are taken
to improve educational-upbringing work, actively to mould the students'
marxist-leninist outlook, and to promote thorough mastery of professional
skills and assimilation of the experience of Soviet and world culture. In
teaching specialized subjects and the social sciences, there is not sufficient
enlistment of highly qualified pedagogues and prominent figures in science
and culture who are capable of teaching professional skills in organic unity
with high ideological and moral qualities, arousing public activeness in
young people, and contributing to the formation of creative individualities.
Party, Komsomol, and public organizations do not always properly take into
consideration the specific nature of educational and upbringing work in post-
secondary institutions and colleges in the arts. The material base of some
educational institutions is in an unsatisfactory condition ...

The creative unions and cultural agencies fail to show the necessary
concern for improving the activity of educational institutions in the arts and
in the professional growth and employment of their graduates, and do not
devote proper attention to young people who are not union members. Few
young staff members in the arts are nominated to elected bodies of the creative unions or to the editorial boards of literary-feature publications, exhibi-
tion committees, or arts' councils.

Since the greatest significance in cultural construction is attached to
work with the young artistic intelligentsia, the CPSU Central Committee
resolves:

1   It is recommended that the central committees of the union republic
communist parties, the CPSU krai and oblast committees, and the central
committee of the All-Union Leninist Communist Youth League work out a
system of measures for the further improvement of ideological and professional training of creative young people, being guided by the proposals put
forward by Comrade L.I. Brezhnev, General Secretary of the CPSU Central
Committee, to the XXV Party Congress.

All work with young artists must be based on a combination of a sym-
pathetic and respectful attitude to them, along with exactingness and principle. The problems and needs of young people must be studied and they are
to be assisted in revealing their talents, which are to be directed along a
creatively promising course. Ties between the young artistic intelligentsia
and life are to be strengthened and diversified constantly; their public activeness is to be developed; young people are to be entrusted with interesting
assignments; they are to be educated as staunch fighters for communist ideals.

It is necessary to take concern for the selection and ideological growth of cadres who teach in arts schools and for improving their professional and pedagogical qualifications.

Guidance must be intensified over the activity of primary party and Komsomol organizations in creative unions, collectives, and educational institutions; the practice of admitting the best representatives of the young intelligentsia to membership in the ranks of the CPSU is to be improved ...

Literaturnaia gazeta, no. 42,   *KPSS v rezoliutsiiakh* XII, 366–70
20 October 1976

5.57
On Enhancing the Role of Oral Political Agitation in
Fulfilling the Decisions of the XXV CPSU Congress   1 February 1977

Despite the importance of agitation work as a technique involving large numbers of party members to disseminate party messages and ideas to the masses and to mobilize people for the achievement of production goals, this resolution stands as the only published decision of the Brezhnev years to deal directly and in detail with the organization and structure of the agitation network. A partial explanation of this lies in the conflict that occurred in the late 1960s over the redefinition of agitation work. The argument put forward in favour of change (whose chief exponent was V.I. Stepakov, head of the Central Committee's Department of Agitation and Propaganda), was that the formal, repetitive, and superficial activities of agitators were no longer necessary in the Soviet Union, which had achieved a level of industrialization characterized by universal literacy, widespread specialized knowledge and expertise, and access by everyone to the mass media. Under these circumstances, it was argued, agitation should be replaced by 'mass political propaganda,' which provided greater and more sophisticated information. This transformation was to be achieved by developing a new category of agitation worker in the person of the politinformator, usually a party or state official, manager, or specialist dealing in a single subject area and communicating with a broad range of audiences (compared to the agitator who is a generalist drawn from worker ranks and who is expected to discuss any matter, but primarily with people in his own immediate work collective or place of residence).

Politinformators did in fact begin to appear in large numbers throughout the Soviet Union in early 1967, indicating that the agitation network might undergo radical transformation. However, after a period of uncertainty and confusion over the status and role of the agitator, the two roles were given equal but different functions in the agitation collective. From the wording of the present document, it seems that the issues were never decisively resolved at the time and that it was only after the XXV Congress, when Brezhnev had reached the height of his power within the party, that an acceptable compromise was imposed on the party apparatus and given public approval. The status of agitation as a form of party activity with the masses was confirmed and the traditional broad definition and functions were retained. However, the politinformator received post hoc party sanction, giving the position the security and status equivalent to the long-standing agitator, as an integral component of a broadened agitation network. Agitation collectives were to remain under the jurisdiction of primary and shop party organizations where they could deal with a specific collective. The groups of politinformators were to be subordinate to local party committees and larger primary party organizations that could use their more specialized information throughout a larger enterprise, association, or territorial unit. What emerged under Brezhnev in the area of ideological work was a more specialized and differentiated structure with three categories of ideological worker: agitator, politinformator, and propagandist.

... Party organizations, relying on the party's traditions of oral political agitation, are finding new and more effective forms and methods of oral political agitation. Question-and-answer evenings, monthly talks on the same date by leading personnel of krais, oblasts, cities, and raions (common Political Days), on-site trips by information and propaganda groups and brigades of agitators, rallies, citizens' meetings, oral magazines, festivals of labour glory, harvest celebrations, celebrations honouring competition winners, initiations of new workers and kolkhozniks, meetings with party, war, and labour veterans and other mass undertakings have become widespread.

There are groups of lecturers working successfully in affiliation with krai, oblast, city, and raion party committees. In many cases, they are led by party committee first secretaries. Groups of politinformators have proven to be useful in explaining pressing questions of socio-political life. Tutorship has become an effective form of professional training, and political and moral education of young people.

At the same time, the CPSU Central Committee notes that party committees do not yet make the fullest use of possibilities for oral political agitation in explaining the domestic and foreign policy of the party and the tasks of labour collectives stemming from the decisions of the XXV CPSU Congress for the further development of the creative initiative and energy of the masses and socialist competition.

In the content and organization of mass agitation work, sufficient consideration is not always given to the educational and cultural level of the people and to the degree to which they are informed through the press, television, and radio. Discussions, political information sessions, and lectures are often limited to retelling generally known truths, fail to answer questions that are of interest to the working people, avoid urgent problems of local life and moral upbringing, and fail to concentrate on the elimination of existing short-comings. There have been incidents when party organizations, in an effort to increase the number of agitators and politinformators, entrust this work to poorly trained comrades, regularly fail to instruct their agitation aktiv or to provide it with necessary guidelines, reference materials, and methodological recommendations, and fail to assign concrete tasks that are urgent for the given collective, city, or raion. At some enterprises, agitation collectives are generally lacking.

Many party committees do not ensure balanced work for the groups of lecturers and do not show proper exactingness toward those communists, specialists in the economy, and leaders who try to withdraw from participation in upbringing work. Mass political agitation is conducted irregularly at the population's residences, primarily during election campaigns. Channels for oral agitation are poorly used to study public opinion, people's attitudes, and demands and for providing an effective response to their questions.

To a certain extent, these short-comings are the result of relaxed attention in some party organizations to oral agitation, a reflection of the incorrect opinion that its significance decreases with a diversified system of mass information and propaganda media. It is necessary to improve oral agitation in every possible way in the interests of further increasing the effectiveness of the political work of party organizations with the masses.

The cpsu Central Committee resolves:

1   The central committees of the union republic communist parties, krai, oblast, city and raion party committees, and primary party organizations are ordered to take measures to enhance the role of oral agitation in the ideological-political, labour, and moral upbringing of Soviet people, in mobilizing them for successful implementation of the decisions of the XXV cpsu Congress and the tasks posed by Comrade L.I. Brezhnev in the Report of the cpsu Central Committee at the Congress and in his speech at the October (1976) Plenum of the cpsu Central Committee, and for a worthy celebration of the 60th anniversary of the Great October Socialist Revolution.

The cpsu Central Committee emphasizes that oral agitation has been and remains an important sphere of party activity and one of the active forms of constant contact of the party with the masses, of their solidarity in their support of the party and its leninist Central Committee, an effective instrument of political leadership. Based on live communication with people, agitation makes it possible, through concrete facts and examples that are clear, close to, and understood by the people, to demonstrate the successes in communist construction, to explain the policy of the party and the decisions of party and state bodies, to influence purposefully the development of competition and the enhancement of the production and social activeness of the working people, to study the sentiments of the masses and respond promptly to them, to conduct an open discussion with audiences on short-comings, difficulties, and ways of overcoming them, and to reach every person with the word of the party. The further development and improvement of political agitation is dictated by the tasks posed by the XXV CPSU Congress regarding a comprehensive approach to organizing the entire business of communist education.

Political agitation must be considered as one of the important means of educating the working people in the spirit of a marxist-leninist outlook, communist convictions, socialist patriotism, and internationalism. It is necessary to make efforts to ensure that mass agitation measures provide a timely and qualified explanation of current events and any questions that the working people may have; these measures should genuinely interest people, arouse their creative energy, direct them to raise labour productivity, the efficiency of production, and the quality of work. By the word of the party and by their labour and moral example, activist-agitators are called upon to cultivate in people a communist attitude to labour and public property and a feeling of responsibility for entrusted affairs. At the same time, they must create an atmosphere of intolerance towards any manifestation of lack of discipline, hooliganism, embezzlement of public property, self-seeking, money-grubbing, foul language and other negative phenomena, and provide sound arguments for unmasking the slanderous fabrications of bourgeois propaganda.

2   The central committees of the union republic communist parties, and the krai, oblast, city, and raion party committees are to improve the basic units of oral political agitation.

It is recognized as necessary to make serious improvements in the activity of agitation collectives created within primary and shop party organizations, to ensure high quality in their work, and not to strive for quantitative indicators. Communists, above all, and the most authoritative non-party activists must be appointed as agitators. It is necessary to enlist more extensively in agitation collectives skilled workers, brigade leaders, and other middle level leaders who can be entrusted with this important party assignment.

The staff of politinformators is to be reinforced with experienced, theoretically trained activists who are able to comment in a qualified manner on questions regarding the political, economic, and cultural life of the country and the international situation, explain the principles and norms of communist morality, and the Soviet way of life. The practice of establishing groups of politinformators affiliated with party committees, as well as with bureaus of primary party organizations that have suitable cadres, has been approved.

A leninist tradition of constant and obligatory participation by leading cadres in the political education of the working people, using diverse forms of work for this purpose, is to be developed in every possible way. The activity of groups of lecturers of raion, city, oblast and krai party committees, and central committees of the union republic communist parties is to be invigorated. Regular talks by leaders to the population on the work of ministries, departments, enterprises, organizations, and institutions that they head are to be ensured.

Fuller use is to be made of the possibilities of personal contacts with people to study and mould public opinion. The questions, proposals, and critical remarks addressed to agitators, politinformators, and speakers are to be systematically generalized and analysed; they should be answered operatively, and the working people should be informed of the practical measures taken on them.

3   In the organization and content of oral agitation, party committees are to take into account the specific nature of people's labour activity in different branches of the economy and regions of the country. Special attention is drawn to the organization of mass agitation work in remote districts that have not been reached by television, in newly established collectives, in areas where female labour predominates, in the sphere of services, in field-camps and specialized livestock sections of farms, in small collectives, and to conducting individual work with people, in particular with young people.

Balanced and systematic mass political work at places of residence of the population is to be strengthened above all among those strata that are not connected with labour collectives and among young people residing in hostels. For these purposes, better use must be made of houses of culture, clubs, libraries, cinema houses, schools, red corners and auditoriums at institutions; the network of summer agitation sites must be expanded. Agitation work must be actively combined with conducting mass cultural undertakings. At voluntary councils in micro-raions, it is expedient to create groups of consultant activists to explain questions that arise to the working people; pedagogues, lawyers, doctors, cultural personnel, and other specialists are to be enlisted widely in this work.

4   The central committees of the union republic communist parties and the krai, oblast, city, and raion party committees are instructed to take measures to improve operational instruction, the theoretical and methodological training of agitators, politinformators, and speakers.

Party committees must regularly work out model themes for discussions, political information sessions, and reports, co-ordinating the themes with articles in the press, television, and radio programmes, and lecture propaganda. They are to send guidelines and other material on pressing questions to party organizations to assist activists in political agitation.

Party committees and party bureaus are to provide concrete, business-like instruction to agitators and politinformators and enlist qualified lecturers and leaders of party, soviet, and economic bodies in this work. Support is to be given to the initiative of party organizations in creating reference-information centres at enterprises and construction sites, in kolkhozes and sovkhozes, organizations and institutions.

Agitators, politinformators, and speakers are not to be overburdened with other social assignments and they should be rewarded for their active work.

More extensive use is to be made of the system of marxist-leninist education for training agitators and politinformators. Schools and seminars for politinformators are considered an integral part of party study. In schools for studies in the fundamentals of marxism-leninism where agitators study, questions relating to the theory and methods of mass agitation work are to be included in the curriculum. Permanent seminars for leaders of agitation collectives are to be organized in city and raion party committees and in large party committees.

The study of problems of political agitation may be expanded in syllabuses for courses in party construction in higher party schools, universities of marxism-leninism, and schools for the party aktiv.

5   Houses and rooms of political enlightenment are responsible for the organization of methodological assistance to agitators and politinformators, for the preparation of reference-information material for them, for recommendations regarding the use of technical media and visual aids in agitation work, and for generalizing experience. Methodological councils on questions of mass agitation work in houses and rooms of political enlightenment are to be created.

6   The magazine *Agitator*, republic magazines on questions of political agitation, and the krai and oblast magazine, *Bloknoty agitatorov*, are to provide systematic qualified assistance to agitators, politinformators, and speakers, taking into account their specific character and functions. These publications must regularly publish model themes for oral presentations and methodological elaborations for discussions arising from the decisions of the XXV cpsu Congress on pressing questions of the domestic and foreign policy of the party, economic and cultural construction, and other instructive and informational material, providing these materials with sound argumentation, interesting facts, figures, examples, comparisons; there is to be a fuller elaboration of the positive experience of mass agitation work.

The editorial offices of central and local newspapers are to give fuller coverage to questions of mass agitation work and the practice of party guidance over oral agitation.

Politizdat is to ensure publication of a textbook on oral political agitation, a 'little library' for the agitator, and brochures generalizing the experience and elucidating the methodology of mass agitation work.

In its plans for scientific research, the Academy of Social Sciences of the cpsu Central Committee is to include the elaboration of theoretical and methodological problems of political agitation in contemporary conditions.

Pravda, 25 February 1977   *KPSS v rezoliutsiiakh* XII, 447–53

5.58
On Some Questions Regarding the Organizational
Structure and Forms of Work of Party Organizations
in the Conditions of Production Associations in Industry   17 March 1977

Increasing numbers of production and science-production associations are
being set up in various branches of industry in accordance with the directions
of the XXIV and XXV cpsu congresses. Over three thousand such associations were in operation by the end of 1976. The associations are producing
more than one-third of the total volume of manufactured products.

In this connection, great significance is attached to questions of
improving the work of party organizations at enterprises forming associations
so that they can make fuller use of their potentials as a qualitatively new form
of management and administration for raising the effectiveness of production on the basis of the concentration, specialization, and acceleration of
scientific-technological progress.

With its decision, 'On the Work of the Party Organizations of the
Gorky Automobile Plant in the Conditions of a Production Association,' the
cpsu Central Committee proposed that the central committees of the union
republic communist parties, and the krai, oblast, city, and raion party committees show daily influence in improving party work in production associations and that they systematically study and generalize the experience of
organizing this work. At the same time, the cpsu Central Committee emphasized that questions relating to the structure of party organizations at associations must be solved in each specific case in accordance with the cpsu Rules,
taking into consideration the interests of the cause and the concrete conditions of production.

At present, three basic variants of organizational structure of party
organizations in associations have emerged, depending on the scope, character and specific features of each production association, its location, and
the legal position of the enterprises forming it.

The first variant. In those cases when the enterprises forming an association are located on the territory of one raion or several raions within a city,
a unified party organization can be formed in accordance with the party
Rules and with the approval of the central committee of the [union republic]
communist party and the krai and oblast committee. All communists in such
a party organization are registered in the raion (city) party committee where
the head enterprise is located; the party organizations of production units
become shop party organizations. According to this principle, for example,
party organizations have been established in the Leningrad associations,
Metallicheskii zavod and the Lenin Optical and Mechanical Plant, the
Moscow association, Moloko, and the Ordzhonikidzeugol association (city of
Enakievo).

The second variant. When communists working at the head enterprise of an association and its branches located on the territory of one raion or several raions within a city form a unified organization. As for the party organizations of production units located in other cities, oblasts, and republics, they retain their independence and, as in the past, are subordinated to the appropriate raion and city party committees according to their location. In particular, such a structure of party organizations has emerged and has completely proven itself in the Gorky Automobile Plant association. Here, the party organizations of five enterprises located in the city of Gorky are united in a single party organization, and five other party organizations located in the Gorky oblast, the Mordovian ASSR, Chernigov oblast in the Ukraine, and in the Tadzhik SSR have remained independent, as in the past.

The third variant. In most cases, the enterprises forming an association are located in different raions, oblasts, and republics, and the creation of unified party organizations in these associations does not present itself as a possibility. Therefore, the party organizations of the constituent enterprises retain their independence and are subordinated to the local raion and city party committees.

All three variants of organizational structure of party organizations in production associations have demonstrated their viability.

As experience has shown, the creation of unified party organizations in associations with a common leading organ at the head makes it possible to carry out party guidance over economic activity more effectively, to concentrate the efforts of communists and all personnel on accomplishing the general tasks of developing production and the scientific-technological revolution, and to achieve greater effectiveness of socialist competition. Unified party organizations in production associations permit labour collectives to enhance their responsibility for the final results not only of their own work, but of the association as a whole. In these conditions, questions regarding the selection and placement of cadres and the reinforcement of lagging sectors of production with qualified personnel are solved better and the right to supervise the activity of the administration is exercised to a fuller extent.

In many cases, enlarged party committees are formed in associations where large party organizations of 1000 and more communists are established. This facilitates the consolidation of ties between the party committee and lower party units and the enhancement of the role and authority of the party committee as an organ of collective leadership. At present, enlarged party committees have been elected in 182 party organizations at associations.

In the production units of associations with more than 500 communists, party committees can also be established in accordance with the CPSU Rules, thus allowing for a considerable improvement in the guidance of shop party organizations and a positive effect on the level of all party work.

In solving the questions of the creation of unified party organizations in associations, however, it is necessary to take into consideration certain circumstances, despite all the positive moments. In particular, it is necessary to take into consideration the fact that, in these cases, an appreciable number of communists move from one raion to another. In this connection, raion committees experience difficulties in solving questions related to the development of the economy of the raions, in conducting social-political campaigns, in involving enterprise collectives in patronage work in rural areas, in organizing public services, in preserving public order, etc. At the same time, as is known, the raion is the basic unit of administrative-territorial division. Consequently, raion party committees bear full responsibility for the accomplishment of the tasks of economic and socio-cultural construction within the territory of their raions when establishing production associations. It is understood that local party organs cannot help but consider the above-mentioned circumstances.

When solving the question of the formation of party organizations at associations, attention must be paid to the fact that enterprises forming associations in large cities are often situated a significant distance from each other and from the head enterprise. It is natural that considerable distances between enterprises create certain complications in the work of party organizations and inconveniences for communists.

Therefore, as a consequence of all these circumstances, the party organizations of enterprises in most associations are independent. In these conditions, questions of the co-ordination of the work of party organizations in associations and of ensuring the necessary harmonization of their plans and actions take on great practical significance. Meetings of the party-management aktiv of the association and mutual exchange of experience and information facilitate this to a considerable extent. Councils of party organization secretaries have proved to be an effective form of such co-ordination. They are successfully functioning in a number of production associations in Moscow and the Moscow, Leningrad, Gorky, and Rostov oblasts, in the Ukraine, Belorussia, and Moldavia.

Proceeding from accumulated experience, the CPSU Central Committee, in its decision on the Gorky Automobile Plant, permitted the central committees of the union republic communist parties and the krai and oblast party committees to create such councils of party organization secretaries in production associations where several independent primary party organizations are operating. In this connection, recommendations have been put forth on fundamental questions relating to the procedure for formation and organization of work and functions of councils of party organization secretaries of production associations that have been formed in practice and fully proved themselves. Their essence consists in the following:

–   a council of secretaries is created by a decision of the central committee of a union republic communist party, krai, or oblast party committee at the location of the head enterprise of an association. The council includes the secretaries of the party organizations of all the branch enterprises. As a rule, the secretary of the party committee or party bureau of the head enterprise is appointed chairman of the council;

–   the council of secretaries is convened periodically to harmonize and co-ordinate the actions of the party organizations on questions of party guidance over production, work with cadres, and the organization of socialist competition;

–   on the basis of collective discussion, the council works out practical measures for organizationally and politically ensuring the fulfilment of the production plans of the association and the plans for introducing new machinery and technology, the assimilation of production capacities, the improvement of efficiency and quality of work, the mastering of new types of products, the economizing of fuel, raw materials, and supplies, the strengthening of labour discipline, the selection, placement and training of cadres, improvement in the business skills of personnel and the accomplishment of other general tasks;

–   the council of secretaries, together with the general management, the trade union committee, and Komsomol organization, considers and resolves questions on the organization of socialist competition, provision of moral and material incentives, and the development and practical implementation of plans for the economic and social development of labour collectives;

–   the council of secretaries, together with the general management, can convene meetings of an association's party-management aktiv for extensive discussion of the long-range development of production and urgent problems in the area of economic activity;

–   the party organizations of all subdivisions of an association are guided by the collectively elaborated recommendations of the council and they are to make efforts to put them into practice consistently;

–   in this context, the council of secretaries does not possess the right to provide recommendations to party organizations of an association on questions within the competence of territorial party organs (regulation of the growth of party ranks, examination of personal cases, registration of communists, payment of party dues, etc.).

The central committees of the union republic communist parties and the krai, oblast, city, and raion party committees are called upon to exert daily influence over the improvement of party work at production associations and to study systematically and generalize its experience. In this, party committees must constantly proceed from the instructions provided in the cpsu Central Committee resolution, 'On the Work of the Party Organizations of the Gorky Automobile Plant in the Conditions of a Production Association,' and take the practical implementation of these instructions under their unremitting supervision.

Partiinaia zhizn', no. 8   *KPSS v rezoliutsiiakh* XII, 462–7
(1977): 9–11

Plenum of the Central Committee   24 May 1977

Brezhnev's report to the May 1977 Central Committee Plenum (*Current Digest of the Soviet Press* XXIX, no. 23, 6–10) set out the official reasons for the introduction of a new Constitution in the Soviet Union. Underlying the document is the marxist idea that a Constitution, as part of the legal superstructure, must be adapted regularly to reflect major, fundamental socio-economic changes that have occurred in the society. According to Brezhnev, the new soviet Constitution reflected two domestic changes since the promulgation of the 1936 Constitution. First, the Soviet economy had 'changed beyond recognition,' especially through the extension of socialist ownership and the impact of the current scientific-technological revolution. Second, Soviet society had become more homogeneous socially, politically, and ideologically, with the working class, peasantry, and intelligentsia all being shaped in their attitudes and behaviour by the socialist environment. This had resulted in the emergence of a 'new historical community of people – the Soviet people ...' Since the completion of the foundations of socialism in 1936, a new stage of socialism had emerged in the Soviet Union, combining the ideas of an 'all-people's state' and a 'developed socialist society.' These socio-economic developments had to be reflected in a new Constitution. Behind the ideological rationalization proposed by Brezhnev lay a more complex story of political differences over the need to introduce a new Constitution and the changes to be incorporated in it. Inability to resolve this conflict was probably reflected in the failure to record that the symbolically important Central Committee resolution on the draft was approved unanimously.

The proposal to amend the old Constitution or adopt a new one originated with Khrushchev. It was implicit in the tone of the XX Congress in 1956, especially in Khrushchev's denunciation of certain aspects of stalinism, and in the call to strengthen socialist legality in the congress resolution on the Central Committee Report (4.5). At the XXI Congress in 1959 there was a call for amendments and additions to the Constitution to reflect the important changes that had occurred in the political and economic life of the Soviet Union and in the international situation. At the XXII Congress in 1961 Khrushchev noted in his Central Committee Report that a new Constitution was being drafted. In April 1962 the Supreme Soviet approved Khrushchev's proposal to draw up a new Constitution and it appointed a Constitutional Commission, with Khrushchev as Chairman. Despite all of these indicators, no draft Constitution was produced under Khrushchev's direction, suggesting that there must have been. strong opposition in principle to the First Secretary's proposal.

The question of a new Constitution was kept alive with the appointment of Brezhnev as the new Chairman of the Constitution Commission in December 1964. Brezhnev made it a political issue in June 1966 when he announced in the context of the campaign for election to the Supreme Soviet that a new Soviet Constitution embodying the achievements of Soviet development over the past half-century should be adopted by the 50th anniversary of the Bolshevik Revolution in November 1967. Apparently Brezhnev's position was not yet strong enough to activate the proposal and there was too much disagreement over the required changes because the only other mention of constitutional matters at this time was Suslov's implicit approval of the existing constitution's ability to provide Soviet citizens with rights and freedoms. Since none of the documents celebrating the 50th anniversary made mention of the proposed new Constitution, it seems that Brezhnev was forced to retreat on this issue. The new Constitution remained in the background as a political issue for almost a decade. The circumspect approach taken to drafting the document after Brezhnev's setback in 1967 is characterized by the remark of the General Secretary as late as the XXV Congress that work on the draft was proceeding painstakingly and without any haste so that every problem would be weighed with the greatest possible precision. In other words, there were still sharp differences over basic points. No deadline was set and no promises were made. After lengthy delay under two leaders, the draft Constitution presented by the Constitution Commission was finally approved by the Politburo and made public at the May 1977 Central Committee Plenum. This announcement was associated with a major personnel change that enhanced Brezhnev's position. N.V. Podgorny was removed from his position as member of the Politburo at the Central Committee meeting. In addition, the plenum was used to announce the appointment of K.V. Rusakov to the Secretariat and the removal of K.F. Katushev from the Secretariat.

5.59
On the Draft Constitution of the
Union of Soviet Socialist Republics   24 May 1977

Having heard and discussed the report of the General Secretary of the CPSU Central Committee, Chairman of the Constitution Commission, Comrade

L.I. Brezhnev, 'On the Draft Constitution of the Union of Soviet Socialist Republics,' the CPSU Central Committee Plenum resolves:
1   To approve in principle the draft Constitution of the Union of Soviet Socialist Republics presented by the Constitution Commission.
2   To transmit the question of the draft Constitution of the Union of Soviet Socialist Republics to the Presidium of the USSR Supreme Soviet and to recommend to the Presidium of the USSR supreme Soviet to bring it to a nation-wide discussion.

5.60
On the State Hymn of the Soviet Union   24 May 1977

To approve the text and musical revision of the State hymn of the Union of Soviet Socialist Republics and to transmit it to the Presidium of the USSR Supreme Soviet for ratification.

Pravda, 25 May 1977   *KPSS v rezoliutsiiakh*, XII, 491–2

Plenum of the Central Committee   3 October 1977

The May 1977 Central Committee Plenum was followed by a rapid succession of events that enhanced Brezhnev's political position along with that of the party. At the June session of the USSR Supreme Soviet it was announced that Podgorny had been replaced by Brezhnev as chairman of the Presidium of the Supreme Soviet, that is, as Head of State. For the first time since October 1964 the leader of the party also occupied one of the two leading state positions. Brezhnev was now accorded the state status that would allow him to steer the Constitution through its formal, public adoption. The summer of 1977 witnessed a national discussion of the draft document, an orchestrated procedure aimed at generating widespread support and legitimacy through the technique of mass participation. When the Central Committee reconvened in October 1977, the stage was set for full approval of the slightly modified document and the recommendation that Brezhnev, in his joint capacity as head of the party, Chairman of the Constitution Commission, and Head of state, usher the document through a special sitting of the Supreme Soviet.

The timing of the May and October Central Committee decisions and the personal role of Brezhnev in the formal proceedings left no doubt about the party's strengthened position in the 1970s (in contrast to 1936 when the party issued no decision on the Constitution). The enhanced position of the party was reflected in its changed Constitutional position. In the 1936 Constitution, the party was mentioned twice, both in broader contexts that assigned it rights, along with other pulic organizations, to exist and to nominate candidates for election to soviets (articles 126 and 141). The new Constitution elevated the Communist Party to a prominent position in a separate article in chapter I (article 6). It was no longer just an association in which the most active and politically conscious citizens voluntarily unite, the vanguard of the working people in their struggle to build communism, and the leading core of all organizations of the working people. The new Constitution now described the party as 'the leading and guiding force of Soviet society and the nucleus of its political system.' The party was granted the Constitutional right to 'determine the general perspective of society's development and the line of internal and external policy of the USSR.' Even this, however, appeared to be something of a compromise. Brezhnev indicated in a speech to the Supreme Soviet in October 1977 that the discussion of the draft produced more extreme suggestions that state functions be transferred directly to the party, including the granting of legislative power to the Politburo (*Current Digest of the Soviet Press* XXIX, no. 39, 5). At the height of his political power, Brezhnev was still taking the position of the moderate broker and emphasizing that in working on the draft '*we stood firmly on the ground of continuity.*'

At the plenum it was announced that K.U. Chernenko and V.V. Kuznetsov had been elected candidate members of the Politburo.

5.61
On the Draft Constitution (Basic Law) of the
Union of Soviet Socialist Republics and the Results
of its Nation-wide Discussion   3 October 1977

1   To approve completely and fully the report of the General Secretary of the CPSU Central Committee, the Chairman of the Presidium of the USSR Supreme Soviet, the Chairman of the Constitution Commission, Comrade L.I. Brezhnev, 'On the Draft Constitution (Basic Law) of the Union of Soviet Socialist Republics and the Results of its Nation-wide Discussion.'
2   To approve in principle the draft Constitution (Basic Law) of the Union of Soviet Socialist Republics presented by the Constitution Commission, with additions, specifications, and amendments introduced into it as a result of the nation-wide discussion. To submit the draft Constitution for consideration by an extraordinary seventh session of the Ninth USSR Supreme Soviet.

To instruct the General Secretary of the CPSU Central Committee, the Chairman of the USSR Supreme Soviet, the Chairman of the Constitution

Commission, Comrade L.I. Brezhnev, to deliver a report on the draft Constitution and the results of its nation-wide discussion at the session of the USSR Supreme Soviet.

3   Party and soviet organs, ministries and departments, trade unions, Komsomol, and other public organizations are to consider carefully all toilers' suggestions and comments received during the nation-wide discussion of the draft USSR Constitution for improving work in concrete sectors of state, economic, and cultural construction and to take the necessary measures for their practical implementation.

Pravda, 4 October 1977   *KPSS v rezoliutsiiakh* XII, 560–1

Plenum of the Central Committee   27 November 1978

Central Committee plenums for discussing the annual plans for economic and social development and the annual budget were held on a regular basis under Brezhnev beginning in 1965. These meetings were convened in the last quarter of the year preceding the year in which the plan and budget were to be implemented. The agenda of the meetings followed a standard pattern. Reports were presented by N.K. Baibakov, Chairman of the USSR Gosplan, and V.F. Garbuzov, the USSR Minister of Finance. The reports were followed with presentations by a number of central and regional party officials and central and republican state officials. On occasion, a representative of the Academy of Sciences, a lower level administrator (e.g. a plant director), or a worker addressed the plenum. Brezhnev invariably began or concluded the discussion of the reports with a major address that served as a 'state of the union' message, set the tone for the coming year, and became part of the public record. The resolutions that emanated from the sessions varied in size and detail from a single sentence expressing approval in principle of the draft plan and budget (nine times) to a more detailed accounting of areas of concern and responsibilities, as well as reference to Brezhnev's speech as a source of direction for party and state officials.

    The tone of Brezhnev's speeches differed from plenum to plenum. On several occasions, Brezhnev projected a very positive and optimistic image, both in his review of the past year's achievements and in his projections for the coming year. At other meetings, he presented a balanced analysis of achievements and shortfalls. Brezhnev also used the annual Central Committee plenum on the draft plan and budget to launch policy initiatives through critical attacks on major short-comings in the economy (for example, in December 1969).

The three Central Committee plenums dealing with the annual plan and budget that preceded the XXVI Congress give the impression of a frustrated and even angry General Secretary trying to explain the shortfalls in his major domestic economic initiatives by pointing to poor administration and management of reasonable policies. In November 1978 Brezhnev dwelt on wastage and loss in metals and fuels; the scattering of capital investments, uninstalled equipment, and unfinished projects in construction; inefficiency in the transportation sector; agricultural losses due to mismanagement, irresponsibility, and negligence; lags in the machine-building industry; and, failure to meet planned investments and output in the consumer goods sector that hindered the system of material incentives. Blame for these problems was placed directly on the shoulders of the executives of the ministries and state committees and the managerial staff responsible for policy development and plan implementation. The failures were explained in managerial and organizational terms – disregard of party and government decisions by managers and failure to work out and co-ordinate decisions with the plan and resources. (*Current Digest of the Soviet Press*, XXX, no. 48, 1–7).

In November 1979 Brezhnev's message was directed towards the same sectors of the economy. This time he spelled out in more detail some of the irregularities creating bottlenecks in each sector (*Current Digest of the Soviet Press* XXXI, no. 48, 1–8). Again the finger was pointed at management for failures to achieve expected levels of quality, efficiency, and labour productivity. However, on this occasion Brezhnev took the logic of his argument one step further, noting that it was not his intention simply to point out existing difficulties once again. Changes were necessary to improve the level of management. Therefore, he called for a toughening of policy through a 'further strengthening of discipline.' This approach involved a number of specific changes. First, the monitoring functions of the Secretariat were to be intensified so that it would hear more frequent reports from responsible state officials. It was expected that the councils of ministers, individual ministries, and party organizations at all levels would duplicate this centralization and intensification of supervision. Second, Brezhnev suggested that mismanagement had to be dealt with more quickly on the spot, through more thorough daily supervision of managerial personnel and, if necessary, more decisive action against irresponsible cadres. Third, Brezhnev called for more stringent laws and the stricter enforcement of laws on the assumption that 'strict, unswerving observance of the law is a necessary precondition for the successful functioning of the entire economic mechanism.' Fourth, Brezhnev noted the intention to introduce a new law strengthening the People's Control agencies in their economic activities.

In October 1980, just months before the XXVI Party Congress, Brezhnev expanded the scope of his criticism by devoting most of his speech to problems in the light industry sector: food supplies, consumer durables, housing, and social welfare programs (*Current Digest of the Soviet Press* XXXII, no. 42, 1–5, 14). Twice in his speech Brezhnev directly linked success in the consumer goods sector and the civilian economy in general to the co-operation of executives, designers, and scientists in the defence branches. Higher levels of production in the consumer sector depended on continued production of consumer goods by heavy- and defence-industry branches and on the sharing of research and design resources to assist civil machine building to develop high-efficiency and high-quality machinery. As in his previous two speeches, Brezhnev came down hard on management. This time, however, he focused on two variations of the issue. He advocated wider use of 'specific-purpose programmes,' by which he meant the development of limited, goal-oriented planning that could easily be assessed in terms of stages, responsibilities, costs, and achievements. Second, Brezhnev brought up the old issue of the correct balance between centralized planning and decentralized administration. After reiterating the need for centralized powers to co-ordinate inter-branch activity and to restrain departmental and parochial pressures, Brezhnev went on to note the need to solve daily problems at the local level, without delay and central consultation. He noted that legislation was being prepared (to be completed before the XXVI Congress) to deal with the reorganization of management.

The resolution reprinted here was the most complete and detailed of the three Central Committee resolutions on the plan and budget, 1978–1980. It included a preamble noting recent successes in socio-economic development, the usual approval in principle of the plan and budget, exhortation of certain key ministries and state agencies to improve production and efficiency, a confirmation of the decisions on agriculture taken at the July (1978) Central Committee Plenum, a reiteration of the importance of socialist competition, and the usual directive for all party organizations to improve their organizational and mass-political work in the economic sphere.

5.62
On the Draft State Plan of Economic and
Social Development for the USSR and the
Draft USSR State Budget for 1979   27 November 1978

... The plenum of the CPSU Central Committee resolves:
2   To approve completely and fully the conclusions and directives set out in the speech by Comrade L.I. Brezhnev, General Secretary of the CPSU Cen-

tral Committee, Chairman of the Presidium of the USSR Supreme Soviet, at the current plenum and to make them the basis of the activity of all party, soviet, trade union and Komsomol organizations, and economic organs. To focus energies on ensuring the fulfilment and overfulfilment of the economic plan for 1979, the fullest utilization of intensive factors of economic development, which will become another important link in the realization of the decisions of the XXV CPSU Congress, the tasks of the Tenth Five-Year Plan, in the implementation of the programme that has been laid out for raising the well-being of the soviet people.

3 The CPSU Central Committee Plenum emphasizes that the further intensification of the struggle for raising the effectiveness of social production and the quality of work are extremely important tasks for ministries and departments, party, soviet and public organizations, and labour collectives. This struggle must be waged on a wide front – in industry, agriculture, transportation, construction and other branches of the economy, in all links of production and administration. Special attention must be directed towards raising labour productivity, introducing the achievements of science and leading experience and new technology into production, mobilizing existing reserves and capacities to increase output and raise the technical level of production under conditions of minimum expenditures.

It is the duty of party, soviet, and economic organizations to take all possible steps to eliminate nonproductive waste and losses and to strive for the thrifty expenditure of metal, fuel, electricity, and all material, financial, and labour resources. It is important that a regime of economy, as one of the main principles of socialist economic management, be carried out consistently in each branch, in each production collective, at each workplace ...

6 The CPSU Central Committee Plenum considers that, in conditions of the steady growth in the scale of the economy and the rise in its qualitative level and the growing complexity of inter-branch and intra-branch ties, more importance be attached to the further improvement of methods of economic administration and management and to the strengthening of organization and co-ordination in work in all sectors of social production. Party, soviet, trade union and Komsomol organizations, and economic organs are called upon to ensure strict observance of plan, production, and labour discipline. Rhythmic, precise work, unconditional fulfilment of the plan for all indices and of obligations for the delivery of output to customers, including for export, must become an immutable law for all units of the economy. It is necessary to strengthen the organizational and mobilization role of the plan, to carry out systematic supervision over fulfilment of established tasks for each enterprise, construction site, kolkhoz and state farm ...

Pravda, 28 November 1978

5.63
On Further Improving Ideological
and Political-Upbringing Work   26 April 1979

Reports of Western observers visiting the Soviet Union, Soviet dissidents, and some recent Soviet émigrés indicate that there has been a significant deterioration in public morale and in mass attitudes towards work, public property, and the belief system on which the Soviet socio-political system has been built. A basic cause for this decline in public morale and behaviour seems to be a failure of the economy to deliver goods and services to the consumer sector, which Soviet citizens have come to expect as legitimate under Krushchev and then Brezhnev. While people are living better than they did a generation ago, improvements in the standard of living have not increased according to the expectations set out by the leadership and according to the expectations that people have set for themselves on the basis of a comparison with the West, with Eastern Europe, and with their image of a socialist society. In the past decade continued growth in the standard of living has been adversely affected by disproportionate investments in heavy industry and the military sector, by crop failures, by mismanagement, wastage, insensitivity to the consumer market, and weaknesses in the distribution system. In turn, these problems have produced a wide spectrum of behaviour patterns that reinforce the low output, poor quality, and inequitable distribution of consumer goods: low labour productivity, alcoholism, and absenteeism among workers; corruption, fraud, embezzlement and theft of state property. Reactions to this state of affairs have been manifested in a number of sub-cultural or counter-cultural patterns. The loss of belief that things will improve by working within the system has led to a wide-ranging and innovative search to satisfy material needs through alternative sources such as bribery and the black market. The loss of belief in the fundamental principles of the system has produced a search for alternative values through religious identification, nationalism (among both Russians and the minority nationalities), and emigration. For many, cynicism and apathy, which involve both a passive rejection of the official norms and the conducting of a double life, have emerged as daily defence mechanisms for coping with the inconsistencies of reality. The party responded in 1979 with two forceful resolutions aimed at coping with the deterioration in public morale and behaviour, one dealing with political socialization and the second with law enforcement.

In May 1979, a party decision on improving ideological work was made public. The criticism of the Soviet political socialization programme contained in this document provided the basis for a proposed wide range of activities aimed at upgrading the effectiveness and responsibility of all organizations that carry out socialization functions in the Soviet Union. Local and primary party organizations, the mass media, professional groups involved in the communications arts, the trade unions, the Komsomol and other organizations in civilian and military life, as well as ministries and state committees responsible for education, were called upon to expand and intensify their ideological work. Each agency, organization and state body was instructed to devote greater resources to its ideological work, improve techniques of propaganda and agitation, relate ideological work more closely to the social and economic tasks of society, and to work out the details of a programme of ideological work that suited its functions and the needs of its audiences.

What is striking about the current resolution is that its authors are guilty of precisely the same sins that they claim have penetrated the socialization network and inhibited its effectiveness. Discussion focuses on symptoms rather than causes. While identifying some of the symptoms, the party fails to place any blame on structural weaknesses in Soviet society or on any basic party policy. Instead, attention is focused on spurious factors such as imperialist propaganda and an ineffective propaganda campaign to counter it, while simultaneously no solutions are offered that will substantially alter the messages communicated through the system or the techniques for conveying those messages. The leadership's concern for the problems prompting the issuance of the present decision on ideological work and its frustration with the apparent lack of impact of ideological work were reflected in Brezhnev's reference to the decision in his report to the XXVI Party Congress. He referred to it as a long-term document in which 'we are talking about a restructuring – yes, this was no slip of the tongue, indeed, a restructuring – of many sectors and spheres of ideological work.' At least in this area, it appears that the General Secretary's power to force change upon the party seems very limited.

... In the press and in mass political work there is still insufficient elucidation of questions such as the acceleration of scientific-technological progress, the introduction of the achievements of science and technology into the economy, the raising of labour productivity and the effectiveness and quality of work, and the most stringent economizing of raw and other materials, fuel, power, and financial resources.

Mass information organs often lack the ability to present and to propagandize in a lively and intelligible manner the best achievements, the leading experience of individual toilers and entire labour collectives. Moreover, they are not able to present them so that the essence of this experience is revealed, so that millions of people are interested by the experience, and so as to help put it into widespread practice.

One still encounters phenomena that are incompatible with the tasks that the party sets out for ideological-upbringing work – a fear of openly bringing up for discussion urgent questions of our public life, a tendency to smooth over and sidestep unresolved problems and sharp questions, and to keep quiet about short-comings and difficulties that exist in real life. Such an approach and an inclination toward window-dressing do not help the cause but only hamper the accomplishment of our common tasks. Direct damage is inflicted on the mass' activeness where criticism and self-criticism are not considered honourable, where there is insufficient openness in public matters. And, indeed, it is precisely the activeness of the masses that is an important source of the socialist system's strength.

The struggle with all means of propaganda and upbringing must be waged systematically, purposefully, and uncomprisingly – from discussions in party organizations and labour collectives to criticism in the press, radio, and television – for the eradication of abnormal remnants of the past hostile to socialism that still frequently exist in our life, such as money-grubbing and bribery, the striving to grab more from society without giving anything in return, mismanagement and extravagence, drunkenness and hooliganism, bureaucratism and a callous attitude to people, violations of labour discipline and public order. In the struggle with these phenomena, it is necessary to use both verbal persuasion and the strict force of the law.

The effectiveness of upbringing work is significantly lowered when a gap between the word and the deed arises, when the unity between organizational, economic, and ideological work is not ensured. When assessing the work of executives and economic cadres, it is necessary to consider not only indicators of the fulfilment of production plans, but also the level of discipline, the moral-political climate in the collective, labour conditions, and daily life.

We must not tolerate the fact that upbringing work often is weak at places of residence, in dormitories, in small collectives, and in remote communities. Ideological-upbringing work with young people at factories, on kolkhozes and state farms, in educational institutions, at construction sites, and in the service sector must become significantly more lively, concrete, interesting, and persuasive.

... imperialist propaganda, with which the propaganda of the Peking chauvinists and aggressors are now openly co-operating, is continuously conducting a fierce offensive against the minds of the Soviet people and, with the aid of the most refined methods and modern technological means, is seeking to poison their consciousness with slander against Soviet reality, to cast a slur on socialism, to embellish imperialism with its predatory and inhuman policies and practices. Distorted information and a tendentious treatment of facts, silence, half-truths, and the simply impudent lie – all these are cast into the fray.

Therefore, one of the most important tasks of ideological upbringing and information work is to aid Soviet people to recognize the entire falsity of this slanderous propaganda, to reveal its insidious methods in a clear, concrete, and persuasive form, to convey to the people of the world the truth about the first country on earth where socialism has triumphed. In doing so, it is always necessary to remember that a slackening of attention toward the elucidation of urgent problems, insufficient effectiveness, questions left without answers are advantageous only to our class enemy.

A major short-coming that substantially lowers the effectiveness of the influence of upbringing work on the consciousness and feelings of people is the frequent appearance of formalism, a propensity for wordy chatter, all kinds of propaganda cliches, materials presented in a dull, 'bureaucratic' style, a reiterative, mechanical repetition of general truths instead of their creative comprehension, and a search for lively and intelligible forms. Sometimes bombast and a superficial, pseudo-scientific language are substituted for theoretical generalization and serious, thoughtful analysis that can enrich readers and listeners, while didacticism and loud phrases are substituted for convincing argument and confidentiality of tone in a discussion with an audience. All this must be resolutely eliminated from practice.

The CPSU considers the communist upbringing of the working people as an important front in the struggle for communism. The course of the economic, socio-political, and cultural development of the country, the full realization of the potentials for developed socialism, the realization of the leninist foreign policy course of the Soviet Union, the strengthening of its international positions depend even more on the successes of ideological and political upbringing work.

The CPSU Central Committee has instructed the central committees of the union republic communist parties, krai, oblast, okrug, city and raion party committees, and primary party organizations to develop and implement concrete measures to improve ideological and political-upbringing work, to raise its effectiveness and quality, to perfect forms and methods, to overcome current insufficiencies. Ideological work must be raised to the highest qualitative level, responding to the requirements of developed socialism and the new tasks of communist construction ...

Pravda, 6 May 1979

5.64
On Improving Work to Safeguard Law and Order
and Intensifying the Struggle against Law Violations   2 August 1979

The party's concern for the breakdown in public morale and behaviour, expressed in the previous document, received additional attention in 1979. Special concern was expressed for behaviour patterns that disrupted work, lowered productivity, and diverted resources from planned distribution. These activities included alcoholism, juvenile delinquency, abuse and misappropriation of state property, and black marketeering. While the previous resolution

focused on techniques for improving socialization as a means of avoiding counterproductive behaviour, the current decision focused on the critical issues of
how to publicize sanctions as a means of discouraging illegal acts and how to
deal with offenders. The solution offered involved a number of approaches.
First, the state agencies and public organizations involved in the socialization
process were to publicize the activities of law enforcement agencies in combatting criminal activity. Second, the law enforcement agencies were to intensify
their work in dealing with violators of public order. Third, party organizations
were to intensify their work in supervising, staffing, and co-ordinating the work
of law enforcement agencies. Fourth, there was a call for public organizations
like the trade unions and Komsomol to reinforce their work in preventing law
breaking. Finally, there was an indication that there would be an attempt to
increase the participation of large numbers of people at the grass-roots level
through the revitalization of a number of organizations that give the flavour of
participatory democracy: the volunteer people's detachments (druzhiny),
workers' meetings, councils of crime prevention, village assemblies, comrades' courts (tovarishcheskie sudy), public stations for safeguarding order
(obshchestvennye punkty okhrany poriadka) and the People's Control Committee.

... the tasks of strengthening law and order are still not being resolved with
sufficient effectiveness. Means of state and public influence and the upbringing of people are not being fully utilized in the struggle against law breaking.
In this work, there is a lack of purposefulness, an integrated approach and
unity of action among party, state, economic, trade union, Komsomol and
other public organizations, and the wide mass of toilers are not often
attracted to it.

The CPSU Central Committee has outlined concrete measures directed
towards the further improvement of the prevention of law breaking, the
strengthening of the struggle against criminal and other anti-social manifestations, the unswerving observance of Soviet laws by all citizens and responsible officials.

Special attention is directed towards the necessity for perfecting the
activity of the agencies of the procurator's office, internal affairs, justice, and
the courts, which are called upon to watch over soviet legality, the interests
of society, the rights of Soviet citizens. The law enforcement agencies must
uncompromisingly and decisively wage a struggle against crime, develop and
strengthen ties between labour collectives and the public. L.I. Brezhnev has
pointed out that the party expects from these agencies 'still greater initiative,
devotion to principle, irreconcilability in the struggle against people who violate the Soviet legal order.'

The USSR Procuracy and the Ministry of Internal Affairs have been
instructed to eliminate existing short-comings in the work of subordinate

agencies, to raise the responsibility of cadres for their assigned work, to strengthen discipline, and to improve the professional training of personnel, to ensure the strictest observance of socialist legality in their activity.

Party committees are called upon to intensify supervision over the work of law enforcement agencies, to take measures to reinforce them with trained cadres, to raise the role of party organizations in the upbringing of personnel in a spirit of complete devotion to the cause of the Communist Party, of irreproachable fulfilment in the performance of their official duties, of critical evaluation of the results of their work, of high political vigilance. They are to show constant concern for the widening and strengthening of ties between law enforcement agencies and the public and for creating an atmosphere of respect and support around them.

Party committees and primary party organizations have been instructed to consider systematically questions of safeguarding law and order and combating law breaking and, together with law enforcement agencies, to draw up and implement concrete measures for further improving this work and enhancing its effectiveness. In doing so, it is necessary to take into consideration the growing intolerance of Soviet people toward any type of antisocial behaviour. There is to be persistent striving to eliminate crime, to mobilize the wide masses of toilers for the resolution of this public task. There are to be assurances that every leader, communist, and Komsomol member is an example of moral purity, a strict observer of Soviet laws, an active fighter for model socialist law and order.

In the struggle against law breaking, party committees must unite and co-ordinate the forces of party, state and public organizations, labour collectives, ideological institutions, family, and school. It is recognized as necessary that comprehensive measures for crime prevention be contained in the long-run and annual work plans of party organizations for the communist upbringing of the toilers.

It has been recommended that the councils of ministers of the union and autonomous republics and the executive committees of the Soviets of People's Deputies enhance the role and responsibility of soviet agencies for strengthening legality and law and order, and the activeness in this work of commissions of Soviet executive committees, deputies' groups and each deputy. These questions are to be discussed regularly at soviet sessions and at meetings of executive committees. They are to hear the accounts and reports of leaders of law enforcement agencies, enterprises, institutions, and organizations on work conducted to ensure public order and the struggle against law breaking.

The following tasks are set out for party, soviet, law enforcement agencies and public organizations:

Improve the safeguarding of public order in cities and other populated areas. Strengthen the patrol and point-duty service of the police. Perfect the work of criminal search and investigation.

Enhance the role of precinct police inspectors in safeguarding law and order, expand their ties with the population. Adjust the day-to-day co-operation between the police and the volunteer people's detachments (druzhiny).

Wage a consistent and persistent struggle against drunkenness and alcoholism. Check progress of the fulfilment of previously taken decisions on these questions and discuss the results in party, soviet, trade union, and Komsomol organizations. Implement more effective measures for the prevention of drunkenness, for intensifying public and legal influences on drunkards, for strict observance of established rules for trade in alcoholic beverages, for expanding the net of addiction treatment institutions, including those at enterprises. Activate anti-alcohol propaganda, make it more persuasive and effective.

Perfect work to prevent law breaking among juveniles at educational institutions, labour collectives, and at places of residence. Improve individual work with young people. Develop tutorship and patronage more widely. Supplementary measures for improving upbringing work and prevention of law breaking among juveniles are to be worked out by soviet, trade union, Komsomol and sports organizations, by cultural institutions, by agencies of enlightenment and professional-technical education, by creative unions, and by law enforcement agencies.

Intensify the struggle against encroachments on socialist property. Establish strict order everywhere in the accounting and storage of materials of value, decisively eradicate mismanagement, wastefulness, report padding and eye washing. Pay especial attention to intensifying the struggle against embezzlement in agriculture, transport, and construction. Improve the activity of the supervisory-auditing apparatus. Reinforce the police service for combatting embezzlement of socialist property and speculation. Intensify the sharpness and devotion to principle of the Procuracy's supervision over laws for safeguarding socialist property.

Activate the struggle against parasitism and speculation. Ensure prompt exposure of persons who evade socially useful labour. See to it that they are employed and attached to collectives. Apply measures provided by the law for influencing those who stubbornly refuse to work.

The basic direction in the prevention of law breaking must become the intensification of this work in labour collectives and at residences. Taking guidance from the CPSU Central Committee resolution, 'On Further Improvement of Ideological and Political-Upbringing Work' [5.63], it is necessary to improve significantly ideological-political, labour, and moral upbringing in each collective, among all groups of the population, and especially among young people, juveniles. An atmosphere of intolerance must be created towards plunderers of the people's property, malicious hooligans, and bribe-takers.

In strengthening law and order, it is necessary to raise the role of workers' meetings, councils of crime prevention at enterprises, village assemblies, and other forms of public influence. The state of discipline and upbringing work is to be considered when summing up the results of socialist competition.

Attention is to be directed to the personal responsibility of leaders of enterprises, construction sites, institutions, secretaries of party and Komsomol organizations, chairman of trade union committees, heads of shops, shifts, sectors, and brigades for the state of discipline and law and order, and for prompt and sharp reaction to reports and signals about cases of anti-social behaviour of individual members of collectives. Those who show indifference and unconcern in this matter must be held strictly accountable.

It is recognized that work in the legal upbringing of the working people is necessary. For these purposes, cultural-enlightenment institutions must be utilized more fully and effectively. The efforts of law enforcement agencies, labour collectives, and the public are to be directed more actively toward preventing various kinds of conflict that arise in family and everyday relations, while observing the necessary tact and consideration. The task has been set of perfecting the study of the bases of Soviet legality in schools, professional-technical institutes, and other educational institutions, in the system of party study, economic education, and Komsomol political enlightenment. Speeches on legal themes during the conducting of unified political days are to be provided. Legal upbringing work is to be intensified among those who commit violations of discipline and public order. The upbringing significance of trials is to be enhanced and they are to be conducted on a visiting basis at enterprises, construction sites, collective, and state farms.

Party, soviet, law enforcement agencies, and public organizations are commissioned to work out and implement practical measures for further improvement of the activity of the voluntary people's detachments, comrades' courts, public stations for safeguarding order, and other public volunteer agencies. The initiative of the working people in ensuring model order in populated areas and at enterprises is to be supported and developed. The positive experience of public participation in the struggle against law breaking is to be generalized and disseminated. A careful and sensitive treatment of suggestions and critical remarks by citizens is to be ensured and they are to be considered more fully in working out and implementing measures to strengthen the struggle against crime. Regular presentations on these questions are to be practised by responsible personnel of party, soviet, and law enforcement agencies in collectives and at places of residence, in the press, on radio and television.

It has been recommended that the All-Union Council of Trade Unions, the central committees, republic, krai, and oblast councils of trade unions work out supplementary measures to strengthen the role of trade union organizations in the prevention of law violations. There is to be more active use of socialist competition as an important means of educating people, strengthening discipline, struggling against truancy, and for the careful utilization of materials of value. Measures are to be taken to improve significantly the organization of leisure and the free time of the working people.

The Central Committee of the All-Union Komsomol and the Komsomol of the union republics, and Komsomol committees are required to enhance the role of Komsomol organizations in the struggle against law violations, to analyse the causes of anti-social manifestations among young people and juveniles, to take concrete measures for overcoming them, to ensure the active participation of each member of the Komsomol in the strengthening of law and order.

It is recommended that the USSR People's Control Committee and its local agencies intensify the struggle against violations of state discipline and laws for the safeguarding of socialist property and decisively stop incidents of deception of the state. They must strive persistently to eliminate the causes of embezzlement, bribery, mismanagement, and various abuses.

It has been recommended that the editors of newspapers and magazines, the USSR State Committee for Radio and Television, the USSR State Cinematography Committee, the USSR State Committee for Publishing, and the Board of the All-Union Knowledge Society improve coverage of issues of the struggle against law violations, drunkenness, parasitism, and money-grubbing, and concretely and persuasively reveal the anti-social essence of these phenomena. They are to reveal systematically the positive side of participation in the preservation of order in work collectives and the community, the selfless labour of the personnel of law enforcement agencies in protecting the interests of the state and the rights of citizens from criminal encroachments.

The USSR Procuracy, the USSR Ministry of Internal Affairs, the USSR Ministry of Justice, and the USSR Supreme Soviet have been instructed to improve the co-ordination of their activities and those of their subordinate agencies and to ensure, on this basis, the comprehensive study of the practice of the struggle against law breaking and the necessary uniformity in the application of the norms of Soviet legislation.

Pravda, 11 September 1979

XXVI Party Congress   23 February–3 March 1981

The XXVI Party Congress was convened amid speculation among Western observers that it would have to face a number of major issues and that changes in personnel and policy were required. External pressures arising from the uncertainties of Soviet policy in Afghanistan and Poland as well as challenges to Brezhnev's policy of detente by the newly installed Reagan administration had threatened to undermine some of the significant advances that had been achieved in the first decade of Brezhnev's leadership. Domestically, the economic growth rates of the late 1960s and early 1970s had been offset, in part, by serious problems in agriculture and energy in the previous five years. The leadership of the party had aged, the Chairman of the Council of Ministers had died, and little had been done to recruit younger members of the political elite and thus facilitate the transfer of power from one generation to the next. Despite these pressures for change in policy and personnel, the XXVI Congress was noted for its continuity with the past.

Brezhnev's Central Committee Report to the Congress (*Current Digest of the Soviet Press* XXXII, no. 8, 3–21 and no. 9, 4–15) was a conservative account of past successes, current problems and future prospects. Emphasis was placed on continuity with existing policies and approaches. Brezhnev continued his long-standing commitment to the agricultural sector by recognizing that agriculture was the key to any improvement in living standards. He also admitted the seriousness of the agricultural situation, especially the supplying of foodstuffs. Brezhnev called for a 'radical solution' to the food supply problem through the development of a special food programme. He then proceeded to recommend to the congress continuation of the line approved at the July (1978) Central Committee Plenum. This boiled down to supporting programmes already set in place, such as continued investments in the rural sector, further integration of agricultural production with storage and processing facilities and the trade network, and a general call for an improvement in efficiency, quality, and productivity. The only suggestions of a somewhat radical departure in agriculture were contained in Brezhnev's recommendations to provide supplementary financial and moral support for the private plots of collective and state farm workers, especially to encourage their production of livestock and poultry, and to provide support to industrial enterprises that run farms which supply their workers with agricultural products. The details of this programme had already been announced in a joint Central Committee–Council of Ministers resolution published in *Selskaia zhizn'* on 18 January 1981 (*Current Digest of the Soviet Press*, XXXIII, no. 5, 15–17).

In his report on economic policy, Brezhnev's accounting of the successes of the past decade and projections for the next five-year period were tempered by a recognition of limits and obstacles that had hindered growth and adversely affected the Soviet standard of living. Brezhnev's analysis of the economy was consistent with his criticism of the last three Central Committee plenums on the annual State Plan and Budget. Difficulties, insufficiencies, and unsolved problems were associated with ministries and state enterprises failing to fulfil their plans, thus creating bottlenecks and disproportions in the economy. Party organs and economic executives were also to blame for violations of discipline and mismanagement. According to Brezhnev, the main factor in explaining the poor economic performance over the past few years related to the failure to overcome fully 'the forces of inertia, tradition, and habits that took shape in that period when the quantitative side of things rather than the qualitative stood out first and foremost.' Brezhnev's solution to the problems of economic management remained conservative: greater discipline, exactingness, and responsibility in fulfilling plans; continued extension of measures to improve co-ordination, such as inter-branch complexes and associations; and a general improvement in the organization of management structures at the association and enterprise level. In his review of the heavy industrial sector, Brezhnev repeatedly emphasized that the success of the economy in the 1980s would depend on the ability to economize, to produce efficiently, and to utilize every single resource and reserve. Improved linkages between science, technology, and production, a long-standing goal of the Brezhnev regime, depended on the solutions to traditional problems: the failure to adhere to priorities, heavy expenditures on the importation of foreign techniques and technology, lack of innovation, low quality of production, and lags in the scientific and design base in the light industry and agricultural sectors of the economy. A major shift in policy (which had already been underway for some time) was reflected in the General Secretary's repeated references to the priorities that had to be assigned to energy development.

Brezhnev extended promises to improve the material well-being of the Soviet people. He called for the equalization of regional social differences, especially through the development of housing, social-cultural amenities, and consumer goods in the northern and eastern regions where the country required an influx of human resources but which had seen a pattern of net emigration. Labour conditions were to be improved, especially for working mothers. When it came to income redistribution through the social welfare system, however, Brezhnev was much more cautious. He suggested improved conditions for pensioners – through employment opportunities in the service sector. Brezhnev's message was that income would be based on continued contribution to economic development and he reminded his audience that the main criterion for distribution under socialism is the quantity and quality of work each individual contributes. He expressed serious concern for the negative effects of any kind of wage levelling and for such phenomena as paying extra wages for simply appearing at work, and not for its real results, and for the awarding of unearned bonuses. He went on to call for the use of all organizational, financial, and juridical methods to close off every opening for parasitism, bribery, unearned income, and encroachments on socialist property. In the consumer goods sector, he called for concrete steps to suppress manoeuvring with 'deficit' goods.

For the most part, Brezhnev's report on the party contained nothing new and little of substance. The import of his message was that positive trends that had been instituted were continuing and that the party was also working hard to eradicate persistent problems. His review of the activities of the central organs of the party (Politburo, Central Committee, and Secretariat) stressed the regularity and frequency of their meetings, the organized and businesslike manner of their proceedings, and the collegial nature of decision making in the Politburo. Praise was directed to local party organs for their contribution to economic development, while a general call was made to enhance their leadership functions. Primary party organizations were exhorted to take a firm and principled stand in their supervision of the activity of administrators to ensure that the party line was enforced in the areas of personnel, plan fulfilment, the improvement of work and living conditions, and inter-departmental co-ordination. Brezhnev once again urged that party executives combine a balance among technical-economic skills, political training, and human relations skills. The area of intra-party communications required improvement, especially vertical communications. Upwards communications had been enhanced to the point where a new Letters Department of the Central Committee apparatus had been formed to handle the approximately 1500 letters per day received by the Central Committee. However, Brezhnev cautioned that many questions that should have been resolved locally were being shifted to the centre. He also expressed concern for 'anonymous slanders' and for the muzzling of honest criticism, both of which the party would not tolerate. Finally, Brezhnev brought up the matter of the Party Programme (see 4.33), noting that the current Programme correctly reflected the laws of social development. However, he criticized Khrushchev's Programme by arguing that the Programme should establish only basic principles. It is impossible and inappropriate to foretell particulars in such a document. Furthermore, the Programme must identify important changes that have taken place in the past two decades in the Soviet domestic economy and in the international arena. Consequently, Brezhnev called for the introduction of necessary amendments and additions in the current Programme through a redrafting by the Central Committee.

While no personnel changes in the party Politburo and Secretariat were announced at the XXVI Congress, a number of important changes had occurred since the XXV Congress. At the Politburo level, three full members had died (Grechko, Kosygin, and Kulakov), one had retired because of health (Mazurov), and one had been dismissed from his positions of power unceremoniously (Podgorny). They were replaced by three new members who had gained candidate status in the Politburo only between 1977 and 1979: Chernenko, Tikhonov, and Gorbachev. One candidate member had died (Masherov) and three new candidate members had been recruited into the Politburo (Kuznetsov, Shevardnadze, and T.Ia. Kiselev). Personnel changes at the level of the Secretariat after 1976 involved the dropping of one member who died (Kulakov), the transfer of another member to work in the Council for Mutual Economic Assistance (Katushev), and the dropping of Ustinov who was appointed Minister of Defence. Rusakov and Gorbachev were promoted to the Secretariat. Ia.P. Riabov had been brought into the Secretariat in October 1976, but he was removed from the body in April 1979 when he was appointed First Deputy Chairman of the USSR Gosplan.

The proceedings of the party congress followed the pattern previously established under Brezhnev. Brezhnev delivered the Central Committee Report and Tikhonov, who had replaced Kosygin as the Chairman of the USSR Council of Ministers in October 1980, presented the Guidelines for the 11th Five-Year Plan. The congress, which was attended by 4994 delegates, elected a new Central Committee consisting of 319 full members and 151 candidate members.

5.65
**On Comrade L.I. Brezhnev's Report: the Report
of the CPSU Central Committee to the XXVI Congress
of the Communist Party of the Soviet Union and the
Party's Immediate Tasks in the Sphere of
Domestic and Foreign Policy**   26 February 1981

Having heard and discussed the report of the General Secretary of the CPSU Central Committee, Comrade L.I. Brezhnev – the Report of the CPSU Central Committee to the XXVI Congress of the Communist Party of the Soviet Union and the Immediate Tasks of the Party in the Sphere of Domestic and Foreign Policy, the XXVI Congress of the Communist Party of the Soviet Union resolves:
1   Wholly and completely to approve the leninist course and practical activity of the Central Committee of the party.
2   To approve the Report of the CPSU Central Committee and to recommend that all party organizations be guided in their work by the propositions and tasks in the sphere of domestic and foreign policy set forth in Comrade L.I. Brezhnev's Report.

5.66
On Preparing a New Draft of the CPSU Programme   26 February 1981

Proceeding from the fact that twenty years has passed since the CPSU Programme was adopted and that during this period extensive experience in socialist and communist construction has been accumulated and new changes and processes have taken place in the international arena, the XXVI CPSU Congress resolves:

To instruct the CPSU Central Committee to make the necessary additions to and changes in the existing Party Programme, which on the whole correctly defines the laws governing world social development and the goals and basic tasks of the struggle of the Party and the Soviet people for communism, and to prepare a new draft of the CPSU Programme for the next party Congress.

In the process, the most important changes in the life of Soviet society and in world social development and the main tasks of the construction of communism must be reflected in the Programme in a thorough and scientific way.

5.67
On Letters and Statements from the
Working People and Appeals from Communists
Addressed to the XXVI CPSU Congress   3 March 1981

1   To take into consideration the fact that the Secretariat of the Congress has examined a large part of the letters and statements from the working people and the appeals from Communists addressed to the XXVI CPSU Congress and has taken the necessary measures.

2   To instruct the CPSU Central Committee to complete the examination of letters and statements from the working people and appeals from Communists addressed to the Congress and to adopt appropriate decisions on them.

Pravda, 27 February 1981
and 3 March 1981

Appendix

Members of the Secretariat, 1952–1964

First Secretary, October 1964–April 1966: L.I. Brezhnev
General Secretary, April 1966–Present: L.I. Brezhnev

Congress	XXIII 1966	XXIV 1971	XXV 1976	XXVI 1981
Brezhnev				
Suslov, M.A.				died 25 I 82
Kozlov, F.R.	to 16 XI 64			
Demichev, P.N.			to 16 XII 74	
Ilyichev, L.F.	to 26 III 65			
Ponomarev, B.N.				
Shelepin, A.N.	to 26 IX 67			
Andropov, Iu.V.	to 21 VI 67			
Poliakov, V.I.	to 16 XI 64			
Rudakov, A.D.	died 11 VII 66			
Titov, V.N.	to 29 IX 65			
Podgorny, N.V.	to XII 65			

Congress	XXIII 1966	XXIV 1971	XXV 1976	XXVI 1981
Ustinov, D.F.	from 26 III 65		to IV 76*	
Kulakov, F.D.	from 29 XI 65			died 19 VII 78
Kapitonov, I.V.	from 6 XII 65			
Kirilenko, A.P.	from 8 IV 66			
Solomentsev, M.S.	from 13 XII 66 to 23 XI 71			
Katushev, K.F.		from 10 IV 68	to 24 V 77	
Dolgykh, V.I.		from 18 XII 72		
Zemianin, M.V.			from 5 III 76	
Chernenko, K.U.			from 5 III 76	
Riabov, Ia.P.			from 26 X 76 to 17 IV 79	
Rusakov, K.V.			from 24 V 77	
Gorbachev, M.S.				from 27 XI 78

*   In April 1976 Ustinov was appointed Minister of Defence. No official announcement of his resignation from the Secretariat was made. He was replaced in the Secretariat by Riabov in October 1976.

Members of the Presidium-Politburo, 1964–

Full Member _____   Candidate Member _____

Congress	XXIII 1966	XXIV 1971	XXV 1976	XXVI 1981
Brezhnev, L.I.				
Voronov, G.I.		to IV 73		
Kirilenko, A.P.				
Kozlov, F.R.	to XI 64			
Kosygin, A.N.				died XII 80*
Mazurov, K.T.			to XI 78	
Mikoyan, A.I.	to IV 66			
Pelshe, A.Ia.	from IV 66			
Podgorny, N.V.			to V 77	
Poliansky, D.S.			to III 76	
Suslov, M.A.				died 25 I 82
Shvernik, N.M.	to IV 66			
Shelepin, A.N.	from XI 64		to IV 75	
Shelest, P.E.	from XI 64	to IV 73		
Grishin, V.V.		from IV 71		
Demichev, P.N.	from XI 64			
Efremov, L.N.	to IV 66			

* Kosygin's health forced his resignation as Chairman of the USSR Council of Ministers in October 1980. However, he apparently retained his seat on the Politburo until his death in December 1980.

Congress	XXIII 1966	XXIV 1971	XXV 1976	XXVI 1981
Kunayev, D.A.		from IV 71		
Masherov, P.M.	from IV 66			died X 80
Mzhavanadze, V.P.		to XII 72		
Rashidov, Sh.R.				
Ustinov, D.F.	from III 65		from III 76	
Shcherbitsky, V.V.	from XII 65	from IV 71		
Kulakov, F.D.		from IV 71	died VII 78	
Ponomarev, B.N.		from V 72		
Solomentsev, M.S.		from IX 71		
Andropov, Iu.V.	from VI 67	from IV 73		
Grechko, A.A.		from IV 73 died IV 76		
Gromyko, A.A.		from IV 73		
Romanov, G.V.		from IV 73	from III 76	
Aliyev, G.A.			from III 76	
Kuznetsov, V.V.			from X 77	
Chernenko, K.U.			from X 77	from XI 78
Tikhonov, N.A.			from IX 78	from XI 79
Shevardnadze, E.A.			from XI 78	
Gorbachev, M.S.			from XI 79	from X 80
Kiselev, T.Ia.				from X 80

Index

Resolutions and Decisions of the Communist Party of the Soviet Union 1898–1981
General Editor: Robert H. McNeal

Volume 1: The Russian Social Democratic Labour Party 1898–October 1917
Edited by Ralph Carter Elwood

This volume treats the period before the October Revolution of 1917. It is the first collection of materials on the early evolution of the Russian Social Democratic Labour Party that deals with the entire movement, so that the interaction of the various factions of the party may be understood as a whole and not merely in a partisan Leninist framework. This volume also breaks new ground in publishing in English vital records of Communist activity during the Revolution of 1917.

Volume 2: The Early Soviet Period 1917–1929
Edited by Richard Gregor

Documents from the period of the October Revolution to the establishment of Stalin's regime emphasize the transformation of the party into a new kind of bureaucratized authority, controlling such areas as the press, trade unions, armed forces, and youth organization. Factionalism within the party and its suppression are a major theme. The volume opens with the documents (previously unavailable in English) concerning Lenin's crisis of control within the Central Committee shortly after the seizure of power, and it goes on to provide extensive material on both Lenin's and Stalin's suppression of critical groups within the party.

Volume 3: The Stalin Years 1929–1953
Edited by Robert H. McNeal

The third volume treats the Stalin era, the early phase of which witnessed a new degree of party intervention in agriculture, industry, and cultural affairs. The ambivalent relation between the party and Stalin's great purge emerges in party decisions of the later thirties, including an archival document never published in the Soviet Union and some little known material on the Central Committee plenum of February-March 1937. The Zhdanov campaign in the arts following the World War is also represented by the party resolutions translated in this volume.

Volume 4: The Khrushchev Years 1953–1964
Edited by Grey Hodnett

Volume 4 covers the rise and fall of Khrushchev. Once again factional activity surfaced in the party, as is manifest in the materials translated here. Khrushchev's diverse campaigns emerge not only in party congress documents, but also in a variety of major decisions that have not been translated into English previously and are too little known. The muted nature of the anti-Stalin campaign, as it appeared in party resolutions, is particularly important to study in view of its contrast with the Khrushchev speeches which have been given much fuller dissemination.